Heartland River

Heartland River

A Cultural and Environmental History of the Big Sioux River Valley

Edited by Jon K. Lauck

THE CENTER FOR WESTERN STUDIES
Augustana University
2022

Publication made possible with funding by the Anne King Publications Endowment and Ronald R. Nelson Publications Endowment in the Center for Western Studies and by the National Endowment for the Humanities. The publisher wishes to acknowledge the assistance of Ana Olivier, Kristi Thomas, Hal Thompson, and Ronelle Thompson.

ISBN: 978-0-931170-96-6
Library of Congress Control Number: 2021948496
Number 3 in the Center for Western Studies Public Affairs Series

The Center for Western Studies (CWS) at Augustana University preserves and interprets the history and cultures of the Northern Plains and seeks to improve the quality of social and cultural life in the region, achieve a better understanding of the region, its heritage, and its resources, and stimulate interest in the solution to regional problems. The Center promotes understanding of the region through its archives, library, museum and art exhibitions, publications, courses, internships, and public affairs programming. It is committed, ultimately, to defining the contribution of the Northern Plains to American civilization.

Visit the Fantle Building for The Center for Western Studies
Augustana University, 2121 S. Summit Avenue, Sioux Falls, South Dakota
605-274-4007 • cws@augie.edu • www.augie.edu/cws • Facebook • Twitter

Front cover photo by Greg Latza / www.greglatza.com: Big Sioux River near Baltic, South Dakota.

Bison effigy image: The original catlinite tablet (c. 1700), exhibiting the incised image of a bison on which this drawing is based, was found by Even Evenson on his Iowa farm near the confluence of the Big Sioux River and Blood Run Creek in the 1930s. Even Evenson Collection, Center for Western Studies.

Printed in the United States of America by Anundsen Publishing Company

For

Rick and Dave,
Sons of the Valley

Contents

Introduction

"A man should have a picture of his river in his head, all of it": Finding the Big Sioux River Valley

Jon K. Lauck
University of South Dakota

Everyone lives in a river valley. It might not seem like it, especially up in the horizontally-oriented Midwestern/Great Plains borderlands, but they do. River valleys and their larger watersheds can be hard to imagine, especially if they are flatter and more remote. Everyone sees the Nile or the Ganges or the Amazon rivers, but the small ones can escape everyday notice. The Big Sioux River, a 420-mile-long prairie river dividing South Dakota and Iowa and Minnesota and a major tributary to the Missouri River, is elusive this way. It has never been the subject of a book—even the sprawling Rivers of America series, which covered 122 rivers, missed the Big Sioux.[1] The river is not short, in relative terms: Caesar's fateful Rubicon is a mere fifty miles long, slightly longer than the River Cam flowing through Cambridge in England. Robert Burns' famous 1783 poem "The Banks O'Doon" is about the river Doon in Scotland, which stretches a mere sixty miles. Shakespeare's River Avon is 95 miles. Italy's mighty Tiber is just 252 miles. Even in our present age of active ecological imaginations and commonplace environmental writing the Big Sioux remains elusive. Thus it is past time for this lost river's moment in the sun.

Recognizing the Big Sioux River is not only a critical exercise in finding a place in an increasingly digital and placeless world, but also

1

an important exertion of cultural identity, a quest for the recognition of a lost watershed in the center of our nation during an era when the coasts dominate our society and the American interior remains neglected. Those who might believe that the Big Sioux River valley can be reduced to a meaningless "geography of nowhere" defined by "emptiness" must be resisted.[2] Against this opposition and disregard, this forgotten valley in the middle of America deserves to be mapped and presented to a world in greater need of grounding and rootedness.

The first critical step in finding a place is situating it in a broader geography. The Big Sioux River is a part of the massive Mississippi River basin that drains the heart of the United States. The main western artery of the Mississippi is the Missouri River, the longest river in the world if traced to the Red Rock Lakes in the Montana Rockies.[3] About halfway up the Missouri's long journey into Montana one will find the mouth of the Big Sioux River. The watershed of the Big Sioux, which is roughly the size of Massachusetts, stretches north up into the corner of northeastern South Dakota, and its boundaries resemble the shape of "Indochina," a formulation found on old colonial maps of Asia, from an era before civil and proxy wars engulfed and splintered the region. The Big Sioux watershed is situated next to the flatter valley of the James River to the west, which gathers north of Jamestown, North Dakota. The James flows south through the western section of East River South Dakota, connecting Aberdeen, Huron, Mitchell, and finally Yankton, where it empties into the Missouri River. To the north of the Big Sioux valley is the watershed of the Red River (of the north, not the Texas version, of John Wayne movie fame), which starts to gather in northeastern South Dakota and then flows north into Fargo and Grand Forks and up into Winnipeg before dumping into Hudson Bay. This means that northeastern South Dakota is the site of the continental divide, or where the water of North America diverges, some flowing south and finally into the Gulf of Mexico and some flowing north into Hudson Bay in northern Canada. The once-prominent North Dakota-born journalist Eric Sevareid made the portage across this continental divide as a young man (he gave a local fishermen two cigars to truck his gear across the two-mile Brown's Valley portage), dropping his canoe into Lake Traverse and paddling north along the Red River and on into Canada.[4] This peculiar formation can cause lots of flooding because the Red River valley is flat—one farmer told me the hydrology is equivalent to spilling a glass of water on a pool table—and because the water at the top of the river melts before the river downstream, so the headwaters are ready to flow before the channel is unfrozen. Some big thinker once tried to re-route some of these headwaters south to mitigate flooding, but the plan fizzled.[5]

To the east of the Big Sioux watershed is the Minnesota River valley. If a drop of rain falls near Summit, South Dakota, it will flow down into the Big Sioux drainage system. But if it falls a bit further east, it will flow into the Whetstone River and then through Big Stone City on the South Dakota/Minnesota border. It will then angle southeast down through the Minnesota River valley through Granite Falls, Redwood Falls, New Ulm, and Mankato (an archipelago of river towns that became Thoreau's last thorough glimpse of nature during a desperate attempt to recover his health) before finally emptying into the Mississippi River in the Twin Cities.[6] To the north of the Whetstone River in northeastern South Dakota lies another twist to this region's, and the continent's, hydrology that could expose a great scandal if it one day drew the spotlight. The area north of the Whetstone is drained by the Little Minnesota River, most of which, oddly, is in South Dakota. Some geologists argue that the real origin of the Big Mississippi is the headwaters of the Little Minnesota River around Veblen, South Dakota. Wendell Duffield, formerly of the U.S. Geological Survey and then a professor at Northern Arizona University, argues that the much-hyped claims of Lake Itasca in Minnesota have blinded scientists to the actual source of the Mississippi. Duffield, who grew up around Big Stone Lake, argues that his fellow scientists have forgotten the massive drainage flows down the Minnesota River from ancient Lake Agassiz (the drainage of which later shifted north) that made the Minnesota the primary contributor to the Mississippi and therefore its proper and original main channel. He wants us to stop being "bamboozled by the Itasca tale" and locate the headwaters properly (it is not a small matter—Montana once claimed control of the Missouri River because it possessed the river's headwaters).[7] All this is to say that the top of the Big Sioux River valley lies just under the headwaters of the grand Mississippi River, a position that further adds to the hydrological centrality of the Big Sioux.

There is another major component to the geological intrigue on the top of the Big Sioux River valley. The reason some water flows to the west, north, and east of the valley is a giant formation known as the Prairie Coteau, French for "Hills of the Prairie."[8] The Coteau is a triangular plateau, a massive earthy wedge, arrow-shaped and pointing south. The Big Sioux gathers up on this plateau, which is the "most conspicuous land form of the Mid-continental United States."[9] The Coteau is 200 miles long and 100 miles wide and rises as much as 700 feet above the prairie around it.[10] About 12,000 years ago, during the Wisconsin glaciation, two piercing ice lobes pushed down on either side of the Coteau. The lobes ground down the area around it even farther and left the noticeable plateau standing out in the middle of the big prairie in the middle of the country.[11] On the west side of the Coteau the James Lobe of the Wisconsin glacier yielded the James River valley, and on the east side the Des Moines lobe of ice descended and within its parameters formed the Minnesota River watershed. One ecologist calls the Coteau a "lucky accident, a freak of nature if you will, spared by the ice lobes and carved from the thick layers of debris left behind by earlier glaciers and the soft sedimentary rock that lay beneath."[12] The Coteau naturally drew attention. According to the artist and explorer George Catlin, a spring freshet, or a flood caused by a rapid spring melt, would draw Native Americans up on to the Coteau to avoid a waterlogged land.[13] Catlin saw the plateau as "classic ground," which Longfellow memorialized in "The Song of Hiawatha" as "the Mountains of the Prairie."[14]

Before the age of the glaciers came and shaped the Coteau there developed another now-hidden and jarring feature of this terrain, or sub-terrain. Below the mouth of the Big Sioux, near Omaha, runs a gigantic rift in the earth. This is the land of the Stable Interior Craton underlying the American Midwest, or the ancient bedrock of North America. The rock here is mostly hidden, deep down, and not exposed on the surface, like in Wyoming or Colorado. Down below is the "basement" of the continent, the stable craton, which once cracked but did not break. Over 1.1 billion years ago a rift developed in the craton (the experts know this land is ancient because the oldest rock in the United States–3.5 billion years old–comes from the nearby Minnesota River valley).[15] The great John McPhee, patron saint of nature writers, sorted out the story of this rift by sitting at the feet of Randy Van Schmus, a geologist at the University of Kansas who grew up in Naperville, Illinois, as the son of a Chicago trust officer.[16] After all his research, McPhee concludes that it "seems likely that the cause of the Midcontinent Rift was a thermal plume from deep in the mantle, a geophysical hot spot doming the crust and then cracking it."[17] If the rifting had persisted, most of the American Midwest "would have departed from North America to end up who knows where and in how many pieces."[18] By ripping the Midwest in half, this rifting would have caused Des Moines and Lincoln to be as far apart as Jersey City and Casablanca and an enormous bay of water to have developed, likely leaving the Big Sioux River valley buried under a sea.[19] But after 22 million years, a relatively short period in geologic time, the rifting stopped and the Midwest held together, leaving a continental scar which jutted up into the Big Sioux River valley near Corson, South Dakota, a physical reminder of the mysteries of Deep Time.[20]

Having avoided a splitting of the Earth and the watery fate of a submerged undersea crevasse, the Big Sioux River valley took shape, high above the Midwestern craton. In the Big Sioux valley there is between 170-820 feet of glacial drift and alluvium above the bedrock, which explains its agricultural future.[21] Glacial drift includes both the rocks and sand directly deposited by a glacier and the outwash deposits, or the sand and gravel left behind by streams of meltwater produced by a glacier.[22] This formation tilts south, guiding water down the modest valley chute toward Sioux City. From the Big Sioux's headwaters around Summit down to Sioux City, over 400 miles, the land falls from an elevation of 1,800 feet above sea level to 1,000 feet by Sioux City, or about two feet per mile. Such a gentle slope does not cause rushing currents of water. By way of comparison, the Platte River drops from an elevation of 11,000 feet in Colorado down to 900 feet at the point where it meets the Missouri River. The Platte gets a head start because it starts in the mountains, up in the Rabbit Ears Range, unlike the Big Sioux, which gathers in grasslands. Whatever the elevation, the principle applies: the land slopes and the water follows. Loren Eiseley, once lying in the Platte River as the water ran, described the feeling—"I had the sensation of sliding down the vast tilted face of the continent."[23]

To find a place is to channel Eiseley and to feel this tilting of the plain and to see this gentle flow of the water and to activate the "rarefied recesses of the mind that consider things like watersheds."[24] We need a "watershed consciousness," as Gary Snyder says, a recognition of "living in space" and its attendant communities and history and geology and a transcendence of geographic ignorance and the digital fog that envelops us.[25] We have guides to consult who can help us escape our narrow everyday vision which may only detect dullness and flatness. "Boredom lies only with the traveler's limited perception and his failure to explore deeply enough," argued William Least Heat Moon in his heartfelt plea to all of us to explore our nation's neglected backroads.[26] "Once in his life," N. Scott Momaday proclaims in *The Way to Rainy Mountain*, "a man ought to concentrate his mind upon the remembered earth....He ought to give himself up to a particular landscape in his experience, to look at it from as many angles as he can, to wonder about it, to dwell upon it."[27] This does not simply mean the Big Places—the oft-traveled oceans and the overrun Everests—but also those unexplored, undiscovered, neglected, marginalized, or never seen places. In Lisa Knopp's work on rivers, she confessed, in her early days, to treating little rivers like the Platte with "condescension"—"More of a creek than a river"—and only taking seriously the big ones, like the Mississippi. But after noticing the Platte and affording it some attention, she "grew to love this sloppy, shallow, loosely knit, prairie river."[28] Paul Gruchow, from western Minnesota, recalled that he used to think "scenery consisted of mountains and waterfalls and deer, rendered on black velvet, and that there was nothing worth seeing in our own tedious flatlands."[29] But then he began to study his home territory, to examine it, and he began to see. One has to begin noticing, taking cues from the great regionalists, like Wallace Stegner smelling the pungent wolf willow along the banks of the Frenchman River in Saskatchewan and remembering his home river valley, part of his quest to find places and all their dimensions.[30] As the Big Sioux River valley's novelist Frederick Manfred believed, a "man should have a picture of his river in his head, all of it."[31]

A first step is simply to see. Perhaps get in a canoe, like Henry and John Thoreau did to see the Sudbury River, and take in the "great hills, and a hundred brooks, and farm-houses, and barns, and haystacks...reeds and rushes waving; ducks by the hundred, all uneasy in the surf, in the raw wind, just ready to rise, and now going off with a clatter."[32] To canoe the Big Sioux is to quickly notice all the turns and loops in the river and to see that the surrounding land is not flat. When rejecting the flatness claim, some geographers deem the territory "gently rolling." "Moderately undulating" seems more accurate in part because I do not comprehend how land rolls. I understand how the land is subtly uneven and interrupted by small rises and hills and how creeks and streams leave crevasses in the prairie and how patches of trees appear, both natural and century-old shelterbelts, but I have a hard time comprehending a "rolling" landscape. Geographers and dictionaries are consistent in their usage, however, so I am not about to contest their decisions, except to maybe stick with "undulating," which I can see. One geographer said the land around Lake Kampeska, a jewel in the heart of the north central Big Sioux basin, "ranges from nearly flat, well drained, and gently undulating to rugged, poorly drained knob and kettle topography," which is more accurate.[33] All this makes John McPhee's point, quite shocking to a *New York Times* reviewer, that the American Midwest "is not quite so flat and dull as it seems" (this reviewer also jabs McPhee for not taking a hysterical turn in his writing and for not yelling, for simply describing a landscape, for "keeping his hands in his pockets and his thoughts to himself").[34] Long before McPhee, the orphaned settler girl Abbie Gardner could see deeper into the valley and behold its charm: "The natural scenery along the Big Sioux is grand and beautiful. From the summit of the bluffs, the eye can view thousands of acres of richest vale and undulating prairie; while through it, winding along like a monstrous serpent, is the river, its banks fringed with maple, oak, and elm."[35] The Coteau, in particular, "harbors a variety of habitats including, forested coulees, wetlands, fens, and lakes."[36]

Another way to begin seeing the river valley is by way of Native American history. Perhaps the first place to look is two Native American historical sites near the river, one of which is a pipestone quarry in western Minnesota. Nearby are the Three Maidens, giant boulders that were once one stone that was carried south by a glacier, making it the "largest ice-transported block known in Minnesota."[37] The Maidens guard the quarry, home to a prized form of malleable stone. In the

1760s a British trader in the area noted that near "the Marble River, is a mountain, from which the Indians get a sort of red stone, out of which they hew the bowls of their pipes."[38] Most of the pipestone pipes used by American tribes across the continent "came from the quarry of the Coteau des Prairies."[39] George Catlin wanted to see this spot so in 1836 he went up the Mississippi River to Fort Snelling, then up the Minnesota River to New Ulm, and then cross country over to the Coteau to see Pipestone (Catlin wanted to claim he was the first white man to see the quarry, but Henry Sibley emphasized that "it is notorious that many whites had been there and examined the quarry long before he came to the country").[40] The ground might have been more open in earlier eras, but by this time it was firmly controlled by the Sioux.[41] In 1838, during the time he was completing his famous map of the upper Mississippi River system, Joseph Nicollet and his assistant, future presidential candidate John C. Fremont, spent three days at Pipestone as part of an expedition exploring the lands between the Mississippi and Missouri River valleys.[42] They stayed for a while because they grasped the significance of this place. According to Native belief, the stones of Pipestone are red because of blood, "buffalo blood from animals slain by the Great Spirit for food, human blood from those who died in an ancient, great catastrophe."[43] The Pipestone quarry is where, some Natives believed, human life began, where "Wakantonka took the red stone, and from it shaped first man, then woman, and the two walked off together."[44] Black Elk also explained how White Buffalo Calf Woman gave her people a pipe in this place before morphing into a baby white buffalo.[45] In 1937 the location was named the Pipestone National Monument and later home to the pageant "The Song of Hiawatha," Longfellow's famous poem, performed in the open air every summer from 1948-2007, often watched by visitors staying at Pipestone's Calumet Hotel, a quartzite fortress.[46]

Further South in the valley, just below Sioux Falls, one finds the remains of the Native settlement of Blood Run. The peoples associated with this Oneota cultural complex probably moved into the Big Sioux River valley around 1300 from parts of the Mississippi River drainage system and then pushed out, by force, the Mill Creek/Over people.[47] The Oneota did not emerge out of the famed Cahokia complex, at least that is what some experts now argue.[48] But Cahokia did collapse around 1250 and the Oneota "occupation of Blood Run coincides with depopulation of the Mississippi River valley" so a connection is possible.[49] In the end, "[w]e simply do not know exactly where these first Oneota settlers in the eastern Plains moved from."[50] Radiocarbon dating, burial mounds, and other findings at Blood Run indicate the beginning of "intensive occupation" about 1500.[51] The people at Blood Run mostly hunted, fished, and gathered and grew corn, beans, squash, and sunflowers.[52] The site was large, with hundreds of mounds, rock circles, and possibly a serpent effigy.[53] The Omaha and Ponca were probably at Blood Run, with some evidence from later years indicating that the Oto, Arikara, and Ioway tribes may have also been in this area, but it is not entirely clear.[54] Because of the potential mixing of these peoples "it is impossible to accurately determine tribal affiliation for the remains at this time."[55] We do not know and cannot know much of what happened prior to the 1700s when Europeans began recording events on paper.[56] Two experts noted that "today it is painfully obvious that just understanding the archaeology of Blood Run is at best fraught with difficulty, to say nothing of comprehending the Oneota archaeological phenomenon in its entirety."[57]

Warfare shaped this landscape. This was an era when "Midwestern tribes were attacked by well-armed warriors of eastern tribes."[58] Anthropologists recognize that "warfare between Indian tribes was a given, probably a pattern from antiquity," but during this era the particularly effective attacks on Midwestern tribes came compliments of the Iroquois.[59] Intra-regional conflict was also common. The Omaha/Ponca group of this time and place may have traveled from Ohio to Missouri to the Des Moines River valley and then over to Pipestone, Minnesota, where they were driven out by the Sioux and then moved south to Blood Run.[60] The historian Beth Ritter explains that the "Pipestone Quarry was a highly contested landscape, and the Omaha/Ponca/Ioway were forced to abandon their settlement at Pipestone due to fierce opposition by the Dakota."[61] When Europeans came through the area in the early 1700s the Blood Run location was already abandoned.[62] Attacks from the Dakota are a large part of the reason nobody remained.[63] "Various Sioux bands, especially the Lakota" who "attacked them repeatedly," meant the end of the Oneota villages at Blood Run.[64] Ritter explains that the "Ponca, Omaha, and Ioway were driven out of their village or villages on the Big Sioux by the Yankton Dakota in a major battle, losing 1,000 warriors in the process."[65] We are fortunate that the Pettigrew brothers (Richard became a U.S. Senator) of early Sioux Falls mapped where the boulders and mounds of Blood Run were located before they were disturbed so that scientists could analyze them in greater detail.[66] We are also lucky that the state archaeologist of Iowa, Dale Henning, was friends with Martin Johnson, the farmer who owned the land around Blood Run, and that Johnson worked to save the materials he found.[67] Later, in 1970, Nixon's Secretary of Interior gave Blood Run landmark status because it was the "largest Oneota site on record" and more recently it became a state park.[68]

After the abandonment of Blood Run followed an age of European exploration and naming and modern identity formation. During the 1600s and 1700s some early but poorly-executed maps of the Missouri River basin emerged.[69] A French map from 1720 refers to what would become the Big Sioux as the LeRocher or Rocher River (meaning rock in French).[70] But later, in the 1790s, after the collapse of French North America, a Welsh explorer named John Evans, working for the Spanish, named the tributaries of the Missouri River.[71] Historians explain that the "Evans map provides the earliest place names for this part of the Missouri basin" and, sure enough, on his map one finds "de Seaux" river.[72] In their journals from their 1804 expedition up the Missouri, during which they used the Evans map, Lewis and Clark also referred to the "Soues River."[73] By the 1830s, steamboats were traveling as far up the Missouri as the Yellowstone River and these steamboats "brought on an avalanche of new and improved maps."[74] In 1839 Joseph Nicollet's expedition took the steamboat *Antelope* up the Missouri and disembarked at Fort Pierre for an overland trip to the Big Sioux River basin.[75] Nicollet's cartographic work, aided by his young charge John C. Fremont, yielded a detailed map of the Big Sioux and its associated chain of lakes.[76] As John Bicknell has noted, "Fremont honed his skills on the Coteau des Prairies" after he received a commission by the Corps of Topographical Engineers, which was under the leadership of Secretary of War Joel Poinsett, whose name lives on in the form of Lake Poinsett in the heart of the valley.[77] On the map produced by the Nicollet mission the river is labeled both Sioux and Tchankasndata and in his *Memoirs* Fremont also refers to the "Tchankasndate River," a Sioux name, or, in English, the "Calumet River."[78] An 1839 map also refers to the Calumet River, which is a reference to the pipe-making quarry near Pipestone, Minnesota.[79] Earlier, around 1700, in another reference to the quarry, the Ioway-Otoe used the name Pipestone River.[80] The name Big Sioux would win out, however. According to the U.S. Geological Survey, the name Sious River was included on a prominent map in 1847.[81] The USGS also reports that Sioux River was on an atlas series created by Colton Maps in 1856.[82] In 1931 the name was made official by the U.S. Board of Geographic Names.

Explorers could see what the valley would become. On July 7, 1839, as Nicollet and Fremont were making their way to the Big Sioux, they spotted a line of trees in the distance at about four in the afternoon, but it took another four hours to reach "the banks of a stream of clear, swift-running water meandering through an immense prairie whose vegetation is better supplied and more varied and where the land seems disposed to provide all the agricultural needs for a civilized society."[83] As they predicted, agriculture was the future. The settlers who came were mostly farmers and they made the basin a Midwestern farming valley, a subset of the broader American agrarian heartland. This region, generally Midwestern tallgrass prairie with deep soils derived from glacial drift, was fertile country.[84] The grasses common to the valley include big bluestem, little bluestem, Indian grass, switchgrass, porcupine grass, and tall dropseed.[85] One study of virgin ground found 232 species of grasses, forbs, shrubs, and trees, "an impressive degree of species diversity typical of prairie remnant areas."[86] This is the more humid East River side of South Dakota, where 26 inches of annual precipitation is common, and not West River, where precipitation averages 13 inches.[87] The 97th meridian runs down through the heart of the Big Sioux River valley, through the South Dakota counties of Grant, Codington, Hamlin, Brookings, Lake, and Minnehaha. Past the next watershed to the West, the James River valley, and close to the Missouri River, a new country appears. This is the transition from the traditional farming Midwest to the plains West.[88] Out by the 100th meridian, made famous by John Wesley Powell, is the Missouri River bifurcation of the state and the line where precipitation declines to a level that changes the land and where farm country turns into ranch country and a more arid ecosystem emerges.[89] Out by the 104th meridian in western South Dakota in counties like Meade is the true High Plains West.[90]

But back in eastern Dakota, the Big Sioux River valley still hugs the humid Midwest and is defined by its agrarian traditions. Lots of Norwegian farmers filled in the valley, as Ole Rölvaag, who made his way from Norway's Arctic Circle to the Dakota prairie, described in *Giants in the Earth*. This is the country where Laura Ingalls Wilder moved with her family. The campaigns of the Populists during the 1890s found some success here. The 1900 national Populist Party convention was held in the heart of the valley in Sioux Falls, where the Cataract Hotel (named after the falls of the Big Sioux) served as the convention headquarters.[91] The agrarian visionary and New Deal economist Paul Taylor, husband to the better-known photographer Dorothea Lange, hailed from the mouth of the valley in Sioux City and became a fierce defender of the valley's small-scale yeomen traditions.[92] The early- to mid-twentieth century farm novels of valley writers such as Ruth Suckow and Frederick Manfred captured the rural rhythms of the watershed. In 1952, when looking for the perfect location to issue his national pronouncements on farm policy, presidential candidate Dwight Eisenhower chose Brookings and South Dakota State College, the state's farm college near the river (also home, naturally, to an Agricultural Heritage Museum). He secured enough of the farm vote to put the GOP back in the White House for the first time in twenty years by speaking from the heart of farm country. This is when 71% of the basin was cropland and another 11% was devoted to grazing.[93] To get a sense of how dense and critical farming is to this valley, consider, for contrast, the Los Angeles River. The LA River once rushed down out of the mountains during the spring melt, but then was subdued via a network of zanja ditches. When ever-expanding LA arranged for the LA Aqueduct to bring in water, the river became marginal, and something of a spring "menace" to be tamed. The days of a trickling pastoral river were over as the Army Corps of Engineers turned the river into a giant concrete storm drain, memorable from scenes in movies such as *Terminator 2: Judgment Day* and *To Live & Die in LA*. This was the era of "squatting, spray painting, drug dealing, and drag racing" for the literally concretized LA River.[94] The river's agricultural orientation vanished, while in the land of the Big Sioux River valley farming remains ubiquitous.

Another way to see the valley is to begin intellectually, through the work of writers and scholars, especially those who help us find places. Reading the valley this way is "surveying the literary cartography of place," as Susan Naramore Maher says.[95] She has traced the intellectual genealogy of the best guides. The fountainhead was the Nebraskan Loren Eiseley, whose book *The Immense Journey* (1957) set the stage for the Iowan Wallace Stegner's *Wolf Willow* (1962), then Missouri's William Least Heat-Moon's deep mapping, then John McPhee, the Princeton man who has explained place to *New Yorker* readers for decades.[96] Since these guides never wrote about the Big Sioux directly, one should consult the valley's minds, like Theodore Schultz, who grew up in Badger, just a bit southwest of Lake Poinsett, during the Depression and went to South Dakota State down in Brookings. Before long he was chair of the prestigious University of Chicago economics department and winning the Nobel Prize for his work on human capital theory, but never losing sight of his roots in the farm country of the Big Sioux River valley.[97] Twenty miles east of Badger, in the heart of the river valley, is Bruce, home to the ecologist Paul Errington, who also went to South Dakota State and then to the University of Wisconsin, where he connected with the Iowan Aldo Leopold and began a life of conservation research.[98] He cut his teeth hunting ducks and trapping furbearers along the Big Sioux and later became an expert on muskrats, authoring books such as *Muskrat Populations* (1963), based in part on his 13 winters of trapping, which paid his college tuition in Brookings.[99] His son, an anthropologist, later donated the Errington family farm in Brookings County to the Fish and Wildlife Service to be returned to native prairie.[100] Ernest Lawrence, born on the river in Canton and a son of Norwegian immigrants, went on to win the Nobel Prize in physics for making the atom bomb possible and always remembered the value of the humble virtues of the valley.[101] A more literary thread can be found in the valley too, including Gore Vidal's father, Eugene, an Olympic athlete from Madison.[102] The once-active Blue Cloud Abbey in Grant County, next to the Big Sioux's headwaters, is where Kathleen Norris, author of *Dakota: A Spiritual Geography* (1996), often found solace, and Brother Stan Maudlin preserved the artifacts of the region.[103] Brother Benet Tvedten, another monk at Blue Cloud, wrote a book about the place.[104] Tvedten often welcomed the writer Jon Hassler, who would come over from Minnesota to stay at the abbey. Starting in 1973, when he was teaching at Brainerd Community College and before he landed at St. John's University as the Writer-in-Residence, Hassler would come to stay at the abbey annually. His writing was sometimes slowed by drinking brandy with Tvedten, who had the key to the liquor cabinet, and by long conversations about their love of Ireland. Hassler came to this place, he wrote, because "on the outside, peace and quiet don't exist."[105] Hassler admired the orderly lives of the Benedictines and thought they "have survived for 1500 years by paying attention to form," or to grounding and place.[106]

Perhaps the writer Frederick Manfred did the most to describe and delineate the contours of this valley. Manfred, raised on a farm in the watershed near Doon, Iowa (named after Burns' "The Banks O'Doon"), in an area settled by Dutch farmers, refused to leave the valley (against the advice of publicists and his friends, including Sinclair Lewis) and is remembered as the "Thoreau for the West."[107] In 1946, in Manfred's third novel, titled *This is the Year*, he describes the spring robins arriving in "Siouxland," and how they "wheeled over the oak-crested, doming hills north of Sioux City" along the Big Sioux River.[108] Manfred said he considered Siouxland to be the area which "encompassed the entire Big Sioux River basin."[109] Tired of citing all the names of the various states of the region he wrote about—the Dakotas, Iowa, Minnesota, Nebraska—he asked, "Why don't I just drop all that state stuff and give the name for that Big Sioux River drainage basin?"[110] He was aware of Hardy's depictions of Wessex and Steinbeck's work to define the Salinas Valley and told his editor at Doubleday, "I feel that it's important for the reader to get a good visual outline of the country, of the farm and its environs, and of Siouxland (my literary territory)."[111] Without Manfred's naming, as the Worthington, Minnesota, writer Paul Gruchow noted, the "region we call Siouxland would, absent Manfred's invention, be almost definitionless."[112]

Along with reading Manfred, the best way to give the valley definition is to get out in it (bring along some Stegner and Eiseley for the trip), to see its details and transcend the abstractions of geology reports and the sterility of road maps and the chirping of GPS. The chapters for this book were due May 1, 2021, so that is when I started to spend some extra energy traveling and seeing the valley and being attentive to its nuances. On May 19, 2021, after my son Henry's baseball practice, I drove north out of Sioux Falls on Interstate 29 farther up onto the Coteau, over the ridge that forces westerly winds upward, turning a hundred wind towers that stalk over the prairie and blink red in the night. I listened to the Audible version of John McPhee's *Crossing the Craton* on the way and heard him describe the giant geographic rip down the center of North America, one that nobody talks about because nobody can see it. Early on May 20 a couple of friends from Madison (Terry Schultz, a seed magnate, and Casey Crabtree, a state senator) and I hit Bitter Lake for some fishing. It was supposed to be clear at 8:30 a.m., but a steady rain delayed our departure from the Game, Fish, and Parks boat ramp on the east side of the lake. By 9:15 a.m. we hit the lake and fished through a drizzle until 10:00, when the sun burned through the clouds and walleyes started biting, some large, some small, and one perch. There are no houses on Bitter, unlike more recreational lakes such as Kampeska and Poinsett, but it has a good reputation in the angling subculture and draws in fisherman from Iowa and Nebraska who know of Bitter's bounty. Not long ago Bitter was several small yeoman farms, and then the floods came—the amount of water in the lake burgeoned ten-fold from 1993-1999.[113] It is mostly a closed basin, meaning it does not usually drain, but if the water becomes too deep it will spill south into the Big Sioux basin. Because it is flooded farms and roads and old rock piles Bitter can be treacherous. My first experience navigating Bitter was with my eight-year-old daughter in the boat, a harrowing affair as the depth gauge spiked from one foot to 25 feet in a matter of seconds. Bitter, which comes by its name honestly, let us off easy that day. My friend Dave O'Hara, a philosopher at Augustana University in the river town of Sioux Falls, almost lost his life on Bitter in a bad boating accident which left him with a fractured skull, vertebrae, and shoulder blade and half his ribs broken.[114]

Later on May 20 my friends and I took our pontoon out on Lake Kampeska to see the new condominium development going up on Stony Point. In 1878 a settler from Berlin, Wisconsin, named Charles M. Williams homesteaded the point because he loved the lake "and the wonderful meadow of wild grasses which lay on its shoreline."[115] Williams became an entertainer and resort owner, first building a confectionary stand along the lake, then cottages for rent, and then bringing in excursion boats, first the *Margaret Mae* and then the famous *Stella Mae*, a 62-foot gas-powered cruiser built by Williams himself in Minneapolis in 1909.[116] Duck hunting and fishing and an annual water carnival were also big draws.[117] Sightings of the Kampeska Creature added to the lake's mystique.[118] Williams later built the Spider Palace on the point, which offered beer, bowling, billiards, and dancing (along with a 300-foot bar, the longest in South Dakota), and then the Spider Web, a roller-skating rink which doubled as a boxing arena.[119] The complex became the "biggest resort west of the Mississippi."[120] The Spider Web's roof caved in due to heavy snows in 1946 and 1978, a not uncommon fate in wintry South Dakota, and it finally went defunct, along with many institutions from the old era of boxing and big bands. In 1971 the Williams family built The Prop, a bar on the site of the old Spider complex and on this day we parked our boat in the sand and had a cold Prop beverage (the "Prop" name comes from the old propeller from the *Stella Mae*, which was attached to the bar's sign until it was taken by a thief in the night).[121] Conda Williams, heiress to the land, served us and later, when she had to run to a doctor's appointment, asked us to finish our cocktails on the picnic table out front. We did so, then hopped in the pontoon and cruised toward the north side of the lake, past the water intake plant that used to pump water from the lake into Watertown. Nearby is the old location of the Casino Ballroom, the site of innumerable barn dances and carnivals that lasted into the 1960s.[122] To the east of this ballroom, during World War II, the military built an airfield to train pilots, which later became the Watertown airport (the thinking was that pilots could simply crash their planes in Lake Kampeska if something went wrong and have a better chance of surviving).[123] The north shore of the lake used to be owned by S.X. Way, the long-time publisher of the *Watertown Public Opinion*, who used to host the state's power elite and on whose kitchen table Way and sculptor Gutzon Borglum planned the carving of Mount Rushmore.[124] Near Way's home (374 North Lake Drive) is where the Chautauqua grounds used to be, which once hosted speakers such as William Jennings Bryan and the saloon-smashing Kansan Carrie A. Nation.[125] We settled into The North Shore bar, The Prop's counterpart on the opposite side of the lake, which for decades had been Lunker's, and enjoyed 50% off burger night and then went back to the cabin and watched *The Terminator*, the original, acquired from the discount bargain bin of the local Walmart.

The shape of Kampeska resembles a giant guppy, a large round torso pointing northeast with a generous fleshy tail on the back pointing southwest. Geographers call it "ellipsoidal."[126] Kampeska is the third largest natural lake fully within the state of South Dakota and it means "shining shells" in Dakota.[127] That day the lake reminds me of the famous bullhead story by Loren Eiseley in which after a day of exploring and literally lying in the Platte River in Nebraska he takes home a bullhead and puts it in a fish tank and it ultimately makes a suicidal jump out of confinement. It was a reasonable jump, Eiseley thinks, one that might have paid off in different circumstances such as being trapped in a shrinking backchannel or pond and needing to find the central channel and the main chance.[128] At Kampeska, we one day found a once-bold northern pike lying dead along the shore. My son noticed a slight filament of a possible fin sticking out of the northern's mouth (in the upper Midwest northern pike is shortened to northern, unlike in other regions, in which it is shortened to just pike, for reasons probably impossible to sort out). I pulled out a pliers and slipped them into the northern's mouth (pliers are a good option when dealing with the spiky-toothed cavernous mouth of a northern) and soon I was pulling out a large sucker, three-quarters the size of the northern itself. This fish had gone for broke on a large supper, literally biting off more than he could chew, and choked out. The incident re-confirmed the aggressive reputation of northerns, which often fight ferociously and snap lines. They are also slimy and bony, hard to filet, and dismissed as "snakes" by fishermen, who prefer the light and near-boneless meat of the prized walleye.

On May 21, before scattering to our jobs and families, we had eggs in Watertown at The Wheel Inn with some local friends. Watertown, which is the central city of the upper reaches of the river valley, was first founded as Kemp Post Office in 1878 and then, at the request of the Kemp brothers, the railroad named the town for their hometown of Watertown, New York, which had been named in 1800 after the falls of the Black River.[129] In 1987 Congressman Jack Kemp began his presidential campaign in Watertown, where he gave a speech at the courthouse and explained how his great grandfather, Oscar Kemp, and his great uncle founded the town because they were "captivated by the Sioux River countryside."[130] After the Kemps came, the next year Arthur Mellette moved to town and began living at Lake Kampeska and commuting to his law office at Kemp and Broadway in Watertown on a small rail line he built.[131] He eventually built a decorous Victorian home up on a bluff in Watertown that surveys the river valley and it can still be toured today.[132] Mellette wanted the capital of South Dakota to be planted between the Big Sioux and Kampeska, a plan that failed, but he did become the state's last territorial and first-elected governor after statehood in 1889.[133] During our time in Watertown it was also political season. A mayor's race was brewing and yard signs jutted up on many street corners. The incumbent mayor was ousted 71%-29% by a local author, legislator, and businessman who had led the effort for a local hockey arena, an increasingly popular sport suitable for long Dakota winters.[134] Watertown also found the political spotlight in the final stages of the Obama administration when it was time to be sure the president had visited every state.[135] Since South Dakota was the only state that Obama had not traveled to as President, his administration arranged for him to speak to the graduating class of the local technical school, Lake Area Technical Institute, whose name nodded to the glacial lakes dotting the Coteau country.[136]

On Monday May 24, 2021, after my son Henry's baseball game on a field next to the Big Sioux River in Sioux Falls (an 8-3 defeat in which he started as pitcher and gave up three runs in two innings, a tough night in Mudville), we hit the Burger King drive-through and headed north through the valley (the boy's spring football games were played at Riverdale Park, also next to the Big Sioux, and his winter basketball team played in the Big Sioux Youth Basketball League). We visited grandpa and grandma in Madison, South Dakota, and then stopped at Memorial Creek in the middle of town. To reduce flooding many years ago, a deep square channel lined with cement and local rocks had been built through the center of town to give Memorial Creek form and direction. Henry asked if it was possible to float from Memorial Creek all the way back to Sioux Falls via the Big Sioux River and I said, yes (Memorial Creek flows east toward Lake Madison and other local lakes and comes out the other end as Skunk Creek, which intersects the Big Sioux in western Sioux Falls). Memorial is just one of several creeks that feed the Big Sioux, including Willow Creek east of Watertown, Stray Horse Creek near Estelline, Hidewood Creek in Deuel County, Peg Munky Run Creek, also in Deuel (a settler pranked the surveyor by telling him it was called Pee Munky Run Creek so it had to be changed later), and Deer Creek, North Deer Creek, and Six Mile Creek, all in Brookings County.[137] Out where the creeks of the town of Madison meet Lake Madison, you will find a U.S. Fish and Wildlife service office near a small park named for Karl Mundt, a Madison man who became South Dakota's longest-serving U.S. Senator and an outdoorsman and conservationist who liked to hunt the area's ducks and geese. In this same area of Lake County, a hunting lodge owner and the county game warden, O.T. "Ole" Hagen, sought to promote pheasant hunting during the 1930s. They were both members of the Izaak Walton League, or the "Ikes," which had a lodge on the north side of Lake Herman for trap shooting and socializing. Naturally, Ernest Hemingway answered the call, arriving in October 1936 at the Wentworth train station for a ten-day pheasant hunt. He regaled the locals with tales of Cuba and Africa, of course, but he also "wanted to know about the Big Sioux River and its tributaries."[138] "This is real prairie," Hemingway said. "You can see for miles." After he dropped his family in Key West after the hunt, Hemingway was off to Spain to write about its Civil War.

As we left Madison that night heading north, a massive, hazy orange sky was developing just ahead of a black sky in the west. We headed north on highway 81 out of Madison and saw the marker for the Lake Badus settlement, where in 1877 Swiss immigrants had set up a colony. Near Arlington, the accumulating fury of an engulfing prairie storm hit us and we had to drive 20 miles per hour through the deluge. By the time we passed the Kones Korner gun store about 10 miles south of Watertown the storm had passed, a bright blue dome had returned, and a crisp post-thunderstorm stillness prevailed. Henry and I were going to spend the night at our Lake Kampeska cabin (the movie that night was *Avatar*) and then go fishing with another dad and his two boys the next day. We targeted that Tuesday for fishing because the weather app showed a clear and warm day. While it was not cold or rainy for a change, it was windy, no small matter on the Dakota plain.

Nevertheless, we left Kampeska and drove up County Road 1 heading to Bitter Lake, only meeting one farm truck during the thirty-mile trek but seeing an assortment of cormorants, blue-winged teal, mallards, pheasants, and turkeys. As we headed out in our boat on Bitter, the wind was 13 miles per hour and we trolled into it, straight across Bitter to the west, trying to keep all the lines straight. Nightcrawlers on chartreuse spinners and bottom bouncers were the offering of the day. We trolled over Bitter's complex lake bottom, including passes over Pike Hump, Three Sisters Humps, Hal's Horseshoe, Two Knob Nuts, Mallard Island, and Butch's Lip, all contours precisely mapped and displayed on our Hummingbird fish finder, into which you can load local topographic data. When we hit the far shore, we drifted back, pulling our spinners and nightcrawlers back to the east side. In a sign of the growing problem of wind, there was not one other boat on the lake. The fishing was slow so the kids fed the seagulls Doritos. At one point we hit a low spot that jolted the boat motor.

After three futile hours on Bitter, we decided to move north to Waubay Lake, where a friend of mine had recently been filming a movie titled *Waubay*. We passed another boat entrance on the east side of Bitter, the one where, the winter before, a fisherman had driven his one-ton pickup and fifth-wheel camper through the ice, where it remained frozen until spring and the subject of much Facebook mockery. Bitter has earned its name. For the glacial lakes of northeastern South Dakota, Bitter is the equivalent of the Great Lakes' Lake Superior, which never gives up her dead. We drove around the north side of Bitter, past a flooded farm which still had trucks and equipment underwater, engulfed by the imperial expansion of Bitter's waters, and into the small town of Waubay, population 500, originally named Blue Lake. The name Waubay, in Dakota, apparently means "to peel or skin a small animal" or "where the wild fowls nest."[139] We pulled the boat across the rail tracks and down an empty main street and past an abandoned bank and an active VFW lodge and saw the sign for the Waubay National Wildlife Refuge. When we reached Highway 12, we turned west by the Purple Cow Ice Cream Parlor, home to a wide selection of meats and ice cream on the shores of Blue Dog Lake (which is also home to a state fish hatchery). We rolled toward Webster, the county seat of Day County and home to the South Dakota Fishing Museum and a number of fishing guides, including the legendary Cory Ewing, and hideouts for fisherman such as The Galley and Pereboom's Café.

Fishing and water have been battlefronts in this area in recent decades. For much of South Dakota history, the state has contended with drought. Think of Dorothea Lange traipsing through the West in the 1930s and the various political battles and scandals relating to the Dirty Thirties and government photography, including the famous case of the manufactured cow skull photos which produced a storm of reaction in the Dakotas.[140] But in recent years, some long-dry lakes filled up with water because of excessive rains that started in the 1990s. Before the '90s, the experts were not sure where the water would flow out of this mostly closed basin because there had never been enough to worry about. When the rains finally came, they found out the water would flow down into the Big Sioux. Emblematic of the era, the water swallowed a farm just east of Webster, leaving cattle stranded on some higher hills and forcing a farmer to ferry out hay and salt licks via boat to the cattle islands. When a hard freeze came during the winter, he drove across the ice and rounded up the cattle for sale.[141] The historic waterlines of the lakes in the area had first been marked by "meandering," or literally walking the shoreline of a lake to determine its typical perimeter. When all the rains came, however, more land was flooded, creating "non-meandered" water which some aggressive anglers fished, even though just below it was a farm recently lost by an unlucky farmer, a victim of the deluge. A political and legal battle ensued and the South Dakota Supreme Court instructed the state legislature to sort out how to handle the non-meandered waters. The solution was to allow farmers to block fishermen from their flooded lands with the exception of 27 lakes specifically set forth in state law.[142]

A few miles north of Webster we turn onto a rough gravel road heading to the Kanago Boat Ramp on the west of South Waubay Lake. The idea was to find some calmer waters, a bit below the stiffer winds, on the west side of the lake. The boys want to explore, so we drop them on Hedke's Island a couple miles into the lake and the dads fish the bay on the island's east side, hugging the shoreline and working calm waters which are protected from the wind by the tall stands of timber on the island. We troll along the shoreline with spinners and then work the fallen timber by casting spoons, hoping to coax out a big northern pike. The fish would not indulge us so we summon the boys from the island via walkie-talkie, have our sandwiches and apples, and begin the trek back. The winds have now increased to 29 miles per hour and the trip home is extremely rough. We joke about Gordon Lightfoot's "The Wreck of the Edmund Fitzgerald." About half-way back our Mercury motor begins to sputter and it steadily fluctuates between 3,000 and 5,000 rpms and finally, a half-mile from the Kanago dock, starts what feels like a final death wheeze. But we have enough power to limp in and load the boat. If the motor had conked out we would have drifted on rough water across five miles of Waubay Lake, but we avoided that fate and dropped the boat at Doug's Anchor Marine in Watertown and asked the mechanic named Earl to review the situation. I had to head home to Sioux Falls to chair a Zoom meeting of the Midwestern History Association the next morning organized to discuss a new intellectual history of the Midwest recently released.[143]

On May 28 I woke up at 5:00 a.m. and gathered several layers of clothes, crossed the Big Sioux River on Minnesota Avenue which bisects Sioux Falls and again headed north into the valley. I met a friend at the first big gas station on I-29 and drove north for some fishing (I had to stop in Colman and get a sixer because the first gas station refused to sell beer before 7:00 a.m.). We left I-29 at the exit for Estelline, population 800, and crossed the Big Sioux again on the west side of town. Our destination was Lake Poinsett, one of the bigger lakes in the archipelago of lakes that act as bladders for the Big Sioux, raising the lake when the river is high and draining the lake when it is low. Several years before, I had served as the attorney in a lawsuit designed to recover documents from the U.S. Army Corps of Engineers related to how they influenced the drainage of Poinsett (we won, mostly, with only a few redactions of the documents). The lake's namesake, Secretary of War Joel Poinsett, lined up cartographer Joseph Nicollet's commission to map the area and also served as Minister to Mexico, from which he brought home a lovely flower, which he named the Poinsetta.[144] To the west, and connected to Poinsett, are Lakes Albert, Mary, Norden, and St. John. Poinsett, while it is a good fishing lake, is also highly recreational and its shores are lined with lake homes, including that of NBA star Kirk Hinrich, who grew up in the mouth of the Big Sioux in Sioux City before going to the University of Kansas and playing for the Chicago Bulls. Poinsett has long been a recreation lake, home to Smith's Resort (where Lawrence Welk played, before it become a Methodist church in a bit of reverse cultural evolution), Mundt's Resort, Edwards Resort, Fish Haven (home of the famous carp sandwich), and Weiland Marine (formerly Ole's Repair Shop and the first Evinrude dealer in this region of lakes and boats).[145] The temperature that morning was a mere 38 degrees and it was lightly sprinkling and the bite was slow. I did, however, have a lunker on the line which snapped my entire spinner and bottom bouncer rig clean off. It was probably a hungry northern pike. After a few hours we give up on Poinsett and drive around the north side of the lake and over to Highway 81 and head further north, past Kones Korner gun store, a Catholic monastery, and a strip club and across the channel that connects Pelican Lake to the Big Sioux on the south side of Watertown. True to form, the pelicans were particularly active that day, both in the channel and in the sky, lazily circling and gliding in a radial line extending out from the chief pelican, who serves as the pivot point. We drove around the north side of Lake Kampeska and across the channel connecting the lake to the Big Sioux and then north, back to Bitter Lake, where we hauled in three sizeable walleyes. My friend headed home and I grabbed the Thursday night special at The North Shore and headed to the cabin to read John Anfinson's history of the Mississippi River.[146]

On May 29, as Memorial Day weekend began, a couple lawyer buddies of mine, Eric Schulte and Ron Parsons, rolled in to our cabin. I had spent the day reading up on the valley for this Introduction, mostly old hydrology reports and more geology by John McPhee. By the time my friends arrived, I was ready for nourishment, so we headed to Harry's, an impressive burger joint on Kemp Avenue in Watertown which includes an old-time barber shop, replete with straight razor shaves. Previously, Harry's had been Past Times, a restaurant owned by Kristi Noem, now South Dakota's governor, and her mother. Afterward, we retired to Dempsey's, a classic Irish pub housed in an old farm implement manufacturing building. We only had one—a local brew called Battle Axe Blonde Ale—and then went back to the cabin because we had an early day of fishing ahead. We were planning to fish a non-meandered lake the next day because one of my friends had been the attorney in the complex litigation that sorted out the meandered from the non-meandered lakes, but the rain in recent days had made the dirt path to the lake too muddy for boats and trucks.[147] We instead headed toward the upper western section of the valley in Clark County, home of the town of Clark and sandy soils suitable for potatoes (thus the annual Clark Potato Days and mashed potato wrestling, a contest my son had won the year before and landed on the cover of the *Watertown Public Opinion*). Clark had recently seen a fair amount of literary activity as the setting of South Dakota State University professor Steve Wingate's novel *The Leave-takers* and the home of Megan Phelps-Roper, the granddaughter of a fanatical Topeka preacher named Fred Phelps who met a lawyer from Clark, reformed her views, and wrote a major book about her journey from fanaticism to a quiet home in the Big Sioux River valley.[148] Our destination that day was Dry Lake no. 2, just outside of the little town of Willow Lake, where my lake neighbor Byron (whom we call Lord Byron, since my wife was an English major) once owned the bar. The name of the lake is a good indication of how this land was once parched and how later rains filled in old fishing holes. Dry Lake no. 2 is not to be confused with Dry Lake no. 1, north of Clark, or Dry Lake (no number) just south of Florence, a town west of Watertown, or Dry Lake (no number), just north of Lake Poinsett. To lessen the confusion, fishermen often say "Dry Lake by Willow Lake" or "Dry Lake by Florence." Surely some entrepreneurial staffer in state government should clear all this up with some naming ideas, although the local anglers probably prefer some mystery and uncertainly to keep the outlanders at bay. On that day on Dry Lake no. 2 in rural Clark County the bite was hot. We trolled an old gravel road, now sunken under 12 feet of water and named 429th Avenue (a level of precision recently added to once-anonymous country roads to help emergency vehicles find their destination). By noon we had caught our twelve walleyes, and a few aggressive and bulky northern pike that we tossed back, and headed home.

On June 12 I drove down through the valley from Watertown past Kones Korner and the Pheasant Motel in Arlington and the town and lake of Sinai and the road to Lake Badus and finally to Ramona (featuring another Dry Lake) to attend a funeral for the former mayor of Madison, Joan Krantz, the mom of one of my best friends as a kid. She was elected mayor in April 1987 by a vote of 1,086-674 over Denny

Rowley, the father of one of my classmates and a hail fellow well met (politics is very small and intimate and friendly in the valley—everyone tends to know everyone else). Although her married name is German, Joan could not have been more Irish. Her maiden name was Dooley and her mother was a Sweeney. The Catholic church in Ramona features a prominent stained-glass window sponsored by the O'Connell family (the neighboring town of Nunda is also famous for its Irish folk).[149] The Catholic cemetery is full of Catholic Germans and Joan's Irish brethren—the tombstones read Dooley, Delaney, McDonald, O'Connell, Sweeney, etc. Ramona used to have its own priest, but the priest that day covered the towns of Howard, Epiphany, and Ramona, a sign of the thinning out of once-large rural Catholic parishes and a declining number of priests. The once-robust small towns of the valley, made lively by the many small farms in their trade area which once had many children, now suffer from the dwindling of main street businesses and have become too oriented toward funerals, occasions for the old-time families of the area to bid goodbye to the dearly departed and an older way of life.

To find where the young families of the valley are increasingly settling visit Sioux Falls, a center point of the Big Sioux River valley and an economic and cultural anchor to the region, so named because of its beautiful falls sloshing through exposed pink quartzite. The falls are perhaps the most iconic part of the river, a place of "high imageability," as the experts say.[150] Sioux Falls is in Minnehaha County, another name taken from Longfellow, via Mary H. Eastman's *Dahcotah; or, Life and Legends of the Sioux Around Fort Snelling* (1849), and supposedly derived from a stream that empties into the Mississippi between Fort Snelling and the Falls of St. Anthony, a "Little Falls." Natives called the falls Mine-hah-hah, or "laughing waters," a name which at least one expert thinks "was the work of white men, although based on Indian roots."[151] Whatever the proper provenance, the name came from Longfellow's widely-known *The Song of Hiawatha*, which was highly popular when Sioux Falls was founded (only four months after the poem was published, the shipbuilder Donald McKay christened a new ship called the *Hiawatha*).[152] Longfellow's work is remembered as the first truly American epic, the artistic work that finally broke free from Europe, an exercise of American cultural independence, the same sensibility that

would underlie future exertions of regionalism in various American lo-
cales, including at the Sioux Falls-based Center for Western Studies.[153]
Sioux Falls has fared much better, over time, than Sioux City (airport
code: SUX), located at the mouth of the Big Sioux and once a prominent jumping off point for settlers heading into the Dakotas and later
a site of some industrial strength.[154] Among valley dwellers, be careful
not to confuse the two. When candidate Barack Obama was campaign-
ing for president in Sioux Falls in 2008 he came on stage at the Arena
to loud applause and shouted "THANK YOU SIOUX CITY!" Not
knowing the name of a place is a failure of recognition, part of a tendency to see interior spaces as undifferentiated nowheres, a sign that it
is time for a valley to make a stronger impression on the map.

Whether booming Sioux Falls or the valley's older small towns or
the treacherous waters of Bitter Lake, it is far past time to find the
varied niches of the Big Sioux River valley. It is important to know a
place, to "become curious about every hill and valley," explained Herbert Krause, the long-time Writer-in-Residence at Augustana University in Sioux Falls and the founder of the publisher of this book.[155] We
hurt ourselves by not knowing our environs. Shortly before he died,
while outlining a piece about the Big Sioux for this volume, University
of South Dakota law professor John Davidson suggested I read *Goodbye to a River*, John Graves's book about the Brazos River in Texas.[156]
Graves canoed the river in 1957 and counseled his readers to see the
world, of course, but also to observe the close-at-hand. He warned that
the "man who cuts his roots away and denies that they were ever connected with him withers into half a man."[157] To avoid such injury we
only need to overcome a lazy blindness. When Robert Pirsig took his
famous motorcycle trip, it included a jaunt out of Minneapolis up into
the Dakotas, which he said was "a kind of nowhere, famous for nothing at all and [having] an appeal because of just that."[158] He was wrong
about it being nowhere, the usual claim of a casual tourist. Every place
is something unto itself and "each place has its own order, its special
ensemble, which distinguishes it from the next place."[159] There is a
particularity of place which shapes people, as the Big Sioux River valley poet David Allan Evans explains.[160] He notes that "just as Darwin's
Finches' beaks differed according to the particular habitat they evolved
in, poets too differ somewhat according to the particular place they

inhabit—especially the place they were born and raised in."[161] Evans says we have to dig to find a place, to go looking, and points us to the Iowa farmer/poet James Hearst's poem "Truth":

How the devil do I know
if there are rocks in your field,
plow it and find out.[162]

To dig down and find out, to locate this lost valley, is our goal here because it will help us care more about this place. As the valley ecologist Paul Errington learned from his mentor Aldo Leopold, "We grieve only for what we know."[163] Once we know this river valley, a new future awaits.

To know this place and its beginnings, a logical first step is to turn to the archaeological record, which is the focus of the first chapter, authored by Renee Boen and Katie Lamie. Together, Boen and Lamie explain how the Big Sioux River served as a critical cultural thoroughfare and trade route between the eastern woodlands and the western Great Plains for thousands of years. In large part, this was possible because the Big Sioux River meets the continent-crossing Missouri River, providing access to a wide trade network across the Northern Plains. Exotic items such as marine shells from the Atlantic and Gulf coasts, native copper from the Great Lakes area, Knife River flint from west-central North Dakota, Bijou Hills quartzite from south-central South Dakota, and obsidian from the Yellowstone region were all traded into the Big Sioux River valley. In return, the locally available red pipestone, also known as catlinite, was traded out all over the Midwest as the raw material for elaborately carved pipes and incised plaques. Boen and Lamie are able to draw on the work of many archaeologists, who have studied this region for over 150 years. They describe the cultural history of the Big Sioux River within the framework of Paleoindian, Archaic, Woodland, Initial Middle Missouri, Oneota, Protohistoric, and Historic periods and provide a summary of cultural adaptions of the first inhabitants along the Big Sioux River through time.

Chapter 2 delves deeper into the archaeological record by examining the history of the Blood Run site from the late pre-contact period up to the eighteenth century. In particular, the historian Joshua Jeffers draws on the archaeological record and oral tradition and explores the connection between Blood Run and the Great Pipestone Quarry in southwestern Minnesota in order to map the economic transition that took place in the region following the introduction of firearms. Separated by less than 40 miles, the relationship of these two sites of great significance offers insight into how Native societies lived in and made use of the region. Jeffers argues that European trade goods merged with a much older system of trade in pipestone, but unlike the pre-contact system, the Euro-Indian trade system was driven mainly by the desire for profit among Europeans and the increasing necessity of access to firearms among Native Americans. As a result, the region devolved into conflict. Blood Run may have been the epicenter of a "catlinite core" where peoples of the Oneota tradition manufactured pipestone products. Archaeological evidence, such as large chunks and preforms as well as finished products, are found in large quantities at Blood Run, suggesting that it was a processing center and that the habitants likely controlled access to the Pipestone Quarry. The introduction of European goods and firearms transformed this system. Traditional economic channels and means of exchange were redirected or given new meaning by the Euro-Indian system of trade. Thus, the significance of control over the Pipestone Quarry and the trade in pipestone was subjugated to the trade in firearms, slaves, and pelts because gaining and maintaining access to firearms was a life-and-death matter. The lifeblood of the pre-contact trade system had been pipestone, which, among other things, symbolized peace. The Euro-Indian trade in firearms coopts this older system with a new instrument of war. The need for guns and the availability of steel goods displaced pipestone as a vital trade good, and when the Indian arms race spread across the region, the ceremonialism associated with pipestone and the trade in pipestone could not dissipate the violence.

In chapter 3 the geographer Chris Laingen sets forth the general geographic scaffolding of the Big Sioux River basin. It begins by situating the basin within the broader geographic context of eastern South Dakota. The river's course from its headwaters in Roberts County to its confluence with the Missouri River at Sioux City is detailed, including descriptions of the counties and communities through which the river flows and a brief discussion as to why the river was used as the state border between Iowa and South Dakota. The chapter then turns its attention to the shaping of the physical landscape through glaciation that took place 20,000 years ago. This process, along with subsequent changes to the region's climate, helped to create the current Big Sioux's fluvial dynamics and ecological setting. The basin's weather and climate are then discussed, as the cyclical drought-deluge conditions present in the northern Great Plains greatly affect the Big Sioux and its tributary's streamflow rates. The landscape's conversion from prairie to farmland is also considered. Over 80% of the basin's grasslands were plowed under between 1870 and 1910. The shift from mixed-grain and livestock farming that once dominated the agrarian landscape to one focused increasingly on cash-grain corn and soybean farming, including livestock and dairy operations, describes the major multi-decadal trend that has been occurring in the basin, though at varying rates, since the 1960s. The chapter closes with a discussion of efforts to remove marginal cropland from agricultural production and return those areas of the basin to more natural land covers through the Conservation Reserve Program. Other environmental "issues" are briefly covered, including the impact of urbanization and the use of agricultural chemicals and their potential runoff into the Big Sioux.

In chapter 4, scientists Matthew Ley, David Swanson, Carter Johnson, and Mark Dixon further elaborate on the trees and wildlife of the valley. The Big Sioux River flows through an agricultural landscape from its source north of Watertown, South Dakota, to its confluence with the Missouri River at Sioux City, Iowa. Land cover in the upper reaches contains larger extents of agriculture and grassland, with smaller, narrower riparian zones dominated by green ash woodlands and willow shrublands. Farther downstream, the diversity of forest types increases, with mature forests dominated by silver maple and cottonwood on wider, more dynamic floodplains. Upland forests, which occur mostly on the middle and lower segments of the river, are dominated by bur oak and several other overstory tree species, with a mix of prairie and eastern woodland species in the herbaceous understory. Riparian forests along the Big Sioux have higher numbers of woody plant species, lower shrub cover, and somewhat different species composition from nearby, flow-regulated reaches of the Missouri River, in part because of differences in flooding frequency. Riparian forests along both rivers, as well as nearby farmstead woodlots, provide breeding and migratory stopover habitat for a wide diversity of land bird species.

The highest number of bird species during the breeding season of these three woodland types occurs along the Big Sioux River. Migrant bird species numbers are also higher in the Big Sioux than in the Missouri River riparian corridor. The future condition of riparian forests along the Big Sioux River may be strongly affected by the spread of invasive plant (garlic mustard) and insect (emerald ash borer) species. Ecological and geomorphic conditions in the riparian corridor and river channel have changed over the past few decades and will continue to be influenced in the future as a function of increased flows due to a combination of a wetter climate, agricultural intensification, and changes in drainage at the scale of the entire Big Sioux watershed. Such changes to the riparian corridor of the Big Sioux River will generate unknown impacts on bird and other wildlife populations dependent on these riparian forests.

Next, the book turns from natural history to human development. The early period of exploration is examined by John Bicknell in chapter 5. In 1838 and 1839 an expedition led by French émigré scientist Joseph Nicollet explored the Big Sioux River valley and the surrounding area. Nicollet's No. 2 was John C. Fremont, who would later gain fame as the "Pathfinder of the West." The 1838-39 expeditions would yield the first accurate large-scale map of the Upper Missouri River basin, including the Big Sioux and the lakes of eastern South Dakota and western Minnesota. Nicollet's detailed map was considered years ahead of its time and became the foundation on which future expeditions and surveys were based. Beyond the scientific value of the map and of Nicollet's report, which included exhaustive lists of the flora and fauna the group encountered, the journey would be an important proving ground for Fremont, who at that time had experience as a wilderness explorer but little scientific training. He would learn by doing with Nicollet, and apply that knowledge to his future and more famous endeavors in the West.

Despite Nicollet's map, the valley did not attract a large population until after the Civil War, when peace, railroads, and the Homestead Act encouraged immigration. As Jeff Bremer explains in chapter 6, the valley was one of the centers of settlement in eastern Dakota, the fertility of its soil offset by limited rainfall. Extremes of temperature, a lack of wood, dangerous prairie fires, and harsh weather challenged settlers, who often lived in sod homes. Immigrants built towns, schools, farms, and churches despite such obstacles. The opportunity for land ownership attracted tens of thousands of settlers, especially Norwegian immigrants, to the area. Farming usually required the work of a family and farmwomen provided crucial labor that helped families survive and prosper. The Great Dakota Land Boom of the late 1870s and 1880s brought hundreds of thousands of settlers to the territory, which ultimately became the separate states of South Dakota and North Dakota in 1889.

The early frontier years were not just about farming, as Sam Herley explains in chapter 7. Ever since their jaunt across Minnesota and into Dakota Territory in the wake of the 1876 Northfield bank robbery, infamous outlaws Frank and Jesse James have left an indelible mark of history, memory, legend, and myth on the Big Sioux River valley. This chapter analyzes the ways in which the river valley and its people–through topographical features, influential speculations, and cultivated traditions–have shaped the story of the outlaws' escape. The result has been the construction of one of the valley's defining characteristics: a strong outlaw legends culture that transcends geographic, social, and ethnic boundaries. Consistent with outlaw legends cultures from around the world and yet also distinctive to the borderlands region of Minnesota, South Dakota, Iowa, and Nebraska, the James brothers' legend has persisted and expanded for generations among area small towns and rural areas while effectively transforming the Big Sioux River valley into nothing less than a riparian Sherwood Forest.

The river saw another tale of pursuit and violence during this time period that has timeless significance, as James Schaap explains in chapter 8. In March of 1857 Abbie Gardner, just 13, was the only member of her family to survive an attack by a Wahpakute band of Dakota who, under the leadership of a headman named Inkpaduta, attacked new Euro-American settlements in northwest Iowa. Abbie was captured but spared from death, some say, because of the bravery she showed after her family members had been brutally murdered. She became one of four women held captive by Inkpaduta's band while they moved north and west to avoid capture and certain death. After four months of captivity, during which two of the four women were murdered, Abbie was released. Some years later she wrote her story, then lost the manuscript in a fire. Still later, she bought 13 acres of her father's original homestead land and moved back to the place where so many family members were killed. Her story, *History of the Spirit Lake Massacre*, was not unusual in the nineteenth century. Captivity narratives were much beloved by the American reading public. Gardner backs away from revelations of brutality that often made such books popular, however. What is more, at times the narrative makes dramatic shifts in tone. As a captivity narrative, it is hardly noteworthy. Schapp examines the *History of the Spirit Lake Massacre* not as another "captivity narrative," but instead as a spiritual (Christian) testimony whose climax is not Abbie's final release from captivity and her return to freedom, but instead her reconciliation with the Santee Sioux people. Both Gardner and the Santee had undergone horrifying suffering, but were able to respect and love each other. When Abbie stands just outside the Santee's River Bend Church in Flandreau, South Dakota, on what she calls her "Day of Realization," she looks at the very spot on the Big Sioux River where she had watched her friend brutally murdered, and she was overwhelmed. That moment is the climax of her story of forgiveness and reconciliation.

The writers and intellectuals of the valley active in the decades after the publication of the Gardner book also left their mark. The countryside surrounding the Big Sioux River, in all directions, has produced a surprising number of accomplished, if unheralded, novelists. In chapter 9, Paul Theobald identifies several of these writers and describes their literary contributions. The list includes Herbert Krause, Frederick Manfred, Ruth Suckow, J. Hyatt Downing, Martha Ostenso, Herbert Quick, Howard Erickson, and several others (less attention is paid to Manfred, since he is the focus of another chapter in this volume, and to Suckow, because she is still remembered in literary circles). With the possible exception of a few books by Krause and Manfred, the novels of these writers have long been out of print and they are largely unknown to the contemporary residents of the Big Sioux valley. This chapter identifies trends common to Siouxland writers, such as accurately handling the physical details of farm and small-town life and characters defined by an uncommon allegiance to community institutions such as the local school or church. Additionally, the chapter analyzes a shifting literary appetite among the American public during the careers of the identified novelists, concluding with commentary concerning how this trend affected Siouxland writers. Theobald seeks to elevate the work of these accomplished twentieth-century Siouxland writers. Their literary contributions deserve not only a contemporary audience, he believes, but additional scholarly attention.

Among these novelists, perhaps Frederick Manfred stands the tallest, literally. Iowa-born Manfred won literary fame for his novels rooted mainly in the area where Iowa and Minnesota meet Nebraska and South Dakota, and especially for his Buckskin Man series set in the Old West period. In chapter 10 Lance Nixon explains how 6'9" Manfred coined the term "Siouxland" for the geography in which he set most of his stories. Manfred himself said in interviews that he toyed with the idea of "Land of the Sioux" before he decided on Siouxland. While the importance of Native Americans in Manfred's fiction is undeniable, they were not the basis of his moniker. In an interview in June 1993, Manfred told Nixon that in the end he chose "Siouxland" based on the fact that the area he intended to spend his life writing about is the drainage of the Big Sioux River—so it is actually a river valley (though one named for an indigenous people group) that gives Siouxland its name. A map of Siouxland that Manfred published inside the front and back covers of his 1947 novel, *This is the Year* (while still writing under the name Feike Feikema), makes it clear that Manfred had a river and its tributaries in mind when he coined "Siouxland." It is also clear from Manfred's letters and his fiction, especially a work such as *Milk of Wolves*, that the rivers of his home region were deeply important to Manfred not only in themselves, but also as metaphors about the writing process and about a life well lived.

In addition to serving as the basis of Manfred's fictional world, the valley also gave rise to perhaps the most influential American historian of China during the twentieth century. John King Fairbank, as Greg Rohlf explains in chapter 11, during his long career at Harvard produced scores of Ph.D.s who went on to staff newly created positions in China studies at universities across the U.S., a field that Fairbank himself helped to create by lobbying for the importance of China studies as part of U.S. diplomatic efforts. His influence was felt in U.S. foreign policy and in public opinion toward China during and after the Cold War. Rohlf sketches out the Midwestern part of Fairbank's proudly cosmopolitan identity, especially his ties and affinities with the Big Sioux valley. The trajectory of Fairbank's life was set by another influential South Dakotan, his mother, Lorena King Fairbank. She was an accomplished person in her own right and is remembered for her many contributions to education and culture during South Dakota's transformation from territory to state and for her work supporting the women's vote. Considered together, the mother and son demonstrate a cosmopolitanism that made them at home in South Dakota and in the world. The chapter brings to light new materials, mainly gathered from newspaper accounts, that detailed their lifetime associations and affinities with South Dakota and the Big Sioux River valley.

Another of the valley's prominent intellectuals was James Everett Seaton, an English professor for 46 years at Michigan State University who challenged many of academia's prevailing orthodoxies, as explained in chapter 12. Seaton was an Iowa native who spent his early and formative years in Sioux City, at the bottom of the valley. Though many—including his colleagues—have cast him as a defender of the so-called "Canon" of established literary classics and a critic of postmodernism, he is better characterized as a champion of what he termed the "Humanistic Tradition" of literary criticism stretching back millennia. What hath Athens to do with Sioux City? According to Seaton, Iowa and the broader Midwest, what Lincoln called the Land of Steady Habits, endures while the Coasts too often secede. This endurance, like a strong marriage, is based not only on love but a humble strength and knowledge of one's flaws leavened by humor rather than despair. These characteristics were embodied by Seaton's family and community, from his self-deprecating WWII veteran father to his enduring marriage to the distinguished playwright Sandra Seaton, which began when a marriage like theirs was still illegal in many states. These family bonds formed the foundation of his character, which formed the foundation of his approach to criticism. It takes humility, for instance, to keep from attempting to resolve ambiguities in Vergil's *Georgics*, or to believe, as Seaton did, that what a literary work said was more important than what it said to him. It takes strength to face what is flawed in one's favorite works as well as in works by one's favorites. The Midwest and Sioux City gave Seaton this humility and strength along with Athens and literature itself.

As suggested by the Fairbanks' and Seaton's cosmopolitanism, the valley also had its artists. The small, if impactful visual artists of the Big Sioux River valley have long dredged the river for pastoral images of natural, if nostalgic scenes of a prairie ecosystem, as Christopher Vondracek explains in chapter 13. These artists include Terry Redlin and John Green and others. But, like the Ash Can School of Art in gritty, turn-of-the-century New York City, which pivoted—if briefly and politically—from the bourgeois perspectives foregrounded by romantic painters of the Impressionist Era to a realistic culture of the worker and the land as-lived, the artists of southeastern South Dakota can draw increased attention to the plight of the river valley and a cultural stasis around ecological issues by informing themselves with the river less as an art object and more as a part of the daily landscape, engrained in the community's livelihood for generations.

Chapter 14 moves from art to politics as Matthew Housiaux discusses the valley's political traditions, figures, and trends. He explores election results in the nine state counties through which the river flows (Brookings, Codington, Grant, Hamlin, Lincoln, Minnehaha, Moody, Roberts, Union), showing how they fit in the broader political history of the state, as well as examining some of the key politicians who were either born or made their homes by the Big Sioux. The picture that emerges is one of a region that has helped define South Dakota political culture as a whole, mainly through its ongoing status as the state's main population and economic hub. Like South Dakota, the Big Sioux valley is a long-time Republican stronghold, prone to occasional bouts of two-party competition that generally correspond with downturns in the agricultural economy. Early settlement patterns, most notably large numbers of Norwegian immigrants in search of land to farm, helped shape the region's political culture even before South Dakota gained statehood in 1889 and would continue to do so for many decades after. More recently, other forces have helped shape the Big Sioux valley and its politics: the growth of Sioux Falls, South Dakota's largest city, and the decline of the region's rural population; the rise of new industries, such as health care and finance; and national political trends, such as growing polarization, that have gradually filtered down to the state level. One thing that has remained constant is the Big Sioux valley's tendency to produce prominent South Dakota politicians, from the state's first governor, Arthur C. Mellette, to its current one, Kristi Noem. Expect the region to remain the focal point of state politics for the foreseeable future.

In chapter 15 Jon Hunter discusses how political decisions have shaped a particular section of the valley. The lakes, streams, and creeks of Lake County are tributaries of the Big Sioux River, but they have a rich history of their own. From dry lakes in the 1930s to flooding events more than a half-century later, water flows and lake levels have been a continual source of debate, politics, speculation, and action, including questionable environmental and surreptitious activity. The watershed begins in northwest Lake County and moves southeast, passing through Lake Herman, Silver Creek (through the City of Madison), Lake Madison, Long Lake, Round Lake, Brant Lake, and Skunk Creek as it exits the county. Each of the lakes has full-time and seasonal homes and a substantial amount of non-resident recreation, including boating, fishing, swimming, camping, and touring. Excess nitrates and phosphorus have contributed to algae blooms in the lakes and uncontrolled waterways have added silt. Substantial efforts over many decades to improve water quality have not yielded much in long-term results. The installation of silt dams leading to Lake Herman have reduced the inflow of dirt and sand and a dredging operation in the 1970s restored depth to that lake. Construction of a sanitary sewer system at Lake Madison was a success, while a similar system at Brant Lake resulted in lawsuits and a huge financial burden for homeowners. A system at Lake Herman has been debated but never constructed. With a growing residential population at all the lakes, as well as pressure from downstream interests, the health of the watershed will only grow in importance.

Dale Potts moves the story of river management beyond Lake County and examines the history of policies that have been pursued by various levels of government to shape the workings of the river. In chapter 16 Potts argues that knowledge of the long-term health of a river system, like the Big Sioux River watershed, requires an understanding of local, state, and federal history while also acknowledging environmental impacts from industrial, municipal, and agricultural sources along the river and its tributaries. Actions to positively affect the health of watershed river systems in South Dakota, as in many states, developed incrementally in the twentieth century, initially reflecting a utilitarian usage of water sources in the nineteenth and early twentieth centuries. From the 1930s Dust Bowl Era to the 1960s modern environmental movement, conservation as a term changed and expanded its meaning in the agricultural Midwest from one focusing on soil health and prevention of topsoil loss to the implementation of large-scale watershed projects to address flooding in urban areas. By the 1960s identifying and correcting point pollution from municipal and industrial sources became more prevalent alongside improved technologies. More complex discussions of the subject of nonpoint pollution sources, ecosystem rehabilitation, and recreational usage, continued to expand interest in the river's health by the end of the century. To understand long-term change in perceptions of the Big Sioux River and attendant actions to address pollution, it is necessary to ascertain the complex interrelationships between industrial and municipal growth, agricultural and livestock practices, as well as the overall health of an interstate, free-flowing water source in the twentieth century.

Many of the policies described by Potts relate to water quality, an issue examined by Kelsey Murray and Linda DeVeaux in chapter 17. The Big Sioux River travels through one of the most sparsely populated regions in the country, where cattle outnumber people 5:1, to the largest urban center in the state. Given the influence of animal husbandry practices of allowing cattle free access to the river, many regions of the Big Sioux River are designated "impaired" by EPA standards, meaning that the levels of fecal coliform bacteria (i.e., *E. coli*) are above the threshold allowed for certain uses, such as recreational use. This affects the downstream recreational usages of the river, including the kayak park inside the city proper. Of particular concern is the nature of the fecal contamination. Certain animals, such as cattle, carry in their guts bacteria that are harmful to humans. One in particular, the *E. coli* bacteria that make "Shiga toxin," causes gastrointestinal distress, which may progress to more severe complications such as kidney failure or death. It may come as no surprise, then, that South Dakota has the highest incidence of this particular disease in the country. Recent floods have likely resulted in the bacterial communities found in agricultural fields, cattle feed lots, and other terrestrial locations being washed into the river. Once these bacteria co-mingle, even those that are relatively harmless can acquire the ability to cause disease. Thus, such severe flooding is likely to result in an increase in cases of Shiga toxin disease. This chapter discusses the incidence of this disease as reported by the CDC and the South Dakota Department of Health, the monitoring of the river quality by the East Dakota Water Development District, and the U.S. Geologic Survey (USGS), and the implications that climate change may have on the rise of this and other emerging diseases.

Beyond the archaeology, geography, history, and biology of the valley are more personal reflections on life in the valley. In chapter 18 Ryan Allen discusses settling in a place created by movement, by the slow accumulation of silt, thoughts, and aspirations. His story is rooted in the Loess Hills of northwestern Iowa and told through the lens of over thirty years of art and literature in *The Briar Cliff Review*, and in the personal family stories and traumas that shape and define our way. Allen argues that we've lost our connection to the forces and fixtures that can guide our path, like family, culture, land and literature, and asks what we might do to re-forge such bonds. Allen considers how to reconcile the unfathomable and examines our capacity to commit to personal and communal change. Drawing inspiration from the natural history of Connie Mutel and her seminal 1989 work on the Loess Hills of northwestern Iowa, *Fragile Giants*, and the personal narratives of individuals like John Price, William Least Heat-Moon, and Annie Dillard, Allen's chapter reflects the paradox of the still-life in motion, how when home we long for travel, and when traveling, we yearn to reach home. Allen describes being a transplant to Iowa and still finding ways to establish and cultivate deep roots. He concludes that our connection to place and our relationship to space is a pathway for self-discovery, transformation, and voice.

Dave Allan Evans, the long-time poet laureate of South Dakota who has lived in valley towns almost his entire life, offers more personal reflections in chapter 19. With a cue from the well-known evolutionary biologist E.O. Wilson, Evans considers his upper-Midwest hometown of Sioux City as a place made up of what Wilson says are the three seminal characteristics of places where human beings have always tended to settle: a savanna; topographical relief, such as hills; and water, such as rivers. Evans considers two main rivers: the Missouri, and the Big

Sioux that flows into it, and especially Sioux City's many hills. Evans also recounts his experiences in a very different landscape—Brookings, South Dakota, a flat town (unlike Sioux City and Sioux Falls), but nevertheless in the vicinity of the Big Sioux. He recalls the highlights of his life as an English professor and Writer-in-Residence at South Dakota State University, and, in the early 1970s, the creation of SDSU's literary magazine, which published not only the writing of students but also regional writers from nearby states. Evans also remembers his time in the University of Iowa Writers' Workshop in the mid-1960s, when heartland writers were often overlooked or disdained by writers and critics from Eastern settings. Such an experience underscores, once again, why we need to find the neglected history and culture of the Big Sioux River valley.

Jon K. Lauck
September 2021
Sioux Falls, South Dakota

Notes

1   The series, organized by Constance Skinner and given lift by Frederick Jackson Turner, was grounded in a tradition of regionalist writing. Nicolaas Mink, "A Narrative for Nature's Nation: Constance Lindsay Skinner and the Making of Rivers of America," *Environmental History* 11:4 (October 2006), 757-58. Skinner planned to write a multi-volume history of rivers, but Turner suggested it would take a lifetime, so the project became focused on just books written about American rivers that she would solicit from other authors "from the various river sections who 'had it in their blood'" and that she would edit. She thought "'rivers' will prove to be only another way of treating 'sections,'" or regions, and river valleys have indeed become a common form of regional study. Constance Lindsay Skinner and Frederick Jackson Turner, "Notes Concerning My Correspondence with Frederick Jackson Turner," *Wisconsin Magazine of History* 19:1 (September 1935), 93; Mink, "A Narrative for Nature's Nation," 758.

2   James Howard Kuntsler, *The Geography of Nowhere: The Rise and Decline of America's Man-Made Landscape* (New York: Simon & Schuster, 1993); Kathleen Norris, *Dakota: A Spiritual Geography* (New York: Ticknor & Fields, 1993), 10 (emptiness).

3   Joseph Kinsey Howard, "Golden River," *Harper's*, May 1, 1945, 511.

4   Eric Sevareid, *Canoeing with the Cree* (New York: The Macmillan Company, 1935), 37.

5	Heather Benson, "What Might Have Been: The Canal to Big Stone Lake," South Dakota Public Broadcasting, January 27, 2020, https://www.sdpb.org/blogs/images-of-the-past/what-might-have-been-the-canal-to-big-stone-lake/ (noting the plan of the Tri-State Drainage Canal Association to build a canal between Lake Traverse and Big Stone Lake in an effort to drain Red River waters to the south and through the Mississippi River system).

6	Gordon V. Boudreau, "West by Southwest: Thoreau's Minnesota Journey," *The Concord Saunterer* 6 (1998): 145-60. Thoreau was "present at the last annuity payment before the Sioux Outbreak, little more than a year later." Walter Harding, "Thoreau and Mann on the Minnesota River, June, 1861," *Minnesota History* 37:6 (June 1961): 225.

7	Kim Ode, "Could the Mississippi River Actually Begin in South Dakota?" *Minneapolis Star Tribune*, 25 July 2016; Howard, "Golden River," 512. Note that the Mississippi River was once just a small tributary to the Ohio River. Raymond E. Janssen, "The History of a River," *Scientific American* (June 1952), 74. In "West from Here," the preface to *The Interior Borderlands: Regional Identity in the Midwest and Great Plains*, ed. Jon K. Lauck (Sioux Falls: Center for Western Studies, 2019), Harry F. Thompson suggests that the Great Plains/West begins not with the Missouri River but with the Big Sioux River, xvi, xx.

8	Alexander Smart, Pete Bauman, and Barry Dunn, "Discover the Prairie Coteau," *Rangelands* 25:6 (December 2003: 39.

9	"Big Sioux River Watershed Strategic Plan" (June 2016), S.D. Conservation Districts, SD Department of Environment and Natural Resources, U.S. Department of Agriculture, 12.

10	"Big Sioux River Watershed Strategic Plan," 12.

11	"Big Sioux River Watershed Strategic Plan," 12.

12	Darby Nelson, *For Love of a River: The Minnesota* (Edina, MN: Beaver's Pond Press, 2019), 23.

13	Theodore L. Nydahl, "The Pipestone Quarry and the Indians," *Minnesota History* 31:4 (December 1950): 203.

14	Nydahl, 193.

15	John McPhee, *Annals of the Former World* (New York: Farrar, Straus and Giroux, 1998), 630.

16	McPhee, 638.

17	McPhee, 658.

18	McPhee, 658.

19	McPhee, 659.

20	Kelli A. McCormick, Kevin R. Chamberlain, and Colin J. Paterson, "U-Pb Baddeleyite Crystallization Age for a Corson Diabase Intrusion: Possible Midcontinent Rift Magmatism in Eastern South Dakota," *Canadian Journal of Earth Science* 55 (2018): 111-17.

21	Jack Kume, "Water Resources of Deuel and Hamlin Counties, South Dakota," U.S. Geological Survey, Water Resources Investigations Report 84-4069 (U.S. Department of the Interior, 1985), 16; Darrell I. Leap, "Geology and Hydrology of Day County, South Dakota," Bulletin no. 24 (Division of Geological Survey, Department of Water and Natural Resources, 1988), 1.

[22] Assad Barari, "Hydrology of Lake Poinsett," Report of Investigations no. 102 (South Dakota Geological Survey, 1971), 4, 8.

[23] Loren C. Eiseley, "The Flow of the River," *American Scholar* 22:4 (Autumn 1953): 453. This essay was later included in *The Immense Journey* (New York: Random House, 1957). Eiseley was a Nebraskan who dedicated the book to the "memory of Clyde Edwin Eiseley, who lies in the grass of the prairie frontier, but is not forgotten by his son."

[24] Scott Pearce, "Road Signs and Watersheds and Gratitude," *Front Porch Republic*, May 10, 2021.

[25] Gary Snyder, "Coming into the Watershed," in Steven Gilbar, ed., *Natural State: A Literary Anthology of California Nature Writing* (Berkeley: University of California Press, 1998), 364, 367. See also Tom Lynch, "Braided Channels of Watershed Consciousness: Loren Eiseley's 'The Flow of the River' and the Platte Basin Timelapse Project," in Tom Lynch, Susan Naramore Maher, Drucella Wall, and O. Alan Weltzian, eds., *Thinking Continental: Writing the Planet One Place at a Time* (Lincoln: University of Nebraska Press, 2017), 137.

[26] William Least Heat Moon, *Blue Highways* (New York: Fawcett Crest, 1982), 283-84.

[27] N. Scott Momaday, *The Way to Rainy Mountain* (Albuquerque: University of New Mexico Press, 1969), 83.

[28] Lisa Knopp, "No Other River," *Iowa Review* 39:2 (Fall 2009): 171.

[29] Paul Gruchow, "Discovering the Universe of Home," *Minnesota History* 56:1 (Spring 1998): 40.

[30] Wallace Stegner, *Wolf Willow: A History, a Story, and a Memory of the Last Plains Frontier* (New York: Viking, 1962), 18-19.

[31] Frederick Manfred, *Milk of Wolves* (Boston: Avenue Victor Hugo, 1976), 248.

[32] Carl F. Hovde, William L. Howarth, and Elizabeth Hall Witherell, eds., Henry D. Thoreau, *A Week on the Concord and Merrimack Rivers* (Princeton: Princeton University Press, 1980), 7.

[33] Assad Barari, "Hydrology of Lake Kampeska," Report of Investigations no. 103, Science Center, University of South Dakota (1971), 4. The "erroneous impression of flatness" has stemmed from the "flatness of the main valley floors and the smoothness of the sky line" and because early settlers tended to travel the valleys first. G. Malcolm Lewis, "William Gilpin and the Concept of the Great Plains Region," *Annals of the Association of American Geographers* 56:1 (March 1966): 51.

[34] David Quammen, review of McPhee, *Annals of the Former World* (New York: Farrar, Straus & Giroux, 1998), *New York Times*, July 5, 1998. Another critic attacked McPhee as a "writer of fabled factuality and unstylishness." Michael Wolff, "No Jokes, Please, We're Liberal," *Vanity Fair* (June 2005). In a sign of his grounded approach, McPhee taught the course "Literature of Fact" at Princeton University.

[35] Abbie Gardner-Sharp, *The Spirit Lake Massacre and the Captivity of Abbie Gardner,* Expanded, Annotated (Byte Books, Kindle Edition), 97. I thank James Schaap, whose work appears in this volume, for opening my eyes to the story of Gardner.

[36] Smart, Bauman, and Dunn, "Discover the Prairie Coteau," 40.

[37] Nydahl, 202.

[38] Nydahl, 196.

[39] Nydahl, 200.

[40] Nydahl, 198-99.

[41] Nydahl, 199, 203.

[42] Nydahl, 200.

[43] Nydahl, 203.

[44] Nydahl, 203. See also Sally J. Southwick, *Building on a Borrowed Past: Place and Identity in Pipestone, Minnesota* (Athens: Ohio University Press, 2005).

[45] Curt Brown, "Sacred Stone Carves a Legacy," *Star Tribune*, August 24, 2012.

[46] Mark Steil, "Pipestone's Hiawatha Pageant to Close after 60 Years," Minnesota Public Radio, December 30, 2007; Denis P. Gardner, "Calumet Hotel Pipestone," *Minnesota History* 63:2 (Summer 2012): 43.

[47] Dale R. Henning and Thomas D. Thiessen, "Regional Prehistory," *Plains Anthropologist* 49:192, *Memoir 36: Dhegihan and Chiwere Siouans in the Plains: Historical and Archaeological Perspectives* (November 2004), 383; Dale R. Henning and Thomas D. Thiessen, "Summary and Conclusions," *Plains Anthropologist* 49:192, *Memoir 36: Dhegihan and Chiwere Siouans in the Plains: Historical and Archaeological Perspectives* (November 2004), 591.

[48] Dale R. Henning and Thomas D. Thiessen, "Regional Prehistory," 384.

[49] Henning and Thiessen, "Summary and Conclusions," 600, 594 ("It is notable that from about AD 1300 to nearly 1500, Oneota populations were rapidly expanding across the upper Midwest, often settling in large villages.")

[50] Henning and Thiessen, "Regional Prehistory," 387.

[51] Dale R. Henning and Thomas D. Thiessen, "Introduction," *Plains Anthropologist* 49:192, *Memoir 36: Dhegihan and Chiwere Siouans in the Plains: Historical and Archaeological Perspectives* (November 2004), 349; "Blood Run National Historic Landmark" (Office of the State Archaeologist, University of Iowa, 2013), 3.

[52] Henning and Thiessen, "Regional Prehistory," 386.

[53] Henning and Thiessen, "Regional Prehistory," 392.

[54] "Blood Run National Historic Landmark," 3; Henning and Thiessen, "Regional Prehistory," 385; Beth R. Ritter, "Piecing Together the Ponca Past: Reconstructing Degiha Migrations to the Great Plains," *Great Plains Quarterly* 22:4 (Fall 2002): 273 (noting that "[w]e can only speculate why the Ponca ancestors and their relatives may have chosen to migrate to the Great Plains").

[55] Henning and Thiessen, "Introduction," 353.

[56] Henning and Thiessen, "Regional Prehistory," 382 (noting that the "archaeological history is extremely complex and has been subjected to a range of interpretations").

[57] Henning and Thiessen, "Introduction," 351.

[58] Henning and Thiessen, "Summary and Conclusions," 595. See generally Richard White, *The Middle Ground: Indians, Empires, and Republics in the Great Lakes Region, 1650-1815* (New York: Cambridge University Press, 1991).

[59] Henning and Thiessen, "Summary and Conclusions," 595.

[60] Ritter, 275.

[61] Ritter, 275.

[62] "Blood Run National Historic Landmark," 3.

[63] "Blood Run National Historic Landmark," 3, 53; Henning and Thiessen, "Regional Prehistory," 392.

[64] Henning and Thiessen, "Summary and Conclusions," 596; Ritter, "Piecing Together the Ponca Past," 275.

[65] Ritter, 275.

[66] Henning and Thiessen, "Introduction," 351.

[67] Henning and Thiessen, "Introduction," 352.

[68] Henning and Thiessen, "Introduction," 349. See also George W. Schurr and James Zangger, "Protection of Mounds at Blood Run in Northwestern Iowa," *Central States Archaeological Journal* 67:4 (October 2020): 244-48.

[69] W. Raymond Wood, "Mapping the Missouri River through the Great Plains, 1673-1895," *Great Plains Quarterly* 4:1 (Winter 1984): 37; Raphael N. Hamilton, "The Early Cartography of the Missouri Valley," *American Historical Review* 39:4 (July 1934): 660.

[70] Virginia Driving Hawk Sneve, *South Dakota Geographic Names* (Sioux Falls: Brevet Press, 1973), 140.

[71] W. Raymond Wood, "The John Evans 1796-97 Map of the Missouri River," *Great Plains Quarterly* 1:1 (Winter 1981): 39 (also noting that Evans created the "first accurate eyewitness map of the Missouri River in what is now North and South Dakota" which showed "all of its principal tributaries").

[72] Wood, "The John Evans 1796-97 Map," 42. Evans worked with James Mackay, but apparently Mackay never went north of the Niobrara. See generally W. Raymond Wood, *An Atlas of Early Maps of the American Midwest*, Scientific Papers, vol. 18 (Springfield, IL: Illinois State Museum, 1983), 1-3.

[73] Reuben Gold Thwaites, *Original Journals of Lewis and Clark*, vol. 1 (New York: Dodd, Mead & Company, 1904), 115; Wood, "Mapping the Missouri River," 37; Wood, "The John Evans 1796-97 Map," 39.

[74] Wood, "Mapping the Missouri River," 37-38.

[75] Wood, "Mapping the Missouri River," 38; Martha Coleman Bray, "Joseph Nicolas Nicollet, Geologist," *Proceedings of the American Philosophical Society* 114:1 (February 1970): 37; Raymond J. DeMallie, Jr., "Joseph N. Nicollet's Account of the Sioux and Assiniboine in 1839," *South Dakota History* 5:4 (Fall 1975): 344-46; Paul R. Picha, "Joseph N. Nicollet and Great Plains Ethnohistory: Interfaces among Nineteenth-Century French Science, Enlightenment, and Revolution," *Plains Anthropologist* 54:210 (May 2009): 158.

[76] Fremont also began to change the popular perception of the middle of the country as a desert. He helped others to more accurately see the territory based on his reports. Andrew Menard, "Striking a Line through the Great American Desert," *Journal of American Studies* 45:2 (May 2011), 267-80.

[77] John Bicknell, "How Fremont Framed the West," *Middle West Review* 7:2 (Spring 2021): 108.

[78] Virginia Driving Hawk Sneve, *South Dakota Geographic Names* (Sioux Falls: Brevet Press, 1973), 140.

[79] David H. Burr, *The American Atlas* (December 31, 1839), noted by "Feature Detail Report for: Big Sioux River" (USGS, February 13, 1980).

[80] Office of the State Archaeologist, University of Iowa 2013.

[81] John Disturnell, *Mapa de los Estados Unidos de Mejico* (December 31, 1847).

[82] "Feature Detail Report for: Big Sioux River" (USGS, February 13, 1980).

[83] Bray and Bray, *Joseph N. Nicollet On the Plains and Prairies*, 88; Nicollet, *Report*, 28.

[84] F. Robert Gartner and Carolyn Hull Sieg, "South Dakota Rangelands: More than a Sea of Grass," *Rangelands* 18:6 (December 1996): 213.

[85] Gartner and Sieg, "South Dakota Rangelands," 213.

[86] Smart, Bauman, and Dunn, "Discover the Prairie Coteau," 40.

[87] Gartner and Sieg, "South Dakota Rangelands," 213.

[88] See Jon K. Lauck, ed., *The Interior Borderlands: Regional Identity in the Midwest and Great Plains* (Sioux Falls: Center for Western Studies, 2019).

[89] Wallace Stegner, *Beyond the Hundredth Meridian: John Wesley Powell and the Second Opening of the West* (Boston: Houghton Mifflin, 1954).

[90] James Davis, "Of Space, Time, Size, Hexagons, Movement, and Memory: A Comparison of County Development in Illinois and South Dakota," in Lauck, ed., *Interior Borderlands*, 40-54.

[91] Orland A. Rothlisberger, "The Populist National Convention in Sioux Falls," *South Dakota History* 1:2 (Spring 1971): 158.

[92] Richard Street, "The Economist as Humanist: The Career of Paul S. Taylor," *California History* 58:4 (Winter 1979/1980): 350.

[93] "Big Sioux River Watershed Strategic Plan," 22.

[94] Vittoria Di Palma and Alexander Robinson, "Willful Waters," *Places Journal* (May 2018).

[95] Susan Naramore Maher, "Deep Mapping the Great Plains: Surveying the Literary Cartography of Place," *Western American Literature* 36:1 (March 2001): 4-24; Susan Naramore Maher, *Deep Map Country: Literary Cartography of the Great Plains* (Lincoln: University of Nebraska Press, 2014); Randall Joorda, "Deep Maps in Eco-Literature," *Michigan Quarterly Review* 40:1 (Winter 2001): 257-72.

[96] Maher, *Deep Map Country*, 119.

[97] John Andrews, "Remembering a Small-Town Boy," *South Dakota Magazine*, May 4, 2020. The long-time historian of South Dakota and the Midwest John E. Miller was planning to write a chapter about Schultz for this volume, but he died, much too soon, in May 2020. Jon Lauck, "S.D. historian Miller passes into history," *Brookings Register*, May 7, 2020.

[98] Robert E. Kohler, "Paul Errington, Aldo Leopold, and Wildlife Ecology: Residential Science," *Historical Studies in the Natural Sciences* 41:2 (2011): 216 (noting how "Errington's ecology and Leopold's ethic were shaped by their own residential trajectories, from the rural Midwest of their youths").

[99] Paul Errington, *The Red Gods Call* (Ames: Iowa State University, 1973), viii-ix; A.W. Schorger, "In Memoriam: Paul Lester Errington," *The Auk* 83:1 (January 1966): 53.

[100] Deborah Gewertz and Frederick Errington, "Doing Good and Doing Well: Prairie Wetlands, Private Property, and the Public Trust," *American Anthropologist* 117:1 (March 2015): 17-31.

[101] Robert M. Berdahl (Chancellor, University of California, Berkeley), "The Lawrence Legacy," Lawrence Symposium, University of South Dakota, December 10, 2001.

[102] Clyde Brashier, "Dakota Images," *South Dakota History* 34:3 (Summer 2004): 290.

[103] Bernie Hunhoff, "All Good Things Must End," *South Dakota Magazine*, June 15, 2012 (noting the Norris connection). The Center for Western Studies at Augustana University is now the repository for the 35,000 distinct images, over 1,000 artifacts, and hundreds of books once collected by Maudlin's Blue Cloud Abbey-American Indian Culture Research Center.

[104] Benet Tvedten, *The View from the Monastery* (New York: Riverhead Books, 1999).

[105] "Memorial by Br. Benet Tvedten, OSB," Saint Benedict/Saint John's, https://www.csbsju.edu/jon-hassler/jon-hassler-memorial-service/tvedten.

[106] "Memorial by Br. Benet Tvedten, OSB."

[107] Keith Fynaardt, "The Presence of Siouxland," *South Dakota Review* 38:3 (Fall 2000): 36.

[108] "Whence Siouxland?" *Book Remarks* (Sioux City Public Library), May 1991, 1-2.

[109] "Whence Siouxland?" *Book Remarks*, 2.

[110] Arthur R. Huseboe, "From Feikema to Manfred, from the Big Sioux Basin to the Northern Plains," *Great Plains Quarterly* 21:4 (Fall 2001): 309.

[111] Huseboe, "From Feikema to Manfred," 310.

[112] Huseboe, "From Feikema to Manfred," 315. Worthington, Minnesota, straddles the eastern boundary of the Big Sioux watershed.

[113] See Colin A. Niehus, Aldo V. Vecchia, and Ryan F. Thompson, "Lake-Level Frequency Analysis for Waubay Lakes Chain, Northeastern South Dakota," Water-Resources Investigations Report 99-4122 (U.S. Geological Survey, U.S. Department of the Interior, 1999), 12.

[114] Jill Callison, "Professor Feels Joy in the Midst of Pain," *Argus Leader*, November 8, 2015.

[115] *Saturday News*, June 27, 1912, quoted in "Stony Point: Entertainment Complex at Lake Kampeska" (Codington County Historical Society Museum, nd).

[116] "Stony Point." These boats are not to be confused with the *Kampeska Belle*, which exploded and sank in 1887. *By the Shores of Lake Kampeska: An Anecdotal History of Its People, Places, and Events* (January 2018), 57.

[117] Joanita M. Kant, "A Historical Geography of Lake Kampeska in the City of Watertown, South Dakota," *Geography Faculty Publications No. 2* (South Dakota State University, 2007), 12.

[118] Jeremy Fugleberg, "The Kampeska Creature," *Watertown Public Opinion*, July 19, 2008.

[119] "Stony Point."

[120]Kant, 12.

[121]*By the Shores of Lake Kampeska*, 58.

[122]Kant, 14.

[123]Kant, 15.

[124]Kant, 14.

[125]*By the Shores of Lake Kampeska*, 42.

[126]Assad Barari, "Hydrology of Lake Kampeska," Report of Investigations No. 103, Science Center, University of South Dakota (1971), 4.

[127]Kant, 9.

[128]Loren C. Eiseley, "The Flow of the River," *American Scholar* 22:4 (Autumn 1953): 456.

[129]Kant, 10; *South Dakota Place-Names*, Part I: State, County, and Town Names, Compiled by Workers of the Writers' Program of the WPA in the State of South Dakota (Vermillion, SD: University of South Dakota, 1940), 165.

[130]Sandy Johnson, "Kemp Runs with Family Ties," Associated Press, April 9, 1987. On Kemp's role as Bob Dole's running mate in 1996 and his return to Watertown, see Tom Raum, "Kemp Goes Solo in Town Great-Grandfather Founded," Associated Press, August 24, 1996.

[131]Kant, 11.

[132]Kant, 11.

[133]Kant, 11.

[134]Grant Evans, "Reid Holien Elected Watertown's New Mayor, Defeating Sarah Caron," *Watertown Public Opinion*, 16 June 16 2021. The new mayor, Reid Holien, is the author of *Skeletons of the Prairie: Abandoned Rural Codington County* (Watertown, SD: Codington County Historical Society, 2000).

[135]David Jackson and Gregory Korte, "Obama Touches Down in His 50th State: South Dakota," *USA Today*, May 8, 2015.

[136]Patrick Anderson, "Obama Praises S.D. Grads, Plugs College Plan in Visit to Watertown," *Argus Leader*, May 8, 2015.

[137]*South Dakota Place-Names*, 49. For early life along the Hidewood, see Robert Amerson, *From the Hidewood: Memories of a Dakota Neighborhood* (St. Paul: Minnesota Historical Society Press, 1996).

[138]Lance Nixon, "A Hemingway Hunting Story They Couldn't Tell," *Pierre Capitol Journal*, September 24, 2013; Ardyce Haberger Samp, Eugene W. Larsen, Sr., and Roger Holtzmann, "Hemingway's Lake County Hunt," *South Dakota Magazine* (September/October 2006).

[139]*South Dakota Place-Names*, 165.

[140]Jon K. Lauck, "Dorothea Lange and the Limits of the Liberal Narrative," *Heritage of the Great Plains* 45:1 (Summer 2012): 22.

[141]Matthew Miller, "Ripple Effects," *Eckleberg Review*, January 16, 2018.

[142]Mikkel Pates, "SD Legislators Reopen Submerged Farmland in Northeast Corner to Fishing Again," *Dickinson Press*, June 13, 2017.

[143]Joseph Hogan, Jon K. Lauck, Paul Murphy, Andrew Seal, and Gleaves Whitney, eds., *The Sower and the Seer: Perspectives on the Intellectual History of the American Midwest* (Madison: Wisconsin Historical Society Press, 2021).

[144]Chuck Cecil, "Poinsett's Enduring Charm," *South Dakota Magazine* (May/June 2009).

[145]Leland Olson Hoel, "Lake Poinsett Nostalgia," October 8, 2016, http://dailypost. wordpress.com/photo-challenges/nostalgia/.

[146]John Anfinson, *The River We Have Wrought: A History of the Upper Mississippi* (Minneapolis: University of Minnesota Press, 2005).

[147]For the case, see Duerre v. Hepler, 892 N.W. 2d 209 (2017).

[148]Steven Wingate, *The Leave-Takers: A Novel* (Lincoln: University of Nebraska Press, 2021); Megan Phelps-Roper, *Unfollow: A Memoir of Loving and Leaving the Westboro Baptist Church* (New York: Farrar, Straus and Giroux, 2019).

[149]See Bill McDonald, *The Nunda Irish: A Story of Irish Immigrants: The Joys and Sorrows of Their Life in America* (Stillwater, MN: Farmstead Publishing, 1990).

[150]Edward Relph, *Place and Placelessness* (London: Pion Limited, 1976), 35.

[151]E.C.G., "Minnehaha Falls and Longfellow's 'Hiawatha,'" *Minnesota History* 8:4 (December 1927): 423.

[152]Cynthia D. Nickerson, "Artistic Interpretations of Henry Wadsworth Longfellow's *The Song of Hiawatha*, 1855-1900," *The American Art Journal* 16:3 (Summer 1984): 49.

[153]Nickerson, 49. For a history of the Center of Western Studies, see Harry F. Thompson, *"Bright, Clear Sky Over a Plain So Wide": The Center for Western Studies, 1964-2020* (Sioux Falls: Center for Western Studies, 2021).

[154]Ralph Brown, "A Tale of Two Cities: Sioux Falls and Sioux City," *South Dakota Business Review* 58:2 (December 2004): 1, 4-20, 19 (noting that in the 1960s Sioux Falls and Sioux City were similar in size, but from 1969-2002 Sioux Falls grew by 60% while Sioux City grew 7%).

[155]Arthur R. Huseboe, ed., *Poems and Essays of Herbert Krause* (Sioux Falls, SD: Center for Western Studies, 1990), 209.

[156]Davidson to author, May 12, 2019.

[157]John Graves, *Goodbye to a River* (New York: Alfred A. Knopf, 1960), 144. See also John Graves, *John Graves and the Making of Goodbye to a River: Selected Letters, 1957-1960* (Houston: Southern Methodist University, 2000).

[158]Robert Pirsig, *Zen and the Art of Motorcycle Maintenance* (New York: Bantam Books, 1974), 3.

[159]Relph, 3.

[160]David Allan Evans, *Remembering the Soos* (Marshall, MN: Plains Press, 1986), 21-28.

[161]David Allan Evans, "'Plow It and Find Out': Midwestern American Poetry," 2, provided by author. An earlier version appeared in *South Dakota Review* 41:1-2 (2003): 33-41.

[162]Quoted in Evans, "'Plow It and Find Out,'" 7.

[163]Aldo Leopold, *Sand County Almanac: And Sketches Here and There* (New York: Oxford University Press, 2020 [1949]), 46.

Part I

Natural History and Indigenous Peoples

Chapter 1

A River Through Time:
Early Cultures on the Big Sioux River

Renee M. Boen
South Dakota State Archaeologist

Katie Lamie
*Repository Manager, Archaeological Research Center,
South Dakota State Historical Society*

O ver the last 11,000 years, the Big Sioux River has been known by many different names. The Ioway-Oto tribe, who lived along its banks around 1700, sometimes called it the Pipe-stone River.[1] The name reflects the river as a link to the soft red pipe-stone that they quarried east of the present-day town of Flandreau. The Dakota had another name for the river, Tehankasandata, or Thick-wooded River.[2] Between 1795 and 1797, Spain sponsored an expe-dition by James Mackay and John Thomas Evans that started in St. Louis, Missouri. Evans, with a small group of men, traveled from Fort Charles, south of present-day Sioux City, Iowa, up the Missouri to the White River in south-central South Dakota in 1797, and then beyond to the Mandan villages in southern North Dakota. He created the first cartographic map of the Missouri River and its tributaries with great accuracy and assigned names to the tributaries, including the Sioux River.[3] Today, cartographers use the name Big Sioux River. Regardless, the river has served as a critical cultural thoroughfare and trade route between the eastern woodlands and the western Great Plains for thou-sands of years. In large part, this was possible because the Big Sioux River meets the continent-crossing Missouri River, providing access to a wide trade network across the Northern Plains. Exotic items, such as marine shell from the Atlantic and Gulf coasts, native copper from the Great Lakes area, Knife River flint from west-central North Dakota, Bijou Hills quartzite from south-central South Dakota, and obsidian from the Yellowstone region, were all traded into the Big Sioux River valley. In return, the locally available red pipestone, also known as catlinite, was traded out all over the Midwest as the raw material for elaborately carved pipes and incised plaques.

The unassuming headwaters of the Big Sioux River are located at the confluence of several intermittent drainages atop the northernmost Coteau des Prairies, a striking flat-iron shaped plateau that represents a biogeographical island[4] that rises 800 feet above the surrounding lowlands (Figure 1). A massive glacier, the Wisconsin, divided at the northern tip of the Coteau during the Pleistocene epoch about two million years ago, scouring the softer geology along the Coteau's eastern and western edges as it moved south, but preserving the plateau itself as an ice-free tableland.[5] Approximately 200 miles long, the Coteau is one of the most prominent topographic features in eastern South Dakota, although its eastern margin becomes less apparent towards the south as the plateau's width expands and its elevation slopes downward.

A sequence of substantial glacial events resulted in the creation of the Big Sioux River on the Coteau. Subsequent glacial events bounded the Coteau on the east with the Des Moines glacial lobe and on the west with the James glacial lobe. Meltwaters from both lobes, carrying massive loads of sands and gravels, drained into the Big Sioux River. As the glaciers melted the volume of water diminished, and the river could no longer support the heavy loads of material. Water backed up behind the tributaries, which were blocked by these dropped sands and gravels, creating a pocked landscape and the complex network of lakes and sloughs seen today, generally only along the glacial terrain west of the river. Some of the blocked tributaries continue to drain portions of the Coteau, while others still feed into the Big Sioux River.[6]

The Coteau represents a unique physiographic and ecological biome that affected the strategic adaptations of its first inhabitants, the Native Americans, who assessed both the potential and limiting factors of this transitional landscape. The valley of the Big Sioux River dissects the Coteau from north to south, exhibiting changes in natural resources along its course, until the river exits southeasterly onto the prairie and continues southward to the Missouri River, north of modern-day Sioux City, Iowa. The glacial lakes near the Big Sioux's headwaters and near its channel, intermittently south through Minnehaha County, provided convenient supplies of fish and mussels, enhancing the seasonal corridor for hunting and trapping migratory birds. While deciduous timber may have been lacking on the northern end of the Coteau, this resource could be found along its steep embankments and on the banks of the river for many miles as it winds its way south. Consisting of soils replenished by frequent flooding, the river's bottomlands were fertile, especially in and around Sioux Falls and Brookings, where, eventually, the hunting and gathering lifestyle was complemented by the farming of corn, beans, and squash.

The southern extent of the Coteau is underlain by a resistant pink quartzite of the Sioux Formation, which extends east into Minnesota, northwestern Iowa, and west towards the Missouri River. This geological layer also includes embedded slabs of catlinite.[7] Taken together, the topography of the plateau, its underlying geology and erosional exposures, natural resources, and waterways, namely the Big Sioux River, set the parameters for the complex cultural developments that archaeologists have aimed to study over the course of the last one hundred and sixty years.

As early as 1860, civil engineer Alfred J. Hill prepared professionally drafted maps of two sets of burial mounds near present-day Sioux Falls. He responded to an appeal from the Minnesota State Historical Society for information on the location and number of Native American mounds encountered by workers and travelers in the greater Dakota Territory area. Hill's later work, in collaboration with Theodore H. Lewis, another professional surveyor with an interest in archaeology, constituted the Northwestern Archaeological Survey from 1880 to 1895. With Hill as financial benefactor and data manager, Lewis traveled over 54,000 miles across several states, mapping burial mounds, cultural earthworks, and stone effigies.[8]

Other early archaeological studies along the Big Sioux River were conducted as gentlemanly antiquarian pursuits from about 1870 to 1920. While impressive "ruined ancient cities" do exist, to some degree, along the river, the main excitement concerning these historic finds was probably related to their opportune location relative to the

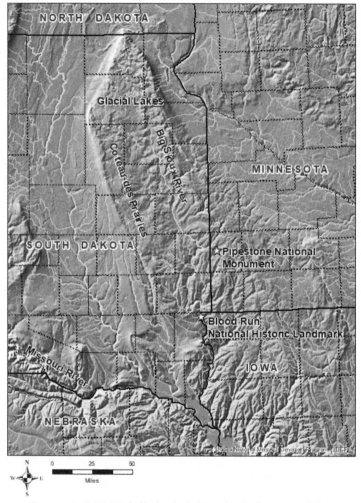

Figure 1. LiDAR hill-shaded digital relief image of the
Coteau landform showing selected features.

bustling young city of Sioux Falls and its landscape-altering agricultural and industrial developments. Local newspaper articles heralded the
sensationalized discovery of the Blood Run/Rock Island site complex,
which contained a *Silent City*[9] of mounds, prehistoric house features,
earthworks, and mysterious pitted boulders on both the South Dakota
and Iowa sides of the Big Sioux River. Among the antiquarians were
brothers Richard F. and Frederick W. Pettigrew, who curated an impressive museum collection while collecting display-quality artifacts,

excavating burial mounds, and mapping sites in and around Sioux Falls.

In the 1920s two archaeological sites on the Big Sioux River, Brandon Village (39MH1) and Split Rock Creek Mounds (39MH6), attracted the attention of William E. Myer of the Smithsonian Institution's Bureau of American Ethnology. Myer supervised the first large-scale excavations at these two sites with the assistance of South Dakota's own William H. Over, the curator and director of the Dakota Museum at the University of South Dakota, Vermillion (now the W.H. Over Museum). In 1939 and 1940 the University of South Dakota sponsored a Work Projects Administration archaeological project at the same two sites, which was, in large part, managed by Elmer E. Meleen.[10] By the mid-twentieth century, much of the professional archaeological work in South Dakota shifted to the Missouri River in advance of federal dam construction projects.[11]

The passage of the National Historic Preservation Act of 1966, as amended, changed the way archaeological pursuits were initiated across the country. Projects on federal land, and those that receive federal funding, require a federal permit, or are subject to federal review, must take historic properties into consideration before construction begins. This legislation also made grant funds available for research projects. As state and federal agencies, contractors, and archaeologists created processes to implement this new, often confusing legislation, a new kind of cultural resource management bureaucracy evolved. In South Dakota, what had started as a largely research-focused program within the University of South Dakota Museum splintered off as the Archaeological Commission in 1973, with J. Steve Sigstad appointed as the first State Archaeologist.[12] This program went through numerous state government reorganizations and is today known as the South Dakota State Historical Society Archaeological Research Center. The Archaeological Research Center continues to be responsible for conducting archaeological surveys and excavations and promoting the preservation of significant cultural sites.

Another major piece of federal legislation, the Native American Graves Protection and Repatriation Act, was passed in 1990. It defines the rights of Native American lineal descendants, Indian tribes, and Native Hawaiian organizations with respect to burials on federal lands as well as directs the repatriation of human remains and funerary objects held in collections across the country. As a result, archaeologists work with Native American tribes if there is the potential for the discovery of human remains during excavation or are associated with a proposed project.

With funding authorized under the National Historic Preservation Act, many tribes established their own Tribal Historic Preservation Offices and lead collaborative preservation efforts. This has allowed tribes to determine archaeological site significance on their own terms. Traditional knowledge, oral histories, and historic documentation from tribal archives are now, with greater frequency, coupled with archaeological methodologies and theoretical frameworks to forge a more academically rigorous and inclusive discipline of archaeology.

Today's archaeologists aim to define and understand cultural patterns through time, using several lines of evidence as interpreted from a multi-disciplinary framework. The archaeological dataset is necessarily limited by the lack of preservation of organic materials, such as leather and basketry, and tends to include animal bone assemblages, bone implements, pottery fragments, charred botanicals, and stone tool technologies at most prehistoric sites. Radio-carbon dating, pollen analysis, molecular studies of catlinite, and residue identification are all methods archaeologists use to fill-in the gaps in the archaeological record. Along with studies of material culture, archaeologists increasingly rely on advanced geological and geographical techniques to interpret the past; geophysical analysis, including non-invasive ground-penetrating radar and Light Detection and Ranging (LiDAR) digital elevation assessments, helps archaeologists identify culturally modified landscapes.

The following discussion is a condensed overview of our current archaeological understanding of the cultural history of the Big Sioux River within the framework of Paleoindian, Archaic, Woodland, Initial Middle Missouri, Oneota, Protohistoric, Historic periods (Figure 2). This narrative is not meant to be authoritative and fixed; future shifts in research topics and paradigms, the near constant development of cutting-edge scientific advancements, the continual discovery of new sites and artifacts, and the reassessment of the significance of the past by each generation will keep the archaeology of the Big Sioux River as dynamic as the geologic processes that created it.

Paleoindian (10,000 to 6,000 B.C.)

A passion of archaeologists is their quest to discover direct, indisputable evidence of the earliest human habitation in North and South America. Studies of ancient DNA add to our knowledge of the peopling of the Americas and have helped archaeologists gauge whether the initial population movement was over the Bering land bridge, along the Alaskan coastline, or as ocean going travel across the Pacific. Each hypothesis comes with its own cult-of-personality and controversy, although some aspects are more generally accepted based on the preponderance of current scientific data. In the Northern Great Plains, this frenzied excitement takes the form of archaeologists playing a role in the investigation of any paleontological megafauna discoveries that *could* be related to human hunting, processing, or scavenging activities at the end of the Pleistocene, as the glaciers retreated.

The Big Sioux River and its environs are a rich source of paleontological treasures. William H. Over's Dakota Museum paleontological catalog record shows a pattern of promising discoveries in the Big Sioux River valley in the early 1900s: about 15 specimens of mastodon/mammoth, 1 giant beaver, 2 musk ox, 17 extinct horses, 1 ground sloth, 8 extinct bison, 5 deer, 6 caribou, 3 "peccary," and 6 unidentified fossilized mammal bones.[13] Most were recovered from gravel and sand pits located in Sioux Falls, Worthing, Tea, Beresford, Hudson, Canton, Parker, Corson, and Vermillion. Other fossils, such as a mastodon found by the Boy Scouts and an extinct bison found in Dell Rapids, were exposed along the cutbank of the Big Sioux River itself. Sioux Falls construction projects in 1916 and a railroad cut in 1901 were discovery sites of paleontological megafauna, and area well-diggers frequently found ancient faunal remains and wood in good condition.

Consequently, in 2001, when kayakers discovered mammoth bones eroding out of the Big Sioux River near Brookings, a team of archaeologists excitedly joined the investigation. Between 2003 and 2005 archaeologists exposed the adjacent riverbank profile and conducted excavations, hoping to find a definitive connection between the 12,000-year-old mammoth and human activity (*Mammuthus columbi* tooth root, radiocarbon age result of 12,485 +/-34 radiocarbon years Before Present). Archaeological materials representing two cultural components were found intact above the mammoth bone layer at what

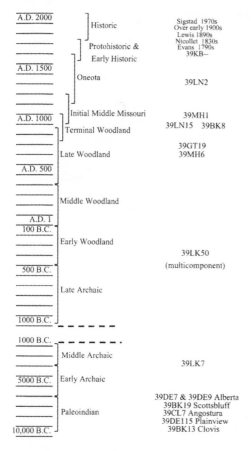

Figure content (chronology chart):

Time	Period	Sites
A.D. 2000	Historic	Sigstad 1970s / Over early 1900s / Lewis 1890s
	Protohistoric & Early Historic	Nicollet 1830s / Evans 1790s / 39KB--
A.D. 1500	Oneota	39LN2
A.D. 1000	Initial Middle Missouri	39MH1
	Terminal Woodland	39LN15 39BK8
	Late Woodland	39GT19 / 39MH6
A.D. 500	Middle Woodland	
A.D. 1 / 100 B.C.	Early Woodland	
500 B.C.		39LK50 (multicomponent)
	Late Archaic	
1000 B.C.		
1000 B.C.	Middle Archaic	39LK7
5000 B.C.	Early Archaic	
	Paleoindian	39DE7 & 39DE9 Alberta / 39BK19 Scottsbluff / 39CL7 Angostura / 39DE115 Plainview / 39BK13 Clovis
10,000 B.C.		

Figure 2. Chronology of the Big Sioux River valley and examples of sites from various time periods.

was later termed the Chalk Rock Site (39BK100); lithics and bison bone were excavated in association with charcoal samples that were radiocarbon dated to circa 9,000 and 10,900 years ago (radiocarbon years Before Present), representing the Late Paleoindian and Early Paleoindian periods. However, a final analysis of the excavated collection has not been completed and the relationship between the mammoth and cultural layers is indeterminate.

The Paleoindian period is a time of big-game hunting and intensive gathering of edible plants across the landscape, most likely in response to animal migrations and the seasonality of important resources. Early Paleoindian populations likely traveled along the Coteau and the Big Sioux River, stalking mammoth and now-extinct species of bison in small interrelated family groups. This mobile lifestyle probably resulted in low population densities and relatively short life expectancies. Little is known about their temporary shelter structures, and they likely carried only a few possessions from camp to camp.

Much of what is known about Paleoindian lifeways in the Big Sioux River valley comes from the ten Paleoindian archaeological sites that have been recorded in the region (including 39BK100). Six of the ten sites include isolated projectile points that were recovered from the ground surface out of their original context. Paleoindian projectile points generally have a lanceolate shape with a concave base, lacking shoulders (Figure 3). Variations in style occur across space and time, including Paleoindian point types called Clovis, Goshen, Folsom, Browns Valley, Scottsbluff, Alberta, and Plainview.[14] Three isolated spear points, a Folsom type (8,950-8,250 B.C.) reportedly discovered in Clark County (39CK2), a Plainview type (8,050-7,050 B.C.) found in Deuel County (39DE115), and an Angostura type (ca. 7,430 B.C.) found in Clay County (39CL7) are among the oldest types found in eastern South Dakota. Other Paleoindian spear point discoveries include Alberta projectile points (7,300-6,900 B.C.) at two additional sites in Deuel County (39DE7 and 39DE9) and a Scottsbluff projectile point (6,800-6,400 B.C.) found in Brookings County (39BK19). Remarkably, the spear point discovered in Clay County (39CL7) was found by a young patrolman with the Vermillion Police Department in a plowed field just outside the city limits of Vermillion, close to the Vermillion River. The patrolman, along with an equally young Clay County Deputy Sheriff, chased burglary suspects through a field of tall corn around 2 a.m. in August 1973. They lost the suspects, but returned the next morning to search for possible stolen items discarded by the burglars. Instead of stolen goods, the patrolman spotted the spear point as he returned across the field.

In addition to the Paleoindian cultural stratigraphy observed at the Chalk Rock Site, there are three other Paleoindian sites in the Big Sioux River region that consist of more than just isolated Paleoindian point finds. A Paleoindian burial site in Browns Valley, Minnesota, (21TR5) was initially discovered in 1933, and included striking Browns Valley Paleoindian projectile points thought to be possible funerary objects.[15] The skeletal remains recovered from the burial appeared to be stained with red ochre and were identified as those of a middle-aged male, which were ultimately radiocarbon dated to over 9,000 years old.[16] A multi-component site in Deuel County, the Winter Site (39DE5), includes evidence of Paleoindian occupation.[17] An incomplete Paleoindian projectile point recovered during 1991 test unit excavations at the multi-component Tangen Site (39BK13), located along the shoreline of Oakwood Lakes, is variously referred to as either Clovis-like or Goshen.[18] Both the Winter Site and the Tangen Site are related to the predictably reliable natural resources that were available in the Glacial Lakes region during Paleoindian times. Lastly, Paleoindian peoples in the Big Sioux River valley are known to have relied on long-distance trade and/or direct procurement of Knife River flint, a high-quality lithic tool-stone found in west-central North Dakota. Many Paleoindian points recovered from the region are expertly chipped from this material, which they obtained through trade, possibly via the Missouri River, or by direct acquisition at the quarry.

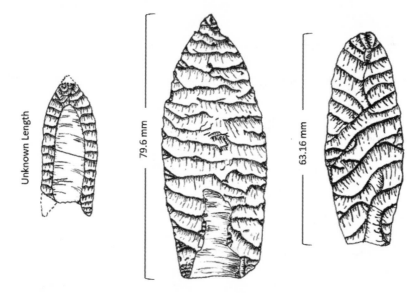

Figure 3. Examples of Paleoindian projectile points (left to right): Folsom projectile point from site 39CK2 (Clark County, SD), Browns Valley projectile point from site 21TR5 (Traverse County, MN), and Angostura projectile point from site 39CL7 (Clay County, SD). Illustrations by Jane Watts 2021, with Browns Valley projectile point adapted from original sketch.[19]

Archaic (6,000-400 B.C.)

Compared to the Paleoindian period, Archaic subsistence strategies are broader based, with a demonstrated reliance on intensive bison hunting and smaller game.[20] Several impressive Northern Plains bison kill sites confirm that Archaic communal hunting strategies could be very productive, especially if opportunistic hunters used steep ravines, sheer cliffs, and marshy terrain to their advantage.

One of the few Archaic sites in the Big Sioux River valley, the Hilde Site (39LK7), is an extensive complex of burial pits and at least one hearth-like feature discovered on the south side of Lake Madison, in Lake County, South Dakota. The glacial gravels along the lake's bluff-top had been commercially mined for years, when in 1981 human remains were found eroding out of the cut portion of the hillside.[21] Over the next four years, the landowners, with occasional assistance from law enforcement and archaeologists, discovered seven to ten burial pits. Forensic analysis of the human remains indicates that 17 to 20 individuals of various ages were represented, although the analysis was complicated by the fact that both primary and secondary burials were identified at the site.[22] The primary burials were characterized by individuals who were interred shortly after their death, in a flexed position with their knees drawn up to their chest.[23] Secondary burials, individuals who were first placed aboveground, possibly in a tree or on a scaffold, included sets of commingled skeletal remains that were later bundled and buried together in the subsurface pits. The presence of both types of burials suggests that deaths occurred during the warmer months *and* when the ground was frozen, which could indicate the site was occupied nearly year-round or that the group returned to the location every year to bury their dead.

Similar to a common Paleoindian burial practice, the skeletal remains of some individuals were treated with red ochre. The artifacts recovered are consistent with Archaic stone tool preform reduction blanks, which are representative of an early stage of the projectile point manufacturing process. Interestingly, four small, nearly identical, asymmetrical stone knives were also recovered. These examples are nearly triangular-shaped, with one edge and the base creating almost a 90-degree angle, opposite to a curved cutting edge. Many of the lithic artifacts were made from Knife River flint, supporting an interpretation that Archaic peoples also utilized long-distance trade routes and/ or traveled to the quarry.[24] The Hilde family submitted samples for radiocarbon dating and received results of circa 3,800 years before present (corrected to 2545-1965 B.C.) and 4,040 years before present (corrected to 2895-2320 B.C.). Thus, the hearth-like feature and burials are consistent with the Middle Archaic.[25]

The human remains recovered from this Archaic burial were ultimately reburied in 1991 under the authority of the State of South Dakota in consultation with tribal representatives, at a place chosen by Arikara spiritual leader Wesley Plenty Chief, along the Missouri River near Fort Pierre. It is important to note that prehistoric and early historic burials on private and state lands are now protected under state law, although in the 1980s, such protections were not yet in place.

Plains Woodland (400 B.C.-A.D. 1200)

In eastern South Dakota, the Archaic hunter-gatherer subsistence strategy and material culture persisted into the Woodland period with few changes and, oftentimes, without clear distinctions. The focus on communal bison hunts continued with spear and atlatl weaponry, although new styles of dart points introduced during the Woodland, called Pelican Lake and Besant, help archaeologists define sites that represent the transition. Woodland groups were not only bison hunters, but exploited the riverine and glacial lakes for fish, mussels, wild vegetables, nuts, berries, deer, elk, and small mammals. Trade for high quality tool-stone, such as Knife River flint from west-central North Dakota, obsidian from the Yellowstone area, and Bijou Hills quartzite from south-central South Dakota, continued from the Archaic into the Woodland. It was not until later, and then not consistently or simultaneously across the landscape, that the hallmarks of Woodland culture emerge, ceramic vessels, the bow and arrow, and earthen burial mounds. These changes reflect influence from eastern Woodland, Hopewell, and Adena cultures that flourished in the Ohio and Mississippi River valleys during this time frame.[26] Finally, the introduction of horticulture emerged during what is known as the Terminal Woodland Great Oasis phase.

Headwaters and Beyond: Grant, Codington, and Hamlin Counties

Several variations of Woodland lifeways are found not only across the Northern Great Plains, but also on the Coteau. The variations in geography, resources, and climate influenced these unique adaptations from north to south. Near the headwaters of the Big Sioux River, on the shore of Summit Lake in Grant County, limited excavations were conducted at a Woodland habitation in 1991 (39GT19). Two dart points and two arrow points suggest the site post-dates A.D. 500, when spear and atlatl technologies, with the larger dart points, were eventually replaced by the bow and arrow, with smaller, broad, notched arrow points.[27] Stone knives and scrapers for hide processing and skeletal elements of at least two bison, a dog or wolf, a dog or coyote, and other small mammals were recovered. Three different ceramic wares are represented, St. Croix (A.D. 300/500-800), Onamia (A.D. 800-1000), and Lake Benton (A.D. 700-1200). These ceramic types are frequently found to the east in Minnesota and beyond and seem to be closely related in style and time frame.[28] Although the dates for the ceramics span A.D. 300-1200, it is quite possible that the time frame for the site is much tighter.

Evidence of Woodland shelters is sparse and typically limited to uncovering a short row or two of soil stains where support posts were set into the ground, called post molds, or fragments of mud and grass used to seal the post structure from the elements, called daub. Excavations at Woodland sites in Minnesota and along the Missouri River suggest that these shelters were pit houses with semi-subterranean excavated floors and a post structure that was covered with thatch or mud and thatch. Circular alignments of stones recorded on the northern Coteau represent weights used to hold down the bottom of a hide covering tipi poles. Tipis were used throughout many time periods, and these do not necessarily represent the Woodland period. Yet they are examples of another type of shelter used by people with a mobile lifestyle. The ephemeral nature of this lifestyle had a limited impact on the landscape, and that, coupled with site destruction from modern development, makes it difficult to identify these architectural features today.

Along the upper Big Sioux, a few series of glacial lakes lie quite close to the river. On the high land overlooking the river and these lakes, archaeologists have recorded many isolated or small scatters of artifacts. Artifact types represented may include stone tools, small flakes of debris from making or sharpening stone tools, animal bone, small fragments of ceramic vessels, or a combination of any of these artifact types. These are evidence of a single individual or a small group traversing the landscape on day trips or short overnight stays, a game overlook for a hunter waiting for an opportunity, or someone looking for edible wild plants. As with stone circle sites, unless temporally diagnostic artifacts are found, they could represent almost any time period. However, several are associated with the Woodland people. Hunter-gatherers would have had a deep knowledge of their home range, its resources, and the season of their availability in order to survive.

Central Channel: Brookings, Moody, Lake and Minnehaha Counties

Small, short-term Woodland base camps have been recorded on peninsulas, islands, and shores of glacial lakes near the Big Sioux River. In Brookings County, the chain of Oakwood Lakes lies about three miles west of the river. Few archaeological surveys have been undertaken in this area and virtually no small artifact scatters have been identified between the river and these lakes; they probably exist and await discovery. In contrast, several archaeological surveys have occurred around Oakwood Lakes, identifying large Woodland camps that were re-occupied repeatedly, conical earthen mounds containing the burials of many individuals, and several small artifact scatters, some of which represent the Woodland period. Following the Big Sioux River into Moody County, a few burial mounds, rock cairns or piles, that may represent "sign posts" or markers on the landscape for travelers, and one stone circle site have been recorded. Little archaeological research has been done in this area.

One camp was excavated on the shore of Lake Herman (39LK50) about 23 miles west of the Big Sioux. It is a multi-component site that includes artifacts and features from the "Euro-American Historic (post 1860), early Native American Historic (ca 1650 to 1868), Late Woodland Lake Benton phase (A.D. 700 to 1200), and Early to Middle Woodland Fox Lake phase (200 B.C. to A.D. 700),"[29] and possibly Oneota (ca 1000 to 1700), Plains Village (A.D. 900 to 1832) or Great Oasis (A.D. 800 to 1250). One of the earliest examples of ceramics on the Coteau, called Fox Lake ware, was found at this site. These ceramics have thick walls with a cord-roughened surface, a conoidal-shaped base, and slight shoulders. Vessel rims are typically straight with trailed-line, cord-wrapped stick, bosses, and tool indent designs.[30]

Another ceramic assemblage at this site, Lake Benton ware, includes decorative techniques such as cord-wrapped stick impressing, dentate stamping, dentates, and single-cord impressing.[31] Little soil development occurred between occupations, resulting in horizontal mixing of the various artifact assemblages, while modern plowing across the site mixed the horizontal and vertical stratigraphy. As a result, clear interpretations of changes through time is limited.

This site also reflects the transition from spear and atlatl weaponry to bow and arrow because both dart and arrow points were found. Stone artifacts, such as knives, hide scrapers, and debris from flint-knapping, although present at the site, changed little through time. On the other hand, a bone garden hoe, fashioned from a bison scapula, suggests that gardening was one of the activities at this site. However, due to the mixing of the assemblages, it could not be assigned to a specific time period.

Once in Minnehaha County, the number of burial mounds on the Big Sioux River intensifies as does the number of recorded occupation sites, many of which represent the Woodland period. The transformation of burial practices and the implied intensification of rituals associated with it reflect an eastern Hopewellian influence. The mounds on the Coteau and beyond are significantly scaled down from the large effigy and other mound types found in Ohio and Illinois. This transformation probably occurred around A.D. 300 and is related to increase in long distance trade, which would also allow for the exchange of ideas.

One of the largest mound groups in eastern South Dakota, about 51 mounds, is situated at the confluence of Split Rock Creek and the Big Sioux River, south of the present-day town of Brandon (39MH6). The mounds were first mapped in 1860 by Alfred J. Hill, who, on the bottom of his map, wrote, "The Eminija [Imnezha] group."[32] *Imniza* is a Dakota word for "rock or rocks," while a similar Dakota word, *heimniza*, means "rocky ridge."[33] In the early years of Dakota Territory, the Dakota Land Company named a townsite near the mounds "Eminja." Hill mapped the mounds with "a small pocket compass the card of which was warped so that the degrees of the circle by no means corresponded with each other."[34] In 1884 T.H. Lewis re-mapped the Eminija Mounds, now known as the Split Rock Creek Mounds.

Although some have been destroyed, the existing mounds are circular, vary from less than one meter to almost two meters in height, and the largest is 25 meters in diameter. A series of amateur and professional excavations occurred at the site as early as 1868 and as recently as 2003, when several were disturbed by a housing development. The Split Rock Creek Mounds may be associated with the Lake Benton phase, although this suggestion is based on only a few rim sherds tentatively identified as Lake Benton ware.

It is suggested that local bands would have congregated to bury their dead year after year, continually adding to the height and breadth as well as the number of mounds.[35] The conversion from subsurface burials to constructing earthen mounds over the burial pits represents a considerable investment of time and labor (Box 1). Bone bangles, ceramics, shell (probably freshwater) disk beads, and conch shell columella beads have been found in burial mounds excavated in Minnehaha County. The conch shell beads would have originated from the Gulf or Atlantic coast, suggesting a wide trade network that linked east and west during this period. Obsidian from the Yellowstone region has been found as far southeast as Arkansas, possibly traded through this region.

Near the Mouth: Union County

In Union County, the Big Sioux River forms the border between South Dakota and Iowa. The floodplain on the west bank of the river varies from one-half to two miles wide as far south as Richland (about five miles north of Elk Point). From Richland south, to the confluence with the Missouri River, the two rivers share a broad triangular-shaped floodplain all the way to North Sioux City. The topography is nearly level except for crescent-shaped remnant scars of old river channels, called oxbows, which were cut off from the winding rivers over the millennia. Some form lakes, other are marshlands, and yet others are dry. Very few archaeological surveys have been conducted along this portion of the Big Sioux River resulting in the recordation of a few artifact scatters and one Woodland burial mound on the terrace of the Big Sioux. Sites on the floodplain would likely have been disturbed or buried under silts deposited during flood events.

Construction of a Burial Mound

For most mounds, especially large ones, construction represents several different building episodes over a period of many years. It was likely an event associated with annual rituals during a gathering of multiple bands from different villages or camps. The initial phase of construction would involve excavating shallow, subsurface burial pits with sticks and other digging tools for one or more bodies or simply placing the body on the original ground surface. Funerary objects, such as shell beads or small bone tools, may or may not be placed with the remains. Bark or wood may be placed on top of the remains. The first layer of soil would have been mounded on top of the burials using baskets, bags, and hands. At some burial mound sites, the location where soil was borrowed to build the mounds shows up as a grassy depression today.

Following a death, the bodies could be treated in several different ways, depending on the time of year and location. In the winter, when the ground was frozen, a body may be wrapped and placed in a tree or on a scaffold until it was time to conduct the burial. Then the remains would be wrapped or bundled; this is considered a secondary burial. Or if the death occurred during a warmer season close to the time of the ritual, it may be a primary burial in a horizontal position or with the legs and arms flexed and placed on its side. In rare cases, there have been evidence of cremation in the burial pit. Ochre, a red mineral, was sometimes rubbed on the body or the skeletal elements and on the funerary objects.

During the next burial season, pits might be dug into the top of the earthen mound, occasionally disturbing a burial below. The mound may represent the burial ground used by a single extended family or closely related individuals. Then, another layer of soil would cover the burials. The burial and building episodes probably continued over and over again for many years, particularly if there were large and many mounds in the group. Often constructed on a high point at the confluence of a river and a secondary creek or stream, the mounds may have also served as territorial markers and guideposts on the landscape, visible from long distances.

Although many of the mounds in eastern South Dakota are conical and circular in shape, less frequently, there are elongated and oval mounds. On some of the early mound maps drafted by T. H. Lewis, a narrow, linear windrow of soil built between two mounds appears. This might indicate a familial relationship between the individuals buried in these two mounds and serve as a visual reminder to the descendants, much like a gravestone, that both mounds contain the remains of their ancestors. However, there is no direct evidence for this suggestion at this time.

Although mounds are generally affiliated with the Woodland period, some, particularly those in the extreme northeastern corner of South Dakota, were used by later groups in the 1700s and 1800s that migrated into the area, including the Dakota tribes.

Terminal Plains Woodland: Great Oasis

Towards the end of the Woodland and the beginning of the Plains Village, there is the Great Oasis phase (A.D. 900 to 1060). First identified in southwestern Minnesota, sites with Great Oasis traits are now recognized in northwestern and eastern Iowa, southwestern Minnesota, western Illinois, southeastern North Dakota, southern Alberta, and eastern South Dakota, including the Big Sioux River and the lower James and Missouri river valleys.[36] These sites, again, with varying degrees of evidence, exhibit eastern Hopewellian influence, such as a ceramic effigy elbow pipe found at Oakwood Lakes (39BK8), and the first definitive evidence of horticulture, such as the charred corn found at 39BK8 and the Heath site (39LN15) southeast of Sioux Falls on the Big Sioux River.[37]

In South Dakota, the greatest density of Great Oasis sites is found around the Big Sioux River, Split Rock Creek, and Beaver Creek in and around the present-day towns of Sioux Falls and Brandon. However, more extensive research on Great Oasis villages has been conducted in Sherman County in northeastern Nebraska, and in northwestern Iowa on the lower terraces of the Big and Little Sioux rivers.[38] Based on this research, Great Oasis houses are usually smaller than, but quite like, those built during the following Initial Middle Missouri period. A shallow rectangular pit, approximately 20 feet wide by 30 feet long, was excavated for the interior floor. Two to six central support posts supported stringers for roof poles that were connected to closely spaced posts set along the exterior walls. Walls and roof were covered with a mixture of mud and grasses, with an opening in the roof to vent the fire pit. A single entrance, typically on one narrow end, sloped downward, opening into a large room. The open floor plan was organized into activity areas, including food preparation, cooking hearths, and sleeping, and areas for storing personal gear. Storage included many small cold-storage root cellars, which are called cache pits. These subterranean straight-walled or bell-shaped cache pits were capped with wood and possibly covered with soil for insulation. A lodge would provide housing for a nuclear family. Typically, houses were arranged along major rivers or streams on the upper terraces almost like individual homesteads with gardens, on an intermediate terrace, along the bottomlands, or on the shore of a glacial lake.[39]

Three villages were mapped by W.H. Over in the 1920s on the lower terraces of the Big Sioux River on the west side of Sioux Falls. In 1922 the Stringham Brothers graded one of the terraces and discovered "many old fireplaces and refuse heaps" as well as artifacts including "pottery (the Mound Builder type), flint arrow points, flint knives, scrapers, and stone implements of various kinds, as well as crushed buffalo bones."[40] This collection is stored at the Archaeological Research Center and includes ceramics typically found at Great Oasis sites; however, it is a small collection and no real conclusions can be drawn from it. The villages do fit the pattern of being located on a lower terrace of the river, but no formal investigations were ever undertaken at the sites. In the 1960s, after the Big Sioux River flooded in Sioux Falls, the river was channeled. Furthermore, the construction of the Great Plains zoo and other development destroyed all or most of these three villages, yet small portions remain intact, but not excavated.

Plains Village-Initial Middle Missouri (A.D. 1000-1300)

While the Woodland innovations set it apart from the Archaic, and the Great Oasis represents small semi-sedentary horticultural villages stretched across the upper terraces or on floodplains, the Initial Middle Missouri Variant is a culmination and magnification of these transformations. Initial Middle Missouri sites occur along the Big Sioux River in northwestern Iowa, up to the Sioux Falls area, west across the lower portion of the James River, and north along the Missouri River as far as the Cheyenne River. Archaeologists have grouped these villages within geographical locations and with similar traits into a series of smaller phases. Those associated with the Big Sioux River watershed are the Big Sioux Mill Creek and Little Sioux Mill Creek phases in northwestern Iowa and the Brandon phase near the present-day town of Brandon.[41] Temporally, Great Oasis overlaps the earliest years of the Initial Middle Missouri and probably represents, at least in some cases, a transition of the same population intensifying the village way of life, broadening the spectrum of gardening into farming, and building larger, more elaborate villages on terraces above the floodplains, while planting crops in the rich soils along the rivers. However, the ability to raise crops was confined to those areas where the climate and soil were favorable, and the growing season was long enough (Box 2). As a result, some groups did not adapt to the agricultural lifestyle, and continued a mobile life-style as hunter-gatherers.

First Farmers

While growing corn is taken for granted in eastern South Dakota today, it is not indigenous to the Northern Great Plains. What became known as North-ern Flint Maize (also called Maiz de Ocho) was a hybrid of varieties out of Mexico that were imported into the southwestern United States. This hybrid was adapted to drier growing conditions, more productive due to the large floury kernels, and easier to grind (Upham et al. 1987). Probably further hy-bridized, it was traded into the eastern Woodlands around A.D. 800 (Smith 1989) and eventually up the Mississippi and Missouri rivers into the Big Sioux River valley around A.D. 900. Based on evidence of charred kernels and fragments of cobs from archaeological excavations on the Big Sioux and Missouri rivers, this northern flint was an 8-row variety. It was hardier and bet-ter adapted to the northern climate and its shorter growing season than earlier 12-row varieties. The northern flint was comprised of at least two varieties, flour and flint, and possibly a third sweet variety, popcorn, all 8-row types. Besides corn, squash, beans, and sunflowers were regularly cultivated by Initial Middle Missouri populations by A.D. 1000. However, bison still played a large role in the villager's diets. (Dennis Toom, "Climate and Sedentism in the Middle Missouri Subarea of the Plains," Ph.D dissertation, University of Colorado, Boulder, 1992).

The semi-permanent villages were laid out in rows of rectangular earth lodges (Figure 4). In some cases, the villages were protected by bastions made from closely spaced wood posts and maybe a dry moat surrounding it. The lodges were built much the same as those seen at Great Oasis sites. Between the lodges were post and pole racks to dry meat or plants such as squash. Cache pits were excavated to store food both in and between lodges. Especially in the Brandon area, bison hunting continued to be a mainstay of the diet, although the emphasis on bison is not as strong in Mill Creek sites in Iowa. Groups, some-times living in temporary structures in small camps, would travel away from the villages along feeder streams to hunt and collect plants, or to collect tool-stone or other resources during the appropriate season.

Village life would have been a vibrant, rich environment, much like a small ethnic neighborhood, with related families living and work-ing together, sharing childcare and food, and participating in celebra-tions and religious activities. The men would have collected stone and

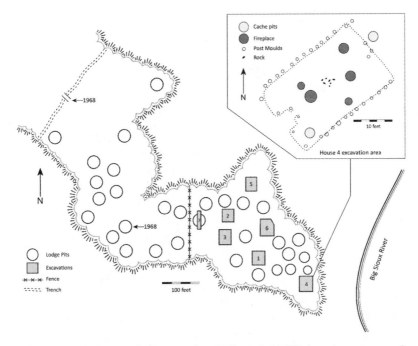

Figure 4. Planview of the Brandon Village (39MH1) and an insert of the floorplan of House 4. Redrawn, based on the 1941 originals.

flintknapped the arrow points for hunting, knives for cutting tools, large scrapers for woodworking, and prepared large stone axes and mauls for cutting trees and pounding stakes. Women planted, tended, and harvested the gardens with bison scapula hoes hafted to wooden handles. They also scraped and tanned hides with bone fleshers hafted with stone endscrapers that were then used to create clothing, bedding, or temporary shelter covers. Sewing kits with different styles of bone awls were used to punch through the leather, which was then stitched with sinew to create the clothing, footwear, and other leather items. The women also made the pottery for storage and cooking. A bone and stone tool kit for making pottery may include a wooden paddle wrapped with cord to shape the exterior and a small flat stone for an anvil to help shape the interior of the vessel, and a series of small bone tools to decorate the pots. The shapes of pots, the style of neck, rim, and lip, the body treatment, and the decorations are all used by archaeologists to help define the culture that created them. They were both utilitarian and works of art, in many cases. The designs were carried down through the female line. A wide array of ornamentation was also created from bone and shell, such as bone bow guards and bracelets, and shell necklaces and pendants. These often reflected a person's status in the village and their family line.

Villages were abandoned when the surrounding timber, game, or other necessary resources were depleted. The villagers would pick another location on the river terrace and rebuild. The evidence indicates that after the resources around an abandoned village were replenished, probably years later, the villages would be repaired, rebuilt, and reoccupied, possibly by the same families or their descendants. However, the Brandon Village (39MH1), near the present-day town of Brandon, was an exception to the rule for long-term occupation. The village was comprised of 37 earth lodges, but the refuse found by archaeologists within and between the lodges was thin, much less than is typically found in villages with a long-term occupation. It may be that the climate changes were enough to result in low returns in the gardens, forcing the occupants to move to a better location. Nevertheless, it was one of the early Initial Middle Missouri villages along the Big Sioux River.

Oneota (A.D. 1250-1700)

Many archaeologists and historians try to work backwards from historic records to track the deep-time genesis of specific Native American tribal groups, periods of tribal fission and fusion, major migrations, and alliances. While this method has been somewhat successful in documenting particular tribal entities from the historic into protohistoric and late prehistoric time periods, this kind of research generally assumes that tribal groups are discrete entities that change in a limited number of predictable ways. Studies of the archaeological record and Native American oral histories, however, suggest that cultural expression and interaction 1,000 years ago along the Coteau of eastern South Dakota were not that simplistic.[42]

Starting at about A.D. 1000, the landscape of the Big Sioux River served as a melting pot, meeting place, and buffer zone for numerous tribal groups, who, despite language differences, developed complex working and warfare alliances.[43] These relationships appear to have culminated in the Oneota cultural component, a well-documented regional lifeway that is characterized by expansive unfortified villages, intensive agriculture (especially maize), catlinite trade and modes of production, shell-tempered pottery, and spectacular zoomorphic iconography.[44] Oneota sites along the Big Sioux River date between A.D. 1250 and 1700 although earlier occupations, dating to around A.D. 900, have been discovered in other areas of the Midwest.

The largest and most significant Oneota site is the 1200-acre Blood Run/Rock Island Site complex, which lies on both the South Dakota and Iowa sides of the river east of the present-day town of Harrisburg. The site once included 275 large conical burial mounds, one possible effigy mound, boulder outlines, earthen enclosures, and conspicuously placed boulders of Sioux quartzite, each covered with several hundred pecked and ground indentations (Figure 5). Archaeologists continue to speculate regarding the meaning of the pocked Sioux quartzite boulders at Blood Run; some theorize that they might represent meteors, while some tribal historic preservationists believe that the indentations represent individually-ground prayers as part of pilgrimage events.

The Blood Run/Rock Island Site complex has been historically documented and mapped as the principal village of the Omaha Tribe from the 1690s to 1714,[45] but it is also known to be associated with the Winnebago, Ponca, Ioway, Otoe, Missouria, Osage, Kansa, and Mdewakonton Dakota.[46] Inscribed catlinite tablets and catlinite pipes, both elbow and disk bowl forms, have been found at the Blood Run/Rock Island site complex (Figure 6); the inhabitants of the village likely facilitated intertribal use of the nearby pipestone quarries and promoted the catlinite trade, which extended as far as Alabama and Oklahoma.[47]

Generally, Oneota villages included multi-family longhouses and large subsurface storage and trash pits. Small triangular arrow points were sufficient to take down bison, and shell-tempered, rounded pots were used for cooking and storage. Exotic goods from across the continent are not uncommon at Oneota archaeological sites. Oneota burials are known to include marine shell mask gorgets, in addition to barrel-shaped and circular disk beads that were also manufactured from conch shells. At Blood Run, European trade goods, such as glass beads and metal, are present in the village setting and were interred within some of the later constructed burial mounds.[48] These trade goods (along with communicable disease) would have reached the village in advance of

the European traders themselves, through well-established protohistoric Native American networks.

Oneota sites were occupied well into protohistoric and early historic times in the Big Sioux River valley, suggesting that this tribal coalition held sway in the region until pressure from neighboring Dakota
groups and increasing Euroamerican settlement led to the dissolution
of the more material aspects of the Oneota culture, although much
of the religious, social, and linguistic structures have been retained in
traditions by the many descendant tribes.[49]

Protohistoric and Early Historic (A.D. 1650-1860)

In contrast to the Big Sioux River valley, the Missouri River is not characterized by a significant Oneota cultural presence during protohistoric
and early historic times. On the Missouri River mainstem, throughout
what is now South and North Dakota, clusters of large earth lodge village sites representative of the Coalescent Tradition are instead prevalent from about A.D. 1300 to 1800 (and even later into North Dakota). Interestingly, Coalescent sites, documented as those core villages
and camps occupied by the ancestors of today's Pawnee and Arikara
(and as later affiliated with the Mandan and Hidatsa), are ubiquitous
on the Missouri River into historic times,[50] but almost entirely absent
along the Big Sioux. Most Coalescent sites along the Missouri River
do include a wealth of catlinite artifacts, which suggests a meaningful
trading relationship with the Oneota farther east.

Beyond the marked Oneota and Coalescent cultural spheres of influence, additional evidence of the early historic Omaha and Ioway-
Oto was discovered in Kingsbury County, South Dakota, at a burial
site that eroded out along Lake Thompson in 1998. The burial, which
is thought to date between A.D. 1760 and 1825, included the skeletal
remains of an adult male, as buried with marine shell beads, white
and blue glass trade beads, and a partial dog skeleton. Based on the
forensic analysis of the remains, the geographical location of the burial,
and the funerary objects, the burial was determined to be most likely
culturally affiliated with the Omaha.[51] The cultural affiliation of this
burial site reinforces the idea that the Big Sioux River valley was the
ancestral home of many different tribal groups, even as Dakota bands

were intensifying their occupation of the region in the eighteenth and nineteenth centuries.

Archaeological evidence of Dakota groups along the Big Sioux River comes in a variety of forms. In addition to the many villages and camps that are mentioned in tribal oral histories and throughout the historic records of traders and explorers, historic Dakota re-use of

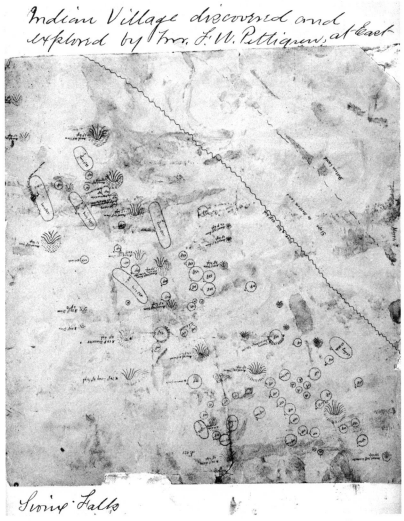

Figure 5: Original sketch of surface features at the Blood Run Site, drafted by F. W. Pettigrew of Sioux Falls circa 1890. Courtesy of Siouxland Heritage Museums (1988.069.00005).

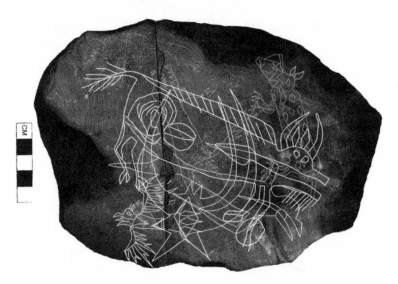

Figure 6: Catlinite tablet found at the Blood Run Site in the 1950s, embellished with tracings to differentiate several of the incised zoomorphic figures. Modified digital image courtesy of Dale Henning, with tracings originally applied in color by Carol Moxham of the Midwest Archeological Center, National Park Service, Lincoln, NE.[52]

Woodland burial mounds is a well-documented practice. This revitalization in the use of ancient burial mounds shows reverence to the past and hints at a complicated relationship with religious missionaries. By roughly 1860, historic records dominate the interpretations of cultural interactions in the area, many times at the disservice of the Native Americans who were still living in the Big Sioux River valley and along the landscape of the Coteau. Archaeological evidence of fur trade posts, early townsites, military posts and associated Dakota scout camps, and tribal communities can be used as a sounding-board to critically evaluate one-sided histories of the Big Sioux River, especially if archaeological research involves tribal partnerships at the outset.

Notes

[1] Office of the State Archaeologist, University of Iowa, "Blood Run National Historic Landmark." *Publications from the Office of the State Archaeologist* (2013).

[2] G. Bie Ravndal, "The Scandinavian Pioneers of South Dakota." *South Dakota Historical Collections* vol. 12 (1924), 297-30.

[3] W. Raymond Wood, "The John Evans 1796-97 Map of the Missouri River." *Great Plains Quarterly* 1:1 (Winter 1981): 39-53.

[4] See Marcel Kornfeld and Alan J. Osborn, *Islands on the Plains: Ecological, Social, and Ritual Use of Landscapes* (Salt Lake City: University of Utah Press, 2003).

[5] John Paul Gries, *Roadside Geology of South Dakota* (Missoula, MT: Mountain Press Publishing Company, 1996), 20-21.

[6] Richard Foster Flint, "Pleistocene Geology of Eastern South Dakota." *Geological Survey Professional Paper* 262 (1955), 6, 64-65.

[7] Gries, *Roadside Geology of South Dakota*, 11, 30-33.

[8] Newton H. Winchell, *Aborigines of Minnesota* (St. Paul: Minnesota Historical Society, 1911), ix-x.

[9] F. W. Pettigrew, "The Silent City." *Sioux Falls Press*, January 4, 1891.

[10] William H. Over and Elmer E. Meleen, "Report on an Investigation of the Brandon Village Site and the Split Rock Creek Mounds." *Archaeological Studies Circular*, no. III (1941).

[11] Thomas D. Thiessen, "Emergency Archeology in the Missouri River Basin: The Role of the Missouri River Basin Project and the Midwest Archeological Center in the Interagency Salvation Program, 1946-1975." *U.S. National Park Service Publications and Papers* 92 (1999).

[12] Mary Keepers Helgevold, "A History of South Dakota Archaeology." *Special Publication of the South Dakota Archaeological Society*, no. 3 (University of South Dakota: Vermillion, 1981).

[13] William H. Over, Paleontological Catalog Record (n.d). Copy on file at the Archaeological Research Center, Rapid City, South Dakota.

[14] George C. Frison, *Prehistoric Hunters of the High Plains* (New York: Academic Press, 1978). Vance T. Holliday, Eileen Johnson, and Ruthann Knudson, eds., *Plainview: The Enigmatic Paleoindian Artifact Style of the Great Plains* (Salt Lake City: University of Utah Press, 2017).

[15] Albert Ernest Jenks, *Minnesota's Browns Valley Man and Associated Burial Artifacts* (American Anthropological Association, 1937).

[16] Scott F. Anfinson, *Southwestern Minnesota Archaeology: 12,000 Years in the Prairie Lake Region* (St. Paul: Minnesota Historical Society Press, 1997), 32.

[17] James K. Haug, "Excavations at the Winter Site and at Hartford Beach Village 1980-1981." *Special Publications in Archaeology*, no. 2 (South Dakota State Historical Society, Archaeological Research Center, 2004).

[18] R. Peter Winham, Edward J. Lueck, and Timothy V. Gillen, "Excavations, Analyses and Site Evaluations: Research in the Lower and Upper Big Sioux Archaeological Regions, 1991" (Archeology Laboratory, Augustana College: Sioux Falls, South Dakota, 1992).

[19] Albert Ernest Jenks, "Recent Discoveries in Minnesota Prehistory." *Minnesota History* 16:1 (March 1935): 10.

[20] Anfinson, *Southwestern Minnesota Archaeology*, 1997), 35.

[21] Linda Hilde, "The Excavation and Evaluation of 39LK7" (1981). Manuscript on file at the Archaeological Research Center, Rapid City, South Dakota. Edward J. Lueck, R. Peter Winham, and L. Adrien Hannus, "Cultural Resources Reconnaissance Survey of Portions of Lake County, South Dakota within the Vermillion Basin and Upper Big Sioux Archeological Regions of South Dakota" (Archeology Laboratory of the Center for Western Studies, Augustana College: Sioux Falls, South Dakota, April 1987). Winham, Lueck, and Gillen, "Excavations, Analyses and Site Evaluations."

[22] John B. Gregg, Report of Investigation of Human Bones Recovered from the Hilde Pipe and Gravel Pit Located Near the Southwestern End of Lake Madison, S.D. on August 1, 1981, in "Cultural Resources Reconnaissance Survey," Appendix 4. See also Lueck, Winham, and Hannus, "Cultural Resources Reconnaissance Survey," 77.

[23] Hilde, "The Excavation and Evaluation of 39LK7" (1981).

[24] Lueck, Winham, and Hannus, "Cultural Resources Reconnaissance Survey." Winham, Lueck, and Gillen, "Excavations, Analyses and Site Evaluations." Hilde, "The Excavation and Evaluation of 39LK7" (1981).

[25] Lueck, Winham, and Hannus, "Cultural Resources Reconnaissance Survey," 77.

[26] Dan F. Morse and Phyllis A. Morse, *Archaeology of the Central Mississippi Valley* (New York: Academic Press, Inc., 1983), 161-64.

[27] Marcel Kornfeld, George C. Frison, and Mary Lou Larson, *Prehistoric Hunter-Gatherers of the High Plains and Rockies,* 3rd ed. (New York: Taylor and Francis, 2010), 130.

[28] Josh Houser, "The Summit Lake Site (39GT19)" *South Dakota Archaeological Society Newsletter* 26:1 (March 1996): 1-6. Scott F. Anfinson, ed., "A Handbook of Minnesota Prehistoric Ceramics." *Occasional Publications Minnesota Anthropology,* no. 5. (Minnesota Archaeological Society: Fort Snelling, 1979). Anfinson, *Southwestern Minnesota Archaeology.*

[29] Ned Hanenberger and Miles Gilbert, "National Register Evaluation of the Lake Herman Site (39LK50), Lake County, South Dakota" (South Dakota Archaeological Research Center, Contract Investigations Series #1655, 2003).

[30] Anfinson, *Southwestern Minnesota Archaeology*, 47.

[31] Hanenberger and Gilbert, "National Register Evaluation of the Lake Herman Site (39LK50), Lake County, South Dakota."

[32] Alfred J. Hill, Personal communication to the Secretary of the Minnesota Historical Society, August 31, 1860, *Northwestern Archaeological Survey Papers,* Box 232, Letter Book 9 (Minnesota Historical Society Archives, St. Paul, 1860), 2. T. H. Lewis Archaeological Survey, Mound Diagrams, Minnesota Historical Society Archives, St. Paul, 1860, Map No. 3.

[33] Stephen Returns Riggs, *A Dakota-English Dictionary* (St. Paul: Minnesota Historical Society Press), 163, 197.

[34] Alfred J. Hill, Personal communication to the Secretary of the Minnesota Historical Society, 1.

[35] Morse and Morse, 163.

[36] Lynn M. Alex, *Iowa's Archaeological Past* (Iowa City: University of Iowa Press, 2000), 138-40. Thomas W. Haberman, "The Bonander Site, 39MH102: A Great Oasis Occupation in Southeast South Dakota." *South Dakota Archaeology* 17 (1993): 1-34. Joseph Tiffany, "The Swanson Site Reexamined: The Middle Missouri Tradition in Central South Dakota." *South Dakota Archaeological Society,* Special Publication no. 12 (2007).

[37] Jeffrey V. Buechler, "Test Excavations at the Volunteer Site (39BK8), *South Dakota Archaeology* 6 (1982): 1-31.

[38] Alex, 138-40. R. Peter Winham and F.A. Calabrese, "The Middle Missouri Tradition," in *Archaeology on the Great Plains,* ed. W. Raymond Wood (Lawrence: University Press of Kansas, 1998), 269-307. M. Anderson, "Archaeological Excavations at the Cowan Site: A Phase II Investigation of 13WD88 Primary Roads Project NHS-75-1-(54)-19-97 a.k.a. 91-97060-1, Woodbury County, Iowa." *Project Completion Report,* vol. 18, no. 10 (University of Iowa, Highway Archaeology Program: Iowa City, 1995). S.C. Lensink, "Rethinking Mill Creek Radiocarbon Chronology" (paper presented at the 15th Annual Meeting of the Plains Anthropological Conference, Lincoln, Nebraska; manuscript on file, University of Iowa, Office of the State Archaeologist: Iowa City). S.C. Lensink, "A Reanalysis of Eastern Initial Middle Missouri Radiocarbon Dates and Implications for Timing of Long-Distance Trade with Middle Mississippian Centers" (paper presented at the Midwest Archaeological Conference, Milwaukee; manuscript on file, University of Iowa, Office of the State Archaeologist, Iowa City). Joseph Tiffany, "An Overview of the Middle Missouri Tradition," *University of Minnesota Publications in Anthropology,* no. 3 (1983), 87-108. Joseph Tiffany, "A Reexamination of the Swanson Site (39BR16), an Initial Middle Missouri Village in Central South Dakota," *Journal of the Iowa Archaeological Society* 50 (2003): 139-57. Joseph Tiffany, "The Swanson Site Reexamined: The Middle Missouri Tradition in Central South Dakota." *South Dakota Archaeological Society, Special Publication,* no. 12 (2007). S.C. Lensink and Joseph Tiffany, "Great Oasis in Time and Space, in *The Cowan Site (13WD88): A Great Oasis Community in Northwest Iowa,* ed. S.C. Lensink and Joseph Tiffany, Office of the State Archaeologist of Iowa, Iowa City, Report 22, 2005), 125-37.

[39] Winham and Calabrese, 269-307. Lensink and Tiffany, "Great Oasis in Time and Space,"125-37.

[40] J. Steve Sigstad and Joanita Kant Sigstad, eds., "Archaeological Field Notes of W.H. Over." *Research Bulletin,* no. 1 (South Dakota State Archaeologist's Office, Vermillion, SD, 1973).

[41] Winham and Calabrese, 269-307.

[42] William Green, ed., *Oneota Archaeology: Past, Present, and Future* (Office of the State Archaeologist, The University of Iowa, 1995).

[43] See Lueck, Winham, and Hannus, "Cultural Resources Reconnaissance Survey."

[44] Dale Henning, "The Oneota Tradition," in *Archaeology on the Great Plains,* 345-414.

[45] Henning, "The Oneota Tradition," 384.

[46] See Dale R. Henning and Gerald F. Schnepf, "Blood Run: The Silent City" (Lyon County Historical Society, Iowa, and the U.S. National Park Service, 2012), 11.

[47] María Nieves Zedeño and Robert Christopher Basaldú, "Pipestone National Monument, Minnesota: Native American Cultural Affiliation and Traditional Association Study" (Bureau of Applied Research in Anthropology, The University of Arizona: Tucson, 2004). Report prepared for the National Park Service Midwest Region.

[48] Colin M. Betts and Dale R. Henning, "Aberrant Earthworks? A Contemporary Overview of Oneota Mound Ceremonialism." *The Wisconsin Archeologist* 97:2 (2016), 101-19.

[49] Henning, "The Oneota Tradition," 404.

[50] Craig M. Johnson, "The Coalescent Tradition," in *Archaeology on the Great Plains*, 309.

[51] Douglas Owsley and Karin Bruwelheide, "Osteological Analysis of a Partial Human Skeleton from Kingsbury County, South Dakota, 39KB11, Accession 99-0066" (Smithsonian Institution, National Museum of Natural History, Department of Anthropology, September 2009). Report on file at the Archaeological Research Center, Rapid City, South Dakota. See also Renee Boen, "South Dakota Archaeological Research Center Burial Report 1999-01, Native American Graves Protection and Repatriation Act Database" (Archaeological Research Center, Rapid City, South Dakota, 1999).

[52] Note that a full color version of this image is posted online through the Office of the State Archaeologist, University of Iowa. See Office of the State Archaeologist, University of Iowa, "Blood Run National Historic Landmark," *Publications from the Office of the State Archaeologist* (2013).

Chapter 2

From Pipes to Pistols: Blood Run, the Pipestone Trade, and the Eclipse of the Pre-Contact Economy in the Upper Midwest

Joshua Jeffers
California State University-Dominguez Hills

In the winter of 1682 Dakota chief Drifting Goose began a winter count, now known as the John K. Bear winter count, by recording a "big battle," which likely refers to conflict with Crees to the north as indicated by Nicholas Perrot, who visited the Dakotas in 1684.[1] Claude-Charles Le Roy de la Potherie, writing from Perrot's journals, observed that the Dakotas "gave all their attention to waging war."[2] Indicative of the proliferation of firearms beyond the Great Lakes, Native peoples warred against one another over access and control within an emerging arms race.[3] In 1688, for example, one Native leader expressed his concern about his Dakota enemies getting guns through trade with the French, telling Baron de Lahontan that "he was extream glad to find that [Lahontan] carry'd neither Arms nor Cloaths to the *Nadouessious*" and that he "had not the Equipage of a *Coureur de Bois*."[4] This leader's concern reflects a broad economic transformation that brought about a transformation in warfare. As the Dakotas rose in power during the late seventeenth century, they expanded westward to the Minnesota and Missouri Rivers and ultimately the Black Hills. But during the prior two centuries, this region had been the peaceful center of a thriving trade. The large settlement at Blood Run on the Big Sioux River, approximately halfway between the Missouri and Minnesota Rivers, was home to Omahas, Ioways, Otos, and likely others. An important trade and processing center for pipestone, or catlinite, products, it was the western terminus of an east-west trade corridor that ran from Omahas, Ioways, and their neighbors at Blood Run to the Mississippi River.[5] The introduction of firearms, the fur trade, and the expansion of the Sioux transformed this trade corridor forcing out the previous inhabitants, marking the end of an era at Blood Run and across the region. The archaeological, documentary, and oral records all indicate a transformation in Native economic life that involved an increase in violence during this period. While Frenchman Nicholas Perrot's visit marked the most memorable event recorded by Drifting Goose for 1684, the following year it was once again war, this time against the Omahas.[6]

The invasion of the Sioux marks the abandonment of Blood Run[7] and the advent of a new social and economic order in the region. The introduction of firearms and the fur trade greatly altered the economic demands confronted by Native people and the social relations necessary to meet those demands. As the need for firearms grew, the need for furs grew apace, and the proliferation of guns and the competitive fur trade overwhelmed the power of pipestone-related alliances and ceremonies to mitigate war and violence, resulting in the abandonment of Blood Run and the decline of the pipestone trade. Evidence suggests that no group lived at Blood Run or the Great Pipestone Quarry after the Omaha left the region in the late seventeenth or early eighteenth century.[8] Prior to this period of conflict, however, Blood Run and the Great Pipestone Quarry were places of great social and economic significance.

Drawing from archaeological evidence, Native traditions, and early European records from the region, this essay first examines the origins of Blood Run and the significance of mound-building for its inhabitants. The essay then looks at the pipestone trade and the connection between Blood Run and the Great Pipestone Quarry, before turning to the effects that the introduction of firearms and metal goods had on this region and economy. Situated at an important regional crossroads, these two remarkable sites offer insight into both the Indigenous economic system in the upper Midwest prior to European contact as well as how Native societies on the periphery of the "Mississippian

Figure 1: Northwest Iowa showing locations of Oneota sites, including Blood Run, and the Great Pipestone Quarry.

shatter zone" to the east confronted the changes wrought by European goods and guns.[9] I argue that European trade goods merged with a much older system of trade in pipestone, but unlike the pre-contact system, the Euro-Indian trade system was driven mainly by the desire for profit among Europeans and the increasing necessity of access to firearms among Native Americans. Thus, traditional economic channels and means of exchange were redirected or given new meaning by the Euro-Indian system of trade. The lifeblood of the pre-contact trade system had been pipestone, which, among other things, symbolized peace. The Euro-Indian trade in firearms coopts this older system with a new instrument of war. Thus, the significance of control over the pipestone quarry and the trade in pipestone was subjugated to the trade in firearms, slaves, and pelts because gaining and maintaining access to firearms was a life-and-death matter. The need for guns and the availability of steel goods displaced pipestone as a vital trade good, and as the Indian arms race spread across the region, the ceremonialism associated with pipestone and the trade in pipestone could not dissipate the violence. As a result, the Dakota Sioux, having acquired guns before their western neighbors, drove Omahas, Ioways, and others from the region.

The Big Sioux drains a broad, canoe-shaped highland that stretches north to south across most of eastern South Dakota known as the Coteau des Prairies, which rises out of the Minnesota River lowland to the east. Philander Prescott, a fur trader sent to the region in 1832, described it as a "great and renowned ridge that divides the waters of the Minnesota and Missouri [rivers]…[which] looked like a blue cloud on the horizon, stretching as far as the eye could reach southeast and northwest."[10] The Big Sioux runs down the center of the length of the landform. Though clearly visible in satellite images, the rise of this flat, seemingly treeless expanse from south to north is subtle, but its northern slopes are marked by valleys and ravines. Though Prescott described the area as a "forlorn and barren country," the Coteau des Prairies and the site at Blood Run in particular served their inhabitants well.[11] Situated at the convergence of several distinct ecosystems, the societies who called the Big Sioux region home benefited from their position between foraging societies to the north and west and more sedentary societies to the east and south.[12] Moreover, the region marks a sort of ecotonic bridge between the mixed-grass prairies to the west and the grassland-forest to the east.[13] These tallgrasses develop thick, extensive root systems that are very difficult to plow, especially without metal implements. But as one descends to the Blood Run floodplain soils become sandier allowing for easier cultivation.[14] The region also boasted large herds of bison, which had initially attracted Native peoples centuries earlier and made it ideal for large, trade fair-type gatherings. Also, less than forty miles from the Great Pipestone Quarry in southwestern Minnesota, the inhabitants of Blood Run were well situated to manufacture and trade pipestone products to surrounding societies on the high plains to the west, the Great Lakes-Ohio Valley to the east, and the Mississippi Valley to the south. As a result, the region became a central crossroads linking the surrounding regions into an extensive network emanating from the Ioway and Omaha villages on the Big Sioux.

The Big Sioux has many names. Called *la Riviere Croche* or Crooked River by the French, the Sioux called it *Tchankasndata*, meaning Thickly Wooded River, though this may have only referred to the lower portion of the river. It was also known as the Calumet River due to its proximity to the Great Pipestone Quarry.[15] For the Ioways it was known as *Pekitanoni*, or Pipestone River, and for the Omaha it was *Xe*, meaning "place where something is buried."[16] This name perhaps suggests that the Omaha were the primary inhabitants of the extensive site at Blood Run, which contained many mounds.[17] Blood Run is the largest site associated with the Oneota cultural complex.[18] The site straddles the Big Sioux River at its confluence with Blood Run Creek along the border of present-day northwestern Iowa and southeastern South Dakota, and given the diversity of materials found at the site, it was clearly a regional trade center.[19] While the primary site, now known as the Good Earth State Park at Blood Run and the Blood Run National Historic Landmark, is believed to have covered about 3,000 acres, extending along both sides of the river, and included at least 158 visible conical burial mounds, as well as storage pits, house sites, one mound enclosure, and a serpent effigy mound, the broader district included no fewer than five discreet mound and village units.[20] Archaeologists estimate that at its height Blood Run was home to six to ten thousand people, contained hundreds of conical mounds, at least two effigy mounds, including a 300-foot long serpentine mound, a 15-acre earthen enclosure, eight pitted boulders, and 150-800 stone circles.[21]

Nineteenth-century accounts put the total number of mounds at 275. In his *Report on the Mound Explorations of the Bureau of Ethnology* (1894), Cyrus Thomas describes multiple mound complexes in the area, with each situated "upon a most beautiful and expansive terrace peculiarly adapted for a permanent village," though "no survey could be made...on account of the high corn crop that covered it." Thomas observed the "stone rings, circular and oblong, made with the granite bowlders [sic] of the prairie." He concluded that these were used to secure the bases of dwellings and thus indicate "the positions of the lodges," though the number of lodges "could not be counted, since about half of the group lies in a field, the original prairie sod of which has been disturbed by the plow of the settler and the stones utilized by him upon his farm."[22] Similarly, Dr. Frederick W. Pettigrew, who excavated at the site in the late 1880s, describes lodges that included a perimeter of rocks along the base of the structure, leaving outlines of where dwellings were located. In 1889, just prior to the removal of such rocks to make way for the plow, Pettigrew published a sketch of these outlines and their relation to nearby mounds.[23] His drawing re-

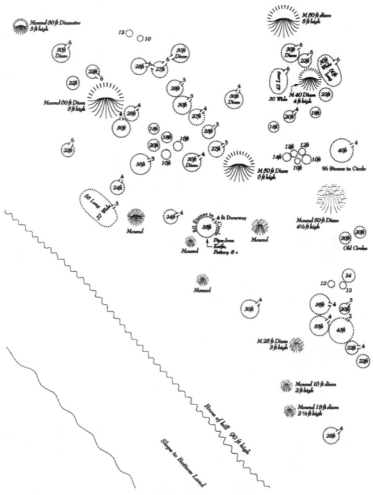

Figure 2: West half, Pettigrew Map the "Silent City," Iowa side, south of Blood Run Creek.[24]

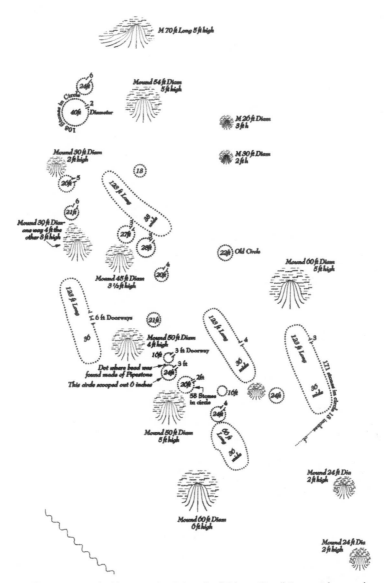

Figure 3: East half, Pettigrew Map the "Silent City," Iowa side, south of Blood Run Creek.[25]

veals tightly grouped mounds interspersed among the wigwams, long-houses, and sweat lodges atop a ninety-foot-high terrace overlooking the river. Most mounds are relatively small, four-to-six-feet high and fifty-to-seventy-feet in diameter, with some as small as two-feet high.

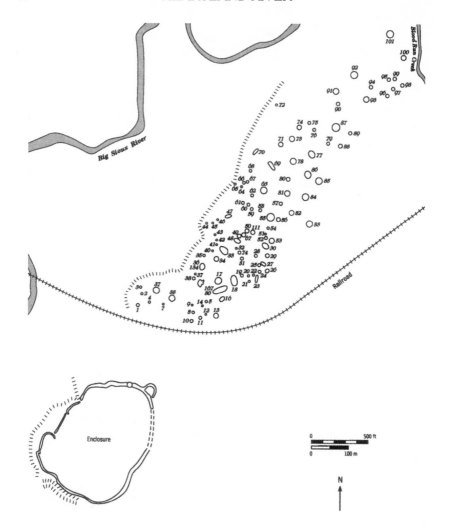

Figure 4: T. H. Lewis map, area south of Blood Run Creek.[26]

Maps by T. H. Lewis, another late-nineteenth researcher who studied the site, similarly reveal the clustered nature of the earthworks in and among social spaces as well as the nearby enclosure and the railroad that bisected the site a couple of decades before. Today, approximately sixty-eight mounds, mostly burial, remain visible, the others being destroyed by some combination of farming, gravel mining, and grave robbing.

Unlike other mound sites, such as those in the Ohio Valley or the Southeast, which exhibit a great deal of symmetry and were often aligned with celestial movements like solstices and equinoxes, villagers at Blood Run seemed to construct mounds more or less at random, tightly packed among village dwellings. Thus, it seems unlikely that they were arranged to represent or mark lunar or solar movements, rather archaeologists believe that it was the process of constructing mounds and going through the associated rituals and ceremonies that was most significant.[27] Similarly, the meaning of the repetitive lyrics of Omaha songs associated with anointing the Sacred Pole "do not appear from the literal words, but must be found in the symbolism of the ceremonial acts...for to the Indian mind the repeated words brought up the varied aspects of the Pole."[28] Like the ceremonies associated with the Sacred Pole, mound construction also served important social functions through symbolism. Mound construction was "a behavioral expression of ideology" in that the process of building the mound was primary, a metaphorical representation of the ceremonial cycles that kept the world in balance.[29] Thus, the mound was both the material product and the symbolic embodiment of the associated rituals, practices, and social connections. The completed earthwork would then remain on the landscape as a reminder and expression of those relationships. All members of society likely participated in some way in the rituals and ceremonies associated with mound construction, which served "to foster social solidarity among seasonally mobile kin groups."[30] In burial mounds the dead were "reincarnated by the adoption with the earth re-created during the course of mound construction," which helps to explain why mounds often contained mundane objects from everyday life, such as personal items and clan heirlooms as well as the pottery, tools, and weapons intended to assist in the afterlife.[31]

In their two-volume work on the Omaha, anthropologists Alice Fletcher and Francis La Flesche, who was the son of Joseph La Flesche, the last recognized head chief of the Omaha tribe, describe Omaha funerary customs, writing that "in olden times...mound burial was the common practice of the Omaha." Burial mounds were made by digging a hole in which the body is placed with personal belongings and then poles are arranged over the opening "upon which earth was heaped into a mound."[32] Some mounds were also "packed" as they were built, resulting in an extremely dense formation, which helps to explain how after more than a century of plowing they remain clearly visible on the landscape. But despite the extent of the mounds at Blood Run, it seems impossible that every death would have been interred this way. There simply are not enough mounds to account for so many people. More likely, mounds were associated with groups, perhaps clans, and served to solidify both intra and inter group cohesion. The mounds at Blood Run then represent a "life-renewal ceremony for re-establishing the relationship between human beings and the spirits of the natural environment" *as well as* social and perhaps political cohesion.[33] Once completed these works demarcated sacred spaces, while also marking the landscape with symbols of collective identity that shaped inter-group alliances and networks of exchange.

Another factor that marks the Blood Run earthworks as unusual is that mound complexes and mound construction are typically as-sociated with the late Woodland and early Mississippian periods, ap-proximately 500-1200 CE. The Oneota cultural complex is in fact distinguished from earlier Woodland cultures in part by the appar-ent absence of mound construction. While considered a "minor yet durable phenomenon" in the Oneota tradition, mound construction among Oneota societies seems to have waxed and waned depending on the needs of the community.[34] For example, some scholars argue that the decline in mound construction between 1400 and 1600 is attributable to the emergence of new rituals like the Calumet Cere-mony, the Sun Dance, and the Spirit Adoption Ceremony that may have eclipsed mound ceremonialism or redirected it away from actual mound construction.[35] And yet the mounds at Blood Run are undeni-able and most were constructed during the seventeenth century. All eleven mounds that have been even minimally examined contained European objects such as glass beads, brass, and iron, indicating that they date to after 1550 and perhaps later. So why the sudden burst of mound building beginning around 1600, and what does it suggest about the significance of Blood Run? This paradox has forced scholars to revise their understanding of both the Oneota cultural complex and the cultural significance of mound construction given that previous analysis of mound construction is for the Woodland period. Archaeologists have identified two periods in the upper Midwest, 1100-1400 and 1600-1725, when mound construction intensified suggesting greater social significance.[36] The first period is typically associated with the process of cultural transformation as the Oneota mode of production emerged out of and displaced its Woodland period antecedent.[37] Then, beginning around 1500, a wave of migrations again transformed the region. This timing also aligns with oral traditions among the Omahas, Ioways, and others living in the region when French traders entered the area.[38] Radio-carbon dating suggests that a period of intensive occupation began in the early sixteenth century, a time when the Mississippian societies to the east and south were fragmenting.[39] Thus, it seems that as the Mississippian civilizations to the east and south were in decline, life in the upper Midwest flourished with its extensive buffalo herds and as the source of pipestone.

While it is not clear if there was a gap in use of the site during the fifteenth or sixteenth centuries, it is clear that by the seventeenth century, mound construction and what archaeologists label "mound ceremonialism" was thriving at Blood Run. Archaeologist Colin Betts and others suggest that social disruptions linked to the previous century of European contact, as Old World products along with environmental changes began to transform networks of trade and power relations in the region, were responsible for this surge in mound ceremonialism and construction. Betts argues that the sudden and extensive outburst of mound construction at Blood Run represents an early example of an Indigenous revitalization movement like those associated with the Delaware prophet Neolin in the 1760s, the Shawnee Prophet Tenskwatawa in the early nineteenth century, and the Ghost Dance of the late nineteenth century. Betts suggests that this revitalization movement "had its roots in the retention of mound ceremonialism as a world renewal ritual among Oneota groups."[40] Thus, mound ceremonialism may have re-emerged as a way to confront threatening or destabilizing forces, such as epidemic disease, warfare, environmental stressors or some combination of these. The introduction of European products and hunting for profit infringed upon the system of trade centered on pipestone and may help to explain the intensification of mound construction. It is also notable that the periods of intensification in mound construction align with two periods of extended lower-than-average temperatures known as the little ice age. There was a drop in average temperatures around 1100, which continued through the fifteenth century. During the sixteenth century, temperatures warmed slightly but colder temperatures returned beginning around 1600. Both periods witnessed widespread crop failures and famine. Some areas were abandoned completely.

Archaeologists have documented a sixteenth-century settlement shift among Oneota peoples from the Mississippi to the Missouri River drainage. The appearance of fortifications has also been documented suggesting an increase in conflict.[41] The reason for this shift has generated much debate, particularly in the context of the introduction of epidemic disease. In 1993 archaeologist William Green proposed that a region-wide depopulation event occurred between 1520 and 1620, which accounted for the shift in settlement, and he argued that this decline in population was due to the introduction of Old World diseases.[42] Others have suggested, however, that the timeframe is simply too early for Old World disease to have reached these populations. The earliest documented European products in the La Crosse region in southwestern Wisconsin, for example, date to around 1625.[43] Despite this, Betts argues that there is "compelling evidence" in the archaeological record for an initial introduction of disease in the upper Midwest between 1625 and 1650 as well as "strong circumstantial evidence" indicating that "disease was largely responsible for the population decline." Betts identifies a 1634 outbreak among the Ho-Chunk in the western Great Lakes as the likely culprit.[44] Archaeologists have also documented outbreaks in the Middle Missouri region by 1650.[45] Omaha traditions, however, refer to famine and warfare but do not reference epidemic disease until the eighteenth century.[46] Nevertheless, while the causes of these population movements and declines will continue to generate debate, it is clear that societies during this time were confronting significant challenges.

Though Blood Run is the most extensive example, there are contemporaneous sites that suggest the intensification of mound construction was not localized at Blood Run, but rather regional in character. For example, the Bradbury phase sites along the Rum River in central Minnesota, the Chariton Locality along the Missouri and Chariton Rivers in north central Missouri, and the Old Fort mounds in Missouri as well as sites in northeast Iowa all attest to a fluorescence of mound construction across the upper Midwest.[47] What puzzles archaeologists is the suddenness and rapidness of mound construction at Blood Run. The people at Blood Run constructed some 275 mounds in approximately fifty years. "The magnitude of human activity between 1500 and 1700," writes one archaeologist, "eclipses all that came before."[48] The extent and intensity of mound construction suggests that Blood Run was a place of great ceremonial significance, and the archaeological record indicates it was of considerable economic importance as well for more than a century. Thus, it seems Blood Run was a regional focal point that may have been the setting for multiethnic rendezvous-type gatherings.[49] As archaeologist Margaret Conkey has argued, such sites would have certain characteristics that distinguish them from other types of sites. Rendezvous sites would be large, situated at river confluences near an abundant, seasonally available food source, and contain many different types of artifacts exhibiting a uniform or standardized style of production and decoration.[50] And such sites may also contain "evidence of the religious ceremonies that dominate[d] these gatherings."[51] One such site called The Pas in Manitoba shares many of the characteristics of Blood Run. It is a site where "archaeological remains are extensive" and there is evidence of large-scale production. It is also situated on a moraine split by a river, "resulting in well-elevated habitation areas on both sides of the river."[52]

The period of fluorescence of mound construction also coincides with a regional intensification in the harvesting of pipestone and the production of pipestone products.[53] The earliest documentations of pipestone disk pipes in the upper Midwest suggest an escalation of pipestone quarrying and processing beginning around 1400. At the Bastion site on the Little Sioux River in Cherokee County, Iowa, for example, dated between 1425 and 1550, there is clear evidence of an intensification in the harvesting of pipestone and the manufacture of pipestone products. The abundance of such products at the site compared to earlier sites, such as Correctionville farther downstream, which was well established by 1300, indicate a significant acceleration of production during the fifteenth and sixteenth centuries. During this time Blood Run emerges as a primary production and perhaps distribution center and "may have had a monopoly on catlinite resources."[54]

The Oneota peoples who lived at Blood Run were ancestors to tribal nations possibly including the Omahas, Poncas, Ioways, Otoes, Osage, Kansas, Winnebagos, Missourias, and perhaps others. It is commonly held that Omahas were the primary group who lived at Blood Run during the seventeenth century. These societies maintained an extensive regional trade that appears to have been largely peaceful in stark contrast to the Iroquois wars known as the "Beaver Wars" taking place across the Great Lakes region during this period. Large Oneota villages lacked palisaded walls, for example.[55] Anthropologist Eric Buffalohead suggests, based on the Omaha Sacred Legend, that Blood Run may have been the site of a historic peace accord established among the Omaha, Ponca, Ioway, Oto, Arikara, and Cheyenne. The identification of Arikara and Iowa style pottery lend support to this idea.[56] Those living at Blood Run also apparently did not seek out European traders.[57] The French only learned of Ioways, Omahas, and their neighbors when Ottawas and Hurons fled west from the Great Lakes to escape Iroquois attacks and met Iowas and Otos living along the Iowa River. Thus, there are no documented encounters between these societies and Europeans until they were sought out by the French in the late seventeenth century, which suggests that their leaders were either comfortable delegating such matters or they expected new trade partners to come to them. During the eighteenth century the Omahas moved south into present-day Nebraska among the Arikaras and Pawnees and thus adopted many cultural elements of Caddoan-speaking Plains Indians.[58] Despite this, it is clear that during the seventeenth century Omahas and Ioways lived on the Big Sioux River at Blood Run, and they were responsible for the mounds constructed during this time.

In his *Omaha Sociology*, the missionary and ethnographer James Owen Dorsey, who lived among the Omahas and Poncas during the late nineteenth century, provides perhaps the most comprehensive account of their migration west of the Mississippi. The migrations presented by Dorsey indicate an extended diaspora from the middle Mississippi or possibly the Ohio Valley. Fletcher and La Flesche also cite oral traditions that begin with the people going down the Ohio River, which Omahas refer to as *Uha'i ke,* meaning "river down which they came."[59] According to these traditions, once reaching the Mississippi, they separate for various reasons into the Omahas, Poncas, Ioways, Kansas, Osage, and Quapaw. After the "final separation occurred... at the mouth of the Osage River," the Omahas and Poncas, "accompanied by the Iowas, proceeded by degrees through Missouri, Iowa, and Minnesota, till they reached the neighborhood of the Red Pipestone quarry....Thence they journeyed towards the Big Sioux River, where they made a fort." Here they remained "a long time, making earth lodges (i.e., permanent villages) and cultivating fields." The representation of this period in Omaha and Ponca oral traditions suggests the nostalgic trappings of a golden age when "game abounded" and life was good. While it is difficult to date these movements, if Dorsey's claim that these movements "must have taken many years, as their course was marked by a succession of villages" is accurate, then they may represent an influx of people to the area of Blood Run during the sixteenth century.[60] Fletcher and La Flesche place the crossing of the Mississippi River described in the Sacred Legend as taking place "considerably more than three hundred years" before the 1830 treaty at Prairie du Chien, which would place the migration in the early sixteenth century.[61] Why these societies migrated west is unclear, but this evidence suggests that the migration took place at least a century before the "Beaver Wars" of the mid-seventeenth century and thus these societies were not fleeing Iroquois raids as other societies in the Great Lakes-Ohio Valley would a century later. The migrations may explain a regional depopulation or "vacant quarter" in the lower Ohio Valley between 1450 and 1550 that has long perplexed archaeologists.[62]

Whatever prompted these migrations, these societies became important economic brokers in the region. Archaeologist Mildred Wedel has shown that an extensive east-west trade existed across the upper Midwest facilitated by Ioways and Otos who maintained peaceful relations with the Sioux to their north and the Ojibwas and Illinois Confederacy to the east, both of whom were enemies of the Sioux. Ioways would trade pipestone, pipestone products, buffalo robes, and doubtless many other things with societies to the east and return to the Big Sioux with European goods.[63] The discovery of a runtee at Blood Run lends support to this scenario. Runtees were produced by Dutch traders for trade with the Iroquois between 1640 and 1690. These artifacts frequently turn up at trade sites in New York and around the Great

Lakes. Many of these sites also contain beads and pendants made of red stone, typically thought to be pipestone. If so, the presence of these pipestone goods along with the runtees discovered at Blood Run and at nearby sites suggest the extent of the trade network in which Ioways and their neighbors served as middlemen.[64] When French traders arrived in the late seventeenth century, they tapped into this regional trade network. Peter Schenk's 1710 map and Guillaume de Lisle's 1716 map both show trade paths connecting the Omaha and Ioway villages on the Big Sioux to the Mississippi.[65]

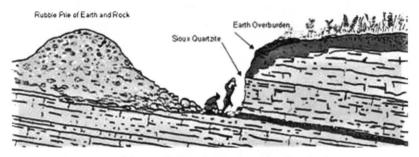

Figure 5: Pipestone excavation.

Figure 6: Section of Peter Schenk map, 1710.

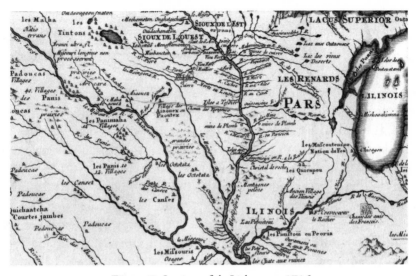

Figure 7: Section of de Lisle map, 1716.

Archaeologists believe this system of trade built around pipestone was centuries old when Europeans arrived. This antiquity engendered an important cultural and economic connection to pipestone and the source of pipestone, the Great Pipestone Quarry.[66] Pipestone is a smooth, workable stone with a pinkish, granite-like appearance, and as Philander Prescott, the first American to document the stone, observed, "Fire does not crack it."[67] Thus, it was ideal for making a variety of products, and the manufacture and trade of pipestone products became deeply interwoven with the society and culture of Omahas, Ioways, and their neighbors. Native traditions suggest that the Pipestone Quarry commanded a certain reverence and any hostilities ceased while engaged with the site. While traveling through the region in the mid-1760s, Jonathan Carver observed "on the plains between the [Minnesota] river and Missouri [river] a large mountain of red marble where all the neighboring nations resort for stone to make pipes. Even those who hold perpetual wars in all other parts meet here in peace. The pipe being the symbol of peace."[68] Based on conversations with Natives living on the upper Missouri in the 1830s, artist George Caitlin[69] reported that people "visited this place freely in former times," and it was once "held and owned in common, as neutral ground, amongst the different tribes who met there to renew their pipes." Even traditional enemies "stayed the [sic] tomahock" when there out of fear of offending the deities.[70] Citing Native traditions, Caitlin wrote that the quarry is the place of the "mysterious birth" of the "red pipe" symbolizing war and the Calumet symbolizing peace. He relates that "at an ancient period" the Great Spirit "called the Indian nations together, and standing on the precipice of the red pipe stone rock, broke from its wall a piece, and made a huge pipe…, which he smoked over them." The Great Spirit told the people that the red rock "was their flesh [and] they must use it for their pipes of peace—that it belonged to them all, and that the war-club and scalping knife must not be raised on its ground." Upon finishing "the last whiff of his pipe" the Great Spirit "went into a great cloud, and the whole surface of the rock for several miles was melted and glazed; two great ovens were opened beneath, and two women (guardian spirits of the place), entered them in a blaze of fire; and they are heard there yet, answering to the invocations of the high priests or medicine-men, who consult them when they are visitors to this sacred place." Pipestone symbolized the blood of the people, and through the pipe, it bound the people together, solidifying political alliances, consecrating social and religious events, and expanding economic networks.

In 1869 Iowa's state archaeologist C. A. White characterized the "Great Red Pipestone Quarry" as the place "from whence the Indians…have from time immemorial obtained the material for their pipes …[and] who, to some extent at least, regard it as a sacred place."[71] White described "the substance of the legends which occur in various forms among the Indians of the North-west concerning this famous locality" explaining that "many ages ago" the Great Spirit descended and stood upon the cliffs that overlook the pipestone, leaving the footprints of a large bird that were apparently still visible in 1869 and a stream issuing from his feet. At this point the Great Spirit "broke a piece from the ledge and formed it into a huge pipe and smoked it." Issuing forth, the smoke created "a vast cloud" that could be seen "throughout the earth," and this became "the signal to all the tribes of men to assemble at the spot from whence [the smoke] issued and listen to the words of the Great Spirit." As the people came and "filled the plain below him, he blew smoke over them all, and told them that the stone was human flesh, the flesh of their ancestors, who were created upon this spot; that the pipe he had made from it was the symbol of peace;…they must ever meet upon this ground in peace and as friends, for it belonged to them all; they must make calumets from the soft stone and smoke them in their councils, and whenever they wished to appease him or obtain his favor."[72] Such powerful spiritual and political connotations coupled with the difficulty of extracting pipestone made it the definitive trade commodity of the period.

Figure 8: George Caitlin, Pipe Stone Quarry and Coteau des Prairies, 1844.[73]

At Blood Run archaeologists have documented large pipestone chunks and preforms, which are rarely found at other regional sites, as well as finished products in large quantities, suggesting that it was a processing center and that the inhabitants may have controlled access to the pipestone quarry.[74] Given the archaeological evidence, it seems clear that by the early sixteenth century pipestone was a vital commodity and the source of a variety of trade goods, including plaques, pipes, bowls, and jewelry.[75] Excavations conducted by Pettigrew in the late 1880s revealed numerous pipestone products, including "one pipestone slab on which is engraved a bird."[76] Subsequent archaeological discoveries at Blood Run include pipestone plaques that "had been illustrated with drawings of hoofed animals and decorative motifs."[77]

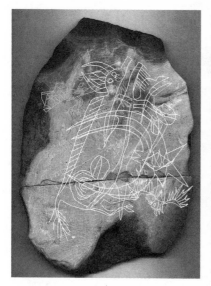 

Figures 9 and 10: Pipestone tablet from Blood Run with incised figures; and pitted boulder with more than 700 pits. While a few pitted boulders have been identified at other sites, their significance and method of construction remain a mystery.

According to archaeologist Dale Henning, these products emanated from a "catlinite core" of Omaha and Ioway villages located between the Minnesota and Missouri rivers. He suggests that this trade network "may have functioned for several centuries prior to contact with Europeans."[78] Thus, by 1600 Blood Run had emerged as "the premier trading center along the eastern Plains," which helps to explain why these societies did not seek out the French for trade, at least not until after the introduction of firearms.[79]

In their extensive anthropological analysis, Fletcher and La Flesche offer insight into the changes brought by the introduction of European goods. They write that "up to the time of the coming of the white trader no Omaha had slain animals for merely commercial purposes," and the new "barter in pelts established by the traders was therefore different in character from any barter that had been practiced between tribes and was destined to give rise to a new industry among the Indians—that of hunting for gain." Fletcher and La Flesche see the simultaneous introduction of metal goods and hunting commercially as "introduc[ing] new motives…not consonant with the old religious ideas and customs."

They argue that the "stimulation of hunting as an avocation" under-mined the persistence of cultural traditions by introducing "different standards of wealth" and reshaping labor relations around commercial hunting.[80] As a result, these customs slowly but inevitably fell into dis-use, which, according to the authors, "weaken[ed] the power of ancient beliefs and introduce[d] new standards, commercial in character; [and] the Omaha became less strong to resist the inroads of new and adverse influences which came with his closer contact with the white race." The introduction of guns was, of course, transformative, but the simultane-ous introduction of metal implements displaced Native pottery and "consequently the pottery industry [i.e., pipestone] was abandoned."[81]

By the late seventeenth century, Native leaders across the region sought to secure close relations with French traders while depriving their enemies of access. The journal of Frenchman Pierre-Charles Le Sueur, who established a fort at the confluence of the Minnesota and Blue Earth rivers in 1700, describes a region in conflict.[82] When he invited Ioways and Otos "to come and make a village near [Fort L'Huillier]" on the Blue Earth River in 1700, warriors of the "Sioux of the East," who are "the masters of the other Sioux, because they are the first with whom we traded, which has given them a good supply of guns," robbed two French traders and took their guns "in revenge for Mr. Le Sueur's settling on the Blue [Earth] river." When some "Sioux of the West" were denied access to the fort over these robberies, they "came to Mr. Le Sueur's cabin to beg him to take pity on them. They wished to weep over his head, according to their custom, and to make him a present of some packages of beaver." Le Sueur's response reveals the character of the new economic system. After "ma[king] them a present," Le Sueur told them, even after agreeing that he knew it was not they but different Sioux who had plundered the traders, "that they shall have no more powder or bullets…and shall not again smoke with [his] calumet," meaning they are no longer friends and trade partners, "until they have given satisfaction for the plunder of the Frenchmen."[83]

Maintaining access to French goods and weapons was vital for the Sioux who feared raids from better-armed Crees and Assiniboins to the northeast who had attained firearms earlier from the English at Hudson Bay.[84] At the same time, Ioways and Otos, previously the middlemen on the east-west trade network from Blood Run to the

Mississippi, "had gone to station themselves on the side of the river of Missoury, in the neighborhood of the Maha [Omaha]."[85] Meanwhile, the Sioux sent a delegation to Le Sueur to make their loyalties clear. With faces "daubed with black," a group of sixteen Sioux, including "several women and children," began weeping for "some ten minutes" while "wip[ing] their tears on Mr. Le Sueur's head and shoulders," asking him to "have pity on his brethren, by giving them powder and ball to defend themselves against their enemies, and to give life to his wives and children who were wasting with hunger in the midst of a country full of all kinds of beasts, having nothing to kill them with." "Behold!" implored the chief, "they will live if thou givest them powder and ball; on the contrary, they will die if thou refuse it."[86] In response, Le Sueur lays out in no uncertain terms the shape and character of the new socioeconomic system. He tells them that "they should reflect that they could not do without the goods of the French" and the only way to secure French trade was to live a sedentary life and not make war on French allies. To emphasize the gravity of his words, Le Sueur gave "a present proportioned to the affair discussed," which included bullets, guns, hatchets, "twelve brasses of tobacco, and a *steel* calumet."[87]

Nevertheless, the Sioux continued to attack societies to the west, including those living at Blood Run and "many Omahas were killed by them." This war with the Sioux marks a turning point when Omahas again uprooted themselves, going first to "the head of Choteau Creek" at present Lake Andes, South Dakota, where they "cut the sacred pole" before traveling up the Missouri to "the country between the Missouri and the Black Hills."[88] While the diplomatic significance of the calumet ceremony persisted through the eighteenth century, the social and political significance of pipestone abated. Though pipestone jewelry and other implements remained somewhat common, the socioeconomic significance of pipestone and the pipestone trade had been eclipsed by the intense demand for lead and steel. As for Blood Run, it remained in silent testimony to an era of transition that witnessed a robust regional economy and way of life collide with the devastating and transformative consequences of contact.

Notes

1. James H. Howard, "Memoir 11: Yanktonai Ethnohistory and the John K. Bear Winter Count," *Plains Anthropologist* 21:73 (August 1976): 1-78, 20.

2. Le Potherie in Emma Helen Blair, ed., *The Indian Tribes of the Upper Mississippi Valley and Region of the Great Lakes* (Cleveland: Arthur Clark Company, 1911), 1:170, 279.

3. See Le Sueur's Journal in Reuben Gold Thwaites, *Collections of the State Historical Society of Wisconsin* 16:180-81, 188.

4. Louis Armand de Lom d'Arce Lahontan, *Some New Voyages in North America,* (1905), 1:176. Though the veracity of Lahontan's account and the belief that he had traveled up the Missouri have long been viewed with skepticism, new research suggests that the account may indeed document an actual trip up either the Missouri or the Minnesota. See Peter H. Wood, ""A Venture to the Plantation of the Sun:" Lahontan's 1688 Journey Across Iowa and Beyond," *Journal of the Iowa Archeological Society* 62 (2015).

5. Named for George Catlin who visited and wrote about the quarry in the 1830s. See Catlin, *Letters and Notes on the Manners, Customs, and Conditions of the North American Indians* (1844).

6. James Howard, "Memoir 11," 20-1.

7. According to tradition, Blood Run Creek is so named for a large Native American battle, which turned the creek red with blood. This tradition, which is likely of Euro-American origin, is not to be confused with the story of Bloody Run, a tributary of the Des Moines River in Humbolt County, Iowa, which was named for an incident in 1854 in which frontier whiskey salesman Henry Lott murdered Sioux Indian chief Sidominadotah and his family and secreted their bodies under the ice of the creek leading to the moniker. See Virgil Vogel, *Iowa Place Names of Indian Origin* (Iowa City: University of Iowa Press, 1983), 9. Another theory suggests that Blood Run Creek was named for a local farm family, the Blud family, who lived near the creek. Still others assert that the water in the creek often had a red hue due to iron ore leaching out of the rock of the streambed, and the name originates from this geological feature. If the name indeed does reference a large Native battle, these wars by the Sioux on the Omahas, Ioways, and their neighbors during the late seventeenth and early eighteenth centuries may be the culprit, but whether or not any battle resulted in the creek running red is not known.

8. Dale R. Henning, *Blood Run: The "Silent City"* (Des Moines: The Iowan Books), 23.

9. See Robbie Ethridge and Sheri M. Shuck-Hall, eds., *Mapping the Mississippian Shatter Zone; The Colonial Indian Slave Trade and Regional Instability in the American South* (Lincoln: University of Nebraska Press, 2009).

10. Donald Dean Parker, ed., *The Recollections of Philander Prescott: Frontiersman of the Old Northwest, 1819-1862* (Lincoln: University of Nebraska Press, 1966), 136.

11. Parker, ed., *The Recollections of Philander Prescott,* 134.

[12] Elizabeth and Dale Henning, "Great Oasis-Mill Creek Interrelationships," in E.A. Bettis III and D. M. Thompson, eds., *Interrelations of Cultural and Fluvial Deposits in Northwestern Iowa* (Association of Iowa Archaeologists, 1982), 11-13; Guy Gibbon, "Cultures of the Upper Mississippi River Valley and Adjacent Prairies in Iowa and Minnesota," in Karl H. Schlesier, ed., *Plains Indians, A.D. 500-1500: The Archaeological Past of Historic Groups* (Norman: University of Oklahoma Press, 1994), 138.

[13] Scott F. Anfinson, *Southwestern Minnesota Archaeology: 12,000 Years in the Prairie Lake Region* (St. Paul: Minnesota Historical Society Press, 1997), 9, 17-19.

[14] William Green and Clare Tolmie, "Analysis of Plant Remains from Blood Run," *Plains Anthropologist* 49:192, Memoir 36: Dhegihan and Chiwere Siouans in the Plains: Historical and Archaeological Perspectives (November 2004), 525-42, 525.

[15] Parker, ed., *The Recollections of Philander Prescott*, 148.

[16] Alice C. Fletcher and Francis La Flesche, *The Omaha Tribe*, 1911 (Lincoln: University of Nebraska Press, 1972), 91.

[17] The antiquity of human occupation and use at Blood Run has long been debated. It is interesting to note that, during excavation for the visitor's center at Good Earth State Park at Blood Run in South Dakota, excavators discovered large geoglyphs just below the topsoil. The visitor's center was resituated in order to preserve these artifacts. An image of one of these geoglyphs is rendered on the floor of the visitor's center, which opened in 2017.

[18] Oneota is the name given by archaeologists to label the mode of production in use in this area during this period. This mode of production was likely practiced by descendants of many, perhaps all, Native societies encountered by the French in this region during this period.

[19] Dale Henning, "The Archaeology and History of Ioway/Oto Exchange Patterns, 1650-1700," *Journal of the Iowa Archeological Society* 50 (2003): 199-221, 213.

[20] Colin M. Betts and Dale Henning, "Aberrant Earthworks? A Contemporary Overview of Oneota Mound Ceremonialism," *The Wisconsin Archaeologist* 97:2 (2016), 101-19, 110; *The Blood of the People: Historic Resource Study, Pipestone National Monument, Minnesota,* 132; "Blood Run Site." *National Historic Landmark summary listing*, National Park Service. Since the site straddles the Big Sioux River, it spans a state border, thus two parks and two names.

[21] Little is known about the origins or purpose of pitted boulders. What is known is that the phenomenon appears to be of human construction, the boulders are completely covered in pits, even on the bottom, and only a few boulders exhibit this feature despite there being many similar boulders in the general area. One theory is that they are boundary markers. Others have proposed that they are symbolic recreations of meteorites. The process by which the "pits" were created is also unclear.

[22] Cyrus Thomas, *Report on the Mound Explorations of the Bureau of Ethnology* (1894), 38-39.

[23] Frederick Pettigrew, *The Silent City* (1889).

[24] Cited in Dale R. Henning and Shirley J. Schermer, "Blood Run Archaeological Investigations," *Plains Anthropologist* 49:192, Memoir 36: Dhegihan and

Chiwere Siouans in the Plains: Historical and Archaeological Perspectives (November 2004), 399-434, 406.

25 Cited in Henning and Schermer, 399-434, 407.

26 T.H. Lewis, Unpublished Field Notes (1881-1895), Minnesota Historical Society Collections, St. Paul; cited in Henning and Schermer, 399-434, 411.

27 Thomas, 38; Colin Betts, personal correspondence, 3 June 2020.

28 The Sacred Pole was the primary sacred object among a pantheon of sacred objects and bundles central to Omaha religion. It was associated with thunder and believed to have been "endowed with supernatural power by the ancient thunder gods." The Sacred Pole was the organizing feature of many Omaha ceremonies. See Alice Fletcher, "The Sacred Pole of the Omaha Tribe," *The American Antiquarian* (1895): 257-68, 268; Fletcher and La Flesche, *The Omaha Tribe*, 236.

29 David Benn, "Continuity in the Woodland Mound Building Tradition of Northeastern Iowa," *Journal of the Iowa Archaeological Society* 56 (2009): 1-31, 1; Colin Betts, personal correspondence with author.

30 Betts and Henning, "Aberrant Earthworks?" 102; David Benn, "Some Trends and Traditions in Woodland Cultures of the Quad-State Region in the Upper Mississippi River Basin" *The Wisconsin Archeologist* 60:1(1979): 47-82, 69; Clark Mallam, *The Iowa Effigy Mound Manifestation: An Interpretive Model* (Office of the State Archaeologist, University of Iowa, Iowa City, 1976), 38.

31 Robert Hall, *An Archaeology of the Soul: North American Indian Belief and Ritual* (Urbana: University of Illinois Press, 1997), 57.

32 Fletcher and Flesche, *The Omaha Tribe*, 592, 83; Francis La Flesche was also the brother of Susan La Flesche Picotte, who was the first Native woman to earn a medical degree, which she received at the age of twenty-one from the Hampton Institute, where she graduated salutatorian of her class before returning to the reservation to serve as a social reformer and physician.

33 Robert Hall, *An Archaeology of the Soul: North American Indian Belief and Ritual* (Urbana: University of Illinois Press, 1997); David Benn, "Continuity in the Woodland Mound Building Tradition of Northeastern Iowa" *Journal of the Iowa Archaeological Society* 56 (2009): 1-31, 2.

34 Betts and Henning, "Aberrant Earthworks?" 101.

35 The Calumet, which refers to both the ceremonies and rituals associated with trade and alliance and the physical pipe that was at the center of these ceremonies, was made of pipestone. While having spiritual connotations, the Calumet was primarily associated with alliance and trade. As one anthropologist writes, the spread of the Calumet ceremony "is better explained in terms of trade and alliance than in terms of missionaries for a nativistic revival." The earliest Calumet ceremony recorded by a European was apparently in 1634 among Plains Apaches, but archaeological evidence, such as the abundance of calumet-style pipes and their inclusion in burials, suggests that ceremonial significance likely emerged during the pre-contact period. See Donald Blakeslee, "The Origin and Spread of the Calumet Ceremony," *American Antiquity* 46:4 (October 1981): 759-68, 759.

[36] Betts and Henning, "Aberrant Earthworks?" 110; Dale Henning, "What Might We Learn from the Mounds on Blood Run? *Newsletter of the Iowa Archaeological Society* 61(2): 8-10.

[37] Paul Kreisa, "Oneota Mounds" (paper presented at the 64th Annual Meeting of the Society for American Archaeology, 1999); David Benn, "Hawks, Serpents, and Bird-men: Emergence of the Oneota Mode of Production" *Plains Anthropologist* 34:125: 233-60.

[38] Fletcher and La Flesche, *The Omaha Tribe*, 72.

[39] Dale R. Henning and Thomas D. Thiessen, "Summary and Conclusions," *Plains Anthropologist* 49:192, Memoir 36: Dhegihan and Chiwere Siouans in the Plains: Historical and Archaeological Perspectives (November 2004), 591-601, 591; Ethridge and Shuck-Hall, eds., *Mapping the Mississippian Shatter Zone.*

[40] Colin Betts, "Oneota Mound Construction: An Early Revitalization Movement," *Plains Anthropologist* 55:214 (2010): 97-110, 98.

[41] Colin Betts, "Pots and Pox: The Identification of Protohistoric Epidemics in the Upper Mississippi Valley" *American Antiquity* 71:2 (2006): 233-59, 235-6; Robert Boszhardt, "Oneota Group Continuity at La Crosse: The Brice Prairie, Pammel Creek, and Valley View Phases," *The Wisconsin Archaeologist* 75:173-236; Robert Sasso, "La Crosse Region Oneota Adaptation: Changing Late Prehistoric Subsistence and Settlement Patterns in the Upper Mississippi Valley," *The Wisconsin Archaeologist* 74: 324-69.

[42] William Green, "Examining Protohistoric Depopulation in the Upper Midwest," *The Wisconsin Archaeologist* 74:290-323, 296.

[43] James A. Brown and Robert Sasso, "Prelude to History on the Eastern Prairies," in David Brose et al., eds., *Societies in Eclipse: Archaeology of the Eastern Woodland Indians, A.D. 1400-1700* (Washington, D.C.: Smithsonian Institution Press, 2001), 211; James A. Brown, "Ground-Stone, Metallic, and Glass Artifacts," in James A. Brown et al., eds., *At the Edge of Prehistory: Huber Phase Archaeology in the Chicago Area* (Kampsville: Center for American Archaeology, 1990), 237-8.

[44] Betts, "Pots and Pox," 250, 252.

[45] Anne Ramenofsky, *Vectors of Death: The Archaeology of European Contact* (Albuquerque: University of New Mexico Press, 1987); Douglas Owsley, "Demography of Prehistoric and Early Historic Northern Plains Populations," in J. H. Verano et al., eds., *Disease and Demography in the Americas* (Washington, D.C.: Smithsonian Institution Press, 1992), 75-86.

[46] Fletcher and La Flesche, *The Omaha Tribe*, 620, 85; George Milner, "Population Decline and Culture Change in the American Midcontinent: Bridging the Prehistoric and Historic Divide," in Alan C. Swedlund, Paul Kelton, and Catherine M. Cameron, eds., *Beyond Germs: Native Depopulation in North America* (University of Arizona Press, 2015), 59-60.

[47] Colin Betts, "Oneota Mound Construction: An Early Revitalization Movement," *Plains Anthropologist* 55:214 (2010): 97-110, 101.

[48] William E. Whittaker et al., *The Archaeological Guide to Iowa* (Iowa City: University of Iowa Press, 2015), 17-18.

49 Benn, "Continuity in the Woodland Mound Building Tradition of Northeastern Iowa," 23.

50 Margaret Conkey, "The Identification of Prehistoric Hunter-Gatherer Aggregation Sites: The Case of Altamira," *Current Anthropology* 21: 609-30, 612; Conkey, "Ritual Communication, Social Elaboration, and the Variable Trajectories of Paleolithic Material Culture," in T. Douglas Price and James A. Brown, eds., *Prehistoric Hunter-Gatherers: The Emergence of Cultural Complexity* (Orlando: Academic, 1985), 299-323, 315.

51 David Meyer and Paul Thistle, "Saskatchewan River Rendezvous Centers and Trading Posts: Continuity in a Cree Social Geography," *Ethnohistory* 42:3 (Summer 1995): 403-44, 410.

52 Meyer and Thistle, "Saskatchewan River Rendezvous Centers and Trading Posts," 413.

53 Hall, *An Archaeology of the Soul*, 57; Betts and Henning, "Aberrant Earthworks?" 103. Pipestone is harvested by excavating the Sioux quartzite to expose the softer pipestone beneath, as shown in figure 5.

54 Henning, "The Archaeology and History of Ioway/Oto Exchange Patterns, 1650-1700."

55 John O'Shea and John Ludwickson, *Archaeology and Ethnohistory of the Omaha Indians. The Big Village Site* (Lincoln: University of Nebraska Press, 1992).

56 Eric Buffalohead, "Dhegihan History: A Personal Story," *Plains Anthropologist* 49:192, Memoir 36: Dhegihan and Chiwere Siouans in the Plains: Historical and Archaeological Perspectives (November 2004): 327-43, 337; Dale Henning, "Study of Pottery from the Blood Run Site (13102) 1985 Excavations," in partial fulfillment of HRDP grant FY 1990-91 from the State Historical Society of Iowa. On file, Archaeological Research Center, Luther College, Decorah, Iowa.

57 In her 1938 master's thesis, Mildred Mott Wedel was the first scholar to connect Ioways with the Blood Run site. Subsequent ethnohistorical research and analysis of tribal traditions has shown that Omahas and Poncas should be included in that habitation as well. "The Native American groups most likely to have lived at the Blood Run/Rock Island archaeological site," writes archaeologist Thomas Thiessen, "are the Omahas/Poncas, Ioways, and Otos." Mildred Mott Wedel, "The Ioway, Oto, and Omaha Indians in 1700," *Journal of the Iowa Archeological Society* 28 (1981): 1-13; Lynn M. Alex, *Iowa's Archaeological Past* (Iowa City: University of Iowa Press, 2000); Dale R. Henning, "The Oneota Tradition," in *Archaeology on the Great Plains*, ed. W. Raymond Wood (Lawrence: University of Kansas Press, 1998), 345-414; 323; Dale R. Henning, "Development and Interrelationships of Oneota Culture in the Lower Missouri River Valley," *The Missouri Archaeologist* 32 (1970): 1-18; Thomas Thiessen, "Who Lived at Blood Run?: A Review of the Historical and Traditions Evidence," unpublished paper produced for the State Historical Society of Iowa, 1998.

58 O'Shea and Ludwickson, *Archaeology and Ethnohistory of the Omaha Indians*, 17-18; Fletcher and La Flesche, *The Omaha Tribe*, 75-6, 80-1.

59 Fletcher and La Flesche, *The Omaha Tribe*, 36.

[60] James Owen Dorsey, *Omaha Sociology,* 3rd Annual Report, Bureau of American Ethnology, 1881-1882, 205-370, 212-13.

[61] Fletcher and La Flesche, *The Omaha Tribe,* 72.

[62] See Charles R. Cobb and Brian Butler, "The Vacant Quarter Revisited: Late Mississippian Abandonment of the Lower Ohio Valley," *American Antiquity* 67:4 (2002): 625-41.

[63] Mildred Wedel, "Peering at the Ioway Indians through the Mist of Time: 1650-circa 1700," *Journal of the Iowa Archeological Society* 33, (1986): 1-74, 45; Henning, "The Archaeology and History of Ioway/Oto Exchange Patterns, 1650-1700."

[64] Colin M. Betts, "Paouté and Aiaouez: A New Perspective on Late Seventeenth-Century Chiwere-Siouan Identity" *Midcontinental Journal of Archaeology* (2018): 1-19, 13-15; Henning and Thiessen, "Summary and Conclusions," 599.

[65] Peter Schenk, *Tabula Mexicae et Floridae : terrarum Anglicarum, et anteriorum Americae insularum, item cursuum et circuituum fluminis Mississipi dicti,* 1710; Guillaume de Lisle, *Novissima tabula regionis Lvdovicianae gallice dictae La Lovgsiane iam olim quidem sub Canadae et Floridae nomine in America Septentrionali,* 1716.

[66] Correspondence with Ioway Tribal Historic Preservation Officer, Lance Foster, in 2015, cited in Theodore Catton and Diane Krahe, *The Blood of the People: Historic Resource Study Pipestone National Monument, Minnesota* (NPS: U.S. Department of the Interior, 2016), 31.

[67] Parker, ed., *The Recollections of Philander Prescott,* 137; Pipestone was formed when layers of clay and sand collected on the ocean's bottom were buried by other sedimentary material and, through time and pressure, turned the sand to quartzite and the clay to pipestone. While the structure of pipestone varies from 10 to 20 inches in thickness, the bands of pure, fine-grained material suited for the manufacture of pipes seldom measures more than three or four inches in thickness. The clay stone gets its reddish color from oxidized hematite. It measures 2.5 on the mohs scale of hardness, which is about the hardness of a human fingernail.

[68] John Parker, ed, *The Journals of Jonathan Carver and Related Documents, 1766-1770* (St. Paul: Minnesota Historical Society Press, 1976), 138-9.

[69] Catlin brought pipestone to the Smithsonian upon his return from Missouri. Considered a novel discovery at the time, it was named "catlinite" in his honor.

[70] Catlin, *Letters and Notes,* 164, 169, 167.

[71] C. A. White, "A Trip to the Great Red Pipestone Quarry" *Annals of Iowa* (January 1869): 60-68, 61.

[72] White, "A Trip to the Great Red Pipestone Quarry," 61.

[73] Catlin, *Letters and Notes,* 165.

[74] Henning, *Blood Run,* 68.

[75] Lynn Marie Alex, "Oneota," Office of the Iowa State Archaeologist (2002), 2.

[76] Frederick Pettigrew, "A Prehistoric Indian Village," *Bulletin of the Minnesota Academy of Natural Science* [1901] 3: 348-55, 353.

[77] Alex, "Oneota," 2.

[78] Henning, *Blood Run*, 77-8.
[79] *The Blood of the People,* 114, 130; Henning and Thiessen, "Summary and Conclusions," 591.
[80] Fletcher and La Flesche, *The Omaha Tribe*, 614-15.
[81] Fletcher and La Flesche, *The Omaha Tribe*, 617.
[82] Le Sueur's Journal in Reuben Gold Thwaites, *Collections of the State Historical Society of Wisconsin* 16:180-1.
[83] Le Sueur's Journal, 16:186-7, 188-9.
[84] Le Sueur's Journal, 16:180-1, 190.
[85] Le Sueur's Journal, 16:180-1, 190.
[86] Le Sueur's Journal, 16:180-1, 191.
[87] Le Sueur's Journal, 16:180-1, 191-2, emphasis mine.
[88] Dorsey, *Omaha Sociology*, 212-13.

Chapter 3

Geography and Land Use in the Valley

Christopher R. Laingen
Eastern Illinois University

1. Location & Setting

The Big Sioux River drains 8,030 square miles of land in eastern South Dakota, southwestern Minnesota, and northwest Iowa. It has four sub-watersheds: Upper and Lower Big Sioux, the Middle Big Sioux Coteau, and the Rock—the latter being the largest single tributary, itself draining 1,740 square miles of southwest Minnesota and northwest Iowa before joining the Big Sioux between Hudson, South Dakota, and Hawarden, Iowa. In the Big Sioux system, "there are approximately 12,000 miles of streams, creeks and slow-flowing sloughs."[1]

The river's headwaters rise in the southwestern corner of Roberts County, South Dakota, near the town of Summit (Figure 1). The headwaters are not picturesque, nor are they singular or certain. If you have ever visited Itasca State Park in neighboring Minnesota and leapt over the Mississippi River in one step at its headwaters, rest assured that you do not need to schedule such a trip to Roberts County. A series of grass-covered, mostly seasonal drainage channels and ditches funnel spring snowmelt and rainfall runoff southward into Grant County where, a few more miles to the southwest of Summit, the river fully channelizes

(Figure 2). Where channelization begins and where running water is found depends upon precipitation amounts of the current season, as well as the previous season(s), and in the driest years the channel may be sporadically or entirely dry as far south as Brookings—80 miles downstream.[2]

Figure 1. The headwaters of the Big Sioux, just west of Summit, South Dakota. In this "wet prairie" numerous grass waterways and seasonal drainageways comprise the river's headwaters before it becomes formally channelized a few more miles to the southwest. Photo by author.

Figure 2. The channelized Big Sioux at 450th Ave. & 146th St., about seven miles southwest of Summit, South Dakota, and two miles directly east of Bitter Lake. Photo by author.

The northwestern-most corner of the Big Sioux watershed is comprised of a closed sub-basin and includes the lakes Pickerel, Enemy Swim, Waubay, Spring, Rush, Blue Dog, Bitter, and several other seasonal sloughs and wetlands. In the late 1990s and again in 2011 lake levels in this closed basin reached historic levels due to years of below normal temperatures (decreasing evaporation) and above normal precipitation. In July 2011 the surface elevation of Waubay Lake surpassed 1,805 feet, and anecdotal evidence showed Bitter Lake neared 1,803 feet.[3] This system accumulates water from underground percolation and flowage between the wetlands that connect Pickerel and Enemy Swim lakes; this water moves southward until it reaches Bitter Lake, a formerly dry wetland, and whose growth has sporadically threatened the town of Waubay.[4]

Hydrologists have estimated that if water level of the Waubay-Bitter Lake system reached 1,811 feet, it would begin to drain southeast into the Big Sioux; though, according to Jay Gilbertson, manager of the East Dakota Water Development District, geologists have never located an ancient (buried) channel that would indicate a natural draining of the Waubay-Bitter Lake system.[5] Rising water levels continue to be offset by evaporation, and the 1,811 mark has yet to be attained. While artificial draining/lowering could be done, digging a channel through the topographic divide would funnel excess quantities of water through private farmland where it was never meant to flow.[6]

The River's Course

The Big Sioux empties into the Missouri River at Sioux City, Iowa, roughly 420 stream-centerline-miles south of its headwaters, or ~200 miles as the crow flies (Figure 3). At the Missouri River the average discharge is 3,800 ft³ per second—a torrent compared to the river's meager beginnings (in high precipitation years such as 2019, average streamflow can exceed 10,000 ft³ per second).[7] Flowing south, the Big Sioux descends from 2,014 feet above sea level to 1,060 feet, a 954-foot difference; an average gradient of nearly 2.3 feet per mile. This might not sound terribly impressive, but it is over five-times "steeper" than the Big Sioux's neighbor to the west, the James River, which drops only five inches over every mile of its course. The James originates in North Dakota and flows for over 710 miles, draining just over 20,000 square miles of territory between the Big Sioux and the Missouri. This difference in slope is due to the James' valley having been flattened by a lobe of glacial ice, whereas the Big Sioux descends from atop the adjacent, and taller, Coteau des Prairies.

Figure 3. The Big Sioux River region. The river and its largest tributary, the Rock River, are shown on the map, along with the watershed (the area inside of the gray boundary), and counties that are used in some of the chapter's statistical analysis of population and land use data are outlined in dark gray. Populous cities and major highways are also shown. Data downloaded from The USGS National Map: https://apps.nationalmap.gov/viewer/. Map created by author.

The Big Sioux channelizes just after crossing into the western part of Grant County, an entirely rural landscape where the river is typically bounded on both sides by a wide buffer of grassland/pasture. The river continues south into Codington County, where it acts as a dual inlet-outlet for Lake Kampeska, the state's third largest natural lake entirely within the state and the most "urban/developed" lake with 13.5 miles of shoreline.[8] "Lake Kampeska was formed thousands of years ago by glacial processes (probably the melting of a remnant ice block) in a zone of glacial stagnation on the boundary between end-moraine till and outwash deposits."[9] "Since the 1940's, the inlet also has served as the outlet after the original outlet along the southeastern part of the lake was blocked during the construction of an airport."[10] The Big Sioux continues south through Watertown, flowing into and out of Pelican Lake in much the same way as it does Kampeska.

The river then enters Hamlin County, passing just to the west of the small town of Castlewood (pop. 619) and is joined by the Stray Horse Creek tributary. Flowing between Estelline (pop. 807) and Lake Poinsett, the Big Sioux, during high water years, again picks up flowage controlled by a flood control structure east of Lake Poinsett—a flowage that drains the lakes of Norden, Mary, St. John, Albert, and finally Poinsett. Two miles south of Estelline, the river enters Brookings County, and a wide floodplain becomes noticeable. Here, center-pivot irrigation units and the Brookings-Deuel-Kingsbury Rural Water System access the underlying Big Sioux Aquifer. Continuing south, the Big Sioux flows past Bruce (pop. 174) before crossing Highway 14 east of Volga (pop. 1,926). Just west of Brookings the tributaries of North Deer and Six Mile creeks join the Big Sioux.

From here, the river's course turns and heads southeast, crossing Interstate 29 about nine miles south of the Brookings Highway 14 interchange and is joined from the northeast by Medary Creek. Once in Moody County, the river abruptly turns back to the west at Flandreau (pop. 2,458). After passing through town, it resumes its generally southern course and skirts the towns of Egan (pop. 354) and Trent (pop. 254) and then enters Minnehaha County. As the river reaches Dell Rapids (pop. 3,660), its southwesterly course abruptly shifts to the west as the river encounters an outcropping of Sioux quartzite. The river then splits into two for about two miles: the western segment of the loop continues west for about a half-mile before continuing south, whereas the eastern segment carved out the "Dells"—40-foot-tall cliffs—of the Big Sioux River from the surrounding quartzite.

Two miles south of where the split merges, the town of Baltic (pop. 1,110) is found on the river's eastern bluffs. Past Baltic the Big Sioux's floodplain again becomes more pronounced as it flows south toward Sioux Falls.

In Sioux Falls (pop. 192,517), the river's natural course makes a large loop south before veering back to the north where another outcropping of Sioux quartzite creates the series of falls for which the town is named. Because one of the largest tributaries, Skunk Creek (which drains nearly 600 square miles to the west/northwest of Sioux Falls), joins the Big Sioux on the west side of town before the river loops back northward, the Army Corps of Engineers, from 1955 to 1961, constructed a flood control system for the city.[11] The system includes 29 miles of floodwalls, levees, and a nearly three-mile-long diversion channel bookended by a dam and a spillway. In flood stage, the diversion channel connects the two "northern ends" of the Big Sioux's loop through central Sioux Falls, leaving the only significant source of incoming water into the Big Sioux (and Sioux Falls) coming from the Skunk Creek drainage. Additional mitigation included the creation of parks and other "greenspaces" atop the river's urban floodplain. If flooding occurs, soccer fields, not homes, get wet.

As it exits Sioux Falls, the river heads northeast toward the town of Brandon (pop. 11,048) where the river, after it turns back to the south, is joined by the Split Rock and Beaver Creek tributaries—both of which drain a sizeable portion of the southwestern Minnesota and far-eastern South Dakota portions of the Big Sioux's watershed.

The River as a State Border

As the river exits Minnehaha County it becomes the border between South Dakota and Iowa—with Minnehaha to the north, the very northwestern tip of Iowa (Lyon County) on the eastern bank, and Lincoln County on the western bank. The river's centerline and the legal border mostly jibe, minus where the river's meandering tendencies continue to sculpt its ever-migrating channel. Along its path to the Missouri, the river passes by the communities of Canton, Fairview, Hudson, North

Sioux City, and Dakota Dunes on the South Dakota side, and Beloit, Hawarden, Akron, and Sioux City on the Iowa side. It is just south of Akron where the Big Sioux finally shares its floodplain with the mighty Missouri, flowing along the eastern edge of the floodplain as the Missouri flows along the western edge until they finally become one at the southern tip of Dakota Dunes.

Why does the Big Sioux not act as the border between South Dakota and Minnesota north of the Lincoln-Minnehaha County line? Minnesota's original Congressional statehood proposal in 1856 indeed described the state's southwestern boundary as the Big Sioux River from the Iowa border north to Lake Kampeska (Watertown).[12] From there the border followed a straight line north/northeast to the southern end of Big Stone Lake, a line that today marks the eastern border of the Lake Traverse Indian Reservation.[13] Had that state border been realized, a sizeable portion of Sioux Falls, all of Brookings, and most of Watertown would all be found in a 3,000 square mile-larger state of Minnesota.

Several theories, all of which unprovable, have been put forward, including lack of federal funding to properly survey the region that eventually became the border, government bureaucracy, and quid-pro-quos between land speculators and Washington, D.C., politicians. Former Minnesota State University history professor William Lass "chalked the change up to a scheme by wealthy St. Paul businessmen and political heavyweights to try to control the lands west of Minnesota. "The heart of the matter was that they wanted the area along the Big Sioux to be left outside of Minnesota," Lass said.[14] The real desire was to control the falls of the Big Sioux. Prominent Minnesotans William H. Nobles and Joseph R. Brown, two of nine men who eventually went on to create the financially lucrative Dakota Land Company, persuaded Washington politicians to opt for the non-Big Sioux River western border for Minnesota.[15] Ultimately, moving the Minnesota border east to its present-day location no doubt lessens what would have been never-ending, red-tape-laden political, economic, and legal headaches, especially for the city of Sioux Falls.

2. Landscape Origins

Glaciation

The Big Sioux River and its basin lie atop and drain the majority of the geologic region known as the Coteau des Prairies—a flatiron-shaped

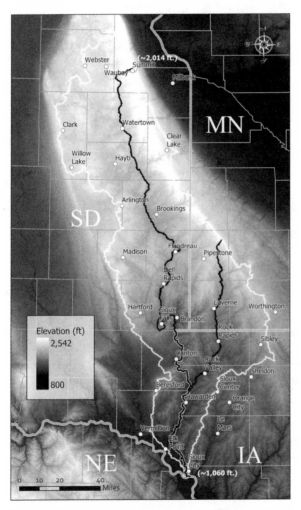

Figure 4. The Big Sioux River and its largest tributary, the Rock River, and the Coteau des Prairies elevation. The "flatiron" shape described by Hogan and Fouberg is clearly evident in this image. To the east of the Coteau the landscape drains into the Minnesota River; to the west into the James River. Data downloaded from The USGS National Map: https://apps.nationalmap.gov/viewer/. Map created by author.

plateau roughly 200 miles in length whose elevation lies between 1,700 and 2,000 feet above sea level, its course following a gradual north to south drop in elevation.[16] Its flatiron shape, the point of which juts into North Dakota, is thought to have been created by the deposition of glacial drift along the region's edges prior to the most recent glacial advance (Figure 4). These barriers of drift acted like a wood splitter, where the southward moving ice sheet was split at the northern tip of the flatiron. Geographers Edward Hogan and Erin Hogan-Fouberg describe it like this: "The Coteau des Prairies is drained by the Big Sioux River, which almost divides the Coteau's watershed in half. The course of the river appears to be a result of the melting of the two ice lobes that flanked the coteau. While both lobes drained into the Big Sioux River, the lobe to the east melted faster than the western lobe. This resulted in the eastern tributaries of the Big Sioux carving stream valleys. The slower melt of the western lobe resulted in glacial drift blocking off former valleys. This resulted in the area west of the Big Sioux River being dotted with perennial and intermittent lakes and sloughs. The largest of these lakes are 5 miles to 10 miles in length."[17]

Weather & Climate

The Big Sioux is found in the heart of the North American landmass. At roughly 45°N latitude, its headwaters are equidistant from the equator and north pole; indeed, the geographic center of North America is found in South Dakota, only a few hundred miles away, just north of Belle Fourche. This "centrality" creates the Big Sioux watershed's "continental" climate, one marked and defined by both annual and long-term weather and climate extremes; where annual temperature ranges can easily surpass 100°F, where precipitation trends alternate between drought and deluge, and where "normal conditions" hardly ever occur. Suffice it to say, this region's weather and climate are two of the most important drivers of how this river system and its landscapes function.

The majority of the Big Sioux's watershed has a Köppen climate classification of Dfa, while a small portion towards the northeastern fringe of the watershed crosses into the Dfb classification.[18] At its broadest categorization, "D" climates are humid continental climates found in the mid-latitudes of North America and Eurasia. Such climates experience all four seasons, have warm to hot summers and cold to severely cold winters, and have no distinct dry season (what the "f" means). While a visitor would hardly notice, the minor difference between the two zones is whether the summer is considered "hot" ("a"), where the warmest month is 71.6°F or above, or "warm" ("b"), where the warmest month's average temperature is below 71.6°F and at least four months average above 50.0°F.

Summit, symbolized in gray on Figure 5, is in the Dfb zone; note the cooler temperatures and lower precipitation totals in March, April, and May, whereas Vermillion is in the Dfa zone and has warmer temperatures and similar or higher precipitation values for most months of the year. Less springtime precipitation in the north has led farmers, historically, to rely upon a small-grains and livestock farming system, whereas locations further south focused on corn and soybean farming earlier on. Not only was precipitation greater, but warmer spring temperatures created a longer growing season, thus increasing the number of growing-degree-days: 3,402 in Vermillion versus 2,430 in Summit.

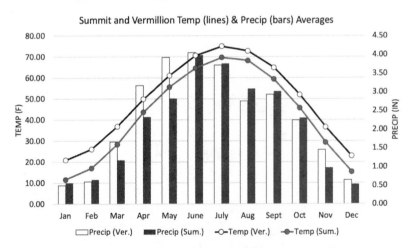

Figure 5. Climate graph for weather stations near the northern (Summit, SD = Sum.) and southern (Vermillion, SD = Ver.) ends of the Big Sioux basin showing temperature and precipitation normals. Data downloaded from South Dakota State University's climate website at https://climate.sdstate.edu/tools/normals/daily.asp. Graph created by author.

Another important climate characteristic that is impactful to the basin, as part of the larger Great Plains region, is the cyclical nature of droughts and deluges (Figure 6). A measurement such as the Palmer Drought Severity Index is useful to visualize the transitions between multiple years of "dryer than normal" (below the 0-line) to "wetter than normal" (above the 0-line) conditions; remembering that "normal" conditions are usually the least experienced and meant only in a statistical sense. Looking at Figure 6, one can easily see important historical events such as the Dust Bowl of the 1930s.

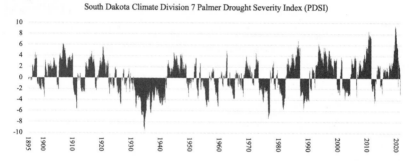

Figure 6. Palmer Drought Severity Index (PDSI) graph for South Dakota Climate Region 7 (east-central SD). Data were downloaded from "Climate at a Glance" website: https://www.ncdc.noaa.gov/cag/divisional/time-series/3907/pdsi/all/1/1895-2021. Graph created by author.

Since the end of the Dust Bowl, periods of higher-than-normal precipitation outnumber (by intensity, or the height of the bars, and in number of continuous years) periods of lower-than-normal precipitation. These long-duration periods of wetter-than-normal conditions, especially those in the 1990s and 2000s, are largely responsible for the filling of the Waubay-Bitter Lake system in the far northern part of the basin.

Trends are also evident in the historical precipitation record kept by the National Oceanic and Atmospheric Administration.[19] Precipitation in South Dakota climate region #7 (east-central South Dakota) has increased at a rate of a quarter inch per decade from 1895 to 2020; the two highest precipitation years (on record) having occurred in 2010 (32.8") and 2019 (38"). In which months precipitation falls has also changed recently when looking at trends from 1990 to 2020 compared to the 1901 to 2000 mean. All months except November have increased precipitation; April through October increased by >0.2", with the most increase having occurred in September and October with 0.54 and 0.58 additional precipitation inches, respectively.

The basin is also warming. Average annual temperature during the twentieth century was 43.4°F. During that century it has warmed 0.2°F per decade, the two warmest years being 1931 (48.5°F) and 1987 (48.4°F). However, the warming does not necessarily mean that summertime high temperatures have been warmer; in fact, daytime high temperatures, especially in the summer months, have been cooler than the twentieth-century means. April through August average maximum temperatures (and October, by >2°F) were cooler over the past three decades than compared to 1901-2000. However, temperature minimums (nightly lows) have been warmer than normal, with the most warming having occurred during the winter, early spring, and late autumn months of the year. So, while summers are actually cooler throughout the watershed, nights have been getting warmer, along with the general warming of the cooler winter, spring, and fall seasons.

Ecological Setting

The Big Sioux basin's pre-European land cover was tallgrass prairie.[20] Across the upper-Midwest, tallgrass prairie ecosystems stretched from Indiana west into the Dakotas, Nebraska, Kansas, Oklahoma, and Texas. West of there was a transitional region of mixed prairie before the landscape, due primarily to lack of precipitation, became fully shortgrass prairie environments.

To better understand the ecological systems at work on the landscape it is often useful to break it up into more manageable areas. These areas are called ecological regions, or ecoregions. "Ecoregions are identified by analyzing the patterns and composition of biotic and abiotic phenomena that affect or reflect differences in ecosystem quality and integrity."[21] The variables used to determine and define ecoregions include geology, soils, landforms, vegetation, climate, wildlife, hydrology, and—what sets U.S. Environmental Protection Agency (EPA) ecoregions apart from other classifications—the consideration of anthropogenic land use.

Ecoregions are nested within one another using hierarchical definitions that get more nuanced as one zooms into smaller spatial areas. The classification system that the EPA uses is numbered from 1 (largest, most general) to 4 (smallest, most specific, but Level 4 regions are too specific for the purposes of this chapter). Broadly speaking, at the Level 1 ecoregion classification scale, the Big Sioux is found within "The Great Plains." This region has been further subdivided into five Level 2 ecoregions—the Big Sioux Watershed found within "The Temperate Prairies" region.

This hierarchical system can best be explained by EPA scientists James Omernik and Glenn Griffith: "For example, within the [*Level 1*] Great Plains, the [*Level 2*] West-Central Semi-Arid Prairies are drier and contain less cropland agriculture than the [*Level 2*] Temperate Prairies to the east and are cooler than the [*Level 2*] South-Central Semi-Arid Prairies to the south. The mosaics of potential natural vegetation and current land use/land cover are markedly different in each of these regions. In contrast to the Temperate Prairies and West-Central Semi-Arid Prairies where corn, soybeans, spring wheat, and barley are major crops, in the South Central Semi-Arid Prairies, winter wheat, sorghum and, locally, cotton are dominant, reflecting a difference in phenology between the regions."[22]

It is only at the Level 3 scale where the Big Sioux watershed splits into two separate and quite distinct regions. The southeastern portion of the watershed that includes the counties of Union, Plymouth, Sioux, Lyon, Nobles, Rock, the eastern two-thirds of Minnehaha and Moody, and the southern half of Pipestone is part of the Western Corn Belt Plains ecoregion (where anthropogenic land uses define the ecoregion), while the remaining counties north and west of those are part of the Northern Glaciated Plains (where glacial actions define the region).[23] This distinction will become clearer as we move into the next part of this chapter, which focuses on land use.

3. Using the Landscape

Tilling the Prairie

Land use within a watershed has been influenced by what shaped the original landscape as well as underlying environmental variables and processes still at work. With the influx of European settlers beginning

in the 1860s, the tallgrass prairie was quickly transformed to one focused primarily on mixed-grain and livestock production. Based on
the 1880 Census of Population and using the sixteen counties[24] that
comprise the Big Sioux Basin, 10% of the total land area had been
converted to what was referred to as "improved farmland."[25] By 1910,
only three decades later, over 80% of the basin's prairie grass landscape
had been brought into agricultural production (Figure 7).

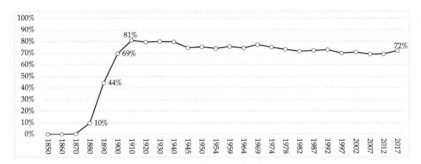

Figure 7. Percent of land area in the sixteen Big Sioux basin
counties considered "Improved Farmland" or "Total Cropland."
Graph created by author.

Since 1910 there has been a gradual loss of ~9% of the basin's
cropland, due mostly to farmers focusing their efforts on only the most
productive croplands.[26] All sixteen counties' cropland trends are somewhat like the trend shown above, though there are sub-trends that are
unique to counties that exhibit similar types of environmental characteristics. The five counties that had the largest percentage of their land
area as cropland in 2017, from 85% to 90%, are all counties found in
the Western Corn Belt Plains ecoregion portion of the basin: Sioux,
Union, Lyon, Rock, and Nobles. Since their initial "peak" from 1900
to 1920, all five counties' cropland areas have either remained steady
or have slightly increased through 2017. The basin's best cropland and
longest growing season are found in these southeastern-most counties,
so it is not surprising that farmers in these counties have and continue
to use their lands thusly.

Counties that had the smallest percentage of their land area as
cropland in 2017, from 55% to 66%, include Day, Minnehaha, Codington, and Deuel. The growth of wetlands and the Waubay-Bitter sys-

tem of lakes and 122,000 acres of undisturbed grasslands explain Day County; the urban expansion of Sioux Falls' exurban developments explains Minnehaha; Codington's lack of cropland is explained by the large number of wetlands to the west of Watertown as well as just over 80,000 acres of undisturbed grasslands; and Deuel is explained by over 110,000 acres of undisturbed grasslands, nearly 28% of the county's total land area.[27]

Contemporary Basin

Even though the Big Sioux is South Dakota's most populated river basin, agriculture is the dominating land use. Over 98% of the basin's land use is comprised of nine categories: corn (34%), soybeans (30%), grass/pasture (16%), developed (6%), water (5%), alfalfa (3%), wetlands (2%), spring wheat (1%), deciduous forest (1%), and ~2% everything else.[28] The majority (85%) is agricultural land, either cropland (as shown in Figure 7) or pastureland, with an increasing amount of cropland as the years go by as the western fringe of the Corn Belt continues its westward and northwestward movement.[29]

In 1925 there were 26,897 farms in the sixteen basin counties. The most farm-dense county was Sioux with 2,860 farms within its 768 square miles; the least-dense was Codington with 1,180 farms within 688 square miles. By 2017 only 12,047 of the Big Sioux's farms remained, but most of them, 95% to 98%, were still family farms. While this decline might seem severe, Big Sioux basin farms have fared much better than what's happened to farms at the national scale where seven out of every ten have disappeared since the 1930s.

Farmland area—all land owned by farmers (cropland, pastureland, idled lands, building sites, etc.)—has changed very little. In 1925 there were 6.1 million acres; in 2017 there were 6.0 million acres. The total percentage of land area in these sixteen counties devoted to farmland dropped, only slightly, from 90% to 88%, a minor change over a nearly century-long period. In 1925 Minnehaha led the way with 95% of its area as farmland. By 2017 Minnehaha had the lowest percentage of land used for farmland at 72%, a result largely of the growth of Sioux Falls' urban and exurban areas. In 2017 the counties with the greatest amount of their land area as cropland were Clark, Sioux, and Union counties, all with 98%.

What has changed, and what has been written widely about over the past decade, are the types of agricultural production systems practiced by the farmers of the basin. Yes, rural to urban land change has occurred. Yes, lake and wetland expansion in recent decades has taken farmland out of production and flooded it. But what has been the most important change is the types of crops produced and the disappearance of widespread livestock production, mostly pastured beef cattle.[30] This shift from mixed-grain and livestock agriculture has been replaced with cash-grain farming focused, increasingly, on corn and soybean production and on large-scale CAFO-based animal production (dairy cattle specifically).

Splitting the region into its two distinct ecoregional parts—the Northern Glaciated Plains and the Western Corn Belt Plains—and selecting a county that is representative of its respective ecoregion, the transition from mixed-grains to corn and soybeans can be seen happening during different periods of time.[31] Hamlin County was chosen as being representative of the Northern Glaciated Plains ecoregion, and Rock County was chosen to represent the Western Corn Belt Plains ecoregion (Figure 8).

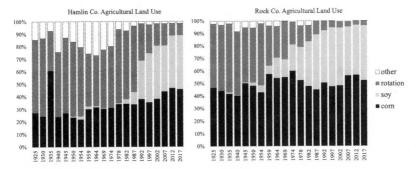

Figure 8. Hamlin County, SD, and Rock County, MN, cropland use trends, 1925 to 2017. Hamlin is representative of trends in the northern (Ecoregion 46) portion of the Big Sioux basin and Rock is representative of the southern (Ecoregion 47) portion of the basin—the latter of which has been involved in corn-soy agriculture for at least three more decades than the northern parts of the basin. Graph created by author.

Modern cash-grain, Corn Belt production can be seen entering Rock County in the late-1950s and early-1960s with the introduction of soybeans. Rotation crops such as wheat, oats, alfalfa, and others quickly disappeared and were replaced within a few decades by corn and soybeans.[32] The same type of transition has occurred in Hamlin County, but much more recently. The lag time involves numerous factors that include differing soil types, climate thresholds such as growing-degree-day limitations that modern corn/soy hybrids have only recently been able to overcome, the emergence of new markets that have urged farmers to grow corn and soybeans instead of small grains and livestock, the introduction of GMO seeds, and other advancements in agricultural technologies, as well as policy changes in U.S. Farm Bills.

Dairy Farming

Livestock farming has long been an important component of the Big Sioux basin's agricultural landscape. In the mid-1920s counties of the basin had 3.1-million hogs and 38-million cattle, of which 3.1-million were milk cows. In 2017 the number of hogs had increased slightly to 3.8-million (although 61% are found on ~600 farms in two Iowa counties), the number of cattle had decreased to just 1.3-million, and milk cows had declined to just under 100,000.[33] The Big Sioux basin finds itself shoe-horned into a transitional zone between the more "core" areas of the hog (CAFO) and beef cattle (feedlot) regions nearby, but the basin, mostly the South Dakota portion of it, has become an important player in the production of milk for the region's growing cheese industry.

Between 2019 and 2020 alone, South Dakota dairy farmers added 14,000 new dairy cows to its stock,[34] a continuation of a nearly decade-long trend, driven by expansion of existing cheese-production facilities, along with new ones, that operate with milk produced on a decreasing number of increasingly productive (and large) dairy farms, some of which have relocated to South Dakota from states such as California. The value of each dairy cow in the state is about $7,100 a year, though other reports have estimated the overall economic impact of each dairy cow in South Dakota as high as $26,000 a year. The state's two largest cheese plants in Lake Norden (Agropur) and Millbank (Valley Queen), are both undergoing significant expansions, and in 2012 Brookings welcomed Bel Brands and its Baby Bel cheese snacks to town.[35]

According to the USDA National Agricultural Statistics Service, in 2013 South Dakota (in sum, not just the Big Sioux basin) had 272 milking operations consisting of 92,000 cows. By 2020 the number of farms had dropped to 171, a 37% reduction, but the number of cows had risen to 127,000, a 38% increase in herd size. Because today's cows produce 11% more milk than in 2013, total milk production has increased from 2.0 billion pounds to 3.1 billion in 2020, a 55% increase over an eight-year period.[36] Driving this change has been a 16% increase in dairy consumption over the past 30 years. According to the USDA, although liquid milk consumption continues to decline, butter consumption has increased 24%, yogurt 7%, and per-capita cheese consumption nationwide has risen 19% in just over the past decade.[37]

Conservation Reserve Program

The landscape of the Big Sioux River watershed has been and continues to be dominated by agricultural land use, with the few exceptions of the basin's larger urban areas, the expansion of lakes/wetlands in the northern part of the region, and some areas where the last remaining stands of native prairie are found.[38] Since settlement and the plowing of the prairie, the most widespread and significant changes to the landscape of the basin have been linked to two large-scale conservation programs that temporarily retired cropland to preserve soil and improve water quality, as well as to help reduce production and regulate the market price of crops: Soil Bank (1950s-60s) and the Conservation Reserve Program (CRP), 1986-present.

The Soil Bank was part of the Agricultural Act of 1956 (the Farm Bill); its threefold purpose was to reduce production of crops, thus lowering surplus and helping to maintain farm incomes, as well as conserving soil.[39] At its peak, the program idled 6% of the country's cropland. In South Dakota, Soil Bank acreage peaked in 1960 with 1.8-million acres idled. The program did not accept new contracts after 1960, but existing contracts kept much of that land idled into 1970, after which most returned to crop production as new export markets in Asia opened and as a new USDA Secretary, Earl Butz, encouraged farmers to farm "fencerow to fencerow."

The second major land transformation began in 1986 after the passage of the 1985 Farm Bill—"The Food Security Act of 1985"—in part, a reaction to the commodities boom of the 1970s and the subsequent economic collapse in the early 1980s that doomed thousands of Midwestern farms.[40] Consisting of 10-to-15-year contracts, the CRP provides participants with rental payments and cost-share assistance for the establishment of long-term resource conserving land covers, which promote the retirement of highly erodible, environmentally sensitive cropland.

Only about 4-7% of the total area enrolled in the CRP since 1986 in the state of South Dakota has been in the counties of the Big Sioux basin; this is not surprising, as some of the state's most productive cropland—thus, least likely to be taken out of production—is located there.[41] Counties with the most acres enrolled as well as the greatest percentage of their area enrolled are in the northern portion of the basin. Day, Deuel, Brookings, Clark, and Codington had between 7% and 14% of their total area enrolled in CRP, with all of them except Clark having the most acres enrolled in the program in 2007 just prior to the passage of the Energy Independence and Security Act (EISA). EISA increased demand for corn, and because 2007 coincided with the expiration of many 10-year CRP contracts, a decline in CRP acreage across much of the northern and central portion of the region occurred.

The counties with the least amount of CRP enrolled, both in total area and percent of total county area, were found in the southern portion of the basin: Rock, Sioux, Nobles, Lyon, and Lincoln—each having between 1% and 3% of their total county area enrolled at any given time. Apart from Lyon County topping-out in 1994 with just over 8,000 enrolled acres of CRP, the remainder of the counties all had their highest CRP enrollment between 2011 and 2018, well after the passage of EISA. This should not be terribly surprising. These counties had much less land enrolled in CRP when the program first began because of the relative lack of "marginal" cropland compared to Big Sioux basin counties further north and west.

These differences also illustrate changes in enrollment practices/opportunities. In the first decade of the program, land was enrolled in CRP in "general signup" contracts. This typically meant that entire fields were enrolled in the program even if the environmentally "marginal" lands were only in a portion of the field's area. Beginning in 1996, "continuous signup" contracts were created. These contracts allowed farmers to enroll smaller—more focused—pieces of land into CRP instead of entire fields. Examples of a continuous application would be the installation of a grass buffer strip along a stream that ran through a field (instead of retiring the entire field from production). Such contracts have become more popular than general signups because of their flexibility in allowing the farmer to keep producing crops on most of their field while still retiring the land where the greatest amount of environmental protection was needed. These contracts are especially appealing in agricultural areas whose landscapes are not widely marginal but where focused, small-scale conservation improvements help to further improve the quality of environmental variables.

Urban Areas

Urban/developed land use accounts for roughly 6% of the Big Sioux basin's landscape. Of the basin's sixteen counties, Minnehaha County has the largest population, and at 197,214 it is larger than the next five largest counties combined. Lincoln (Sioux Falls), Sioux (Sioux Center), Brookings (Brookings), Codington (Watertown), and Nobles (Worthington) comprise the next largest cohort, all with populations between 20,000 and 50,000, with Lincoln having jumped into second place overall by 2010 as major growth areas of Sioux Falls occurred in northern Lincoln County, along with continued growth of nearby commuter towns such as Harrisburg, Tea, and the county seat of Canton which is found along the Big Sioux fifteen miles south-southeast of Sioux Falls. The remaining cohort of ten counties have populations ranging from just shy of 3,837 (Clark) to 16,811 (Union) and are largely rural. Except for Lincoln County's exceptional growth since the 1990s (65,161), the rank of these counties in terms of population has been largely the same since 1940.

4. In Closing

The primary goal of this chapter was to "lay the geographical groundwork" for this book–to orient the reader as to the physical environment of the Big Sioux basin as well as to describe some of its most important land uses. As agricultural practices continue to transition from historically relevant mixed-grain and livestock systems to those resembling the corn-soybean systems of the Corn Belt, land transformations continue to take place. Pasturelands no longer needed have, in many cases, been plowed and are now used to grow crops. Much has been written about grassland-to-cropland change in this region of the country,[42] however, much of the change that has been documented has been simply the non-renewal of CRP (grassland) contracts as the agricultural market has once again favored production over conservation.[43]

Indeed, conservation-based land uses impact water quality of the Big Sioux River. One of the most effective methods for addressing water impairments involves restoring and/or maintaining riparian buffer areas.[44] As the name implies, these areas provide a buffer between potential contaminant sources (animals and their waste, farm chemicals or nutrients) and the particular water resource. In these natural (or restored) strips of grassy vegetation, most ranching and conventional farming practices are either restricted or altogether prohibited. Protection is obtained in several ways. The grass itself acts as a filter, trapping sediment that might have otherwise been carried into a stream by water or wind erosion. Root systems can absorb excess nutrients that may be moving through the soil with water before those nutrients make their way to the stream. Finally, prohibiting livestock from the buffers ensures that nutrients and bacteria from manure do not contaminate the stream.

Nitrate levels are another important water-quality issue. In large part, high nitrate levels in both surface and groundwater sources throughout the Midwest have been linked to excess agricultural nitrogen application. Because the central and northern portions of the Big Sioux basin have yet to undergo large-scale sub-surface agricultural tiling in the same way the southern portion of the basin has, nitrate monitoring in the Big Sioux River revealed increased levels at testing sites near municipal water treatment facilities.[45] Increased levels–though still well below safe drinking water standards–have also been noted near testing sites where the Medary Creek (Brookings) and Split Rock Creek (Minnehaha) tributaries enter the Big Sioux. The tributary with the most troubling trends has been the Rock River, which drains parts of southwestern Minnesota and northwestern Iowa and enters the Big Sioux near Hudson. These landscapes have been extensively drained (both surface and subsurface networks), in some places for nearly a century, whereas throughout much of the South Dakota portion of the Big Sioux basin, landowners have only recently just begun such practices.

Notes

1   "Portrait of a Watershed," Friends of the Big Sioux River, accessed August 25, 2021, https://www.friendsofthebigsiouxriver.org/blog/portrait-of-a-watershed.

2   Edward P. Hogan and Erin H. Fouberg, *The Geography of South Dakota*, rev. ed. (Sioux Falls: The Center for Western Studies, 1998), 16.

3   M. T. Anderson and D. G. Driscoll, "Lake Levels in Northeastern South Dakota Reach Historical Maximum Elevations in 2011" (paper presented at the annual meeting of the American Geophysical Union, Fall 2011), https://ui.adsabs.harvard.edu/abs/2011AGUFM.H51K1355A/abstract.

4   "Waubay Chain of Lakes, South Dakota, USA," LakeLubbers.com, accessed August 25, 2021, https://www.lakelubbers.com/waubay-chain-of-lakes-2019/.

5   Jay Gilbertson, interview with author, July 24, 2020.

6   Amanda Fanger, "Commissioners are Looking into Draining Waubay, Bitter Lake," *Reporter and Farmer*, July 6, 2020, http://www.reporterandfarmer.com/index.html.

7   "USGS 06485950 Big Sioux River at Sioux City Iowa," USGS National Water Information System: Web Interface, accessed August 25, 2021, https://waterdata.usgs.gov/nwis/inventory?agency_code=USGS&site_no=06485950.

8   Bryan D. Schaap and Steven K. Sando, "Sediment Accumulation and Distribution in Lake Kampeska, Watertown, South Dakota," *USGS Water Resources Investigations Report 02-4171* (2002), 1-37: https://pubs.usgs.gov/wri/wri024171/pdf/lakekampeska.pdf.

9   F.V. Steece, "Geology of the Watertown Quadrangle," *South Dakota Geological Survey Geologic Map* (1957).

10 Ken R. Madison, "Diagnostic/Feasibility study of Lake Kampeska, Codington County, South Dakota," *South Dakota Department of Environment and Natural Resources* (January 1994): 1-174, https://denr.sd.gov/dfta/wp/tmdl/tmdl_kampeska.pdf.

11 "Flood Control," City of Sioux Falls Public Works online archive, accessed August 25, 2021, https://web.archive.org/web/20110108022715/http://www.siouxfalls.org/PublicWorks/water_conservation/flood_control.

12 Mark Stein, *How the States Got Their Shape* (New York: Harper Collins Publishers, 2008), 149-50.

13 David Montgomery, "Part of Sioux Falls Almost Was Minnesota," *Argus Leader*, September 2, 2014, https://www.argusleader.com/story/news/2014/09/02/section-sioux-falls-almost-minnesota/14951607/.

14 Montgomery, "Part of Sioux Falls."

15 William E. Lass, *Shaping the North Star State: A History of Minnesota's Boundaries* (St. Cloud: North Star Press, 2014), 103-51. Chapter 4, *Determining the*

Western Boundary, details how Minnesota's western border (South Dakota's eastern border) came to be.

[16] Hogan and Fouberg, 16.

[17] Hogan and Fouberg, 18.

[18] Markus Kottek, Jurgen Grieser, Christoph Beck, Bruno Rudolf, and Franz Rubel, "World Map of the Koppen-Geiger Climate Classification System, Updated," *Meteorologische Zeitschrift* 15:3 (July 2006): 259-63, DOI: 10.1127/0941-2948/2006/0130. Data for use in GIS available here: http://koeppen-geiger.vu-wien.ac.at/usa.htm.

[19] "Climate at a Glance," National Oceanic and Atmospheric Administration, accessed August 31, 2021, https://www.ncdc.noaa.gov/cag/divisional/time-series. At this site, from the drop-down menus users would select "South Dakota," "Climate Division 7," "Annual Precipitation," and the range of years that they would like to graph.

[20] August W. Kuchler, "Potential Natural Vegetation of the Conterminous United States," *American Geographical Society*, Special Publication No. 36 (1964): https://databasin.org/datasets/1c7a301c8e6843f2b4fe63fdb3a9fe39/.

[21] James M. Omernik, "Ecoregions of the conterminous United States. Map (scale 1:7,500,000)," *Annals of the Association of American Geographers* 77:1 (1987): 118-25, https://www.jstor.org/stable/2569206.

[22] James M. Omernik and Glenn E. Griffith, "Ecoregions of the Conterminous United States: Evolution of a Hierarchical Spatial Framework," *Environmental Management* 54 (2014): 1253, https://link.springer.com/article/10.1007/s00267-014-0364-1.

[23] Level III and IV Ecoregion descriptions can be downloaded from: ftp://newftp.epa.gov/EPADataCommons/ORD/Ecoregions/us/Eco_Level_III_descriptions.doc.

[24] Because natural regions such as watersheds do not always align with political boundaries such as states or counties—boundaries used to collect and report statistical information on population and agricultural land use—counties were a part of the Big Sioux River watershed if the majority of their area fell within it. The one exception made to this rule was the inclusion of Day County, South Dakota, because of the unique nature of the enclosed, non-draining sub-basin of the Big Sioux watershed found in eastern Day. Counties included in the basin for the purpose of statistical analysis can be seen in Figure 3. County population was obtained from the U.S. Census Bureau, various years, at: https://www.census.gov/.

[25] Pamela J. Waisenen and Norman B. Bliss, "Changes in Population and Agricultural Land in Conterminous United States Counties, 1790 to 1997," *Global Biogeochemical Cycles* 16:4 (2002): 1-19, https://agupubs.onlinelibrary.wiley.com/doi/pdf/10.1029/2001GB001843. Up through 1920, the "improved land in farms" category defined a consistent time series. In 1925 and later years, the term "improved land in farms" was no longer used and the term "cropland" was introduced. The category "total cropland" included the subcategories of harvested cropland, crop failure, idle cropland, cropland in summer fallow, and plowable pasture.

[26] John C. Hudson and Christopher R. Laingen, *American Farms, American Food: A Geography of Agriculture and Food Production in the United States* (Lanham: Lexington Books, 2016), 131.

[27] Pete Bauman, Joe Blastick, Cody Grewing, and Alexander Smart, "Quantifying Undisturbed Land on South Dakota's Prairie Coteau," *South Dakota State University report to The Nature Conservancy* (June 30, 2014), https://www.nature.org/media/southdakota/assessing-untilled-sod-prairie-coteau-report-2014.pdf.

[28] Percentages calculated using the U.S. Department of Agriculture's "Cropland Data Layer" statistics found at https://nassgeodata.gmu.edu/CropScape/. The boundary of the Big Sioux River watershed was used to select land cover data from the interface; data were then summarized by category.

[29] Chapter 3, "The Corn Belt" from Hudson and Laingen, *American Farms, American Food* describes this expansion. An in-depth study in the driving forces at play can be found in Roger Auch, George Xian, Christopher R. Laingen, Kristi L. Sayler, and Ryan R. Reker, "Human Drivers, Biophysical Changes, and Climatic Variation Affecting Contemporary Cropping Proportions in the Northern Prairie of the U.S.," *Journal of Land Use Science* 13: 1-2 (2018): 32-58, https://doi.org/10.1080/1747423X.2017.1413433.

[30] John Fraser Hart, *Changing Scale of American Agriculture* (Charlottesville: University of Virginia Press, 2003), 14-39.

[31] The southeastern portion of the watershed that includes the counties of Union, Plymouth, Sioux, Lyon, Nobles, Rock, the eastern two-thirds of Minnehaha and Moody, and the southern half of Pipestone is part of the EPA's Western Corn Belt Plains ecoregion (47), while the remaining counties north and west of those are part of the Northern Glaciated Plains (46). Level III and IV Ecoregions of the Continental United States. Maps and descriptions: ftp://newftp.epa.gov/EPADataCommons/ORD/Ecoregions/us/Eco_Level_III_descriptions.doc.

[32] Christopher R. Laingen, "The Agrarian Midwest: A Geographic Analysis," in *Finding a New Midwestern History*, ed. Jon K. Lauck, Gleaves Whitney, and Joseph Hogan (Lincoln: University of Nebraska Press, 2018), 143-60.

[33] "Census of Agriculture, 2017," U.S. Department of Agriculture National Agricultural Statistics Service, accessed 25 August 2021, https://www.nass.usda.gov/Publications/AgCensus/2017/.

[34] Bart Pfankuch, "S.D. Dairy Industry Growing Fast to Meet Needs of Cheesemakers," *South Dakota News Watch,* March 3, 2021, https://www.sdnewswatch.org/stories/special-report-s-d-dairy-industry-growing-fast-to-meet-needs-of-cheesemakers/.

[35] Donna Berry, "South Dakota Sets its Sights on Disrupting the Dairy Industry," *Food Business News*, October 2, 2018, https://www.foodbusinessnews.net/articles/12608-south-dakota-sets-its-sights-on-disrupting-the-dairy-industry.

[36] Data were acquired from USDA NASS Quick Stats: https://www.nass.usda.gov/Quick_Stats/.

[37] Data were acquired from USDA Charts of Note: https://www.ers.usda.gov/data-products/chart-gallery/gallery/chart-detail/?chartId=81223.

[38] Bauman, Blastick, Grewing, and Smart, 10-16.

[39] J. Douglas Helms, "Brief History of the USDA Soil Bank Program," *USDA Natural Resource Conservation Service, Historical Insights* no. 1 (1985): https://www.nrcs.usda.gov/Internet/FSE_DOCUMENTS/stelprdb1045666.pdf.

[40] David Danbom, "The Indistinct Distinctiveness of Rural Midwestern Culture," in *The Rural Midwest since World War II*, ed. J. L. Anderson (DeKalb: Northern Illinois University Press, 2014), 303.

[41] County-level CRP data was acquired from the USDA Farm Service Agency webpage: https://www.fsa.usda.gov/programs-and-services/conservation-programs/reports-and-statistics/conservation-reserve-program-statistics/index.

[42] Christopher K. Wright and Michael C. Wimberly. "Recent Land Use Changes in the Western Corn Belt Threatens Grassland and Wetlands," *Proceedings of the National Academies of Science* 110:10 (2013): 4134-39, https://doi.org/10.1073/pnas.1215404110. See also Carol A. Johnston, "Agricultural Expansion: Land Use Shell Game in the U.S. Northern Plains," *Landscape Ecology* 29 (2014): 81-95. https://doi.org/10.1007/s10980-013-9947-0.

[43] Michael C. Wimberly, Larry L. Janssen, David A. Hennessy, Moses Luri, Niaz M. Chowdhury, and Hongli Feng, "Cropland Expansion and Grassland Loss in the Eastern Dakotas: New Insights from a Farm-Level Survey," *Land Use Policy* 63 (2017): 160-73, https://doi.org/10.1016/j.landusepol.2017.01.026.

[44] Barry Berg and Matt Johnson, "Protecting Riparian Buffers: A Good Idea for Everyone," *South Dakota Rural Water's Quality on Tap* 12:3 (2017): 6-7, http://www.sdarws.com/assets/0117-qot-sdarws.pdf.

[45] Berg and Johnson, 7.

Chapter 4

Land Use, Forests, and Birds of the Big Sioux River Valley

Matthew J. Ley
Colorado State University

W. Carter Johnson
South Dakota State University

David L. Swanson
Missouri River Institute,
University of South Dakota

Mark D. Dixon
University of South Dakota[1]

Introduction

R iparian corridors–ecosystems bordering streams and rivers–are ecologically distinct transitional zones between aquatic and terrestrial habitats. Flooding prominently influences riparian zones as erosion and sediment deposition create a dynamic heterogeneous environment,[2] with certain species of trees and shrubs uniquely adapted to tolerate these conditions.[3] Riparian forests provide a host of beneficial ecosystem services including wildlife habitat, water quality protection, stream bank stabilization, biodiversity conservation, and aesthetic enjoyment and recreational opportunities for people.[4]

Pervasive human effects on riparian zones occur on regulated rivers where dams, levees, channelization, and bank stabilization reduce flooding and the dynamic riparian habitats reliant upon floods.[5] These modifications have occurred along most major river systems and have often been accompanied by large-scale land use conversion. This is particularly evident in the U.S. Midwest, where large tracts of native riparian vegetation were removed and converted to agricultural use since the onset of Euro-American settlement.[6] These threats to ecological function, combined with the value of riparian corridors for providing ecosystem services, highlight the importance of understanding and conserving these areas.

Geography of the Big Sioux River

The Big Sioux River drains approximately 9,000 square miles of eastern South Dakota, northwestern Iowa, and southwestern Minnesota[7] (Figure 1). From its origins in southern Roberts County in South Dakota, the Big Sioux flows 420 miles southward to its confluence with

Figure 1. The Big Sioux basin drains approximately 9,000 square miles in Minnesota, Iowa and South Dakota, including the Coteau des Prairies and much of South Dakota's Prairie Pothole region. It originates in southern Roberts County, SD, and flows 420 miles southward to its mouth at the Missouri River at Sioux City, IA. The upper, middle, and lower segments of the river, as described in this chapter, are shown.

the Missouri River near Sioux City, Iowa. In contrast to many other midwestern rivers, the Big Sioux has a largely intact riparian corridor and little flow regulation except for a few low-head dams that raise upstream water levels a few feet, but do not greatly affect downstream flows. The river flows through a largely agricultural landscape that contains several population centers, including Watertown, Brookings, and Sioux Falls, South Dakota, and Sioux City, Iowa, making the Big Sioux the most highly populated basin in South Dakota.[8] The cumulative effects of agriculture and urban land uses throughout the basin have contributed to serious water quality problems.[9]

Historical and Current Land Cover and Vegetation along the Riparian Corridor

Historical Conditions

The General Land Office of the U.S. Government conducted surveys in eastern South Dakota in the 1870s, including areas along the Big Sioux River, to describe the parcels of land to be offered to immigrants through the Homestead Act. Notes and maps from townships in Brookings County show that riparian trees at that time (e.g., elm, willow, ash, boxelder, hackberry) were the same as today, although cottonwoods are not mentioned (Figure 2). Tree coverage was low (about 4% of the area), confirming the dominance of grassland in the township. The confinement of trees to riverbanks and lake margins suggests

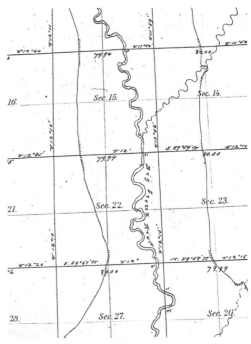

Figure 2. General Land Office Survey map and transcribed notes for a portion of Brookings County, early 1870s. Channel configuration of the Big Sioux River between section lines is approximate, as these areas were not surveyed.

Brookings County GLO survey

T109N 50W—This township contains a large amount of rich bottom lands situated on both sides of the Big Sioux River. The uplands are generally rolling and well adapted to cultivation. Timber chiefly Elm and Hackberry, willow and oak, situated on the Big Sioux River and Lake Campbell. The area of timberland in this township is estimated at near 1,000 acres. There is a considerable quantity of stone on the shores of Lake Campbell, chiefly granite. Lake Campbell is a beautiful lake of clear, deep and fresh water with sand or rocky shores except in the north and northwest which are low and marshy. This township is much above the average and will sustain a large settlement.

Timber elm, willow, ash, box elder.

T110N R51W—The Big Sioux River in the township is a deep, clear sluggish stream with a gravelly bottom.

the effects of fire. The high fuel loads of grasses on the productive floodplain soils would have produced intense fires un-survivable by woody plants. Trees found refuge on and near the riverbanks where continual deposition of river-borne sediments favored riparian trees over grasses. In contrast, the water quality described by the surveyors differs sharply from that of today. They describe the Big Sioux River as a "deep, clear sluggish stream…with a gravelly bottom" (Figure 2). Today, the Big Sioux is a river with high sediment load, turbid water, and shallow depths. The erosion of uplands in the watershed due to farming and other land uses has oversupplied the river with fine sediment compared to the heavily grassed watershed and protected soils of a century and a half ago.

Current Land Cover

Using aerial imagery, Ley[10] mapped land cover within a one-and-a-quarter-mile-wide corridor along the lower 358 miles of the Big Sioux River. The upper 62 miles of the river (above Watertown) were excluded given the diminutive nature of the headwater stream, small floodplain, and scarcity of woody vegetation within this area. The rest of the river was divided into upper, middle, and lower study segments, with boundaries that corresponded to ecoregional boundaries[11] or the confluences of major tributaries (Figure 1). The upper segment flows from Watertown, South Dakota, to northeast of Flandreau, South Da-

Big Sioux Corridor Land Cover

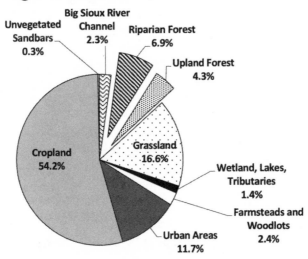

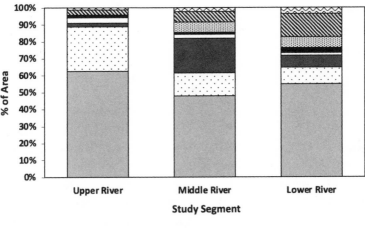

Figure 3. Relative area of different land classes in the Big Sioux riparian corridor (1.25 miles wide) for the entire study area and in the upper, middle, and lower study segments.

kota. The middle segment extends downstream to the confluence of the Big Sioux with its largest tributary, the Rock River, near Hudson, South Dakota, and includes the Sioux Falls metropolitan area. The lower segment includes everything downstream of the Rock River confluence. Below this confluence, the annual discharge of the Big Sioux approximately doubles and the size of the river and its floodplain area increase dramatically. Downstream from Richland, South Dakota, the Big Sioux River runs across the broad Missouri River floodplain to its confluence with the Missouri River at Sioux City, Iowa.

Overall, agricultural cropland is the dominant land use type along the river corridor, covering 54% of the total area, while grassland covers 17%, urban land use 11%, riparian forest 7%, and upland forest 4% (Figure 3). Among the segments, the upper segment has the highest proportional coverage of agricultural cropland (63%) and grassland (26%), but the lowest coverage of urban lands (2.4%), riparian forests (2.7%), and upland forests (0.2%). The middle segment, with the towns of Dell Rapids, Canton, and the greater Sioux Falls area, has the highest proportional area of urban land use (20.3%). Nearly all the upland forest (99%) and riparian forest (88%) occurs on the middle and lower river segments, with the highest proportional cover of riparian forest (14%) on the most downstream segment.

Riparian Forest Community Types

The riparian corridor contains a mosaic of vegetation communities influenced by river processes, disturbance history, basin geology, geography, and land use practices. These include riparian forests, which were classified into six community types based on species composition and forest successional stage.[12] The youngest, early successional shrublands are dominated by sandbar willow (*Salix interior*), along with varying abundances of peachleaf willow (*Salix amygdaloides*) and eastern cottonwood (*Populus deltoides*) saplings. This community often occurs along the river margin and is frequently flooded. The community type adjacent to these flooded shrublands represents the next stage of forest succession and contains young peachleaf willow and cottonwood trees between 20 and 40 feet tall. Occurring next in the successional sequence are forests with larger cottonwood trees in the canopy and variable abundances of other tree species. These include forests with abundant silver maple (*Acer saccharinum*); those with green ash (*Fraxinus pennsylvanica*) and boxelder (*Acer negundo*), but not a significant silver maple component; and those dominated by cottonwood without a significant presence of the other tree species. The final community type is a conglomerate of forest stands lacking large cottonwoods and is dominated by green ash, boxelder, hackberry (*Celtis occidentalis*), and American elm (*Ulmus americana*). This community type represents the latest successional stage, where cottonwoods have senesced or are absent for other reasons (e.g., selective harvest). Together, the mature maple-elm-cottonwood and ash-boxelder forests make up more than three quarters (77%) of the riparian forest cover in the basin, with the other two mature cottonwood forest types together comprising 5%, the young cottonwood-peachleaf willow woodland 14%, and the early successional willow shrubland 4% (Figure 4).

Riparian forests in the upper study segment are narrow, isolated, and lack diversity in age structure and community types (Figures 3, 4). Here, late successional ash-boxelder forest is the most common forest type, with young cottonwood-peachleaf willow woodlands and willow shrublands composing most of the rest (Figure 4). The limited forest area may occur on an immature floodplain where the river's natural flooding cycle does not have the ability to consistently create new habitats for colonization by riparian vegetation. Agricultural land uses within the basin also remove or prevent establishment of riparian vegetation and most private land forests in the upper river segment are intensively grazed, further modifying these habitats and altering their ability to regenerate naturally.[13]

Riparian forests in the lowest segment of the river reside on a much wider floodplain where annual overbank flooding, migration of the channel, and oxbow lake formation have created a heterogeneous and dynamic vegetation mosaic. Here, mature silver maple-elm-cottonwood forest is the dominant riparian forest type (59%), with the late successional green ash-boxelder forest and the earlier successional cottonwood-peachleaf willow forest comprising 17% and 16% of the riparian forest area (Figure 4). Forests within the middle river segment represent an intermediate condition between the upper and lower segments. Coverage of silver maple forest declines sharply from the lower to the middle river segment, until it drops out completely

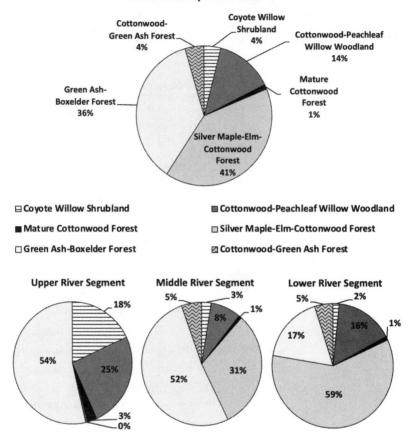

Figure 4. Relative areas of different riparian forest types across the study area and in the upper, middle, and lower river study segments of the Big Sioux River.

near Flandreau, South Dakota, where the northern-most boundary for silver maple within the basin and the state of South Dakota occurs.[14] These longitudinal changes are consistent with findings from other river basins, where the simplest forests occur in upper river reaches and the more complex (i.e., larger areas, greater diversity in age classes and vegetation types) forests occur in the downstream areas.[15]

Common Name	Scientific Name	Growth Form	Frequency (%)	Mean Cover (%)	IV
Canadian woodnettle	*Laportea canadensis*	Forb	62.69	56.34	34.63
Reed canary grass	*Phalaris arundinacea*	Grass	55.22	29.81	18.44
Cutleaf coneflower	*Rudbeckia laciniata*	Forb	43.28	8.62	6.90
Smooth brome	**Bromus inermis*	Grass	20.15	5.00	6.63
Ground-ivy	**Glechoma hederacea*	Vine	22.39	20.71	5.80
Canadian honewort	*Cryptotaenia canadensis*	Forb	32.09	5.50	5.34
Whitegrass	*Leersia virginica*	Grass	30.60	8.24	4.78
Clearweed	*Pilea pumila*	Forb	34.33	6.00	4.73
Virginia wildrye	*Elymus virginicus*	Grass	29.85	8.50	4.73
Green ash	*Fraxinus pennsylvanica*	Tree	33.58	4.11	4.10
Stinging nettle	*Urtica dioica*	Forb	29.10	4.46	4.08
Woolly blue violet	*Viola sororia*	Forb	27.61	6.39	3.89
Riverbank grape	*Vitis riparia*	Vine	29.85	4.01	3.62
Common buckthorn	**Rhamnus cathartica*	Tree	22.39	7.28	3.32
Smooth-cone sedge	*Carex laeviconica*	Sedge	14.93	14.66	3.12
Grape woodbine	*Parthenocissus vitacea*	Vine	20.90	5.66	2.82
Boxelder	*Acer negundo*	Tree	23.13	2.90	2.60
Common dandelion	**Taraxacum officinale*	Forb	15.67	6.79	2.26
Little-leaf buttercup	*Ranunculus abortivus*	Forb	20.15	1.90	2.10
Ontario aster	*Symphyotrichum ontarionis*	Forb	13.43	5.02	1.74
Tall beggar's ticks	*Bidens vulgata*	Forb	15.67	1.27	1.55
Maple-leaf goosefoot	*Chenopodium simplex*	Forb	14.18	2.50	1.54
Silver maple	*Acer saccharinum*	Tree	14.93	1.26	1.47
White goosefoot	**Chenopodium album*	Forb	14.18	1.66	1.45
Common hackberry	*Celtis occidentalis*	Tree	14.18	1.59	1.44
Other (143 species)			-	-	66.92

Table 1. Summary of most common plant species in the herbaceous layer of riparian forests across 35 sites along the Big Sioux River, in descending order of importance value (IV). Importance values was calculated by summing relative frequency and relative cover for each species. An asterisk (*) indicates the species is considered non-native.

Plant Species Richness and Composition in Riparian Forests

Across 35 riparian forest sites on the upper, middle, and lower segments of the Big Sioux River, Ley recorded 175 plant species, of which 75% (131) were native and 25% (44) non-native.[16] Numbers of species sampled per site ranged from 5 to 56 with a basin-wide average of

28. Canadian woodnettle was the dominant species within the herbaceous ground layer, occurring in 62% of sample plots and averaging 56% ground cover (Table 1). Other important species included reed canary grass, cutleaf coneflower, Canadian honewort, and whitegrass. Although considered a native species in our analysis, reed canary grass is often considered an invasive, non-native species, as introduced European cultivars may have largely replaced or hybridized with native varieties.[17] Common non-native species in the ground layer included smooth brome grass, ground ivy, seedlings of common buckthorn (an invasive tree species), and common dandelion. The most abundant tree species was boxelder (27% of sampled trees), followed by green ash (21%), eastern cottonwood (17%), and silver maple (13%). Abundances of different sapling or shrub species varied, generally representing the dominant overstory tree or shrub species in each riparian forest type (e.g., sandbar willow, cottonwood, silver maple), except for the green ash-boxelder forest, where invasive buckthorn was the most common shrub/sapling species.

Tree and shrub species composition and shrub cover differ from nearby reaches of the Missouri River.[18] Shrub cover averaged much lower in Big Sioux forests and some common species in the Missouri River forests, such as roughleaf dogwood (*Cornus drummondii*), common buckthorn, eastern redcedar (*Juniperus virginiana*), and Russian-olive (*Elaeagnus angustifolia*) are scarce along the Big Sioux.[19] Conversely, silver maple, the dominant tree species on the lower Big Sioux, is nearly absent on the nearby Missouri River. Dean found higher numbers of tree species, lower dominance of cottonwood, and higher abundances of boxelder, silver maple, and elm along the Big Sioux River, along with bur oak (*Quercus macrocarpa*) on adjacent upland habitats.[20] Some of these vegetation differences may be related to contrasting flooding regimes on the two rivers, as upstream dams and channel incision have greatly reduced flooding on the Missouri River, whereas the Big Sioux continues to flood regularly and has even increased in mean streamflow over the last 70 years.[21]

Upland Forest Vegetation and Community Types

Six upland forests sites (22 plots) were also sampled, with all but one of these sites occurring downstream of Sioux Falls, South Dakota.[22] A to-

Common Name	Species	Growth Form	Frequency (%)	Mean Cover (%)	IV
Virginia waterleaf	*Hydrophyllum virginianum*	Forb	86.36	16.99	15.62
Canadian woodnettle	*Laportea canadensis*	Forb	40.91	47.33	14.52
Clayton's sweetroot	*Osmorhiza claytonii*	Forb	45.45	27.79	12.34
Virginia creeper	*Parthenocissus quinquefolia*	Vine	72.73	14.32	10.27
White snakeroot	*Ageratina altissima*	Forb	50.00	15.83	8.10
Common hackberry	*Celtis occidentalis*	Tree	63.64	10.62	7.27
Common buckthorn	*Rhamnus cathartica*	Tree	54.55	11.43	6.38
Hophornbeam	*Ostrya virginiana*	Tree	54.55	9.23	6.23
Bristly greenbriar	*Smilax tamnoides*	Vine	50.00	5.80	4.46
Bloodroot	*Sanguinaria canadensis*	Forb	59.09	4.35	4.39
Fragrant bedstraw	*Galium triflorum*	Forb	40.91	8.95	4.39
Starry false Solomon's seal	*Maianthemum stellatum*	Forb	54.55	5.87	4.06
Missouri gooseberry	*Ribes missouriense*	Shrub	54.55	6.77	3.97
Green ash	*Fraxinus pennsylvanica*	Tree	50.00	7.39	3.96
Hairy wildrye	*Elymus villosus*	Grass	50.00	6.22	3.58
Common woodland sedge	*Carex blanda*	Sedge	40.91	5.99	3.21
American lopseed	*Phryma leptostachya*	Forb	31.82	7.25	2.80
Riverbank grape	*Vitis riparia*	Vine	40.91	3.25	2.62
Maryland black snakeroot	*Sanicula marilandica*	Forb	31.82	6.08	2.62
Upright carrion flower	*Smilax ecirrhata*	Vine	31.82	4.86	2.15
Other (81 species)			-	-	77.05

Table 2. Summary of most common plant species in the herbaceous layer of upland forests across six sites along the Big Sioux River, in descending order of importance value (IV). Importance values was calculated by summing relative frequency and relative cover for each species. An asterisk (*) indicates the species is considered non-native.

tal of 108 plant species were observed of which 90 (83%) were native. Of the 108 species, 30 were unique to upland forest sites, whereas 78 species were found in both upland and riparian environments within the Big Sioux basin. Upland sites tended to be more diverse than riparian sites, with an average of 42 species per site. Virginia waterleaf was the most abundant species within the herbaceous layer, occurring in over 86% of the plots (Table 2). The next most important species were Canadian woodnettle, Clayton's sweetroot or sweet cicely, Virginia creeper, and white snakeroot. Bur oak comprised nearly half of the trees sampled in the upland sites, with other common species in-

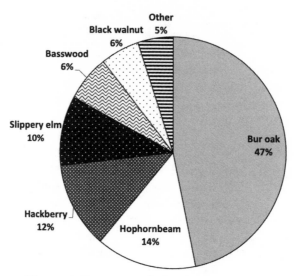

Figure 5. Percent totals for the most common tree species sampled within six upland forest sites along the Big Sioux River.

cluding hophornbeam (*Ostrya virginiana*), hackberry, and slippery elm (*Ulmus rubra*) (Figure 5).

The most common upland forest type, occurring in portions of five of the six study sites, was a forest with an overstory dominated by bur oak and other associates (elm, hackberry, and hophornbeam) and an understory dominated by hairy wildrye grass (*Elymus villosus*), bristly greenbriar (*Smilax tamnoides*), Virginia creeper, and Clayton's sweetroot.[23] Forest sites in the southern portion of the basin had middle/lower slope areas dominated by a diverse overstory including American basswood (*Tilia americana*), bur oak, hackberry, green ash, black walnut (*Juglans nigra*), hophornbeam, and elm. The understory of these forests was composed of similar species to the riparian forests, such as Canadian woodnettle, common moonseed (*Menispermum canadense*), cutleaf coneflower, starry false Solomon's seal (*Maianthemum stellatum*), and stinging nettle (*Urtica dioica*), but also contained species with a more eastern North American affinity, including red columbine (*Aquilegia canadensis*), bloodroot (*Sanguinaria canadensis*), upright carrion flower (*Smilax ecirrhata*), and jack-in-the-pulpit (*Arisaema triphyllum*). Forests along dry ridge tops represented a transition between the upland forest of lower slopes and the tallgrass prairie remnants commonly adjacent to these forests, with the overstory dominated by bur oak, with elm, eastern redcedar, and hophornbeam also forming a significant component. The understory was a mixture of dry prairie grasses, such as little bluestem (*Schizachyrium scoparium*), indiangrass (*Sorghastrum nutans*), and buffalograss (*Bouteloua curtipendula*), and upland species, such as hairy wildrye (*Elymus villosus*), bristly greenbriar (*Smilax tamnoides*), and starry false Solomon's seal.

Riparian Forests as Bird Habitat

Woodlands are generally scarce in prairie landscapes and cover less than 3% of the total area in eastern South Dakota counties through which the Big Sioux River flows.[24] Despite their rarity, woodlands are disproportionately rich habitats for birds, supporting higher bird abundances and diversity than other habitats in the region.[25] Riparian forests, which historically were the primary woodland habitats in the region, have been greatly reduced in area, fragmented, and degraded since Euro-American settlement. Several studies compared woodland use by breeding and migrating birds in Big Sioux and Missouri river riparian corridors with non-riparian farmstead woodlots in the region.[26] During the breeding season, Big Sioux sites had the highest bird species richness (63 species total), with Missouri River forests intermediate (55 species), and farmstead woodlots with the lowest (47 species) values. Bird densities, however, showed the opposite trend, with densities greatest in woodlots, intermediate in the Missouri River corridor, and lowest along the Big Sioux River. Nesting success (the proportion of nests for which at least one young bird survived) was comparable in Big Sioux riparian forests to other riparian and non-riparian woodlands in the region.[27]

During migration, bird abundances were similar on Missouri River and Big Sioux River forests in spring but greater along the Missouri River in fall, primarily due to very high numbers of migrating warbling vireos (*Vireo gilvus*) there.[28] Species richness, however, was generally greater along the Big Sioux River.[29] Farmstead woodlots had similar or higher bird species richness and abundance during both migration seasons than Missouri and Big Sioux River riparian forests.[30] Missouri River sites provided enough food resources for migrant birds to add

Breeding	Spring Migration	Fall Migration
House Wren *Troglodytes aedon*	Yellow-rumped Warbler *Setophaga coronata*	American Redstart *Setophaga ruticilla*
Gray Catbird *Dumetella carolinensis*	Orange-crowned Warbler *Leiothlypis celata*	Wilson's Warbler *Cardellina pusilla*
Rose-breasted Grosbeak *Pheucticus ludovicianus*	Tennessee Warbler *Leiothlypis peregrina*	Orange-crowned Warbler *Leiothlypis celata*
Black-capped Chickadee *Poecile atricapillus*	Swainson's Thrush *Catharus ustulatus*	Nashville Warbler *Leiothlypis ruficapilla*
American Redstart *Setophaga ruticilla*	Yellow Warbler *Setophaga petechia*	Red-eyed Vireo *Vireo erythropthalamus*

Table 3. Top five bird species by abundance from point counts (highest to lowest abundance listed top to bottom) in Big Sioux River woodlands during breeding and spring and fall migration.

Figure 6. Bird species common to Big Sioux River riparian forests during breeding and migration seasons (see Table 3 for scientific names). Bird species pictured are (A) House Wren, (B) American Redstart, (C) Rose-breasted Grosbeak, and (D) Yellow-rumped Warbler. Photo Credits: Terry Sohl.

fat to fuel the next leg of the migratory journey, suggesting that these represent high-quality habitat.[31] Most migrant bird species feed on arthropods (insects and spiders), and arthropod abundance was similar or greater at Big Sioux River sites than at Missouri River sites in both spring and fall.[32] Collectively, these data suggest that Big Sioux River riparian forests also serve as high quality migration habitat.

The most common group of birds occurring in Big Sioux River woodlands during both breeding and migration seasons (Table 3, Figure 6) are the Nearctic-Neotropical migrants, which include flycatchers, vireos, thrushes, and warblers, among other species. These birds breed primarily in North America north of Mexico and winter primarily south of the U.S.-Mexico border. This group includes many bird species of substantial conservation concern because habitat loss or degradation can impact populations across all stages of the annual cycle. Consequently, conservation measures must provide sufficient areas of suitable habitats for the breeding, wintering, and migratory phases of the life cycle of these species.[33]

Threats to Big Sioux River Forests

The forests within the riparian corridor of the Big Sioux River provide important habitat for a diversity of birds and other wildlife, as well as supporting other ecosystem services and amenities valued by people. These services and amenities may be compromised on regulated rivers like the Missouri, making unregulated rivers like the Big Sioux particularly valuable. Understanding historical and present conditions in Big Sioux riparian forests and their impacts on wildlife habitat and provision of ecosystem services will be useful for setting priorities for conservation and targets for ecological restoration, as human land use and climate change continue to modify the landscape and invasive species increase, potentially altering riparian forest communities.

An invasive plant, garlic mustard (*Alliaria petiolata*), and an invasive insect, the emerald ash borer (*Agrilus planipennis*), are particularly of concern. Garlic mustard was encountered regularly by Ley[34] along the Big Sioux in both Iowa and South Dakota. This Eurasian species can have a devastating effect on forest understory habitats, due to its ability to invade, persist, and eventually dominate undisturbed forest communities.[35] The Big Sioux basin is an invasion front for this species as it moves west into woodland habitats in the Great Plains. Hence, strategic management efforts should be instituted to help stem the spread of this species before it becomes dominant in the forest communities along the Big Sioux and establishes within riparian and upland forest communities elsewhere in South Dakota.

The spread of the emerald ash borer may have even more serious effects. Ash borer larvae feed underneath the bark, forming galleries (tunnels) that interfere with the ability of the tree to transport water and nutrients, potentially killing the tree within two years. This non-native beetle, inadvertently introduced to North America from east Asia in the early 2000s, has killed tens of millions of ash trees as it spread across the eastern United States.[36] By July 2020 trees infested by the borer had been identified in portions of South Dakota counties (Minnehaha, Lincoln) through which the Big Sioux River flows.[37] Green ash comprises a significant component of the forests along the Big Sioux and other riparian corridors throughout the state, as well as plantings in urban areas and shelterbelts. These woodlands may be dramatically altered if the borer continues to spread in South Dakota over the next decade.[38]

Historical legacies and ongoing changes in land use in the basin also strongly affect the river and its riparian corridor. Stream flows have increased dramatically over the last several decades in the Big Sioux basin[39] because of climate change-induced increases in precipitation and increased agricultural run-off.[40] Chronically increased flows have led to substantial widening and straightening of stream channels, which may reduce riparian habitat and degrade water quality.[41] Such effects could be further accentuated by recent conversion of grasslands to corn and soybeans in the basin, driven by higher commodity prices.[42] Defining sustainable solutions to these problems will require cooperation among the wide variety of stakeholders invested in the Big Sioux River basin.

Notes

[1] Funding for Matt Ley's thesis work came primarily from a State Wildlife Grant from the South Dakota Department of Game, Fish, and Parks to the Biology Department at the University of South Dakota. Bird work was supported by grants from the South Dakota Department of Game, Fish, and Parks and U.S. Fish and Wildlife Service. We thank Jon Lauck and other, anonymous reviewers for providing editorial comments that improved the chapter. We also

acknowledge the invaluable contribution of our late friend and colleague, Gary E. Larson, for his expert assistance with plant identification.

[2] Robert J. Naiman and Henri Décamps, "The Ecology of Interfaces: Riparian Zones," *Annual Review of Ecology and Systematics* 28 (1997): 621–58.

[3] U.S. Fish and Wildlife Service, *A System for Mapping Riparian Areas in the Western United States* (Arlington, Virginia: Division of Habitat and Resource Conservation, Branch of Resource and Mapping Support, 2009).

[4] National Research Council (NRC), *Riparian Areas: Functions and Strategies for Management* (Washington, D.C.: National Academy Press, 2002).

[5] N. Leroy Poff et al., "The Natural Flow Regime: A Paradigm for Conservation and Restoration of Riverine Ecosystems," *BioScience* 47 (1997): 769-84.

[6] Mark M. Brinson et al., *Riparian Ecosystems: Their Ecology and Status* (U.S. Fish and Wildlife Service: Eastern Energy Land Use Team [and] National Water Resources Analysis Group, 1981).

[7] David L. Galat et al., "Missouri River Basin," in *Rivers of North America*, ed. Arthur C. Benke and Colbert E. Cushing (Oxford: Elsevier, 2005) 427–80.

[8] Craig L. Milewski, Charles R. Berry, and Douglas Dieterman, "Use of the Index of Biological Integrity in Eastern South Dakota Rivers," *The Prairie Naturalist* 33:3 (2002): 135-52. East Dakota Water Development District (EDWDD), *East Dakota Riparian Area Restoration and Protection Project*. Project Summary available at: http://denr.sd.gov/dfta/wp/319apps/2010/edwdd.pdf, 2010.

[9] Douglas Dieterman and Charles R. Berry, "Fish Community and Water Quality Changes in the Big Sioux River," *The Prairie Naturalist* 30:4 (1998): 199-24.

[10] Matthew J. Ley, "Riparian Forest Vegetation Patterns and Historic Channel Dynamics of the Big Sioux River, South Dakota" (M.S. thesis, University of South Dakota).

[11] James M. Omernik, "Ecoregions of the Conterminous United States," *Annual Association of American Geographers* 77 (1987): 118-25.

[12] Ley, "Riparian Forest Vegetation"; Don Faber-Langendoen, ed., *Plant Communities of the Midwest: Classification in an Ecological Context* (Arlington, VA: Association for Biodiversity Information, 2001).

[13] Randy L. Smith and Lester D. Flake, "The Effects of Grazing on Forest Regeneration along a Prairie River," *Prairie Naturalist* 15:1 (1983): 41-44.

[14] Elbert L. Little, Jr., *Atlas of United States Trees, Volume 1, Conifers and Important Hardwoods*, Miscellaneous publication 1146 (Washington, D.C.: U.S. Department of Agriculture, Forest Service, 1971).

[15] David L. Rosgen, "A Classification of Natural Rivers," *Catena* 22 (1994): 169–99; Naiman and Décamps, *Annual Review*.

[16] Ley, "Riparian Forest Vegetation."

[17] http://www.fs.fed.us/database/feis/plants/graminoid/phaaru/all.html#TAXONOMY

[18] Mark D. Dixon, W. Carter Johnson, Michael L. Scott, and Daniel Bowen, *Status and Trend of Cottonwood Forests along the Missouri River*, final report to U.S. Army Corps of Engineers, 2010. Christopher J. Boever et al., "Effects of a Large Flood on Woody Vegetation along the Regulated Missouri River, USA," *Ecohydrology* 12:1 (2019): e2045.

[19] Ley, "Riparian Forest Vegetation."

[20] Kurt L. Dean, "Stopover Ecology of Neotropical Migrant Songbirds in Riparian Corridors in the Northern Great Plains" (Ph.D. dissertation, University of South Dakota, 1999).

[21] Galen K. Hoogestraat and John F. Stamm, *Climate and Streamflow Characteristics for Selected Streamgages in Eastern South Dakota, Water Years 1945–2013*, U.S. Geological Survey Scientific Investigations Report 2015-5146, 2015.

[22] Ley, "Riparian Forest Vegetation."

[23] Ley, "Riparian Forest Vegetation."

[24] Thomas L. Castonguay, *Forest Area in Eastern South Dakota, 1980*, Research Note NC-291 (St. Paul, MN: U.S. Dept. of Agriculture, Forest Service, North Central Forest Experiment Station 291, 1982).

[25] Deborah M. Finch and Leonard F. Ruggiero, "Wildlife Habitats and Biological Diversity in the Rocky Mountains and Northern Great Plains," *Natural Areas Journal* 13:3 (1993): 191-203. Kristel K. Bakker, *A Compilation and Synthesis of Avian Research Completed in South Dakota*. Wildlife Division Report No. 2003-09 (Pierre, South Dakota: South Dakota Department of Game, Fish and Parks, 2003).

[26] Dean, "Stopover Ecology." David L. Swanson et al., "Riparian and Woodlot Landscape Patterns and Migration of Neotropical Migrants in Riparian Forests of Eastern South Dakota," in *Bird Conservation Implementation and Integration in the Americas: Proceedings of the Third International Partners in Flight Conference*, ed. C. John Ralph, C. John and Terrell D. Rich, vol. 1, Gen. Tech. Rep. PSW-GTR-191 (Albany, CA: U.S. Dept. of Agriculture, Forest Service, Pacific Southwest Research Station, 2005), 191: 541-49. Dale J. Gentry, David L. Swanson, and Jay D. Carlisle, "Species Richness and Nesting Success of Migrant Forest Birds in Natural River Corridors and Anthropogenic Woodlands in Southeastern South Dakota," *The Condor* 108:1 (2006): 140-53.

[27] Gentry et al., *Condor*.

[28] Dean, "Stopover Ecology"; Swanson et al., *Bird Conservation*.

[29] Dean, "Stopover Ecology."

[30] Dean, "Stopover Ecology"; Swanson et al., *Bird Conservation*.

[31] Ming Liu and David L. Swanson, "Stress Physiology of Migrant Birds during Stopover in Natural and Anthropogenic Woodland Habitats of the Northern Prairie Region," *Conservation Physiology* 2:1 (2014): cou046.

[32] Dean, "Stopover Ecology."

[33] John Faaborg et al., "Conserving Migratory Land Birds in the New World: Do We Know Enough?" *Ecological Applications* 20 (2010): 398-418.

[34] Ley, "Riparian Forest Vegetation."

[35] Victoria Nuzzo, "Invasion Pattern of the Herb Garlic Mustard (*Alliaria petiolata*) in High Quality Forests," *Biological Invasions* 1 (1999): 169-79. Erik Welk, Konstanze Schubert, and Matthias H. Hoffmann, "Present and Potential Distribution of Invasive Garlic Mustard (*Alliaria petiolata*) in North America," *Diversity and Distributions* 8:4 (2002): 219-33. Betsy Von Holle, Hazel R. Delcourt, and Daniel Simberloff, "The Importance of Biological Inertia in Plant Community Resistance to Invasion," *Journal of*

Vegetation Science 14:3 (2003): 425-32. Kristina Stinson et al., "Impacts of Garlic Mustard Invasion on a Forest Understory Community," *Northeastern Naturalist* 14:1 (2007): 73-88.

[36] Therese M. Poland and Deborah G. McCullough, "Emerald Ash Borer: Invasion of the Urban Forest and the Threat to North America's Ash Resource," *Journal of Forestry* 104:3 (2006): 118-24. W. Keith Moser et al., "Impacts of Nonnative Invasive Species on US Forests and Recommendations for Policy and Management," *Journal of Forestry* 107:6 (2009): 320-27.

[37] https://emeraldashborerinsouthdakota.sd.gov/.

[38] W. Carter Johnson et al., "Forty Years of Vegetation Change on the Missouri River Floodplain," *BioScience* 62 (2012): 123–35.

[39] Hoogestraat and Stamm, *Climate and Streamflow.*

[40] Ley, "Riparian Forest Vegetation." Y-K Zhang and K. E. Schilling, "Increasing Streamflow and Baseflow in Mississippi River since the 1940s: Effect of Land Use Change," *Journal of Hydrology* 324:1-4 (2006): 412-22.

[41] Ley, "Riparian Forest Vegetation." C. F. Lenhart et al., "Adjustment of Prairie Pothole Streams to Land-use, Drainage and Climate Changes and Consequences for Turbidity Impairment," *River Research and Applications* 28:10 (2012): 1609-19. Christian F. Lenhart et al., "The Role of Hydrologic Alteration and Riparian Vegetation Dynamics in Channel Evolution along the Lower Minnesota River," *Transactions of the ASABE* 56:2 (2013): 549-61.

[42] Christopher K. Wright and Michael C. Wimberly, "Recent Land Use Change in the Western Corn Belt Threatens Grasslands and Wetlands," *Proceedings of the National Academy of Sciences* 110:10 (2013): 4134-39.

Part II

Explorers, Settlers, Outlaws, and War

Chapter 5

"A stream of clear, swift-running water": Nicollet, Fremont, and the Exploration of the Big Sioux River in 1838

John Bicknell

O n a high bluff on the eastern bank, less than ten miles from the confluence of the Big Sioux and Missouri rivers, lie the remains of Sergeant Charles Floyd, the only member of the Corps of Discovery to die on the transcontinental trek of Meriwether Lewis and William Clark. After burying Floyd on August 20, 1804, the Corps camped just north of the site, at a creek named in honor of their comrade. The next day, they proceeded on past the mouth of "the Soues River" and up the Missouri. The captains did not venture onto the Big Sioux but did make note of it in their journals: Their interpreter told them it was "navigable to the falls 70 or 80 Leagues and above these falls Still further, those falls are 20 feet or there abouts and has two princepal pitches, and heads with the St. peters passing the head of the Demoin, on the right below the falls a Creek coms in which passes thro Clifts of red rock which the Indians make pipes of."[1]

Mountain men, fur magnates, trappers, traders, freelancers, missionaries, artists, and the merely curious would follow in the wake of Lewis and Clark. Stephen Long's aborted 1819 expedition might have as well, but it halted south of Council Bluffs and Long was reassigned to an exploration of the Platte. American Fur Company trader Philander Prescott is credited with being the first white American to visit the falls of the Big Sioux in 1832. Prescott found a river "about 20 yards wide" and a falls ten feet high with "so many broken rocks and crevices that you cannot see much water about the falls when the water is low." He later established a trading post up the river near the present site of Flandreau, South Dakota. Although government-sponsored expeditions would explore some of the surrounding area, the next official expedition would not explore the Big Sioux River until 1838.[2]

That expedition was led by French émigré Joseph Nicollet and included John C. Fremont, who would later gain fame as the "Pathfinder of the West" and as the first Republican presidential candidate in 1856, when the upper Midwest would be an electoral bastion for the new party. Traveling from St. Louis to Fort Snelling, then on to Traverse des Sioux and Pipestone Quarry before turning toward the Big Sioux, the party explored a large chunk of the Missouri River drainage. Nicollet and his group would follow the Big Sioux nearly to its source and chart much of its watershed (more than 8,000 square miles). Nicollet and Fremont returned to the region the following year, venturing farther north. Combined, the 1838-39 expeditions yielded the first accurate large-scale map of the Upper Missouri River basin.

"The American age of exploration"

Joseph Nicollet was born in France in 1786. He studied geography, astronomy, and mathematics, and taught the latter two at the university level, developing a considerable reputation among European academics. In 1825 he was awarded the Legion of Honor, France's highest award. But the July Revolution of 1830, which overthrew the restored Bourbon monarchy, disrupted Nicollet's professional life and left him nearly destitute. In 1832 he emigrated to America. Nicollet made contacts in Washington and spent the better part of three years traveling in the South, finally landing in St. Louis in 1835. From there, he launched an expedition to the source of the Mississippi River funded by the American Fur Company and Pierre Chouteau Jr., a leading St. Louis magnate and scion of a famed fur trading family.[3] That expedition's success recommended Nicollet to Secretary of War Joel Poinsett, who agreed to pay Nicollet $8 a day and ten cents a mile for a new expedition—twice what Army topographical engineer and second lieutenant Fremont would earn.[4]

The fatherless Fremont enjoyed the patronage of a series of powerful men, beginning with Poinsett, a fellow resident of Charleston, South Carolina. Poinsett had given Fremont his start as an explorer with a railroad survey to Cincinnati and a reconnaissance of Cherokee lands in 1837. The Nicollet expedition would be an educational experience for Fremont, who knew his way around in the wild but had little formal scientific training. Now, he would be learning by doing alongside an acknowledged expert, with virtually all their time "occupied in astronomical & Geological observations."[5]

Fremont's fame would eventually grow far beyond that of Nicollet's, and the leading historian of the Corps of Topographical Engineers would call Fremont the "dominant personality" in topographical exploration in the years following the Nicollet expedition. But historian Vernon Volpe noted that "while Fremont's exploits garnered public acclaim, the foundation for his success was laid by" Nicollet, Poinsett, and John J. Abert, chief of the Corps of Topographical Engineers.[6]

The Nicollet expedition came in the heart of the six-decade period that William H. Goetzmann called "The American Age of Exploration." Goetzmann also noted that Fremont, "if anyone did, fitted perfectly the requirements of the romantic hero-symbol of an age of expansionism." And Nicollet gave Fremont what he lacked: a firm grounding in the disciplines of science.[7]

Poinsett wanted to shift from the haphazard wanderings of mountain men to a systematic, scientific, government-led project. To that end, the government focused in the 1820s and 1830s on a great triangle west of the Mississippi and north of the Missouri that reached to the Canadian border. Sparked by competition with Britain over the fur trade and alliances with natives, the push for surveys increased as settlers began moving into the territory. The search for knowledge was coupled with the government imperative of replacing the "unconstrained" life of the Indians with the "constraints of civilization."[8]

Leading the way would be the Army Corps of Topographical Engineers. The Army Reorganization Act of 1838 had created this separate organization out of the Topographical Bureau of the Army Corps of Engineers that had been in place since 1831. The Corps of Topographical Engineers comprised 36 officers led by Abert, who recommended Nicollet to Poinsett. Minnesota fur trader, pioneer, and politician Henry Hastings Sibley referred to the three of them as "kindred spirits," and under Abert's hand—with an assist from Fremont and a cadre of territorially aggressive politicians—the Topographical Corps would become the advance guard of Manifest Destiny.[9]

This first expedition of the Topographical Corps was planned as a two-stage journey tasked with exploring the area between the Mississippi and Missouri rivers. The first year, the party would extend westward from Fort Snelling to the Missouri; the second year, it would move up and beyond the Missouri into the western and northern watershed, building on Nicollet's 1835-37 explorations of the upper Mississippi.

Nicollet's reputation made him the obvious choice to lead the expedition. He was among the first to use a barometer to measure altitude, allowing for more precise descriptions of small variations in the landscape and providing a three-dimensional picture of the prairie for those back east who still had visions of the featureless "Great American Desert" in their heads. These small variations were also important to those thinking about military matters, and Abert had noted to Poinsett that Nicollet's work was "peculiarly adapted for the basis of a system of military defenses."[10]

No botanist had been assigned to the expedition. At his own expense, Nicollet hired Charles Geyer, an 1834 immigrant from Dresden, Germany, whom Nicollet had met in St. Louis. Geyer, an "amiable and agreeable" man according to Fremont, would catalog 23 pages of trees, herbs, and other flora for the expedition, and he would add yet another bit of international diversity to the company.[11]

Although Nicollet was highly respected in Washington, he was not without his critics. George William Featherstonhaugh, an Englishman who had lived in the United States for thirty years by the time of the Nicollet expedition and the first geologist employed by the U.S. government, had traveled the Fox and Mississippi rivers in 1835 and was bidding to return. He was not above a little negative advertising—and foreigner bashing—to make his case.

Having heard that Nicollet was in line for the Missouri expedition, Featherstonhaugh lashed out at Nicollet in a letter to Abert in May 1837, complaining that Nicollet was

> yet at Fort Snelling and from what I hear is engaged
> writing a book of travels. I am sorry for this as I do not

believe he will make a figure that way. Having been fifty or sixty miles further than [Henry] Schoolcraft at the sources of the Mississippi, and observed that the small lakes, which Schoolcraft has fixed upon as the probable sources, were in fact fed by some insignificant streams, extending a little farther the idea of playing the role of Christopher Columbus has got into his head, and true frenchmanlike he is writing a book of discovery. I really am sorry for it, he will make a miserable book of it, and will incite a prejudice against his reputation, which ought to be very great, if he would only raise it upon his acknowledged ability and experience as a barometrician.[12]

Perhaps Featherstonhaugh was simply a disagreeable character. In addition to criticizing the genteel Nicollet, he had also slammed the ubiquitously praised fur trader Joseph Renville for a supposed lack of cordiality and allegedly taking advantage of him in business dealings.[13]

Nicollet was actually spending this time in "the study of the Chippeway and Sioux languages," a useful endeavor for a man in his trade, and "continuing my observations on the customs of the Indians, assisting at all their medicine dances, and their winter and spring ceremonies." He also was considerably more gracious to Featherstonhaugh than Featherstonhaugh had been to him: Nicollet wrote in his report that Featherstonhaugh "well described" the route along the Minnesota (then sometimes called the St. Peter's) River, although Nicollet also noted "some ambiguity in the geographical names of places" in Featherstonhaugh's report.[14]

"Occasionally surpassingly beautiful"

Nicollet's circle of acquaintances in St. Louis was wide, and included William Clark, the patron of western exploration. Another Army engineer was also busy in the city: Captain Robert E. Lee was leading a Corps project to divert the flow of the Mississippi. Fremont arrived in May 1838 and found his future Civil War adversary "an already interesting man" with an "agreeable, friendly manner."[15]

Clark couldn't have been a very active member of the society of the new generation of explorers. He suffered from a multitude of ailments for which he sought out cures, including gleet, whooping cough, consumption, bleeding piles, toothache, and headache; he was bedridden for long periods; and he would die on September 1. But the symbolic passing of the torch to the new generation of American explorers had taken place that spring.[16]

Nicollet, Fremont, and Geyer left St. Louis aboard the fur company steamboat *Burlington* on May 18. They did not fritter away their time on the way up the river. "Every day—almost every hour I feel myself sensibly advancing in professional knowledge & the confused ideas of Science & Philosophy [with which] my mind has been occupied are momently arranging themselves into order & clearness," Fremont wrote to Poinsett. Nicollet, whom Fremont referred to as the "Pilgrim of Science," was the man doing the arranging, inspired by "his almost extravagant enthusiasm in the object of his present enterprise wh[ich] he seems to think the sole object of his existence."[17]

They arrived after a week's travel at Henry Sibley's trading post, a short run up the Minnesota River from Fort Snelling, "on the borderline of civilization," near the confluence with the Mississippi. Sibley, a fur trader (and later the first governor of the state of Minnesota) provided the company with the French-Canadian boatmen, known as *voyageurs,* they would need to make their way westward.[18] The party, which included the Sioux wives of two of the *voyageurs*, left Sibley's on June 9 in two groups. Fremont, still a bachelor, wrote to his mother that he expected to be gone three months and that she should expect to "receive no news from me" during that time."[19] "Our party, tho' small, is well armed, at least sufficiently so to secure us in the event of an accidental rencontre. & Mr. Nicollet's knowledge of the Indians justifies us in believing that we shall meet with no serious difficulty," Fremont told Poinsett.[20]

Nine members rowed up the Minnesota River, the other seven traveled overland. The overlanders—including Nicollet, Fremont, and Geyer—traveled along the south side of the river 115 miles to the lower end of the Traverse des Sioux, the site of a river crossing along an ancient Indian trail. There, the two groups came back together and another *voyageur* joined up. Arriving June 14, they camped at the spot for four nights.

Camp material (hauled in one-horse carts manned by the *voya-geurs* on loan from the American Fur Company) focused on wilderness needs: a hatchet, an axe, a crowbar, a large kettle. Nicollet also brought along "a nice little store of Coffee, Chocolate, Tea, prepared Soup &c in addition to the more substantial articles of food" such as dried beef, pork, hams, sausages, pemmican, corn, flour, and biscuits. Also on hand were a few luxuries: tobacco, cognac, and wine.[21]

From Traverse des Sioux, the reunited party moved on foot along the Cottonwood River to the lower section of the Coteau des Prairies, the 5-million-acre plateau that separates the Mississippi and Missouri rivers. As Fremont described it, "the prairie air was invigorating, the country studded with frequent lakes." Nicollet also noted the existence of Sisseton Sioux villages along the route and relentlessly attended to the scientific project. In contrast to Featherstonhaugh's derisive tone, Fremont noted Nicollet's complete devotion to duty. "In all this stir of frontier life, Mr. Nicollet felt no interest and took no share....His mind dwelt continually on the geography of the country."[22] Nicollet took enough notice of frontier life to describe the "boundless and fer-tile prairies" as "a beautiful arrangement of upland and lowland plains, that give it an aspect *sui generis*." Fremont, too, remarked that the scen-ery "was occasionally surpassingly beautiful."[23]

But all the beauty did not deter the company from worry. Stand-ing guard at night and during daytime breaks, they took precautions against the possibility of attack by the Sioux who shadowed their move-ments. The "exaggerated precautions proved useless," Fremont noted; the Indians did nothing but guardedly watch the travelers. On the con-trary, Nicollet noted in his journal how the natives' "presence adds so much to the character of the country."[24]

As they approached Pipestone Quarry, a sacred gathering place for the natives, the relatively dry weather the expedition had enjoyed thus far gave way to a thunderstorm in the early afternoon of June 29. Fre-mont was so taken with Pipestone that he told Sibley, "I should have been satisfied if we had made the journey merely for the purpose of seeing it." He must not have been the only one who liked it; the party stayed there for six days and celebrated Independence Day by plant-ing an American flag on "a large, sharp-cornered rock, 23 feet high, standing isolated in front of the hill....It is necessary to jump from the top of the hill to the summit of the rock…a surface 2 feet square, and the space between it and the hill is 5 feet wide," Nicollet recorded. "Fremont was assigned this perilous operation."[25] The respite over, the expedition headed northwest toward the Big Sioux River.

"A stream of clear, swift-running water"

One of the earliest documents to mention the Big Sioux was French trader Pierre Charles Le Sueur's map, published in Paris in 1701. It shows a 300-mile long fur trader's trail from the falls of the Big Sioux to Prairie du Chien, a rendezvous point for Indians and French fur traders on the Mississippi. Jean Baptiste Trudeau passed the river's mouth in 1794 before building Pawnee House, the first trading post on the Upper Missouri, near the site of Fort Randall in South Dakota.[26]

Nicollet noted in his post-expedition report that the Sioux called the river "Watpa ipakshan, the river which bends"— so much so that they considered it to be two rivers. (Nicollet would apply a different Sioux name to the map that accompanied the report.) The French called it Crooked River (*la viviere Croche*), an equally apt name, as anyone who has traveled its winding length can attest. It was also referred to as the Calumet, the French word for the pipes made at Pipestone Quarry, about 15 miles to the east. Nicollet called it "the Big, or simply the Sioux river" and noted its "importance to the country through which it flows."[27]

The shortest route to the river from Pipestone would have been due west, and Nicollet considered taking that route. But he changed his mind and instead headed northwest, dedicating more time to taking readings on the Couteau des Prairies. That roundabout route used up all of July 6. The group broke camp on the 7th at 5:15 a.m. and headed north of west. Along the way, the travelers spotted traces of buffalo but no animals, although Nicollet predicted that "herds are confidently expected to be met with here at all seasons of the year." They spotted a line of trees in the distance at about four in the afternoon, but it took another four hours to reach "the banks of a stream of clear, swift-running water meandering through an immense prairie whose vegetation is better supplied and more varied and where the land seems disposed to provide all the agricultural needs for a civilized society."[28] Later pioneers attributed the clarity of the water to the ubiquity in the river's drainage basin of big bluestem, a perennial grass that "acted as a vast natural filter."[29]

The river "flows through a beautiful and fertile country," and the corps would have been surrounded by the pleasant midsummer riverine scents of damp bank, muddy water, fresh fish, and ragweed— accompanied by the incessant buzzing of mosquitoes "in myriads on each squarefoot!" Nicollet wrote. The pests had not bothered the group traveling across the high prairie, but along the banks of the Big Sioux, "the suffering they made us endure in the midst of the fertility raises the question where on earth is man well off?" The second night was no better than the first: "The mosquitoes devoured us."[30]

Perhaps in part because of a lack of sleep the previous night, horses and men were given a longer rest than usual on the morning of July 8, affording a chance to explore. At the campsite (west of modern Brookings, South Dakota) they found the river "50 or 60 feet wide and about 1½ feet deep" and rife with freshwater mussels.[31] From there, the party headed northwest, with the Big Sioux on their right, to a collection of lakes amid a "country full of grandeur and beauty." Nicollet named the largest of the lakes after Poinsett as a thank-you to the patron of the expedition. The lake southwest of that was named in honor of Abert, although the name was bastardized into Albert before the 1880s. The others, including John, Dry, and Norden were named by later settlers. The group spent two days there looking for outlets before breaking camp on July 10 and heading north of east and again encountering the winding Big Sioux at its confluence with Stray Horse Creek, called *Tchan Shasha Yankedan* by the Sioux, meaning "where there is redwood." On the 11th, they broke camp and headed northeast, with the river on their left, the beginning of the journey home.[32]

Nicollet did not reach the river's headwaters in modern Roberts County, but speculated (incorrectly) in his final report that "its sources are at the head of the Coteau des Prairies, not more than a mile from those of the St. Peter's, and separated only by a low ridge." He estimated its length at not less than 350 miles (it's 419 miles long), and described "two principle bends—the more southerly and smaller being terminated by a fall"—Sioux Falls—"said to be the only obstacle to its entire navigation." He used the indigenous name for Lake Kampeska on the map he would make, but did not apply names to many of the other bodies of water in the area.[33]

From Stray Horse Creek, the group followed the lead of guide Joseph Renville, Jr., to Lac qui Parle and a trading post established by fur trader Joseph Renville, Sr.—who had been part of Zebulon Pike's 1805 Mississippi expedition and acted as an interpreter for Stephen Long on the Minnesota in 1823. Nearby was the Lac qui Parle Mission, which served as a sort of neutral zone for natives and whites. Nicollet used the settlement, "the only retreat to travelers to be found between St. Peter's and the British posts, in a distance of 700 miles," as a base to explore the surrounding country.[34]

From there, it was the road and river home. "We have returned without having a single tale of danger or suffering to relate," wrote Fremont, who neglected to mention that he had almost drowned in the northern reaches of the Des Moines River in late June. "No one sick no accident—we have not even starved a little," a claim Fremont would not always be able to make about his later expeditions.[35]

"It is the water that matters"

Nicollet and Fremont got an earlier start in 1839, leaving St. Louis on April 4 aboard the steamship *Antelope*. It was slow going up the swift and snag-filled Missouri. Not until May 9 did they reach the mouth of the Big Sioux, where they disembarked to climb the hill to visit the grave of Sergeant Charles Floyd.

"By the time Mr. Fremont and I reached the summit," Nicollet wrote, "the men of the steamboat were already busy lifting up the piece of wood bearing an inscription. It had been blown to the ground by the wind. I am embarrassed to admit that more than once I have been left behind by men who are often described as 'common' in the observation of this sad and sacred duty which *voyageurs* of the solitudes always faithfully perform for one another."[36]

It had been almost thirty-five years since the Corps of Discovery had passed this way, but the memory and the connections were still strongly felt, even amid rapid change. Anticipating the future of speedier river travel on the Missouri, Nicollet noted his June 12, 1839, arrival at Fort Pierre meant that the corps was "sixty-nine days in ascending a distance of 1,271 miles, which, on the Mississippi, and with a steamboat of the same power, could have been accomplished in twelve days."[37]

From Fort Pierre, established by and named for Pierre Chouteau, Jr., the man who had funded Nicollet's Mississippi River expedition, the explorers fanned out to finish the job they had started: map the watershed of the upper Missouri. On that map—*Hydrographical basin of the upper Mississippi River from astronomical and barometrical observations, surveys, and information*—the river is labeled both the "Sioux" and the *Tchankasndata*, or "river that is continuously wooded." The map was based on 90,000 instrument readings and 326 astronomical points. Goetzmann, the premier historian of the U.S. military's exploration of the West, called the results of Nicollet's expeditions of 1837-39 "the first important scientific achievement west of the Mississippi by the Topographical Bureau since the Long expedition of 1819-20" and rated his map and report "years ahead of their time."[38]

Gouverneur K. Warren, an Army engineer who would gain fame for his role at Gettysburg, called Nicollet's map "one of the greatest contributions ever made to American geography" and Nicollet himself "indefatigable in the use of the telescope for observing occultations and eclipses, and of the sextant, with which he was very skillful; with these, a pocket chronometer, artificial horizon of mercury, and barometer, he obtained results possessing remarkable accuracy for the means employed."[39]

Nicollet's report, written as he was suffering from the illness that would kill him in September 1843, was "disorganized and incomplete," in the words of one historian, and does not do full justice to the accomplishment of the accompanying map.[40] As Nicollet biographer Martha Coleman Bray noted, "on a modern highway map, the thin lines of the waterways are all but invisible and their names infinitesimally printed. But on Nicollet's map, it is the water that matters."[41]

Notes

[1] Reuben Gold Thwaites, *Original Journals of Lewis and Clark*, vol. 1 (New York: Dodd, Mead & Company, 1904), 115.

[2] Philander Prescott, *The Recollections of Philander Prescott: Frontiersman of the Old Northwest, 1818-1862*, ed. Donald Dean Parker (Lincoln: University of Nebraska Press, 1966), 141.

[3] Biographical details for Nicollet from Henry Hastings Sibley, *Memoir of Jean N. Nicollet* (St. Paul: Minnesota Historical Society, 1872), 184-87; and Martha Coleman Bray, "Joseph Nicolas Nicollet, Geologist," *Proceedings of the American Philosophical Society* 114:1 (February 16, 1970): 37-39.

[4] John J. Abert to Joel Poinsett, April 7, 1838, in Martha Coleman Bray and Edmund C. Bray, eds. and trans., *Joseph N. Nicollet on the Plains and Prairies: The Expeditions of 1838-39 with Journals, Letters, and Notes on the Dakota Indians* (St. Paul: Minnesota Historical Society Press, 1976), 219-20; Abert to John C. Fremont, April 16, 1838, in Donald Jackson and Mary Lee Spence, eds., *The Expeditions of John Charles Fremont, Volume 1, 1838 to 1844* (Champaign: University of Illinois Press, 1970), 3.

[5] Fremont to Poinsett, June 8, 1838, in Jackson and Spence, *Expeditions of John Charles Fremont,* 12.

[6] Frank N. Schubert, ed., *The Nation Builders: A Sesquicentennial History of the Corps of Topographical Engineers, 1838-1863* (Fort Belvoir, VA.: Office of History, U.S. Army Corps of Engineers, 1988), 54; Vernon L. Volpe, "The Origins of the Fremont Expeditions: John J. Abert and the Scientific Exploration of the Trans-Mississippi West," *The Historian* 62:2 (Winter 2000): 246.

[7] William H. Goetzmann, "The West and the American Age of Exploration," *Arizona and the West* 2:3 (Autumn 1960): 267; Goetzmann, *Exploration and Empire: The Explorer and Scientist in the Winning of the American West,* 1966 (Francis Parkman Prize Edition, History Book Club, 2006), 241-42.

[8] Tom Chaffin, *Pathfinder: John C. Fremont and the Course of American Empire* (New York: Hill and Wang, 2002), 43.

[9] Sibley, *Memoir of Jean N. Nicollet,* 189.

[10] J. J. Abert to Joel Poinsett, January 17, 1838, in Bray and Bray, *Joseph N. Nicollet On the Plains,* 216.

[11] Fremont to Ann Hale, June 6, 1838, in Jackson and Spence, *Expeditions of John Charles Fremont,* 10; Joseph N. Nicollet, *Report Intended to Illustrate a Map of the Hydrographical Basin of the Upper Mississippi River,* 28th Congress, 2nd Session (Blair and Rives, 1843), 143-65.

[12] George William Featherstonhaugh to J. J. Abert, May 19, 1837, Abert Family Letters, Missouri Historical Society: https://mohistory.org/collections/item/resource:189075. Henry Schoolcraft made an expedition to Lake Itasca, the source of the headwaters of the Mississippi, in 1832 and published his findings in *Narrative of an Expedition Through the Upper Mississippi to Itasca Lake* (New York: Harper and Brothers, 1834).

[13] Gertrude W. Ackerman, "Joseph Renville of Lac qui Parle," *Minnesota History* 12 (September 1931): 240.

[14] Nicollet, *Report,* 11-12; 67. The Minnesota River's name change came at the behest of Martin McLeod, an early pioneer, when he was serving in the territorial legislature in 1852. See Charles J. Ritchey, "Martin McLeod and the Minnesota Valley," *Minnesota History* 10 (December 1929): 394.

[15] John C. Fremont, *Memoirs of My Life,* repr. ed. (Cooper Square Press, 2001), 31.

16 William Clark Papers, 1830-1838, n.d, Clark Family Collection, Box 14, Missouri Historical Society.

17 Fremont to Poinsett, June 8, 1838, in Jackson and Spence, *Expeditions of John Charles Fremont*, 12.

18 Fremont, *Memoirs of My Life*, 32.

19 Fremont to Ann Hale, June 6, 1838, in Jackson and Spence, *Expeditions of John Charles Fremont*, 10.

20 Fremont to Poinsett, June 8, 1838, in Jackson and Spence, *Expeditions of John Charles Fremont*, 12.

21 B.L.H., "Supplies for the Nicollet Expedition of 1838," *Minnesota History* 19 (June 1938): 192-93; Fremont to Ann Hale, June 6, 1838, in Jackson and Spence, *Expeditions of John Charles Fremont*, 10; also see vouchers in Jackson and Spence, *Expeditions*, 31-36.

22 Alexander Smart, Pete Bauman, and Barry Dunn, "Discover the Prairie Coteau," *Rangelands* 25 (December 2003): 39; Fremont, *Memoirs of My Life*, 33, 35; Nicollet, *Report*, 13.

23 Nicollet, *Report*, 7, 10; Fremont to Sibley, July 16, 1838, in Jackson and Spence, *Expeditions of John Charles Fremont*, 20.

24 Fremont, *Memoirs of My Life*, 35; Bray and Bray, *Joseph N. Nicollet On the Plains and Prairies*, 64.

25 Fremont to Sibley, July 16, 1838, in Jackson and Spence, *Expeditions of John Charles Fremont*, 20; Bray and Bray, *Joseph N. Nicollet On the Plains and Prairies*, 79.

26 Harry F. Thompson, ed., *A New South Dakota History*, 2nd ed. (Sioux Falls, S.D.: Center for Western Studies, 2009), 49.

27 Bray and Bray, *Joseph N. Nicollet On the Plains and Prairies*, 89; Nicollet, *Report*, 27-28.

28 Bray and Bray, *Joseph N. Nicollet On the Plains and Prairies*, 88; Nicollet, *Report*, 28.

29 "The Big Sioux: A Brief Environmental History," EcoInTheKnow.com, http://ecointheknow.com/uncategorized/the-big-sioux-a-brief-environmental-history/

30 Nicollet, *Report*, 28; Bray and Bray, *Joseph N. Nicollet On the Plains and Prairies*, 89.

31 Bray and Bray, *Joseph N. Nicollet On the Plains and Prairies*, p. 89.

32 Bray and Bray, *Joseph N. Nicollet On the Plains and Prairies*, 90, 94; Virginia Driving Hawk Sneve, *South Dakota Geographic Names* (Sioux Falls, SD: Brevet Press, 1973), 287, 311, 333, 351. See *South Dakota Historical Collections*, vol. 10, South Dakota State Historical Society, 87, for reference citing the name of Lake Albert having been changed by 1884.

33 Nicollet, *Report*, 27-28.

34 Ackerman, "Joseph Renville," 238; Nicollet, *Report*, 12.

35 Bray and Bray, *Joseph N. Nicollet On the Plains and Prairies*, 63, for Fremont's near drowning; Fremont to Sibley, July 16, 1838, in Jackson and Spence, *Expeditions of John Charles Fremont*, 21.

36 Bray and Bray, *Joseph N. Nicollet On the Plains and Prairies*, 156.

37 Nicollet, *Report*, 41.

[38] Joseph N. Nicollet, *Hydrographical basin of the upper Mississippi River from astronomical and barometrical observations, surveys, and information.* U.S. Senate, 1843, https://www.loc.gov/resource/g4042m.ct001419/?r=0.321,0.688,0.11,0.042,0; Goetzmann, *Army Exploration in the American West, 1803-1863* (Lincoln: University of Nebraska Press, 1959), 72; Goetzmann, *Exploration and Empire*, 313.

[39] Gouverneur K. Warren, *Memoir to Accompany the Map of the Territory of the United States from the Mississippi River to the Pacific Ocean* (Washington, D.C.: War Department, 1858), 40-41. For a detailed history of the mapping of the Missouri River, see W. Raymond Wood, "Mapping the Missouri River Through the Great Plains, 1673-1895," *Great Plains Quarterly* 4 (Winter 1984): 29-42, which lists Nicollet's map as part of the eighth generation of Missouri-basin maps.

[40] Raymond J. Mallie, Jr., "Joseph N. Nicollet's Account of the Sioux and Assiniboine in 1839," *South Dakota History*, 5:4 (1975): 346.

[41] Martha Coleman Bray, *Joseph Nicollet and His Map* (Philadelphia: American Philosophical Society, 1980), 200.

Chapter 6

The Big Sioux River Valley Frontier, 1851-1889

Jeff Bremer
Iowa State University

The Big Sioux River flows through eastern South Dakota, entering the Missouri River at Sioux City, Iowa. Its watershed includes parts of southwestern Minnesota and northwestern Iowa. The first significant non-Indian presence in the Big Sioux River valley were European and American fur traders, but the region took decades to attract a significant white population. By the 1850s Europeans and Americans were beginning to settle in northwest Iowa and trickling into South Dakota. Starting in 1851 the first of a series of treaties and cessions opened the Dakotas for white emigration. Four years later Sioux City was founded at the junction of the Big Sioux and the Missouri River. Congress established the Dakota Territory in 1861. The end of the Civil War and improved transportation brought more immigrants, as did liberal land policies such as the Homestead Act. Railroads tied the territory to eastern cities and encouraged even more immigration in the 1870s and 1880s. Most people settled in eastern Dakota, with the Big Sioux valley one of its population centers. The Great Dakota Boom (1878-1887) added hundreds of thousands of people to the territory, pushing its population to 600,000 in 1890. Towns blossomed and the Dakota countryside filled in, full of the Americans and the foreign-born chasing their dreams of farm ownership.[1]

This chapter surveys the history of European and American settlement along the Big Sioux River from the early 1850s until South Dakota's statehood in 1889. The vast prairies of the Great Plains were initially seen as an obstacle to settlement. Emigrants avoided the plains and headed farther west to Utah, California, Oregon, and Colorado before the Civil War. Powerful native tribes also kept settlement away. While the soil was fertile, rainfall was limited to about 25 inches a year in the valley. In many years too little rain fell for successful farming and the river was barely a stream. Rolling prairies dominated an almost treeless landscape, which seemed strange and alien to those from eastern woodlands. Harsh weather was normal in eastern South Dakota, which suffered from extremes of hot and cold since it was distant from the moderating effects of oceans. All of these things made life tough for migrants, who often lived in primitive sod homes. Immigrants were optimistic though, stoically building towns, schools, farms, and churches in an often hostile place. They adapted to a new environment, endured, and most found success. Northern Europeans, especially Norwegians, saw potential in the Big Sioux area. Life was challenging but the allure of land ownership pulled many thousands to the valley.[2]

The Homestead Act of 1862 offered 160 acres of land to the heads of households or unmarried adults, male or female. Applicants had to be citizens or those who intended to become one. They had to pay a ten-dollar fee, make improvements to the property, build a home, and live on the land for five years. Then they received title to it. The Homestead Act, passed the year after Dakota Territory was organized, helped spur migration to the region as well as across the Midwest and West. The law resulted in some homesteading in the Big Sioux River valley in the late 1880s but most claims in North and South Dakota occurred from 1901-1915. About 41% of South Dakota was patented by homesteaders. In North Dakota it was about 45%. Free land attracted many to the Dakota frontier in the late 1800s, wrote historian Gilbert C. Fite. The Homestead Act ensured much of the public domain went to poorer settlers.[3]

The white settlers of Dakota Territory existed in a raw place, full of environmental difficulties. Calamities occurred in the first couple years of the territory's existence. In 1861 prairie fires scorched the countryside in the autumn. A brutal winter afterwards killed some farmers caught in blizzards. In 1862 a dam of ice created a huge lake that covered the Missouri River valley for sixty miles below Sioux City. Farms were abandoned, as settlers fled for their lives with their animals. But the ice melted, the valley drained, and that year found a bounty of crops and increased immigration. Farmers often found themselves whipsawed between extremes of disaster and plenty in Dakota Territory.[4]

The land was fertile but it was hard to start farming on the plains. The prairie soil was a rich black loam, covered with a thick layer of tangled roots. The Big Sioux valley was covered by tall and mid-size grasses, such as big bluestem, switchgrass, and needlegrass. Grasses were shorter in the northern parts of the valley. This sod was tough to plow, but the soil was full of decomposed and nutrient-rich plant material. Up to ninety percent of a prairie plant's mass was underground; roots could penetrate more than six feet below the ground. Breaking prairie sod "often required as many as seven yoke of oxen to pull a single plowshare," wrote Thomas E. Fenton and Gerald Miller. Once the sod was broken a farmer had to plow the soil again to further break up the surface. Then farmers could plant wheat or a family garden. Hay for animals could be cut from the vast prairies.[5]

The Dakota Territory was established on March 2, 1861, but attracted few immigrants in its first few years. It was a vast place, including the current states of North and South Dakota, as well as Montana and parts of Wyoming. The Civil War and a revolt by the Minnesota Sioux (Santee) in 1862 drastically slowed settlement. The Sioux in Minnesota had been left starving by the U.S. government. Hundreds died on both sides and bloody fighting continued in Dakota Territory until 1864. The Santees were defeated and exiled to Canada and a reservation in the territory. European and American immigrants lived in the southeastern part of the territory, usually along waterways. Only about 500 white people lived near the Missouri and Big Sioux rivers in 1860. Yankton was the territory's first capital and most important early town. Most newcomers came from nearby states such as Minnesota, Iowa, or Wisconsin, traveling by steamboat or overland. The 1900 federal census showed that 31,047 South Dakotans had been born in Iowa, making Iowa the birthplace for more residents than any state other than South Dakota. The U.S.-Dakota War of 1862 led to the abandonment of all settlements in Dakota except Yankton. Droughts and grasshopper invasions, plagues that would return in the following decades, helped push out many who remained in 1864 and 1865. The end of the Civil War and the displacement of the Sioux opened it once again to immigration.[6]

Some moved to claim land as soon as the territory officially opened for emigrants. Israel Trumbo and three relatives lived near Vermillion in the winter of 1861, cutting wood and hunting in the sparsely occupied region. Trumbo wrote to his family that "there is no money here" and that he could not earn anything. But their claims were safe. There were plenty of turkeys and deer to hunt. The men earned two dollars a day for their labor, but were paid "in trade mostly." He wrote, "people here are very kind" and helped each other in good friendship. But he warned his wife of "pretty hard times here" for a year or two after his family joined him. He promised they would soon raise all they needed to live on. Trumbo's letter is an example of the stoic optimism of those who moved to the Dakota Territory.[7]

Dakota's early territorial government primarily consisted of a federally-appointed governor, a secretary, and three judges. The legislature first met in March 1862, choosing Yankton as the capital and Vermillion as the eventual location for a university. They wrote civil and criminal laws, partially copied from Ohio. Most education in the first years of the state was through private schools. The first permanent school was in Vermillion, built during the winter of 1864-1865. A land office was established in the same town, which recorded one of the first Homestead Act claims in the country shortly after midnight on January 1, 1863. The court system was impeded by the great size of the territory, as well as "a generally lax attitude toward maintaining law and order," wrote historian Herbert S. Schell.[8]

The late 1860s and early 1870s experienced the first wave of immigration into the Big Sioux River valley. A rail line reached Sioux City in 1868, easing migration. Peace also encouraged new settlement. Farm families began to settle along the Big Sioux River starting in 1865, when Fort Dakota was established at Sioux Falls. The United States Army cavalry was stationed there until the fort was abandoned in 1869. The first settlers moved into Brookings County that year. After 1870 settlement along the Big Sioux progressed rapidly. The land office at Vermillion was moved to Sioux Falls in 1873 because of the demand for land in the area. By September of that year the town had 593 inhabitants and it had hotels, mills, a brick yard, and a brewery. The arrival of railroad lines at Yankton in 1873 and at the eastern border of the territory in 1878 tied the area to markets in the east and encouraged the founding of farms and towns. Farmers sold wheat and flour to the Mississippi River valley. New stores provided access to goods from outside the territory. Even more settlers moved to live along the upper Big Sioux, aided by rail lines, and joined in the Great Dakota Boom of the late 1870s and 1880s.[9]

Will C. Robinson, who lived in Lyon County in southwestern Minnesota, came to the Big Sioux valley in 1878 to claim land. The grasshopper "scourge" had kept emigrants out of Dakota Territory in the mid-1870s. He found the town of Gary "filled with land hunters, every one was hopeful and enthusiastic." He stayed with a friend who lived on a homestead near Watertown. The man had hauled wood 75 miles from Minnesota with an ox team to build his house. The northern reaches of the valley were still sparsely settled, with only two settlers staying in the area over the winter. Robinson and his friends each claimed three 160-acre plots, one under the Homestead Act and the other two with a pre-emption and a timber claim. "In those days the land laws were administered rather loosely," he noted in a reminiscence. They visited Medary in Brookings County to make their formal claims.[10]

Immigrants did not just come from American states. They also came from western and northern Europe. Norwegians, Swedes, Danes, and Germans came to the Dakota Territory and the Big Sioux valley. Foreign-born settlers in Dakota Territory were more than one-third of the total population from 1860-1880. In 1866 Norwegians from Minnesota moved to live near the town of Baltic, and the valley became a center of Norwegian settlement in Dakota Territory. More than 3,300 lived in Brookings County in 1900. In that year nearly 37% of Minnehaha County was Norwegian. By 1873 Swedish settlers had filed more than 200 claims in Clay and Lincoln counties in the southern part of the valley. More than 500 German immigrants from Russia also came in 1873, settling in northern Yankton County. They had lived in Russia for about 100 years, having been invited by Catherine the Great in 1763 to settle on the country's vast steppe. The Russian government taxed them lightly and let them run their own schools and churches. But in 1871 Czar Alexander II began to remove the concessions of his predecessor. Thousands then left Russia. More than 100 Danes lived in Turner County in the early 1870s; by the end of the decade there were more than 600 in Turner, Clay, and Yankton counties. Neither an economic depression in the mid-1870s nor a grasshopper invasion could drive these groups out of the area. Few left and thousands of other foreign-born immigrants followed in the 1870s and 1880s.[11]

Watertown was but a townsite with a few buildings until April 1880, when it began to grow quickly. Its land office, opened during the Great Dakota Boom, did extensive business, as people flooded into the valley. The author of an 1881 history of southeast Dakota wrote that as many as one hundred carpenters labored, with "continual pounding from morning till night." Within a year the town had more than 1,000 inhabitants. By then it had five hotels, grain elevators, two banks, two newspapers, three churches, and a schoolhouse. Eight general stores, two painters, a shoemaker, three druggists, two saloons, at least seven law firms, and an undertaker provided their services to the area.[12]

Villages and towns had many businesses for those who came to visit, but most people lived in the countryside. Their lives revolved around their homes, local churches, and schools. The first schools in the Big Sioux River valley were makeshift, often a sod house. Students from age five to 21 went to school together. A teacher in Brookings County earned twelve dollars a month around 1870. Eventually, school districts were formed and one-room schoolhouses were built of wood. Families in Minnehaha County built a school, which also served as a church. Until ministers could be found, singing hymns and Bible reading made up church services. Traveling ministers often held meetings in cabins. Local families provided labor or a bit of money to assist in building churches and schools. Churches in the countryside were often started by immigrants. About 1,100 churches—about half of those that existed in the state in 1926—were founded by immigrants.[13]

Towns and farms in and around the valley prospered, even though parts of the upper Big Sioux valley were unsettled. The number of inhabitants in Dakota Territory grew quickly in the late 1870s, reaching 136,000 in 1880. In the 1880s South Dakota's population increased by 256%; North Dakota grew by 416%. In 1883 one thousand people came to the territory each day. Yankton had 3,434 people in 1880, while Sioux Falls had 2,163. Canton, Watertown, and Elk Point all had about 700 people. Counties on the upper Sioux had a smaller population, with Codington County having about one-quarter the population of Minnehaha County, which had 8,252 inhabitants in 1880. The major city in the valley, Sioux Falls, thrived. Its land office sold 200,000 acres of land in April 1878. At one point in May 1878, 160 acres of land were sold every three minutes, a prime example of the term "doing a land-office business," wrote Gary D. Olson. The city's hotels and boardinghouses were continually crowded, its dozen saloons and two houses of prostitution busy. Sixty-one percent of the city was male, with 37% of all independent adults foreign born. The vast majority of residents were from northern states or Europe. Ten percent of the immigrant population was from Norway, six percent from Ireland, and five percent from both Germany and Sweden. More than half of the women in the town were employed as domestic servants, but females were represented in many occupational categories, including cooks, teachers, bakers, and dressmakers. One woman was a hotel keeper and two ran houses of prostitution.[14]

The influx of settlers brought men like Fred Fleischman to the region. Fleischman came to homestead near the village of Oldham in 1879, about 30 miles west of Brookings. He left Wisconsin to settle in Kingsbury County, where the 1880 census reported only twelve farms. He bought lumber for a house, broke twenty acres of sod for $60, and began to grow wheat. In the next few years, he bought cows, hogs, and chickens and sold butter and eggs for additional income. He was lucky—crops were good and prices were high when he first came to the area. But drought and low prices hurt farmers in the late 1880s. Wheat prices fell by half and hard times afflicted the plains through the early 1890s. Despite this, Fleischman persevered and continued to live on his farm until his death in 1929.[15]

A farm usually required a spouse, though plenty of single men and women lived on the plains. As many as one-third of homesteads in Dakota Territory may have been held by women in 1887. Homesteading was hard but satisfying work that provided independence to women. Few wanted to return back east. The labor of married women was varied and endless. They made goods necessary for family survival, produced and cared for children, working both within and outside the home. Women juggled labor from cooking and butter-making to breaking sod and herding cattle. The daughter of one Norwegian woman called her mother's home a "pioneer factory," due to her proficiency at knitting, spinning, sewing, and soap-making. Women baked bread, made cream and butter, processed wild game into meals, dried fruit, butchered hogs, did laundry, and completed a thousand other tasks. One woman in Dell Rapids, about twenty miles north of Sioux Falls, gave birth to ten children while helping her second husband raise seven more. Single farm women had fewer domestic chores due to the absence of a family though. But they often worked outside their home at paid jobs in teaching or domestic work. Income earned from female labor often made family farms successful, with cash from butter and eggs keeping farms afloat in lean years. Married or single women tried to convert their primitive housing into pleasant homes. One woman learned how to plaster, secured needed materials, and filled in the many holes in her walls of her home near Brookings. She noted that early Dakota houses had many drawbacks but that they could be made into a nice home. With scrubbed floors, whitewashed walls, and window sills with flowers, homes were "by no means unattractive in the pioneer country."[16]

The Dakota Territory attracted a huge number of migrants but it rarely made their lives easy. The absence of wood forced many newcomers to live in sod homes, which were built out of prairie sod cut into pieces about three-feet long. It was stacked like brick to form four walls, with room left for a front door and windows. Walls were usually three or four feet wide at the base and about half as wide at the roof, which was built of cottonwood poles, often obtained from a nearby stream. Cottonwood rafters were covered with brush and grass, with a layer of sod on top. Clay was used to fill open spaces in the walls. Such shelter was primitive but cost little, helpful to thousands of people of limited means. It was often temporary, but many pioneers began life in the Big Sioux valley in a "soddie." Families usually moved into a normal wood-framed house as soon as they could. Abbie Mott Benedict lived in a sod home with her husband, Albert, and their three children in Clay County in northwest Iowa from 1869 to 1871. Her brother sometimes lived with them too, making a small home even more crowded. She described it as desolate and windswept, but warm in the winter. Their sod shanty was fourteen by twenty feet, with heavy posts in corners to hold up a hay roof. Frances Olsen Day described one as "a snug shelter but rather lacking in niceties of civilized life." A soddie that she visited in northwest Iowa was very small and dim, with only two small square windows. Wood frame houses were cheaply built and not very warm. But, they were "brighter and airier," Day wrote.[17]

In 1869 Horace C. Webb and his family homesteaded on 160 acres near Sibley, Iowa, about 75 miles northeast of Sioux City. Their land sat on the southeastern edge of the Big Sioux River valley. Webb was an infant and his family of five lived in a "little shack" of ten by twelve feet, he wrote. There was not a tree to be found for a few miles; men had to travel 25 miles to the Rock River for lumber. Winter was an endless series of blizzards and the wind "whistled through that single-boarded house like nothing on earth. Ice froze in the wash basin," he recalled. To stay warm, they twisted hay into bunches and burned it in their stoves. Some families burned buffalo chips—dried bison dung—or corncobs to stay warm. Those who could afford it purchased coal from nearby towns. The Webbs struggled to produce a good crop, battling droughts and grasshoppers their first few years. They sold their land for $1,000 and moved to Sibley by the time Horace started school.[18]

Winters in Dakota Territory were usually harsh, as Horace Webb observed, with some blizzards lasting more than a week. Extreme cold and heavy snow, as well as unrelenting wind, made life miserable. The winter of 1880-1881 was especially severe and January 12, 1888, was known for its great blizzard, probably "the greatest one-day weather disaster in South Dakota history," wrote historian Richard Maxwell Brown. The blizzard struck without warning all over the state just before noon, a day that had been warm and pleasant. It killed at least 170 people who were away from buildings, including teachers, children, and farmers. The winter of 1880-1881 was known as a hard winter, when more than eleven feet of snow fell. Telegraph wires were buried under great drifts of snow. Train service was halted for months in some places. In February 1881 one blizzard lasted nine days. Farmers had to dig tunnels through mountains of snow to reach their barns and livestock. Hattie Phillips remembered a blizzard in 1873 that hit Minnehaha County. "It came without warning," she recalled, and hit her house with a crash. It was a terrible day, with two children that her family knew killed in the storm.[19]

Droughts also provided challenges for settlers beyond a lack of rain. Dry weather pushed massive swarms of locusts, which were a highly mobile form of grasshopper, out of the Great Plains. They invaded eastern South Dakota, western Iowa, and other states in the mid-1870s. One writer compared a grasshopper invasion to an immense snowstorm—a vast cloud of specks that moved with the wind. "Their ravages were so wide-spread in extent, and the destruction following in their wake so complete, that many families were left destitute," the *History of Southeastern Dakota* noted. Minnehaha County organized an aid society in 1875 to distribute food, clothing, and seed sent by Americans in the east. Horace Webb wrote, "the sun was clouded as though a bad storm was coming" when the insects appeared. They consumed his family's garden in a few hours. "That winter all we had to pull us through was sent to us through the Government and church communities," he wrote. The insects ate everything, especially living plants. They also consumed wood, paper, cotton, bark, and even the wool off of sheep. They were too numerous to exterminate. Hogs and turkeys that ate grasshoppers all summer tasted like the insect. Once they arrived, usually in mid-summer, locusts stripped the countryside bare of crops and garden vegetables. They often laid eggs, which hatched in springtime and portended further agricultural calamity. Grasshoppers last appeared in 1877 on the plains. But they helped halt settlement in Dakota and drove many farmers out of the region.[20]

Prairie fires terrified Big Sioux farm families, as they could destroy homes, crops, and years of work in a few minutes. Fire was a danger when grass was dry in the fall or spring. Flames could move at thirty miles an hour and sometimes devastated entire townships. One conflagration in 1889 consumed more than 400 square miles and destroyed most of the town of Leola. Another fire in 1871 leapt across both the James and Vermillion rivers. Seven homes were lost in less than a half hour in Turner County, southwest of Sioux Falls in 1889. One man was terribly burned, his horses killed while still in their harnesses. Walborg Strom Holth described fires in 1882 around her family's home in northeast Dakota Territory. They raged around the horizon for several weeks but spared their homestead. She noted that farm families usually plowed several furrows around buildings and hay stacks to protect them. But a year of crops could be lost with high winds that pushed flames over barriers. Will C. Robinson wrote that a prairie fire swept down upon a small settlement near Lake Oakwood, close to Brookings, in the spring of 1878. "It made some lively work for a time and it is doubtful if, but for the assistance of our party of five men, the houses could have been saved," he recalled. People took shelter in dugouts or even wells when necessary. One woman in Dakota Territory in 1859 crawled into a water well with her child, surviving through "sheer nerve and resourcefulness," wrote historian Everett Dick.[21]

By the time South Dakota achieved statehood, the Big Sioux River valley had filled with settlers. Sioux Falls had more than 10,000 inhabitants in 1890. Farms dotted the countryside, with villages and towns providing services and entertainment to residents. Railroads connected the area to the outside world, bringing new people and carrying away wheat and other agricultural products. It was a tough place to make a living, but thousands came chasing their dreams of land ownership. Some took advantage of the Homestead Act to start their farms. Men, women, and children sought independence on the mostly treeless prairies, struggling against droughts, blizzards, prairie fires, grasshoppers, and fluctuating farm prices. They often lived in rudimentary sod homes, built from the same prairies that they uprooted to found their dreams. While the Dakota Territory could be an unforgiving environment, it provided opportunity for Europeans and Americans, who relentlessly pushed settlement west in the nineteenth century.[22]

Notes

[1] Jon K. Lauck, *Prairie Republic: The Political Culture of Dakota Territory, 1879-1889* (Norman: University of Oklahoma Press, 2010), 4-6; Arthur R. Huseboe, "Sod Busting in Fact and Fiction in the Sioux River Valley," in *Big Sioux Pioneers*, ed. Arthur R. Huseboe (Sioux Falls: Nordland Heritage Foundation, 1980), 5; Norman K. Risjord, *Dakota: The Story of the Northern Plains* (Lincoln: University of Nebraska Press, 2012), 102-08, 116-18, 133-34.

[2] David B. Danbom, *Born in the Country: A History of Rural America* (Baltimore: Johns Hopkins University Press, 1995), 135-38; Arthur R. Huseboe, 5-6; Christopher R. Laingen, "Geographies of the Borderlands," in *The Interior Borderlands: Regional Identity in the Midwest and the Great Plains*, ed. Jon K. Lauck (Sioux Falls: The Center for Western Studies, 2019), 9; Jon K.

Lauck, "Crossing the Center Line: In Search of the Midwest/Great Plains Borderlands," in *The Interior Borderlands,* xxxvii-xxxix.

[3] David B. Danbom, *Born in the Country,* 113-14; Gilbert C. Fite, "Agricultural Pioneering in Dakota: A Case Study," *Great Plains Quarterly* 1(Summer 1981): 170; David B. Danbom, *Sod Busting: How Families Made Farms on the Nineteenth-Century Plains* (Baltimore, Johns Hopkins Press, 2014), 9; Richard Edwards, Jacob K. Friefeld, and Rebecca S. Wingo, *Homesteading the Plains: Toward a New History* (Lincoln: University of Nebraska Press, 2017), 10, 112, 117-19, 202.

[4] *History of Southeastern Dakota, Its Settlement and Growth, Geological and Physical Features—Counties, Cities, Towns and Villages—Incidents of Pioneer Life—Biographical Sketches of the Pioneers and Business Men, With a Brief Outline History of the Territory in General* (Sioux City, IA: Western Publishing Company, 1881), 21-23.

[5] Thomas E. Fenton and Gerald Miller, "Soils," in *Iowa's Natural Heritage,* ed., Tom C. Cooper (Des Moines: Iowa Natural Heritage Foundation and the Iowa Academy of Science, 1982), 81; Daryl Smith and Paul Chris Hansen, "Prairies," in *Iowa's Natural Heritage,* 166-17; Harry F. Thompson, ed. *A New South Dakota History* (Sioux Falls: Center for Western Studies, 2009), 29-30; Norman Risjord, *Dakota,* 140-42.

[6] Herbert S. Schell, *History of South Dakota* (Lincoln: University of Nebraska Press, 1961), 77-80; Thompson, *A New South Dakota History,* 89; Bruce E. Johansen, *The Native Peoples of North America: A History* (New Brunswick: Rutgers University Press, 2005), 263-64. In 1900 160,220 people claimed birth in South Dakota, 31,047 in Iowa, 24,995 in Wisconsin, and 18,515 in Minnesota. See *Twelfth Census of the United States-1900,* vol. 1 (Washington, DC: United States Census Office, 1902), 686-89.

[7] "A Pioneer's Letter Home," *South Dakota Historical Collections* 6 (1912), 201-03.

[8] Schell, *History of South Dakota,* 93-102.

[9] Schell, 109-15; *History of Southeastern Dakota,* 53-60.

[10] Will C. Robinson, "Some Pioneers of the Upper Sioux," *South Dakota Historical Collections* 7 (1914), 549-53.

[11] Thompson, 124-35; Gary D. Olson, "The Historical Background of Land Settlement in Eastern South Dakota," *Big Sioux Pioneers,* 24; John P. Hohansen, "Immigrant Settlements and Social Organization in South Dakota," Agricultural Experiment Station, South Dakota State College of Agriculture and Mechanic Arts, *Bulletins,* June 1937, 7.

[12] *History of Southeastern Dakota,* 159-63.

[13] Carolyn Sands, "Frontier Architecture of the Big Sioux Valley, 1865-1885," *Big Sioux Pioneers,* 40-41; Hohansen, "Immigrant Settlements," 5.

[14] *History of Southeastern Dakota,* 32-34; Gary D. Olson, "A Dakota Boomtown: Sioux Falls, 1877-1880," *Great Plains Quarterly* 24 (Winter 2004): 20-29; Schell, 170; Danbom, *Sod Busting,* 65-66.

[15] Fite, "Agricultural Pioneering in Dakota," 169-75; Danbom, *Sod Busting,* 66-67.

[16] Glenda Riley, "Farm Women's Roles in the Agricultural Development of South Dakota," *South Dakota History* 13 (Spring/Summer 1983): 87-92, 95-99, 101.

17 Risjord, *Dakota,* 140-41; Frances Olsen Day, "More About Life on the Prairie," 1-3, State Historical Society of Iowa, Iowa City (SHSI-IAC); Glenda Riley, *Prairie Voices: Iowa's Pioneering Women* (Ames: Iowa State University Press, 1996), 150-53; Glenda Riley, *Frontierswomen: The Iowa Experience* (Ames: Iowa State University Press, 1981), 39-40; Danbom, *Sod Busting,* 34-35.

18 H. C. Webb Reminiscence, 1-3, SHSI-IAC; Frances Olsen Day, "Pioneering," 1-4, SHSI-IAC.

19 Everett Dick, *The Sod-House Frontier, 1854-1890* (Lincoln: University of Nebraska Press, 1954), 227-29; Richard Maxwell Brown, "The Enduring Frontier: The Impact of Weather on South Dakota History and Literature," *South Dakota History* 15 (Spring/Summer 1985): 28-34; Dana Reed Bailey, *History of Minnehaha County, South Dakota* (Sioux Falls: Brown and Saenger, 1899), 243-44.

20 Mary K. Frederickson, "The Grasshopper Wars," *Palimpsest* 62:5 (Fall 1981), 150-60; Frank C. Pellett, "Some Farm Pests of Pioneer Times," *Iowa Journal of History and Politics* 41 (April 1943): 196, 199-201; Cyrus Carpenter, "The Grasshopper Invasion," *The Annals of Iowa* 4:6 (1900): 437-39, 441-45; H. C. Webb Reminiscence, 2-3, SHSI-IAC; *History of Southeastern Dakota,* 56-57; Dick, *The Sod-House Frontier,* 204-06; Jeffrey A. Lockwood, *Locust: The Devastating Rise and Mysterious Disappearance of the Insect That Shaped the American Frontier* (New York: Basic Books, 2004), 27.

21 Lorna B. Herseth, ed., "A Pioneer's Letter, "*South Dakota History* 6 (June 1976): 314; Robinson, "Some Pioneers of the Upper Sioux," 552; Schell, 182; Everett Dick, 217-18. Dick does not identify where the woman lived, but she would have mostly likely been in southeast Dakota Territory along the Missouri River.

22 Olson, "A Dakota Boomtown," 18.

Chapter 7

From Northfield to Springfield: The Escape of the James Brothers from History into Legend along the Big Sioux River

Sam Herley
University of South Dakota

Desperate, dirty, and exhausted, the two brothers crossed the border, entered the valley, and neared the water. Swarms of posses hunted them in the endless rain. Wounded and having lost nearly everything, the brothers were on the run as never before. The last two of their outfit not to have been killed or captured in the fallout of a bloody shootout from ten days ago, they had had to use all their skill, tenacity, and guile to make it this far. Already since the botched robbery, they had traveled–by walk, crawl, or horse–some 200 miles, by coincidence nearly the exact distance of the fabled ride by infamous English highwayman Dick Turpin from London to York. Now here at the river's edge, they encountered a new obstacle. Yet they also found an ally that would serve as a safe harbor not just for their lives in the moment but also for their own story long after they were gone. They surely could not pause to ponder such matters. They had to keep moving down through the river and beyond. For them, in the moment, time was short.

Time itself, with all its abundance, has an irresistible persistence in sculpting rivers, memories, legends, and myths, usually in that order. By the time Frank and Jesse James had arrived at the Big Sioux River in the aftermath of the robbery in Northfield, Minnesota, in September

1876, the river already had existed for ages. In the nearly 150 years since its encounter with them, the river valley has become a riparian Sherwood Forest destined to be linked to the legend of the James brothers for ages more. Their tale has become as inextricable from the river as the quartzite that permeates its valley. It was here that a new chapter of the robbery's aftermath began. And it was here that the escape took a turn–geographically, historically, and mythologically–that affected not only immediate events but also the entire Jesse James mythos. The Big Sioux River valley thus shaped the story of the James brothers' flight from the Northfield robbery in at least three ways: first, its position and physical features had a direct effect on the brothers' route and method of escape; second, the people of the valley were responsible for much of the speculation that spread lasting theories and myths about the brothers' supposed arrivals and actions in adjacent communities; and third, the river valley serves as a classic borderlands locale for a traditional outlaw legends culture that has crossed geographic, social, and ethnic boundaries.

The Northfield bank robbery precipitated the brothers' journey through the Big Sioux River valley in September 1876. Writers have called the crime "the most famous bank robbery in American history" or "the most famous bank robbery of all time."[1] Its outcome signaled the destruction of the James-Younger Gang. Many essentials of the robbery and early aftermath are well chronicled. Frank and Jesse James, two brothers who had honed their abilities as Confederate guerillas during the Civil War, conducted a series of bank and train robberies across the middle United States for a decade. Some historians have described their path as a turn to a life of crime. Others have called it a continued insurgency of a war that, to the brothers, had never ended. Frank and Jesse combined with the Younger brothers Cole, Jim, and Bob and other men to form the James-Younger Gang by the late 1860s. In summer 1876 they decided to rob far to the north of their usual crimes. They settled on the First National Bank in Northfield after scouting for targets in Minnesota.

The reasons for the gang's fateful choice for faraway Minnesota remain numerous and contentious for scholars. Among the logistical explanations is that some gang members wanted to rob in a place where they would have freedom of movement and contend with only unsuspecting law enforcement. Other versions emphasize a personal vendetta, with Jesse James's desire for revenge against attorney Samuel Hardwicke, who had moved to St. Paul after representing a Pinkerton Detective Agency member accused of involvement in the 1875 bombing of the James family home at Kearney, Missouri. The explosion killed Frank and Jesse James's fourteen-year old half-brother, Archie Samuel, and destroyed the arm of their mother, Zerelda.[2] Finally, recent historians have emphasized political motivations. The raid, they allege, had deeply intentional North-South overtones and was an attempt to hit an easy target in the enemy's own home. In effect, the gang intended the raid to strike at federal Reconstruction policy. According to Bob Younger in jail afterward, the gang settled on the Northfield bank because Adelbert Ames, a Radical Reconstructionist and postwar military governor of Mississippi, was among its investors.[3]

The robbery occurred on September 7. Bank clerk Joseph Lee Heywood delayed the gang while armed citizens gathered outside. The townspeople, in a series of actions celebrated for heroism ever since, fought back. They killed gang members Clel Miller and Bill Chadwell in the street and drove off the rest of the gang.

The remaining six gang members fled to the southwest. They used their guerilla experience with rivers and forests to hide their movements in south central Minnesota where possible during a days-long pouring rain.[4] On September 14 they decided to split: the James brothers went one way, and the Younger brothers went another with fellow member Charlie Pitts. A posse hunted down and captured the Youngers and shot Pitts to death on September 21. The James brothers stole horses and accelerated across the vast, treeless southwestern Minnesota prairie toward Dakota Territory. Because of so many witnesses, testimonies, and physical pieces of evidence, the events of the Northfield raid and the arrest of the Younger brothers are well documented. The precise actions of the James brothers thereafter are not.

They escaped, continually dodging a swelling fray of lawmen and bounty hunters. When they reached the Big Sioux River valley, the brothers already had crossed at least a half-dozen major waterways, including the Minnesota River, Blue Earth River, Des Moines River, and Rock River, all of whose shores today are lined with tales of the incident. Biographer T. J. Stiles has called the flight from Northfield across Minnesota and down the Big Sioux River "the most desperate ride of their lives."[5] Author Mark Lee Gardner has described it as "the largest manhunt in U.S. history at that time."[6] Writer Wayne Fanebust has asserted that the escape was crucial in launching Jesse James into a different level of criminal superstardom; had James failed to escape and instead gone to prison, he still would have been a bandit of some note but never would have approached apex outlaw mythology status.[7]

Why the Younger brothers and especially the James brothers went westward rather than straight south home to Missouri has been another longstanding question. "Nobody knows why they went west," tour coordinator at the Northfield Historical Society Earl Weinmann said in 2009. "Perhaps they got lost or were just trying to elude pursuit."[8]

Other researchers have pointed to possible if not obvious reasons. A primary goal appears to have been Dakota Territory itself, an area not only beyond Minnesota jurisdiction but also one immersed in the notoriety of a wide-open frontier with fewer settlers, towns, laws, and law officers. Other experts have noted the Jameses' pattern through the years of robbing in Iowa and then fleeing to places where they had friends, family, or safe houses along the Nebraska side of the Missouri River.[9] Like the nearly parallel Rock River of Minnesota and Iowa, the Big Sioux flows into the Missouri River. Theories persisted that the brothers made their way to the Missouri, commandeered a vessel and floated to safety, as the Big Muddy flowed right back nearly to the doorstep of their family farm in Clay County, some 300 miles from the mouth of the Big Sioux.[10]

The consensus route of the brothers—based on reports from posses and area residents—took them near Luverne, Minnesota, and then into Dakota. Although most researchers do not think the Jameses had any familiarity with the Big Sioux River before entering its valley ten days after the robbery, testimonies suggest that they arrived somewhere near what is now known as Palisades State Park and the towns of Valley Springs and Garretson. The Big Sioux River distinguished itself from the aforementioned rivers associated with the escape in that the James brothers followed its waters, whereas the others were obstacles for them to cross. The brothers, historians believe, entered Dakota Territory on September 17. They followed the Big Sioux River—sometimes crossing it back and forth—through September 21. The brothers allegedly left it near Canton if not miles farther to the south. In all, they followed the river for at least 30 miles, perhaps as many as 100. No other single river along the entire escape route occupied their attention and presence for so long a time or distance.

Aside from the Big Sioux's position just inside Dakota Territory, the river's southern valley into which the James brothers descended was in many ways ideal for them. Historians and folklorists often have described Frank and Jesse James as highwaymen, but in a practical sense the brothers were outlaw river men. To a remarkable degree, from the time they were boys fighting as guerillas in the Civil War, rivers comprised a primary component of their modus operandi.[11] Using river valleys for cover, food, water, and shelter, as well as finding ways to cross rivers as large as the Missouri in order to elude pursuers, had been a routine part of their lives for years.

The physical characteristics of the lower Big Sioux thus offered key advantages. Located in a region that still receives the highest precipitation levels of what became the state of South Dakota, the southern valley historically has featured tall grasses that have reached up to six feet in height.[12] Although the tree cover has changed, the Big Sioux River has been and remains "a forested gash in the prairie."[13] Since as early as the 1830s, Euro-American explorers, surveyors, and settlers in the region claimed that a local Native American word for the Big Sioux, "Tchan-kans-data," translated to "thick-wooded river" or some variant such as a river "continuously lined with wood."[14] Finally, although there are more trees across much of the prairie now than in the late nineteenth century because of settlement and the reduction of prairie fires, studies have shown that many of the northern plains rivers such as the Big Sioux actually declined from the late nineteenth through the late twentieth centuries as a result of modern agricultural practices.[15]

It is plausible that the brothers had acquired a map or otherwise had an idea of where they were headed. They angled their southwestward journey into the area of the Big Sioux where it transitions from an open, flat plain to a valley filled with bluffs and forests that resembled those of their native Missouri.[16] In addition to providing dense cover, the Big Sioux River valley by late September provided not only water but also ripe plums, chokecherries, serviceberries, and possibly acorns.[17] In sum, by choice or chance, Frank and Jesse James appear to have entered the valley at the point where it becomes hillier, more densely wooded, more familiar, and more suited for hiding and sustenance. If the open prairie of the southwestern Minnesota presented a danger to the brothers, the terrain of the Big Sioux River valley reset the chessboard much in their favor. Yet the brothers found an even more versatile resource for hiding not only their immediate whereabouts but also their ultimate legend in the region: the valley's people.

Locals who encountered the Jameses at first usually had no idea who the brothers were. The pair used ruses to conceal their identity and tribulation, and they reportedly received food and comfort at various farms and households along their way. Fanebust has argued that such ploys were at least as important to the brothers' escape as the area's landscape.[18] Some researchers have traced the route of the Jameses directly into Sioux Falls, which then was still undergoing incorporation as a territorial town and had a population of fewer than 1,000. A marker now stands in the city where the brothers allegedly stopped a stagecoach and asked the driver about surrounding roads. Reports of the incident emerged with details that the Yankton sheriff's office originally anticipated that the robbers would try to head west and cross the Missouri River at Springfield, Dakota Territory.[19] In the tiny town's vicinity were forested bluffs, multiple ferries, ample sandbars to ford during the autumnal low-water season of the river, and spots where criminals reputedly crossed into what is now known as the Outlaw Trail area of northeastern Nebraska.[20]

As word spread about the robbers, local newspapers tried to keep up with the action. In addition to covering reports of law agents and claimed sightings of the brothers, writers and editors also from early on speculated as to where the "Northfield robbers" were headed. At the time, many reporters prognosticated on the robbers' intent to cross the Missouri River into Nebraska or western Dakota Territory. Arthur Linn, editor of the *Sioux Valley News* in Canton, wrote that the robbers would cross into Nebraska somewhere between Sioux City, Iowa, and Springfield, Dakota Territory, "where friends were waiting for them, to shelter and take care of them."[21] If the robbers could pull it off, the thought went, they were as good as gone.

Thus, began the connection–real or imagined–of various places along or just outside the Big Sioux River valley to the James brothers and the supposed route of their ultimate escape. Numerous communities in Iowa's northwest corner claim some connection to the James brothers' route. From Sioux City to the city of Le Mars, to the unincorporated community of Beloit and East Orange Township, stories of the brothers coming through the area in the final stages of their Northfield escape abound.[22] Many accounts are subject to serious question. Yet there is consensus among twenty-first century researchers that the brothers probably did escape into Iowa before heading back to Missouri, with a key moment being a well-documented encounter of the pair with a Dr. Sidney Mosher north of Sioux City. Gardner has gone so far as to trace the brothers' route toward Ida Grove, Iowa, based on testimonies and newspaper reports, and his book touches on the tale of a girl's offering Frank and Jesse James a piece of potato near the town.[23] Nonetheless, the early speculations of a westward route out of the Big Sioux River and along the Missouri River lingered, saw a boom in the 1920s and 1930s, and have remained entrenched ever since.

Despite the lasting influence of local news reports, they came to an abrupt stop after the brothers vanished. There is a noticeable late-nineteenth century dearth in the literature on the James brothers' jaunt through the region, even as their reputations and myths soared in the years following Jesse's murder in 1882. The delay in coverage affected the memory and historiography of the event ever since. Reasons for the pause are not clear. Fanebust argues that the primary cause was the desire for local newspapers in eastern Dakota Territory to promote the stability of their communities and to attract safe settlement. Such publications attempted to "accentuate the positive" and guard against negative press coming from the East that sometimes painted the West as a wild and dangerous frontier.[24]

Published accounts increased in the early twentieth century. Although it might have existed earlier, the fabled leap of Jesse James over Devil's Gulch across Split Rock River, a tributary to the Big Sioux, to elude pursuers near what is now Garretson, South Dakota, only appeared in earnest by then. It has since become one of the most famous, celebrated, and debated singular acts in the entire Jesse James mythology–or history, depending on one's view. Gary Chilcote, director of the Jesse James Home in St. Joseph, Missouri, has called the Devil's Gulch jump "the best-known piece of Jesse James lore that you can never prove or disprove." Most outside researchers tend to dismiss the jump as folklore, but local residents often favor its possibility if not insist on its fact.[25]

In the early twentieth century the story of the James brothers' ride through the valley underwent a transformation because of what folklorist Graham Seal has identified as one of the most important characteristics of the traditional outlaw legend: the tale of the great escape in which an outlaw hero, skilled at the artful dodge and the coy disguise, overcomes fantastic odds in outwitting and ultimately eluding his pursuers.[26] By the 1920s there already were enough stories to blur the lines of history and myth that Sioux Falls *Argus Leader* reporter J.A. Derome set out to accomplish the impossible: find the truth. He interviewed numerous area residents who had been alive in 1876 and still had memories of the event. Derome's series on the topic in 1924 was among the first and most important of many publications in the 1920s and 1930s that began to flesh out speculations and claims of encounters with the James brothers in the Big Sioux River valley and beyond. James biographer Ted Yeatman called the Derome articles "valuable sources of previously overlooked primary-source information."[27]

Derome also brought attention to the debated idea that the brothers crossed the Missouri River into Nebraska somewhere between Sioux City and Springfield.[28] A minority of experts since has endorsed the Springfield route. Historian Robert Barr Smith, for example, admitted that the conclusion was "guesswork" but described the course as the brothers' "most likely route away from danger."[29] Although Derome's articles promoted such serious tones and aimed for truth and history, ironically they also added more fuel to the growing legends and myths.[30] His work was among the first of many publications that have illustrated how the escape and its theorized passages serve as threads of history, legend, and myth that sew the area's peoples together from across the geographic, social, and ethnic boundaries.

Seal observes that outlaw heroes "ride between the border of history and mythology," and that the historical circumstances of many episodes of banditry are "frequently related to transitional, unsettled or otherwise uncertain divisions, the liminal space between them forming a kind of no-man's land for bandits."[31] The flight of the James brothers along the Big Sioux serves as the standard for the region. In addition to its elements of a great escape, the story has created a common outlaw borderlands legend that allows for different views based on geography and any number of associated social factors in the region. Seal notes that "different perceptions of outlaw heroes across borders of state, ethnicity, language, and class are found around the world," and such distinctions apply to the ride of the James brothers through the valley.[32]

Stories of Jesse James exist from California to Missouri to Maine. The late John Koblas in his exhaustive *Jesse James Ate Here* documented more than 100 locations in Minnesota alone that had featured at least one prominent Jesse James story, if not many more. He also wrote works that documented countless other such places in Iowa and northeastern Nebraska.[33] In the Big Sioux River valley nearly all such stories stem from the historical aftermath of the Northfield raid. The valley itself serves as a thematic demarcation for the memory of the event. In much of Minnesota to this day, for example, there is a celebration of the defeat and expulsion of the James-Younger Gang. Northfield celebrates an annual "The Defeat of Jesse James Days" and highlights it with a reenactment. There is likewise an annual reenactment of the capture of the Younger brothers.

In contrast, the Big Sioux River and much of its adjacent areas to the west in South Dakota and Nebraska memorialize the successful escape of the James brothers. There is Devil's Gulch and the "Jesse James Days" celebration in Garretson. Along Split Rock River near Garretson, there have been Jesse James Pontoon Rides in which customers can see the cave in which Jesse James supposedly hid.[34] Near Canton, Newton Hills State Park's reputation as a James hideout has been no small selling point.[35] Such is barely the beginning. Just upstream from Springfield on the Nebraska side of the Missouri River is the town of Niobrara, which has highlighted the James brothers in its celebrations of "Desperado Days." The town's museum features a Jesse James display as its most prominent exhibit, topped by a saddle the outlaw allegedly stole in Minnesota during his flight from Northfield.[36]

The saddle itself has connections to stories of the James brothers' supposed hiding in nearby Devils Nest, a notorious den for nineteenth-century thieves in unusually thicketed and gullied terrain not far from the town of Santee. The Santee Sioux Nation, which the federal government removed to its current reservation in the aftermath of the U.S.-Dakota War of 1862, claims one of the most famous Native American connections to the James brothers. In the 1930s a Santee man named Joseph James Chase publicly claimed to be the son of Jesse James.[37] Chase was born in 1870, and stories emerged that the James brothers had been familiar with the area for years and thus used it as a safe haven in the aftermath of Northfield.

Today at the Santee Sioux Tribe Museum in the town of Santee, Nebraska, one can find numerous documents discussing the reputed relationship. A note in *Santee Dakotah Genealogy* makes the disclaimer: "There is no proof to date that Joseph's father was the outlaw Jesse James as oral history suggests."[38] Nonetheless, many people Native and non-Native both on and off the reservation believe the Chase story, which the late Santee tribal historian Duane Whipple characterized as "probably true."[39] The internet, from Ancestry.com to findagrave.com, is replete with family trees, message board forums, and web pages that discuss and debate the veracity of the genealogical connection.

Other tales of the James brothers on the Santee reservation show evidence of influence from outlaw myths that originated elsewhere. For example, one of the most universal tales in outlaw mythology world-wide is the story of the outlaw hero who helps a widow in distress with an onerous landlord, loan shark, or banker. Sometimes he gives her the money to pay her rent or debt and then steals it back.[40] Such stories of Jesse James have existed for decades throughout the United States, including the northern plains, and the Big Sioux River valley, as well as the Nebraska Santee Reservation.[41]

There are other noticeable social divisions in the area regarding the legend, such as those between the academic urban establishments and the rural areas with small towns. Larger museums in Sioux Falls and Sioux City feature no displays or exhibits on the James brothers. Small museums in places such as Garretson, Niobrara, and Santee–towns with populations under 1,200–all feature notable displays or collections of information on the duo. Similarly, a review of the indexes of academic works such as *History of South Dakota* (2004) by prominent state historians Herbert Schell and John Miller or *A New South Dakota History* (2009) by a collection of respected scholars reveals plenty on Wild Bill Hickok and Calamity Jane but no mention of Jesse James.[42] Rather, the James escape story continues to live in the hearts, minds, and voices of the area's residents, especially in small towns and rural areas. Such conditions are consistent with other traditional legends and myths around the world for areas where historical outlaw figures operated.[43]

New evidence might emerge someday, but history might never record the exact route that the James brothers used to escape through and from the Big Sioux River valley. Until it happens, researchers are the latest posse giving chase for targets who already have succeeded in escaping history into myth. As Seal argues, more important than raw sets of facts or data surrounding such episodes is how the reframing of the past through combinations of history, memory, and folklore creates representations that affect actions in the present.[44] And despite all the myths and legends that spread thicker than a riparian forest, the tale also holds lessons in historical methodology. Although Minnesotans, South Dakotans, Iowans, and Nebraskans might be partial to their own perspectives, historian Herbert T. Hoover argued that state boundaries are often arbitrary, and so state history itself must be regional and thematic.[45] The James brothers' escape created a common outlaw legend culture for the region, but also one with diverse geographic, social, and ethnic characteristics. Such diversity has ramifications, for outlaw traditions have different meanings to different groups.[46] John Newman Edwards, the Missouri newspaperman who was more responsible than any other individual for the creation of the outlaw hero myth of Jesse James, perhaps summarized the James brothers best not long after the Northfield raid and escape: "By some intelligent people they are regarded as myths; by others as in league with the devil."[47]

From Devil's Gulch to Devils Nest, from Northfield to Springfield and along countless fields in between, the story of the James brothers' escape through the Big Sioux River valley has bedeviled posses of historians, folklorists, writers, antagonists, and admirers across cultures in every part of the borderlands between Minnesota, South Dakota, Iowa, and Nebraska. The legend might not last as long as the waters will run. But just as when the brothers first arrived in the valley, their story keeps moving down and through the river. And beyond.

Notes

1 See Mark Lee Gardner, *Shot All to Hell: Jesse James, the Northfield Raid, and the Wild West's Greatest Escape* (New York: Harper Collins, 2013). Reviews of this work are also particularly apt to describe the robbery in such terms.

2 Wayne Fanebust, *Chasing Frank and Jesse James: The Bungled Northfield Bank Robbery and the Long Manhunt* (Jefferson, NC: McFarland & Co., 2018), 26.

3 T. J. Stiles, *Jesse James: Last Rebel of the Civil War* (New York: Vintage Books, 1999), 317.

4 Ibid., 342. See also Gardner, 66-67.

5 Stiles., 335.

6 "What Drove Wild West's Jesse James to Become an Outlaw?" *All Things Considered*, NPR, August 17, 2013, https://www.npr.org/2013/08/17/212374395/what-drove-wild-wests-jesse-james-to-become-an-outlaw.

7 Fanebust, email to author, March 27, 2021. See also Fanebust, *Chasing Frank and Jesse James*, 3.

8 Ried Holien, "Did Jesse James Jump?" *True West Magazine*, January 1, 2009, https://truewestmagazine.com/did-jesse-james-jump/.

9 Dan Eshelman, "Infamous Criminal Had His Start in Iowa," *Clarinda Herald-Journal*, May 22, 2019, https://clarindaherald.com/townnews/crime/infamous-criminal-had-his-start-in-iowa/article_97b88dfe-7cbb-11e9-9afc-37285999e1c6.html.

10 Ted P. Yeatman, *Frank and Jesse James: The Story Behind the Legend* (New York: Fall River Press, 2000), 184.

11 Stiles, 100. See also http://www.tjstiles.net/bio.htm, section on Guerilla Tactics.

12 Harry F. Thompson, ed., *A New South Dakota History* (Sioux Falls: Center for Western Studies, Augustana College, 2009), 30.

13 Marshall Damgaard, email to author, Jan. 10, 2020.

14 I. N. Nicollet, *Report Intended to Illustrate a Map of the Hydrographical Basin of the Upper Mississippi River* (Washington: Blair and Rives Printers, 1843), 27.

15 Kurt L. Dean, "Stopover Ecology of Neotropical Migrant Songbirds in Riparian Corridors in the Northern Great Plains" (Doctoral diss., University of South Dakota, 1999), 137.

16 See Matt J. Ley, "Riparian Forest Vegetation Patterns and Historic Channel Dynamics of the Big Sioux River, South Dakota" (Master's thesis, University of South Dakota, 2012), Table 1.8, 48. See also *Report on Sioux River, South Dakota*, U.S. Army Corps of Engineers, House Document No. 93, 56th Congress, 2d session, 1900.

17 Damgaard, email to author, Jan. 10, 2020.

18 Fanebust, telephone conversation with author, notes, March 24, 2021.

19 *Yankton Daily Press & Dakotaian*, September 19, 1876.

20 *Springfield Times*, September 14, 1876. See also Mary Lou Livingston, ed., *History of Running Water* (1989), 7-10.

21 John Koblas, *Faithful Unto Death: The James-Younger Raid on the First National Bank, Northfield, Minnesota, September 7, 1876* (Northfield: Northfield Historical Society Press, 2001), 125.

22 Koblas, *Jesse James in Iowa* (St. Cloud: North Star Press, 2006), 145-49.

23 Gardner, 194.

24 Fanebust, email to author, March 27, 2021.

25 Holien, "Did Jesse James Jump?"

26 Graham Seal, *The Outlaw Legend: A Cultural Tradition in Britain, America and Australia* (Cambridge: Cambridge University Press, 1996), 9.

27 Yeatman, 428, endnote 5.

28 J. A. Derome, "Canton Thrown into Wild Stage of Excitement When Report Was Given That Bandits Were Near," *Sioux Falls Argus Leader*, May 10, 1924.

29 Robert Barr Smith, *The Last Hurrah of the James-Younger Gang* (Norman: University of Oklahoma Press, 2001), 153. The same theorized route is described, though not necessarily endorsed, in Koblas, *Jesse James in Iowa* (St. Cloud: North Star Press of St. Cloud, 2006), 146.

30 Fanebust, email to author, March 27, 2021.

31 Seal, *Outlaw Heroes in Myth and History* (London: Anthem Press, 2011), 12, 88.

32 Seal, email to author, April 7, 2021.

33 Koblas, *Jesse James At Here* (St. Cloud: North Star Press of St. Cloud, 2001). See also Koblas, *The Jesse James Northfield Raid: Confessions of the Ninth Man* (St. Cloud: North Star Press of St. Cloud, 1999).

34 Beth Warden, "Jesse James Pontoon Ride in Garretson Provides Laughs, History at a Great Price," ksoo.com, August 3, 2018, https://ksoo.com/jesse-james-pontoon-ride-in-garretson-provides-laughs-history-at-a-great-price/

35 J. D. Collins, "Kickin' Country Small Town of the Day 'Canton, SD,'" kikn.com, June 5, 2013, https://kikn.com/kickin-country-small-town-of-the-day-canton-sd/.

36 Valorie Zach, "Saddle makes history come alive just in time for Desperado Days," *Niobrara Tribune*, July 23, 2015.

37 "Joe Chase Claimed to be Jessie [sic] James Son," *Crofton Journal* (Crofton, NE), Dec. 7, 1939, reprint from *Omaha World Herald*.

38 Vicky L. Valenta, *Santee Dakotah Genealogy: A collection of family histories for early Santee* (n.p., 2015).

39 Duane Whipple, interview by author, notes, Santee, Nebraska, January 8, 2020.

40 Seal, *The Outlaw Legend*, 9.

41 Marita Placek, *Legends & Lore of the Outlaw Trail: Nebraska's Scenic Byway Highway 12* (Plainview, NE: Northeast Nebraska RC&D, 2011), 17.

42 See Herbert S. Schell and John E. Miller, *History of South Dakota* (Pierre: South Dakota State Historical Society Press, 2004), and Thompson, ed., *A New South Dakota History*.

43 Seal, *The Outlaw Legend*, 182.

44 Ibid.

45 Herbert T. Hoover, oral history conducted by Mike Manascaqua, June 1, 2007, AIRP 2333, South Dakota Oral History Center, University of South Dakota.

[46] Seal, *The Outlaw Legend*, 182.

[47] John N. Edwards, *Noted Guerrillas, Or, The Warfare of the Border* (St. Louis: Bryan, Brand & Co., 1877), 450.

Chapter 8

Abbie Gardner, the Spirit Lake Massacre, and Reconciliation on the Big Sioux River

James Schaap
Dordt University

Without the horror, the blood, the grief, the lifelong sadness, there could not have been the triumph. That's the story line here. Abbie Gardner was just thirteen when her family set down a perilous homestead out front of the wave of white newcomers to a region of the country few Euro-Americans had ever seen: Iowa's northwest corner.

Years after Inkpaduta and his Wahpakute[1] (Waa-pa-koot'-ee) band wreaked bloody horror on the Gardner family and the thirty-some others they also murdered, Abbie wrote a memoir about what she'd suffered at the hands of those who'd killed her mother, her father, and her little brother, and then held her in frightful bondage for about four months.

Her memoir, *The Spirit Lake Massacre and the Captivity of Miss Abbie Gardner* (1885), told the story and contributed to a genre that had already gathered fascinated readers here and abroad, ever since the publication of a seventeenth-century predecessor, *A Narrative of the Capture and Restoration of Mrs. Mary Rowlandson* (1682), a memoir subtitled *The Sovereignty and Goodness of God*. Rowlandson's *Capture and Restoration* is often considered America's first "best-seller," a white woman kidnapped and mistreated by hideous warriors in bright red war-paint. It was also the progenitor of a genre scholars refer to as "captivity narratives," stories that attract audiences by what is often unthinkably repulsive and therefore undeniably fascinating.

Abbie Gardner Sharp (she married soon after her freedom was purchased) likely knew something of the popularity of captivity narratives. If she didn't, someone in her acquaintance would have. That she did, however, doesn't mean the book she wrote—and later peddled herself at the scene of the crimes—was just dime novel material. *The Spirit Lake Massacre and the Captivity of Abbie Gardner* is an honest, heartfelt and fascinating read—of both tale and teller.

That the Spirit Lake Massacre is common knowledge among those who live in the neighborhood is probably not a valid assumption. For descendants of Iowa pioneers like the Gardners, the dark tales that rose from Manifest Destiny are easier *not* to remember. Most Iowans know little about the Ioways, even less about how it is the Ioway tribe has lived in Oklahoma for almost 200 years.

Some background is relevant. Be warned: it's bloody. In March of 1857, the Gardner family had just moved to land in a region unsettled by Euro-Americans. They were the cutting edge of a cultural wave that had begun in 1620 at the Plymouth Colony: white folks assuming the land to be free and open for settlement, even though their squatting threatened the indigenous who lived there.

Winter never departed that particular March, the temperatures as low as temperatures can dip here, deep snow sharply crusted to make walking any distance almost impossible. For the Gardners, a band of Indians coming to their door that day was not rare. Neither was talk. When the Wahpekutes came, Abbie's father picked up his rifle; but her mother, Abbie remembers, told him to put it down. "If we have to die," she told him, "let us now die innocent of shedding blood." Thus, the Gardners allowed Inkpaduta's men into their cabin and cooked up pancakes for breakfast.

Later, when their guests returned, they demanded flour. When Abbie's father turned to get what little they had, one of them shot him through the heart. Her mother attempted to push a rifle barrel away and was clubbed, then dragged outside and killed "in the most cruel and shocking manner," Abbie says. Abbie was little more than a child. In a few moments, both her parents lay dead.

That left her alone with three children. Two were her brothers, the other belonged to an older married sister who happened to be away. The Wahpakutes grabbed the children, dragged them outside, and clubbed all three to death:

> After ransacking the house, and taking whatever they thought might be serviceable, such as provisions, bedding, arms and ammunition; and after the bloody scalping knife had done its terrible work; I was dragged from the never-to-be-forgotten scene. No language can ever suggest, much less adequately portray, my feelings as I passed that door.[2]

What happened at the Gardner cabin was the first terrible act in a string of atrocities along the lakeshore, a string that, a day later, extended into the town we know today as Jackson, Minnesota. The night before that attack, Abbie remembers seeing the same warriors dress once again for battle, her own family's killers. They might have murdered all the residents of the village had there not been a warning. Even so, Inkpaduta's men plundered what they could and killed seven more settlers, including another eight-year-old boy. To say those victims were murdered *unmercifully* seems redundant, but consider it understatement. In all, Inkpaduta's band killed as many as 40 settlers in the three-day rampage and took four women captives, including young Abbie Gardner.

Any telling of the story cannot deny that the Wahpekutes had cause, as their descendants will explain; the existence of the tribe and their freedom as a people were at stake. From an indigenous point of view, what Inkpaduta accomplished was what he and his band had set out to do: clear the area of white settlers, the illegal immigrants. That, they did—for a time.

Even before the massacre, Inkpaduta, the "chief" of the Wahpekute band, was considered dark as sin itself by white settlers—and for good reason. He'd committed his band to the area of the Little Sioux River, where he had managed to make few friends among the settlers. But the level of hideous carnage the band had reached that late winter day was new and beyond white folks' imagination.

Like several other Sioux headmen, Inkpaduta refused to buy into the treaty/reservation system, the white man's view of how "Indians" should live. He despised the enforced settlement created by treaties.

The Minnesota State Historical Society describes the Treaty of 1851, signed just north of St. Peter, Minnesota, just six years previous, this way:

> At Traverse des Sioux, the Sisseton and Wahpeton bands of the Dakota ceded 21 million acres. At Mendota, the Mdewakanton and Wahpekute bands ceded about 14 million acres. The combined payment was about $3,075,000. Most of this money was to be paid in the form of annuities. At Traverse des Sioux, Dakota leaders signed—some later said they were tricked into signing—the infamous "Traders' Paper." This agreement turned over most of the Dakotas' cash payments to their mixed-blood relatives and to traders, who had allowed debts to mount over the years in expectation of tapping into the flow of the government's "Indian money."[3]

Signing the treaty meant being forced to live and stay within the boundaries of a territory twenty miles wide along the Minnesota River. Buffalo hunts west of the Missouri River kept people in food for some time; more than that, however, the hunt had become a ritual with cultural and religious significance. Not being able to leave the reservation meant the death of a way of life. Inkpaduta was unwilling to cede that to the Great Father in Washington or the settlers swarming into a region they'd always considered free. Moreover, annuities were frequently late; some never came. Some were disgusting.

Inkpaduta had lost a friend and blood relative who had been brutally murdered, along with his wife and children, all of them killed by a white man, a much-hated liquor peddler. After the murders, that man had gone farther west to avoid prosecution. When, later, Inkpaduta attempted to secure justice from white man's courts, he came away claiming he'd received nothing but indifference.

That the Waupekutes had cause to fight the new settlers is understandable: white people had no right to take land that had always been theirs. But the Wahpakutes' brutality left pioneer families throughout the region repulsed and fearful and therefore vigilant. For hundreds of miles in every direction, the new settlers were greatly fearful.

Meanwhile, for three long months, Abbie Gardner, captured by her family's killers, became a slave to the Inkpaduta's band, until she was sold for horses and blankets and ammunition. During her captivity, her suffering was immense. However, if anxious readers of other "captivity narratives" expected to find multiple gruesome descriptions of the degradation she suffered, they may well have been disappointed. Her telling does not deliver the tabloid spectacle readers a century ago—or even today—might have expected or still expect. Not only does her story not indulge in sensational details, but her rendition also takes odd turns into unexpected lyrical descriptions of time and place, descriptions that seem created by someone seemingly unaffected by the suffering she was going through.

When Inkpaduta ran from the settlers he knew would come after him, he went north and west to open country and arrived at the eastern banks of the Big Sioux River, near what is Flandreau, South Dakota, today. The orphaned Abbie Gardner, clearly taken in by the landscape around her, seems unperturbed by the fact that each day, each hour, takes her farther and farther west, away from safety and into wilderness:

> The natural scenery along the Big Sioux is grand and
> beautiful. From the summit of the bluffs, the eye can
> view thousands of acres of richest vale and undulating
> prairie; while through it, winding along like a monstrous
> serpent, is the river, its banks fringed with maple, oak,
> and elm.

She understands that this bit of reverie is out of place amid the horrors she was suffering, so she adds what needs to be said: "But alas, how could we! The helpless captives of these inhuman savages could see no beauties in nature or pleasures in life."[4]

While the band and its captives are at this very spot on the Big Sioux River, she describes the fate of the last of the four women taken captive during the Spirit Lake Massacre. Two of them were "sold," then released; the other two were murdered. One, 19-year-old Elizabeth Thatcher, who was pregnant, sensed real danger one day and whispered to Abbie to tell her husband, should she die, that she loved him. That day, Elizabeth was beaten to death while struggling to stay afloat in the Big Sioux. Abbie watched her being tortured, then murdered by killers who made a game of her dying. When Elizabeth swam against the current and made it back to shore, her tormentors did not let her get out of the water:

> She was here met by some of the other Indians, who were just coming upon the scene; they commenced throwing clubs at her, and with long poles shoved her back into the angry stream. As if nerved by fear, or dread of such a death, she made another desperate effort for life, and doubtless would have gained the opposite shore; but here again she was met by her merciless tormentors and was beaten off as before. She was then carried down by the furious, boiling current of the Sioux; while the Indians on the other side of the stream were running along the banks, whooping and yelling, and throwing sticks and stones at her, until she reached another bridge. Here she was finally shot by one of the Indians in another division of the band, who was crossing with the other two captives, some distance below.[5]

Oddly enough, just a few pages before the description of that vicious murder Gardner describes the famous pipestone quarries in a passage whose style could well be lifted from a travel brochure:

> Our journey led through the famous pipe-stone quarry, in Pipestone county, Minnesota. It is situated on a small tributary of the Big Sioux, called Pipestone Creek. The surface of the country is broken and picturesque, abounding in bluffs and cliffs. But its principal attraction, of course, is a layer of peculiar and beautiful rock, highly prized by the Indians and no doubt valuable to the whites. The cliffs here are similar to those at Luverne, but smaller. Beneath these, on a level tract of land, is found the precious pipestone. The stratum is about fourteen inches thick and is overlaid by four feet of other rock, and about two feet of earth, which must be removed before the coveted rock is reached. It is softer than slate, entirely free from grit, and not liable to fracture. When first taken out, it is

soft and easily cut with ordinary tools, hardly dulling
them more than wood does. On exposure to the air, it
becomes hard and is capable of receiving a high polish.
It had already been used for mantels, table-tops, and
the like, as well as for ornaments, and is doubtless
destined to more extensive use. In color it varies from
light pink to deep, dark red; while some of it is mottled
with all these shades, giving great variety.[6]

Similar emotional disjunctions in the story she wrote are a problem
that one Amazon reader correctly observed: "I felt like she very lightly
touched on her childhood, the Massacre, her captivity. There was a lot
of back and side history of the Sioux and other tribes, the US government, etc. I was hoping for more of what she actually endured personally."

What Abbie did endure is there in the memoir, but details are
sometimes hidden beneath and behind other official reports of the
events and her own interest in both the region and its aboriginals.[7] If
Abbie Gardner knew what "captivity narrative" readers were looking
for, she didn't deliver the details, even though the brutal truth of what
happened is here.

Why? For what reason would Abbie Gardner Sharp hesitate to do
what she might have done in her own book? It seems clear that her
reluctance to overdo the violence did not originate in emotional reti-
cence. She wrote the story first just a few years after her release, but a
house fire destroyed that manuscript. The 1885 version clearly took
her more years to write and publish, but she was not shy about touting
it. Her life post-capture was not without difficulty; married at 14, she
lost children, suffered a divorce, then moved back, oddly enough, to
the lakeshore. When, years later, she and her son could afford it, she
bought the very log cabin from which she'd been taken captive and
where her family was murdered, then lived there for the rest of her life.

Once in residence, she set up her own gift shop, where she sold her
memoir and told her story to vacationers who had begun to make Lake
Okoboji a popular tourist destination. She became Lake Okoboji's own
Buffalo Bill, a showman, a carnival barker right there where her sadness
began, just beside Arnolds Park's famed wooden roller coaster.

Abbie Gardner admits witnessing her family's brutal death, as well as her horrifying captivity, prompted something akin to PTSD: "Never have I recovered from the injuries inflicted upon me while a captive among the Indians," she tells her reader late in the memoir. "Instead of outgrowing them, as I hoped to, they have grown upon me as the years went by, and utterly undermined my health."[8]

She does not seem to have been emotionally silenced by the brutality she suffered, however; she spent many years retelling it. If that's true, then why does the tone of the narrative so frequently seem reluctant and scattered, even off-key? How can we explain the oddly disjointed memoir of a woman who returned to the scene of her horror only to replay the story a thousand times and turn the cabin itself into an Okoboji tourist sideshow?

Abbie's hawking her book requires psychological analysis I won't attempt, but the book's mottled character may have suffered from its being misunderstood—by both reader and writer.

Without a doubt, I read her book with an agenda, but I would like to believe that the style and the character of *The Spirit Lake Massacre and the Captivity of Miss Abbie Gardner* can be best understood by the author's own testimony late in the book. In the chapter titled "The Epoch of Advancement," she explains that she wrote her memoir twice, then edited again when she gained blessed relief from what she described as her own lifelong pain.

How exactly did that lifelong pain disappear? The agent, she testifies, was a newfound Christian faith. She says Jesus Christ granted her spiritual, healing powers she discovered by way of Mary Baker Eddy and Christian Science:

> ...after long meditation I resolved to give this new yet old religion a trial, with little faith or hope that I could be relieved by its ministry. However, to the great surprise of all who knew me, I was healed by this demonstrable truth.[9]

The passage is "testimony": she believed a newfound faith brought her to "the living Christ," she says, "who forgives our sins, and heals all our diseases."

In *Massacre and Captivity*, Abbie Gardner Sharp is herself conflicted by two stories of her life as a captive of the band that slaughtered her family. One of those stories is something of a "captivity narrative," replete with bloody evidence to describe her suffering and explain her hatred for the murderers. But a different Abbie created a subsequent and different edition. That Abbie claimed to have been healed and blessed, even forgiven by that same "living Christ."

The narrative includes descriptions one might expect from victims of such crimes. Abbie Gardner includes lengthy reports, one of them written by a man who led a search team looking for others "who alike fell victims to the merciless savages' inordinate thirst for human blood."[10]

She too had cause to speak the way that man did. But in her "captivity narrative," she at times goes out of her way to lend sympathy, not to the killers but to the plight of "the Indian." She takes the opportunity to offer admonition to her own people as well. At one point, she describes the culture of Dakota men who, as boys, are given eagle feathers when they kill their first enemy warrior. At that point, she stops and gives this warning:

> It seems to me that Christian statesmen, and all those who have a duty to perform toward the rising generation in civilized nations, might find a lesson in this. Is there not altogether too much glorification of deeds of blood? Too much talk about gunpowder and glory? Patriotism is a noble emotion; but love of country is one thing; love of war is quite another.[11]

One can't help but wonder whether, after the conversion she describes and relishes, she didn't herself determine that the story of her suffering could have a more blessed effect on her readers if she included less bloody spectacle and more reconciliation, more healing and forgiveness, less war and more peace.

Evidence for the spiritual power of her conversion, not just in soul but in body and strength, seems to me to be evident. Perhaps her "conversion" lends the narrative a softness readers would not have expected in a "captivity narrative," a softness that makes the story feel broken or disjointed. She could well have made the book a greater financial and even artistic success if she'd done more to fulfill expectations of the story of her captivity undoubtedly held; but, as she maintains, finding

God changed Abbie Gardner, made her story less terrifying, and therefore less marketable.

Read instead as what we might call something of a traditional Christian testimony, the whole story feels different. After her conversion to "the living Christ," Ms. Gardner's attempt at a dramatic climax begins with her rescue by three Dakotas, three "farmer Christians,"[12] but it doesn't conclude there, or with her return to "civilization." The story doesn't end with Abby being freed.

The climax of the story, what she herself might call the *eternal* climax of the story, occurs when she travels to Flandreau, South Dakota, where what she might have considered an impossible reconciliation happened, an event that would not have happened without war, but neither could have happened without both sides—Ms. Gardner and the Santees—wanting to reconcile, or at least, in the language of her own Christian conversion, wanting peace in their hearts.

Flandreau, South Dakota, is a small town somewhat less than an hour west of the greatly revered Catlinite quarries at Pipestone, Minnesota. A few white settlers were in the region when, in 1868, 11 years after the massacre, many Santee Sioux families, some Wahpeton and others Wahpakute, moved north and east from their reservation in Nebraska to claim farmland there, around a bend in the Big Sioux River.

Abbie Gardner begins her narration of the Flandreau story this way:

> On Sunday, September 26, accompanied by C. H. Bennett and wife, and H. L. Moore and wife, a drive of some fifteen miles was made to Flandrau [sic], visiting on this occasion the Indian Episcopal and Presbyterian churches. It seemed as though a miracle had been wrought in this region and the day of realization was at hand. Here at Flandreau the red man and the white man are brought face to face in daily contact, living, as it were, next door neighbors, the Indians commanding the utmost respect of the white residents.[13]

What she says she witnessed in Flandreau is a degree of shalom she had never seen before on the frontier. Something that clearly thrilled her was going on in this small South Dakota town, something she found to be what she might well have called a miracle.

Understanding her incredulity at the "utmost respect" she witnessed there in Flandreau, once again, requires some historical background. Historians have claimed—as Ms. Gardner does in her memoir—that the Dakota of the Minnesota River reservation were emboldened by Inkpaduta's crimes and his having escaped punishment. That he and his band roamed free after the slayings meant depredations against settlers exhibited the white man's disregard for what the Wahpakutes had done: in short, Inkpaduta's escaping punishment made more attacks easier. After all, well-defined links exist between the blood shed on the shores of Lake Okoboji in 1857, and Lake Chetek and New Ulm in 1862, in the Dakota War. The Wahpakutes and the Santees spoke a similar language; they were all Dakota Sioux people.[14]

What Abbie Gardner doesn't say in her description of the Flandreau visit is that there may have been a handful of Santees at Flandreau who, years earlier, were part of Inkpaduta's bloody band. In that town, in two churches, she had to know not only that they were Native people but that they were themselves related.

But on Sunday, September 26, 1892, Abbie Gardner Sharp wasn't the only soul in those churches who had suffered horrors; so were the Santees who were that day sitting in hand-cut pews. She doesn't mention their suffering, but, again, it's difficult to believe she didn't know. It was the Santees, led by their headman Little Crow, who had raided the Lower Sioux Agency at Redwood Falls on August 18, 1862, the frontier town of New Ulm a day later, and Fort Ridgely on the 20th and the 21st. During the Dakota War, the total number of settlers murdered in a solitary month of raids will never be known; historians estimate between 450 and 800, all of them murdered after the bloody fashion of Abbie's own family and their neighbors.

During the Dakota War, hate boiled over into slaughter throughout the Minnesota River valley. When it was over, trials, some no more than five minutes long, determined the fate of the more than 400 Dakota warriors accused of atrocities. When tallied, the military tribunal found 303 men guilty of rape and murder, and thereby sentenced to be hanged.

In December 1862 the nation was preoccupied with the Civil War. The list of convicted warriors was sent to Washington, where President Lincoln surveyed names and stories' charges, then narrowed the list of guilty to 39, one of whom was later exonerated. Thus, on December 26, 1862, 38 Dakota men were hanged when a man whose wife and family had been killed at Lake Shetek massacre pulled a rope on the gallows erected in Mankato, Minnesota, for the public to witness.

A thousand more Santees, mostly women and children, were imprisoned on Pike Island, near Fort Snelling, where hundreds died of infectious diseases that winter. The 275 convicted men who'd not been hanged were, early the next spring, shipped down the Mississippi to a fort near Davenport, Iowa, where they spent the next two years as prisoners.

The rest of the Dakotas interned on Pike Island were also sent down river, then up the Missouri to Crow Creek, South Dakota, where they suffered through drought and heat and long hard winters, before begging the government to let them go south to Missouri River land and a reservation in northeast Nebraska.

Hundreds of women, children, and old men were moved once more to the place where some of their descendants live yet today, a small Santee reservation where the tribal museum includes photographs of some of those warriors, freedom fighters, who were hanged at Mankato. The museum's prize possession is mounted in a window box on the south wall—the rifle of Little Crow himself, killer to some, hero to others.

During that deathly winter on Pike Island, something fierce happened to the Dakota people amid their suffering. It is not easy to talk about the phenomenon because historians do not propose eternal answers to spiritual questions. But what happened just before those who were hanged sang their death songs was what one might call a mass "conversion." An immense spiritual about-face was somehow passed along from death row and into the internment camp, where their families were shivering and too often dying in a Minnesota winter. While fevers and disease raged, so did a full-blown religious awakening. Missionaries who stayed with the Santee people before and after incarceration and were angrily reviled for visiting "the savages," claimed the Holy Spirit came upon the people and created a mass conversion.

The Rev. Stephen R. Riggs, who spent his life as a missionary to the Dakota, explained what happened this way:

> The circumstances were peculiar, the whole movement was marvelous, it was like a "nation born in a day."

> The brethren desired to be divinely guided; and after
> many years of testing have elapsed, we all say that was
> a genuine work of the Holy Spirit."[15]

While I and others may be less sure of what occurred than was Rev. Riggs, my judgement of what happened spiritually in Mankato, and then on Pike Island, or even to Abbie Gardner, what ignited religious enthusiasm or sustained it, is not my concern. Believers claim such "conversions" happen in a thousand ways. What interests me is the effects of a spiritual experience that changes hearts and minds of people who believe they have come into the presence of a being they consider to be "the living God." What is of importance to Abbie Gardner's story and the book itself is what happened in the lives of people—of Abbie and the Santees—as a result of their "conversions."

In 1869 some of the Santees from that small Nebraska reservation determined to take up farming on their own land in a big bend in the Big Sioux River, near Flandreau. What Abbie Gardner doesn't tell her readers is that many of the people she met on that visit to Flandreau would never forget their own tribulation, the great sadness of the Dakota War, just seven years—and so much suffering—in the past. Abbie Gardner doesn't tell the reader that Santee story, but it is a story she almost certainly had to know.

When she met the Flandreau Santees, descendants of those who'd fought in the 1862 war, she stood before men and women who knew very well what had happened to her 35 years before. Inkpaduta was Santee. Clearly more important to her was that she also stood before people she believed were, as she had been, washed in the blood of the lamb. "It seemed as though a miracle had been wrought in this region," she says, "and the day of realization was at hand."

The climax of Abbie Gardner's story is not her physical release from captivity of Inkapaduta, which occurs two-thirds of the way through the memoir, but her visit to Flandreau, where she had herself witnessed the horrible death of her friend on the Big Sioux River, where she was held captive herself by those who had slaughtered those she loved. But what she'd recognized that day at the Flandreau church, where she had met and spoken with Santee men and women who had experienced, in outline, a similar story of suffering, people who, by their own testimony, had experienced immense depths of sadness, but also what they all would have called peace. Everyone in those two Flandreau churches had suffered greatly but felt themselves redeemed. Without the horror, the blood, the grief, the lifelong sadness, and without subsequent spiritual renewal, the triumph of that particular moment in the company of those particular people would have been impossible. That reconciliation is the heart of the story Abbie Gardner wants told in this odd, old blessing of a memoir.

That grand moment of peace, not war, what Abbie Gardner calls her very own "day of realization," is the climax of the story because that moment was, for her, the most amazing event of all, an occasion for reconciliation, not degradation. She couldn't help feeling their mutual faith brought her and the Santees together.

And all of that, she says so emphatically, happened within sight of the very place on the Big Sioux River where she could never forget the horrible death of her companion in captivity—19-year-old, pregnant Elizabeth Thatcher:

> On an elevation about one mile north of town…a charming view can be obtained of the picturesque valley of the Big Sioux. From this point I beheld a promising young city (named in honor of the man who conceived the plan of my rescue[16]), two Indian churches, and the river where I stood on the bridge of driftwood and witnessed the death of Mrs. Thatcher some thirty years ago.[17]

Standing there before the church at Flandreau, she was so close to that riverbank, she claimed she could see the place where Mrs. Thatcher was beaten to death in the swirling rush of water:

> The past and present scenes rose up and passed before me like a living, moving panorama, and the change that had come to pass on the stage of life seemed truly marvelous. We attended the services in these churches, listening to impressive sermons, delivered in the Sioux tongue, to large, well dressed, and attentive congregations. What had once seemed an impossibility, had become a living reality—a body of Sioux Indians, with religious thought, congregated together to praise Him whose name is Love![18]

Some readers may have anticipated the publication of her memoir as yet another "captivity narrative." Those readers couldn't help but be disappointed because Abbie Gardner could not tell her story accurately without the stunning moments of reconciliation at Flandreau. She wanted badly to claim she'd been healed of those maladies that kept her an invalid, freed by her belief in Jesus. For that woman, standing in the circle of men and women who could have murdered her family, men and women she knew to be mutual sufferers, then professing their mutual faith, was a "truly marvelous" event unlike any she says she could ever have imagined. It is a stunning moment.

Does all of that make Ms. Gardner's book a better memoir? I don't believe so. *Massacre and Captivity* still feels uneven, strangely disjointed, an awkward mix of horror and beatitude amid a file drawer full of historical reports, and a memoir that may well be withholding some of its own secrets. But this reader, so many years later, finds it much easier to understand the memoir as a Christian "testimony" than a captivity narrative; and so may others, especially, I suppose, those who share Abbie Gardner's faith in a person she describes as "the living Christ."

I'd like to believe that Abbie Gardner's memoir describes a very specific place in Flandreau, South Dakota, just up the hill from town where, today, stands "the oldest continuously used church in the state," or so the sign out front says—River Bend Church. The building was constructed in 1873; the original structure still stands on the grounds of the Moody County Museum, in Flandreau.

River Bend Church sits quite reverently away from things, a quiet and beautiful place. A cemetery, which stands just west of the building, tells its own incredible stories, gravestones etched with Bible verses in both English and Dakota. It just seems fitting that even the much-hated and much-loved Dakota headman Little Crow is here too, in peace, in a far corner.

If you stop sometime, you'll almost certainly be alone. But I'm guessing that's where Abbie Gardner stood one day in September 1892 and saw before her both death and life in a vision somewhat akin to a new heaven and new earth, on a day she calls her "Day of Realization."

It is unlikely that anyone will ever know who wrote the epithet on the stone over the grave of Abbie Gardner Sharp, if she did not. It sits a few steps east from the cabin where Abbie lived for decades after watching her family murdered right there. The words on the stone speak to a similar place in the human heart, a place she would have called "the soul":

ORPHANED AND ENSLAVED BY HOSTILE SIOUX
SHE LIVED TO EMBRACE
IN CHRISTIAN BENEVOLENCE THE AMERICAN
INDIAN AND ALL MANKIND

Notes

[1] Inkpaduta's Wahpakute band was one of four distinct lingual branches of Dakota people. History suggests that the Dakotas, along with the Nakota and Lakota, once shared a common language with many other tribes (among them the Mandan, Crows, Winnebago, Omaha, and Iowa). The name "Santee" makes a broader reference to those Dakota people who lived in the eastern edges of what Euro-Americans called Dakota Territory. Inkpaduta's band were Dakotas, but more specifically, they were Wahpakutes, and would have considered themselves as such.

[2] Abbie Gardner-Sharp, *The Spirit Lake Massacre and the Captivity of Abbie Gardner*, Expanded, Annotated (Big Byte Books, Kindle Edition), 37.

[3] http://www.usdakotawar.org/history/treaties/minnesota-treaty-interactive.

[4] *Massacre and the Captivity*, 97.

[5] *Massacre and the Captivity*, 97.

[6] *Massacre and the Captivity*, 94.

[7] Her description of the Yanktons, for example, proposes that the Yanktons who lived on the west side of the Big Sioux River had never seen a white woman before, speculation which is doubtful but not impossible.

[8] *Massacre and Captivity*, 157.

[9] *Massacre and the Captivity*, 173.

[10] *Massacre and the Captivity*, 76.

[11] *Massacre and Captivity*, 119.

[12] The term "farmer Christian" refers to those Dakota men who had both assented to worship a white-man's God and demonstrated that pledge by giving up their tribal identity and willingly begun to work the soil, to farm, i.e., taking up the way of life the missionaries preached and taught. One of those rescuers, a devoted Christian Dakota man named John Other Day, played a significant role in ending the captivity of hundreds of homesteaders—mostly women and children—whom Dakota warriors similarly captured in the 1862 war fought throughout their reservation, the Dakota War. Gardner describes him in the story and tells a significant part of his story, even explaining how he was mistreated by his own people after undertaking her release from Inkpaduta.

[13] *Massacre and the Captivity*, 174-75.

[14] The Santee people who had taken up reservation residence along the Missouri River were from two branches—Wahpakute and Mdewakanton.

[15] Stephen Return Riggs, *Mary and I: Forty Years with the Sioux* (Chicago: W. G. Holmes, 1880), 189.

[16] *Massacre and the Captivity*, 174.

[17] *Massacre and the Captivity*, 176.

[18] *Massacre and the Captivity*, 175.

Part III

Writers, Scholars, and Artists

Chapter 9

Unheralded Novelists of Siouxland

Paul Theobald
Wayne State College

It is fitting, I think, that the four-state area that makes up the watershed of the Big Sioux River received its vernacular name, "Siouxland," from a writer, Frederick Manfred, in 1946. The region is conspicuous for the number of writers it has produced as well as the quality of their work. Manfred, born in Doon, Iowa, lived in Siouxland for most of the years of his life. He died at age 82 in Luverne, Minnesota. Manfred may be the most successful Siouxland novelist, along, perhaps, with Ruth Suckow from Hawarden, Iowa (sometimes referred to as "Iowa's Willa Cather"). Since Manfred will receive special attention from another contributor to this volume, he will remain largely outside the scope of this chapter.

If one were to stretch the boundaries of Siouxland to the east, the region could claim two Pulitzer Prize winners. Wallace Stegner, who won the award in 1972 for *Angle of Repose*, was born in Lake Mills, Iowa. Margaret Wilson won the Pulitzer Prize in 1924 for her novel, *The Able McLaughlins*. Wilson was born and raised in Traer, Iowa. But there is no need to stretch boundaries. The region of Siouxland mapped out in Manfred's *This is the Year* (runner-up for the Pulitzer in 1948) has produced many talented, if unheralded, novelists. It is the goal of this chapter to identify several of them and relay their literary contributions. If I were to approach the matter chronologically, the analysis would likely start with Herbert Quick, born in 1861 and raised on a farm near Grundy Center, Iowa, but spent much of his adult life in Sioux City; indeed, he served as mayor of the city near the end of the nineteenth century. But, instead, I will approach the chapter from my own conception of literary talent. In that regard, along with Manfred and Suckow, Herbert Krause looms large.

Herbert Krause

Born in 1905 on a farm in Friberg Township near Fergus Falls, Minnesota, Herbert Krause was raised as a member of the Missouri Synod Lutheran Church. As a young boy, Krause excelled in the local one-room school and reportedly resolved to become a writer at the age of ten.[1] He entered St. Olaf College in 1931 eager to learn from O. E. Rölvaag, who gained literary renown for his best-seller, *Giants in the Earth*.[2] Unfortunately, Rölvaag died before Krause arrived at St. Olaf, but he remained steadfastly determined to make a literary contribution chronicling the lives and hardships of German Americans in a manner similar to Rölvaag's contributions for Norwegian Americans. In fact, Krause began work on his first novel, *Wind Without Rain*, while still an undergraduate.

Having taken college work at Park Regional Academy, Krause was able to receive a B.A. from St. Olaf in 1933. He then moved to Iowa City for graduate work at the University of Iowa, receiving an M.A. in English in 1935. While at Iowa City Krause completed *Wind Without Rain*, although it would not be published until 1939. The novel introduced American readers to the German-American farming communities of western Minnesota and to the xenophobia that often defined them, the intense religious schisms that often divided them, and to the all-too-frequent weather exigencies that rendered farming extraordinarily difficult for them. The character development is extremely detailed, and conversations betray an intimate knowledge of the way German Americans spoke to, and behaved with, one another. The book won an award as the best Midwestern novel of 1939 from the Friends of American Writers, but it did not engender the attention it deserved.

Krause began an academic career in 1938 as a member of the English Department at Augustana College in Sioux Falls, South Dakota.

He later served as head of the department and as founder and director of Augustana's Center for Western Studies. A professor at a teaching-heavy liberal arts college, his literary production was necessarily slow, although his approach to writing was painstaking regardless of other circumstances. All of his three novels took years to write, including his second one, *The Thresher*, which was selected as a Literary Guild alternate and sold over 400,000 copies. Of it, one reviewer noted, "It could not have been finished sooner; it could not have been written quicker." Said another, "I feel as if I had really seen inside human hearts, seen things too dark to be told except in poetry, too beautiful to be forgotten. Bitter as black frost, radiant as the sun on the snow, as satisfying as ripe fields of wheat and beautiful—beautiful beyond bearing—is this book." Stephen Vincent Benet predicted "Herbert Krause is going to be one of our essential authors." Wallace Stegner said of him, "The beauty of his style doesn't dilute the honesty of his scenes, yet even in the bitterest of these scenes his words sing."[3] While his work garnered high praise from members of America's literary elite, Krause never became a member himself, and his work was never elevated into what some literature scholars refer to as the "canon," the essential work of the essential writers.

Krause's third novel, *The Oxcart Trail*, was published in 1953 and was his least successful among the reading public, but it did sell 10,000 copies, "making it one of Bobbs-Merrill's better-sellers."[4] With *The Oxcart Trail*, Krause shifted gears to some degree, writing a novel of territorial Minnesota during the 1850s, noting "I wanted to preserve a chapter in the history of the northwest which is being rapidly forgotten." With his typical painstaking preparation, Krause immersed himself in his chosen topic: "I spent several weeks of some of the past four springs in the northern Manitoba bush region, and have traveled some 2000 miles in a nineteen foot canoe with a companion and two Cree guides." According to Krause, "without the background of day to day trail life, I would have had a difficult job re-creating the atmosphere of the oxcart trail itself."[5]

Krause also wrote and published poetry, essays, plays, and a newspaper account of Custer's 1874 expedition to the Black Hills. He taught generations of students while at Augustana and contributed significantly to the school's academic reputation. Krause never married and when he passed away at 71 years in 1976, he bequeathed his personal 9,000-volume library to the Center for Western Studies he had founded.[6]

J. Hyatt Downing

Like Krause, John Hyatt Downing remains an unheralded, largely unknown, Siouxland novelist. Born in 1888 in Granville, Iowa, Hyatt actually grew up in Hawarden, as did Ruth Suckow (born in 1892). In fact, Downing later reminisced, "I remember how I sighed at the long sermons of her father, who was our pastor."[7] At age 13 Downing moved with his family to a ranch near Blunt, South Dakota, the town destined to become the setting for Downing's first two novels. Downing was an adventurous young man working at the family ranch for a time, as a railroad company surveyor, a hotel night clerk, and as a shepherd in Wyoming and in the Black Hills, all before finally graduating from the University of South Dakota in 1913.

Upon graduation, Downing worked for the Internal Revenue Service in Aberdeen, South Dakota. In 1921, after contracting tuberculosis, Downing and his wife moved to Carlsbad, New Mexico, to get to a dryer climate. He managed an alfalfa farm while there. With a son in tow, the family moved back to the Midwest in 1925, settling in St. Paul, where he sold insurance. It was during his St. Paul years that Downing began writing for publication, concentrating on short stories. His story "Closed Roads" was published by *Scribner's* in 1925, and many others followed quickly. Downing didn't try his hand at novels until the late 1930s. *A Prayer for Tomorrow* was a semi-autobiographical account of ranch culture in South Dakota, published in 1938. *Hope of Living* followed a year later; again, a novel dealing with the futility of trying to make an agricultural region out of the arid plains of central South Dakota.

Downing's break-out novel, *Sioux City*, was published in 1940, named for the city to which the family had recently moved. A Book of the Month Club selection and *New York Times* bestseller, Downing sold the rights to *Sioux City* to Hollywood movie producers. In fact, at their invitation, Downing moved his family to Los Angeles, but for some reason, the movie was never made. Nevertheless, Twentieth Century Fox hired Downing to write publicity and radio scripts. While in

Los Angeles, Downing published *Anthony Trant*, a moderately successful sequel to *Sioux City*. In 1944 Downing published *The Harvest is
Late*, the story of an enterprising farmer in eastern South Dakota who
establishes a small-town bank and works hard on behalf of his neighbors (and depositors) to withstand the Great Depression. A final novel,
Four on the Trail, a paperback western, was only released in England.
During the late 1940s and 1950s, Downing returned mainly to producing short stories, his last one published in *Readers Digest* in 1963.
Downing passed away in 1973.

Martha Ostenso

Born in Norway in 1900, Martha Ostenso (pronounced Austin-
so) moved with her family to Winnipeg in Canada, in 1902. As a
result, both Norway and Canada sometimes lay claim to Ostenso's
literary talent. But Ostenso's family remained in Canada for just
two years before moving to Siouxland. Martha spent the next
thirteen years of her life moving from one small town to another in
South Dakota and Minnesota, never far distant from the Big Sioux
River. She started writing at a very young age. In fact, at the age
of only eleven, she was paid 80 cents for each regular contribution
to the "junior page" of the Minneapolis *Journal*. She was living
in Benson, Minnesota, when as a 16-year-old, she and her family
returned to Winnipeg. Once there, Martha enrolled at Brandon
Collegiate. A year later she acquired a teaching certificate and
took a position at a one-room schoolhouse over one hundred miles
northwest of Winnipeg. As was common at the time, she boarded
with an area family, an experience that proved to be a crucial
experience for the production of her first, and arguably best, novel,
Wild Geese (1925).

In 1919 Martha enrolled at the University of Manitoba, taking
two English courses from a professor by the name of Douglas Durkin,
a published novelist, 16 years older than Ostenso. Durkin was married with children, a circumstance upended by his growing relationship
with Ostenso. In 1920 Durkin moved to New York where he taught
English at Columbia University, leaving his wife and children in Winnipeg. A year later Ostenso joined him in New York and once again

became his student. That was the beginning of a 40-year relationship, although they had to wait decades before they could marry, as Durkin's wife never consented to a divorce. When she passed away, Durkin and Ostenso were married.

The extent to which Durkin and Ostenso collaborated on *Wild Geese* and all subsequent novels is unclear, but it clearly was a partnership. *Wild Geese* was wildly successful, went through multiple print runs, was translated into seven languages, and was produced as a film starring Belle Bennett (a second film rendition came out in 1941, and a third one in 2004). As well, Ostenso won a $13,500 award for the best first novel by an American author. That was an enormous sum for the time and enabled the couple to devote full-time to writing. *The Dark Dawn* and *The Mad Carews*, both set in rural Minnesota, were published in 1926 and 1927 respectively. Thirteen more novels followed, most set in rural western Minnesota. *Love Passed this Way* (1942) was set in eastern South Dakota. The last novel, *A Man Had Tall Sons*, was published in 1958. It was the least successful of her novels, although still very well done.

Martha's health began to fail in the years after her final novel was published. She and Douglas decided in 1963 to move to Washington to be closer to his two sons. Martha became sick on the train to Seattle and never recovered. A biographer contends that Ostenso became increasingly addicted to alcohol in her last years and ultimately died of psoriasis of the liver.[8] She was only 63 years old.

Herbert Quick

John Herbert Quick was another Siouxland novelist who died too young, also at age 63. Quick was born on a farm near Steamboat Rock, in Grundy County, Iowa. After a few years as a country schoolteacher, Quick read law, passed the Iowa bar exam, and made his way to Sioux City where he established a law practice. An attorney for 19 years in Sioux City, Quick became its 27th mayor in 1898. Life as a politician did not agree with Quick, however, and he served as mayor for only a two-year term. Thereafter, he turned to writing, although he supported himself practicing law. In 1904 he published *Aladdin and Company*, a novel depicting a booming Sioux City, similar in theme to Downing's *Sioux City*. Of Quick's first novel, Clarence Andrews remarked, "compared with *Sioux City*, Quick's novel comes off a poor second. Downing's characters seem much more real and believable."[9]

Several novels followed quickly, *Double Trouble* in 1906 (which actually became the basis for a silent motion picture in 1915 starring Douglas Fairbanks in his first film), *The Broken Lance* in 1907, *Yellowstone Nights* in 1911, *The Brown Mouse* in 1915, and *The Fairview Idea* in 1919. It was not until Quick reached 60 years of age, however, that he produced his very best literary work. *Vandemark's Folly* was published in 1922, the first of a trilogy that chronicled the initial settlement and development of Iowa. *The Hawkeye* followed in 1923, and *The Invisible Woman* in 1924. While the latter trailed off in quality, *Vandemark's Folly* and *The Hawkeye* have been widely praised by reviewers and literature scholars—they were his bestselling works among the general public.

Herbert Quick moved to a farm he called "Coolfont" in West Virginia after serving on President Wilson's Federal Farm Loan Board during World War I. It was there that he wrote his trilogy and two final pieces of nonfiction, *The Real Trouble with Farmers*, and an autobiography, *One Man's Life*. Quick suffered a heart attack and died on May 10, 1925, while on his way to give a lecture at the University of Missouri.

Josephine Donovan

Josephine Donovan was born in Granville, Iowa, almost five months to the day after J. Hyatt Downing was born in the same small town. If you drive through Granville today, you will find no markers commemorating the birthplace of either author, although there is one small sign in Granville that says "Home of Black Soil." Few area residents likely know the origins of the sign, but it is a reference to Josephine Donovan's sole novel, *Black Soil*, published in 1930. The daughter of Thomas Barry, an area farmer, Josephine went off to the University of Iowa and graduated in 1909. Almost immediately thereafter, she married a young physician by the name of William Donovan.

Little is known about her life over the next 20 years, but in 1929 she re-entered the University of Iowa as a graduate student in the School of Letters. Whether she had begun work on *Black Soil* before entering graduate school is unknown, but she offered the manuscript as her M.A. thesis. Wallace Stegner noted that the manuscript "was accepted,

but before she could finish the degree, the novel was bought for publication, won a two-thousand-dollar prize, and was being dickered for
by the movies. So Ms. Donovan lost interest in the academic M.A."[10]
Black Soil indeed became a *New York Times* bestseller, a fact that makes
her literary disappearance curious. She never published another book.
Donovan passed away in 1984 and is buried in Iowa City.

One reviewer listed *Black Soil* as "one of the ten best books of 1930,"
although subsequent literature scholars, such as Roy Meyer, have been
much more circumspect as to the quality of the novel. I nevertheless
found it to be an engaging tale of early settlement in northwest Iowa
(specifically, O'Brien County). It is a little unusual as the main characters, Tim and Nell Connor, are Irish and Catholic in an area dominated
by Dutch and German immigrants. Beyond that, the story covers familiar ground, chronicling the hardships of early settlement, prairie
fires, swarming locusts, severe drought, and transportation difficulties.
In a particularly poignant part of the story, a young German farmer, so
despondent over uncontrollable circumstances, commits suicide. In yet
another unusual development the Connors adopt an orphan, Sheila,
who as a young adult marries a Native American, Wild Goose. *Black
Soil* therefore offers a very early instance of interracial marriage in an
American novel.

Walter Muilenburg

Five years after the birth of Downing and Donovan, and a mere seven-
teen miles west of their birthplace, in Orange City, Iowa, Walter John
Muilenburg was born. In 1911 he made his way to the State University
of Iowa and developed a keen interest in writing fiction. While still
an undergraduate, he published two short stories in the new journal
founded by John T. Frederick, *The Midland*. Both stories dealt with
farming—the first, entitled "The Prairie," was an account of a young
couple just starting out, which ended badly. The young wife dies in a
fire and the young husband begins to drift, homeless. The second story,
"Heart of Youth," is an account of father-son discord on the farm. It
was published subsequently in a volume entitled *The Best Short Stories
of 1916*. The volume's editor, Edward O'Brien, remarked that he expected to see great things in the future from Muilenburg.[11]

Sadly, with one notable exception, he didn't see much. After graduating from the State University of Iowa in 1915, Muilenburg spent two years teaching in country schools and contributing to small-town newspapers. In 1917 he was hired by the English Department at the University of Iowa and he taught there until 1926 when he joined the English Department at Michigan State College. The 1925 publication of his only novel, titled simply *Prairie*, likely aided his successful move to East Lansing.

Prairie was received well by literature scholars and the general reading public. In the novel, he went back to the theme of father-son discord that he handled so effectively in "Heart of Youth." Elias Vaughan, the main character, rebels against his exacting father and decides to marry Lizzie, a young woman from a family not well thought of in his Iowa neighborhood. Reaching the end of his rope, Elias' father gives his son $900 and tells him that he is through with him. Elias outfits a prairie schooner and takes his new bride west to Kansas. There the young couple endures prairie fires, snowstorms, hail, and drought, to acquire, ultimately, a small farm. As fate would have it, Elias and Lizzie have a son, Joey, and as he comes of age, he too rebels against Elias, much as Elias had once done with his own father. But Joey's departure was a terrible blow to Lizzie who dies about a year later. On her deathbed, she asks for Joey and ultimately Elias feels compelled to tell his delirious wife that he is Joey. She dies peacefully believing she is holding Joey's hand.

Although the novel is painful, it is gracefully written and all too authentic in the way it portrays the often-troubled relationships of patriarchal farm fathers who make man-sized demands of their sons. For reasons that are unclear, like Donovan, Muilenburg never published another novel.

Howard Erickson

Howard Erickson is, perhaps, the most unheralded of the unheralded novelists chronicled in this chapter. Erickson was born and raised in Royal, Iowa. Like several others from the far northwest corner of the state, he went off to the University of Iowa as a young man. After graduating in 1913 he was hired by the *Omaha World Herald*. In 1917 he became the Sunday issue editor, a position he held into the 1930s.

He published short stories on the side. His story "The Debt," published in *Munsey's* in 1921, received honorable mention by the committee selecting O. Henry's Best Short Stories for that year.

Erickson's only novel, *Son of Earth,* is a rare Siouxland novel in that its focus is on an immigrant "hired man," rather than the more common focus on farm owners. In the rural Midwest, hiring out was very common for both young men and women. Young men worked the fields, and with livestock, alongside farm owners for a monthly wage, plus room and board. Young women were hired for housework and for help with young children, also for a monthly wage along with room and board. Occasionally, this circumstance gave rise to sexual assault, something that surfaces in Erickson's novel, and was generally only hinted at by other rural novelists, such as Willa Cather.

Tolf Luvversen, son of Danish immigrant parents, lost his father at a very young age. His mother remarries another immigrant Tolf refers to merely as Jacobsen. For his part, his stepfather refers to Tolf only as Luvversen. The new family (Jacobsen has two older sons, Tolf has two younger sisters) is able to purchase a small farm in northwest Iowa and as Tolf grows older, he is encouraged to hire out and does so. As was typical during the first quarter of the twentieth century, parents expected their hired sons and daughters to give their wages to their parents. Tolf follows the tradition, but becomes disillusioned, since his step-father is a poor farmer, rarely completing jobs, leaving machinery in the fields, etc. Jacobsen's sons had long since left home, striking out on their own. With Tolf "working out," the burden of caring for the farm fell squarely on Jacobsen, and he wasn't up to the task.

Eventually, Tolf breaks from tradition and keeps his own money, returning home only for brief visits. An ambitious young man, Tolf wants to work for what he calls an "English" farmer and marry an "English" girl. Not without considerable hardship, Tolf eventually secures a hired-man position for an English farmer recently moved from Indiana to northwest Iowa. As well, a sister accompanies the wife of the Hoosier farmer, and Tolf falls hopelessly in love with her. It didn't turn out well for Tolf. The girl treated him poorly, but well enough to give Tolf hope. Eventually she moves back to Indiana and marries someone else. Tolf is devastated and drifts for a while, drinking too much. He is saved by a widower farmer, a Swedish immigrant, for whom he once worked. The recent widower had a hired girl, Christine, also a Swedish immigrant, for cooking and housework. With no family, the widower wills his farm to her, since she had taken care of him as he grew older. The farmer's death left Christine and Tolf alone in the home. Christine suggests marriage and Tolf agrees, believing that such an arrangement would make him a farm owner. It doesn't happen. Christine keeps the farm and Tolf, eventually, settles into a disappointed life. The marriage produced an heir, however, and Tolf takes consolation in the fact that his son will one day own the farm.

Roy Meyer's review of *Son of Earth* was not charitable, "characters are largely caricatures, dialogue is wooden, and many events (such as Tolf's reaction to his unhappy love affair) are overdrawn."[12] The review surprised me, as I found the novel compelling and written with an authentic knowledge of the subject. As it turns out, Mari Sandoz agreed. After reading the novel, she felt compelled to write to Erickson "to tell you how much I enjoyed *Son of Earth*." She went on,

> I have read many so-called farm novels and generally with little approaching enjoyment. They are usually frankly back-to-the-farm propaganda or sugary pseudo-farm stories written by nice ladies in small towns or what is still worse, if possible, brutal behind the barn scenes by oversexed young New Yorkers. In *Son of Earth* I find a good story told sincerely and honestly.[13]

Mr. Erickson was impressed. He wrote in a return letter: "Thank you for writing me about *Son of Earth*. Words of appreciation are always welcomed by us of the writing craft, particularly if the words are from a craftsman."[14]

Alvin Johnson

Alvin Saunders Johnson was born on a farm near Homer, Nebraska, in 1874. He attended a country school and later made his way to the University of Nebraska where he majored in classics, graduating in 1897. In 1902 Johnson earned a Ph.D. in economics at Columbia University in New York. He then began a very long professorial career, teaching at various times for Columbia, Stanford, the University of Texas, the University of Nebraska, the University of Chicago, and The New School for Social Science Research. In fact, Johnson later became president of The New School and led a crusade to rescue German scholars threatened by Hitler's regime. During World War II, he orchestrated a similar campaign to bring exiled French scholars to The New School.

During the worst years of the Depression, Johnson decided to try his hand at fiction, writing *Spring Storm*, which was published in 1936. Accompanying the manuscript, Johnson included a letter to Mr. Alfred Knopf, of Knopf Publishing. Said Johnson,

> Perhaps I ought to offer an apology to the craft of novelists in breaking in to their mystery. I was once an ardent classical scholar; then an economic theorist; then an editor of a liberal journal; then an encyclopaedist; then an educational administrator: what training could such a career offer for serious fiction? The history of literature has, however, reserved a modest place to the outsider. At least he has from time to time brought into literature additional material. The craft itself is the guardian of form, but form takes on life only when abundant and appropriate material is at hand.[15]

By any measure, *Spring Storm* was a success. It became a Book of the Month Club selection. The novel is generally considered semi-autobiographical, as it focuses on a family who purchased a rather large piece of land on the Nebraska side of the Missouri River. Julian, the only son of Mr. and Mrs. Howard, grows from adolescence into manhood during the years of the novel, and he is able to keep his father from making costly mistakes. Sadly, Harriet Howard, Julian's mother, passes away during his teen years. Living alone with his father proved difficult. To complicate matters further, Julian fell in love with the young wife of an older neighbor. The drama culminates in two choices faced by Julian, either run away with the woman he loves, a move that would severely disappoint his father, or go off alone to the university in Lincoln. He chooses the latter. A young college-bound woman seated next to Julian on the train strikes up a conversation, and the novel ends.

Conclusion

It should be stressed that this list of "unheralded" novelists is not nearly exhaustive. As mentioned at the start, Frederick Manfred is the subject of another chapter in this volume and consequently not dealt with here. Similar to Johnson, although perhaps not in terms of quality, there have been many non-writers who published autobiographical novels at the end of their careers. For example, Tom McHale, born in Sioux City in 1902, but a real estate executive in Dallas for most of his career, published a novel at the age of 70 about his Irish Catholic upbringing in Sioux City entitled *Dooley's Delusion*. Mary Worthy Thurston enlisted the help of her daughter, Muriel Breneman, to write a novel loosely based on her childhood on a farm in eastern South Dakota. They used the lives of Mary's parents as the main characters. They decided to combine their names into Mary Worthy Breneman for publication of *The Land They Possessed*. It was released by Macmillan in 1956 and was moderately successful. It was republished by the South Dakota Committee on the Humanities in 1991. Lucille Fargo, who spent many of her young years in Dell Rapids, South Dakota, went on to have a distinguished career as a librarian in Washington state. She published an autobiographical novel about a girl growing up in South Dakota called *Prairie Girl* in 1937.

Like Wallace Stegner, who was born just east of Siouxland, Curtis Harnack, from Remsen, Iowa, squarely within Siouxland, doesn't qualify as "unheralded." He had a long career as a writer of fiction and nonfiction plus a widely applauded memoir, *We Have All Gone Away* (1973). After graduating from Grinnell College, Harnack moved to New York City for graduate work at Columbia University. The city was destined to become his home, although most of his literary work centered on his experiences growing up on the Iowa prairie. Harnack was involved as president of Yaddo, the artists' retreat in Saratoga Springs, New York, and he also served as the president of the School of American Ballet in New York City.

In addition to O. E. Rölvaag, Siouxland holds some claim to Laura Ingalls Wilder and Rose Wilder Lane as well, but, again, they hardly qualify as unheralded. Still, taken together, those who acquired a national following (with work still in print), and those who did not (and their work long out of print), the number of novelists emanating from Siouxland during the twentieth century is truly impressive, and their literary contributions merit twenty-first century readers.

Notes

1 Marcia Noe, "Herbert Krause" in *Dictionary of Midwestern Literature*, vol. 1, ed. Philip A. Greasley (Bloomington: Indiana University Press, 2001), 303.

2 Publisher's Note: O. E. Rölvaag's *Giants in the Earth*, as well as the other two novels in his "prairie trilogy," all originally written in Norwegian, is set in the Big Sioux River valley, northeast of Sioux Falls. For these novels, he drew upon the recollections of the second-generation immigrants he met while working during the 1890s on the Sivert Eiden farm at Elk Point, South Dakota. Rölvaag also drew upon the experiences of Andrew and Karen Berdahl, settler pioneers on Slip-Up Creek, near Garretson. He came to know the Berdahls through their sons John and James, fellow students at Augustana Academy, in Canton, South Dakota, which he attended once he had saved enough money from farm work. They, in turn, introduced him to their sister, Jennie, who later became Rölvaag's wife. For an account of the historical basis of Rölvaag's novels, see Clarence Berdahl, "The Slip-Up Settlement and Ole Rölvaag," in *A Common Land, A Diverse People: Ethnic Identity on the Prairie Plains*, ed. Harry F. Thompson, Arthur R. Huseboe, and Sandra Olsen Looney (Sioux Falls: Nordland Heritage Foundation, 1987), 41-49.

3 Reviewer quotations taken from book jacket of Herbert Krause's second novel, *The Thresher* (Indianapolis: Bobbs-Merrill, 1946).

4 Arthur R. Huseboe, ed., *Poems and Essays of Herbert Krause* (Sioux Falls: Center for Western Studies), 31.

5 Quotations from Herbert Krause are from the book jacket of his third novel, *The Oxcart Trail*, (Indianapolis: Bobbs-Merrill, 1954).

6 All of Krause's novels, poems, and essays, including a separate collection of his ornithological essays, are available in print from the Center for Western Studies.

7 Clarence A. Andrews, *A Literary History of Iowa* (Iowa City: University of Iowa Press, 1972), 38.

8 Joan A. Buckley, "Martha Ostenso: A Critical Study of Her Novels" (Ph.D. diss., University of Iowa, 1976).

9 Andrews, *A Literary History*, 70-71.

10 Wallace Stegner, "The Trail of the Hawkeye," *Saturday Review of Literature*, July 30, 1938, 3-4.

11 Edward O'Brien, ed., *The Best Short Stories of 1916* (Boston: Small, Maynard and Company, 1917), 378.

12 Roy W. Meyer, *The Middle Western Farm Novel in the Twentieth Century* (Lincoln: University of Nebraska Press, 1965), 210

13 Mari Sandoz Collection (MS 0080). Archives & Special Collections, University of Nebraska–Lincoln Libraries.

14 Mari Sandoz Collection (MS 0081).

15 Letter is quoted verbatim on the book jacket of Alvin Johnson's *Spring Storm* (New York: Alfred A. Knopf, 1936).

Chapter 10

The Origins of "Siouxland"

Lance Nixon

In an otherwise insightful essay about Frederick Manfred, fellow novelist Wallace Stegner shows what may be a common misunderstanding about a key feature of Manfred's work: the origin of the name "Siouxland" that Manfred gave to that part of Iowa, Minnesota, South Dakota, and Nebraska in which he set many of his novels. Stegner seems to suggest that Manfred coined the term for the setting of his regional fiction because he wrote about the area once dominated by the Sioux Indian tribes in one of the most colorful periods of the region's history. Stegner writes: "As I have indicated, he seems to me more successful in his historical and more romantic fiction than in his realistic stories of contemporary farm and town people: the very fact that he calls his chosen country Siouxland rather than Cornland or Hogland is an indication of where his imagination hankers."[1]

Stegner, who won both a Pulitzer Prize and a National Book Award for his own remarkable fiction, here interprets "Siouxland" as an appeal to history and romanticism in contrast to a more contemporary term that might better reflect the region's agriculture-driven economy—as though the "Siouxland" that Manfred had in mind is something like the Edward S. Curtis photograph "In the Land of the Sioux." In that image from the third volume of his portfolios of Native America, Curtis photographed three Oglala Sioux men, Red Hawk, Crazy Thunder, and Holy Skin, crossing a wet area in the prairie on horseback as they accompanied the photographer on a trip into the South Dakota Badlands.[2] In fact, what Stegner implies is not a bad supposition, for Manfred did indeed toy with the idea of "Land of the Sioux" as one of a number of variants before settling on "Siouxland."[3]

Stegner is certainly right that Manfred's most successful fiction deals with the colorful history of the region's frontier days. Manfred's novel about the epic crawl of mountain man Hugh Glass across part of what is now central South Dakota, *Lord Grizzly*, and four of his other frontier novels make up the celebrated Buckskin Man Tales. Manfred once explained those works as his own attempt to provide a written past for his region, since there were no earlier authors on whose work he could build. Manfred wrote: "I wanted echoes of an earlier American time in my novels. By writing about Hugh Glass and others, I'd be my own progenitor. I would father myself. Once I had determined that, a whole new concept of my role as writer sprang into my head. I'd create a long hallway of literary murals, from 1800 and on to the day I died, of life in Middle America. It would be a history, in fiction, of our country."[4]

Because several of the Buckskin Man Tales deal with the Sioux Indians at least in part—and at length in *Conquering Horse* and *Scarlet Plume*—it is easy to assume that Manfred coined "Siouxland" solely as a way of acknowledging their presence and importance in the region. Even University of South Dakota scholar John R. Milton, a great student and promoter of Manfred's work and South Dakota literature in general, seemed to suggest that was the source of the name. Milton wrote of *Lord Grizzly*, "As a portrait of Western Man it has been filled out by four additional novels, all set in the region once inhabited by the Sioux, a region Manfred calls 'Siouxland.'"[5]

But as this essay will show, the deciding factor in why Frederick Manfred chose the name was a matter of geography, not history—because the Big Sioux River and its watershed define the physical geography of his home region. In a 1993 interview, Manfred made it clear that "Siouxland" ultimately derives from the river valley, although the fact that the river was named for the Sioux Indians—the people who identify themselves as the Dakota, Nakota, and Lakota peoples—is an important secondary consideration.

Frederick Manfred was still writing under the name Feike Feikema when he first conceived a map of Siouxland in 1946, publishing it inside the front cover and back cover of his 1947 novel, *This is the Year*. A glance at that map shows clearly that Manfred's Siouxland is not romantic geography stranded in Old West history. The map shows the borders where the present-day states of Minnesota, Iowa, South Dakota, and Nebraska come together, and it includes such landmarks as "Sioux Indian School" in Flandreau, South Dakota, and the present-day cities of Sioux Falls and Sioux City.[6] Also, a map of "Pier's Farm and neighborhood," referring to the protagonist of the novel, occupies the page next to the Siouxland map inside the back cover,[7] an indication that both maps were offered up to readers as present-day geography to the characters in that novel.

Furthermore, it quickly becomes apparent to one studying Manfred's map that what dominates it is the river systems—Big Sioux River, its tributaries, and the Missouri River. Included on the map are both real and fictional places from Manfred's writing. This "fictive region," writes John Calvin Rezmerski, is "a kind of alternate world in which there is a town called Bonnie where our world has a town named Doon, in which Savage has been replaced by Brokenhoe and Luverne is named Whitebone, and in which nevertheless, Sioux Falls is still Sioux Falls and Minneapolis and St. Paul are still the Twin Cities."[8]

It would seem that Manfred is using the physical and cultural geography of a real place as a stage on which his characters are acting out the stories of his novels, using both real and fictional locations as props against which the action plays out. It's so effective that by now, as Rezmerski goes on to say, the term "Siouxland" has come to epitomize, at least for Midwest readers, Frederick Manfred's literature of place. "He coined the name 'Siouxland' to refer to the region in which most of his work is set: Minnesota, South Dakota, Iowa, and Nebraska, and especially the region where those states meet near the confluence of the Big Sioux and Missouri rivers. The name 'Siouxland' has entered the vernacular and is now used by both scholars and business people to describe the region once ranged by the tribes called Sioux, an area with its own characteristic pattern of social, economic, and cultural evolution."[9]

But in Manfred's writing, it's clear that an actual waterway, the Big Sioux River, is the seam that runs through Siouxland to help sew it all together. For example, in his 1979 reminiscence of a 1934 hitchhiking trip, *The Wind Blows Free*, Manfred tells of getting into a debate in his mind with the writer O. E. Rölvaag, the Norwegian immigrant author of the classic novel about prairie homesteading in Dakota Territory, *Giants in the Earth*. In Manfred's imagination, the debate is about whether Siouxland should ever have been plowed or been left to ranching instead. What is noteworthy is that Manfred gets into this imaginary discussion about Siouxland while hitching his first ride west through gullies and deep ravines as the wooded country along the Big Sioux River comes into view near the town of Canton, South Dakota.[10]

It's also apparent from Manfred's writing and from his own experience that physical rivers were important to him, both as part of the landscape of the area he loved and for their utility as metaphors. Manfred's 1976 novel, *Milk of Wolves*, ends with a chapter telling how his protagonist follows the Big Rock River in southwest Minnesota (one of the features included on Manfred's 1946 map of Siouxland) to its point of origin.[11] Manfred made it clear in an interview that he once spent two days making that same hike to the river's source.[12]

As he's about to set off on that journey, Manfred's protagonist in *Milk of Wolves*, Juhl Melander, tells himself, "A man should have a picture of his river in his head, all of it."[13] And as he arrives at the source of the Big Rock River, Melander observes, looking back on his own life as a stonecutter, "The whole river of it was worth having."[14]

Just as in his fiction, Manfred uses the metaphor of a river in his correspondence, too. A letter to William Van O'Connor in January 1949 discusses T.S. Eliot's "objective correlative"—Eliot's term for a formula a poet uses to evoke a certain response in the reader. For Manfred, that requires a style that uses "as clear a stream as possible, so that as it courses along we can sometimes see, when the river-bed deepens, the terrible rocks below, so that we can see, when the river-bed shallows, the lovely stones in the ford."[15] In speaking of *Riders of Judgment*, Manfred once likened writing the first draft of a novel to "trying to swim across a river with a rope in your mouth. And once you're across you know how to get the rest of the bridge over."[16]

What went into Manfred's thinking as he coined "Siouxland" as the name for his home geography? I asked him that question once when, as a graduate student in English searching for a possible thesis topic, I had the chance to interview the novelist. The interview took place in Manfred's work room, just above grass level in the prairie at his house near Luverne, Minnesota. It was a Friday, June 18, 1993. I was a journalist for the *Grand Forks Herald* newspaper in North Dakota at the time and a graduate student at the University of North Dakota. I recorded the interview and made a transcript shortly afterward, though I didn't do a thesis about Manfred, in the end.

When I asked Manfred about Siouxland, he gestured to a map on one wall and said:

> Right up there it is. Nineteen forty-six I drew the map. It came out in the pages of *This is the Year*. And after that it was picked up everywhere around here. The reason I did that, I got tired when I was doing *This is the Year* of mentioning Norfolk, Nebraska, Sioux Falls, South Dakota, Sioux City, Iowa, and Worthington, Minnesota. And I got to thinking: Those people who read this are going to think, My God, they've got to travel a hundred miles to get a loaf of bread. But we never mention the states. We just say we're going to Norfolk, or we're going to Sioux Falls, or we're going to Sioux City or Worthington. We never mention it. Nobody pays any attention to state lines here. The only reason is the Mann Act, a man's not supposed to transport a woman across state lines and screw her, he could go to jail for that. I got sick of that and I thought, I've got to find a name for the area that I'm going to spend most of my life writing about. It hit me that this is really the Big Sioux River drainage basin, of which the Rock River is a part and the Vermillion River and so on. They all flow down to the Missouri at Sioux City. So I had different names for it, Land of the Sioux and so on, and finally I decided on Siouxland.[17]

The second page of Manfred's Prelude to that 1947 novel confirms that it is indeed a watershed that Manfred has in mind as he introduces the word "Siouxland." Describing a robin's spring migration north, Manfred writes: "At last, in late March, he arrived in Siouxland. He wheeled over the oak-crested, doming hills north of Sioux City, flew up the Big Sioux River, resting in elms and basswoods....He flew on, over Last Chance, Iowa, and Welcome, South Dakota, over the Big Sioux Bridge that tied the two together."[18]

Amazingly, it seems that Manfred's pondering and his subsequent choice of a term for his home geography supplied something that was lacking in the public discourse, for soon after his 1947 novel appeared, "Siouxland" became a common term in the area. As the Sioux City Public Library's *Book Remarks*, a monthly newsletter, noted in an article in May 1991, the term was pressed into service as early as summer 1948 by *Sioux City Journal* sports editor Alex Stoddard. Also in that year, Orlyn A. Swartz renamed the business he had just purchased "Siouxland Finance Co."—the first of many regional businesses with similar names. By 1990 the Sioux City telephone directory listed sixty-five businesses or entities using Siouxland or variations in their names (Sioux Land, Soo Land, Sooland). The Sioux Falls directory listed eleven such businesses.[19]

Clearly the term remains popular in 2021. An internet search on May 14, 2021, quickly turned up such examples as Siouxland District Health, in Woodbury County, Iowa; Siouxland Libraries in Sioux Falls; Siouxland Ethanol in Jackson, Nebraska; Siouxland Energy Cooperative in Sioux Center, Iowa; Siouxland Machine Inc. of Rock Valley, Iowa; Siouxland Oral Surgery of Sioux Falls, Mitchell, Brookings, and Yankton, South Dakota. There are many more such instances where "Siouxland" is part of a name for an organization or event.

Perhaps the closest parallel to the success of Siouxland in the way it has been embraced by its regional public is in the way variations of A. B. Guthrie, Jr.'s term "the Big Sky," from his novel of the same name, have come to be used by residents of the state of Montana to refer to their home geography. Coincidentally, Guthrie's novel about the fur trade era in Montana appears in 1947, the same year in which Manfred's "Siouxland" is introduced. The irony is that Guthrie didn't actually come up with the term, "the big sky"—his publisher did while reading some of Guthrie's autobiographical notes while casting about for a title for Guthrie's novel.[20] Manfred's perhaps hasty judgment of A. B. Guthrie and his novels *The Big Sky* and *The Way West*—"much overrated" Manfred wrote in a letter on Christmas Day 1954,[21] even though Guthrie had already won a Pulitzer Prize in 1950 for *The Way West*—overlooks the way Guthrie, like Manfred, has coined a distinct term for his chosen geography that will quickly be embraced by the public. Arguably, it is the most powerful, pithiest prose either author ever wrote—conjuring the essence of a real place into a single word or phrase.

What is particularly noteworthy about Manfred's term is the pleasing ambiguity of "Siouxland." The word evokes in most readers images of a Plains Indian tribe, but it also speaks a river's name. In that June 1993 interview, discussing how "Siouxland" was embraced by the region, Manfred made it clear that many area residents had leaped to the same conclusion that readers such as Wallace Stegner had in thinking the name referred solely to the Sioux Indians. Many area residents misunderstood his intent to suggest the geography of the Big Sioux River basin, and they also introduced variations of "Siouxland" that seemed to Manfred to be inaccurate characterizations of Sioux Indians.

Manfred said: "And it was picked up everywhere. Sioux City was the first. Within a month they were broadcasting over the radio, 'Serving greater Siouxland.' See, I didn't pay attention to all the states, I just said 'Siouxland.' Sioux Falls did the same thing, but then they got nervous because they didn't want the same thing Sioux City had, so then they called it 'the Sioux Empire.' I've written a couple letters to the paper there telling them this is silly, the Indians were the last people to think of empires. They lived in bunches of fifty, fifty families, and they were nomads. But that's the white man's notion, see, he's always got to be a conqueror."[22]

Manfred's designation of Siouxland has been so influential that there is now a Wikipedia entry discussing the term. The discussion at that page makes it clear, however, that there is broad disagreement over the boundaries of Siouxland and the communities it includes. The website lists no less than twenty-nine Iowa communities that are usually considered part of Siouxland, twenty-two Nebraska communities, ten South Dakota communities and only one Minnesota community

(Luverne, Minnesota, where Manfred lived for much of his life).[23] Yet the Wikipedia list leaves out several communities that are clearly shown on Manfred's original map of Siouxland from his 1947 novel (Tea, Salem, Baltic and Flandreau, in South Dakota, and Pipestone in Minnesota).[24] Arguably, what the list from the website represents is the Sioux City region's early acceptance of the term Siouxland, and perhaps a lack of understanding that Manfred was thinking of the Big Sioux River watershed when he coined the term.

Importantly, the Wikipedia entry does note that there are changing conceptions of Siouxland in its discussion of the related term "Sioux Empire," noting that several counties around Sioux Falls as well as portions of southwest Minnesota are "part of Manfred's original conception of Siouxland." Observing that the major cities in Siouxland are Sioux City and Sioux Falls, the online encyclopedia's entry adds that Norfolk, Nebraska, is another prominent city in the area "but this city is marginally in what is considered to be Siouxland." The same discussion makes no mention of Worthington, Minnesota.[25] Yet in the passage from the June 1993 interview cited above, Manfred clearly includes those two cities along with Sioux Falls and Sioux City as major communities within Siouxland.

Perhaps more important than what "Siouxland" signifies to readers is what it signified about Frederick Manfred the novelist. It marked him as a regionalist, as Joseph M. Flora noted in a 1974 monograph about Manfred's decision to live and write in Luverne, Minnesota. "While the Big Sioux River Valley had long been a fertile part of Manfred's imagination and the setting for many novels and stories, he was coming home to Siouxland—his name for that area of South Dakota, Minnesota, Iowa, and Nebraska—as if to confirm his dedication to the task of completing a series of novels that would give an accurate picture of this Upper Midlands country from 1800 to his death." [26]

In the June 1993 interview, asked whether his close ties to Siouxland make him destined to be remembered as a regional writer, Manfred seemed to bristle, and then embrace the term, linking it with a similar term—"provincial." It's fitting to note here that novelist Wallace Stegner, in the same passage in which he described Manfred as "a gigantic and gifted primitive, intelligent, vastly energetic, pretty much self-educated," also offered his opinion that Manfred was "a shade too provincial in his point of view."[27] Manfred, in turn, said Stegner "hasn't really made up his mind whether he is West or East."[28] Manfred may have had that discussion in mind when he responded to my question about whether he is marked as a regional writer. He said: "Well then, then Cervantes is regional when he writes about La Mancha. And Steinbeck is, (writing) about Salinas Valley, Faulkner is, writing about down there. And Hardy is, about Wessex. And in a kind of curious way, Shakespeare is, too. He writes about the royalty in London. That's provincial, too. I think almost everybody living east of the Hudson River is very provincial."[29]

Manfred went on to suggest that being pigeonholed as regional is "the Easterners' way of putting you down" and he began discussing different writers in terms of how much they were the products of urban versus small-town or rural environments—clearly a topic he had discussed before.

> I was doing that one time with a bunch of guys from New York. They said, 'Well, what about Melville?' 'Well,' I said, 'he was raised near Albany, which was a little, small town at that time. And he lived in Pittsfield when he wrote *Moby Dick*. And he finally went to New York in his old age when he thought he was a failure. He worked for the government then in the customs house. And they tried to list some other ones, but if you look at it closely, they really are small-town. Like Hemingway. Well, he was born in Oak Park. That was sort of a dormitory town to Chicago, but it really was a small town. Faulkner was born in a small town, Steinbeck in a small town. Fitzgerald was born in Saint Paul, although at that time Saint Paul was a small place. But that's why he never became great, because he was exposed to too much city. You get to see the whole stratification of society in a small town. You get to see all the different grades there. The upper crust, the banker and the preacher and the mayor, and then down below that are your other stratifications, and then down below that are your plebeians and your lowly worker types.[30]

Here it is important to note that Manfred is not alone among writers in believing that he senses an Eastern prejudice against Westerners. Pulitzer Prize-winning novelist Marilynne Robinson, who has won critical acclaim for novels such as *Gilead* and *Housekeeping*, expresses a similar thought in one of her essays. She writes: "I went to college in New England and I have lived in Massachusetts for twenty years, and I find that the hardest work in the world—it may in fact be impossible—is to persuade Easterners that growing up in the West is not intellectually crippling. On learning that I am from Idaho, people have not infrequently asked, 'Then how were you able to write a book?'"[31] Robinson confides that she has sometimes let puzzled Easterners believe it was her education at an eastern college that taught her to write; but in her essay she tells that it had more to do with her own intellectual life as "a bookish child in the far West."[32]

Similarly, Siouxland was formative for Manfred for more than its geography. In a figurative sense, it provided the rich soil of a rural area in which language and storytelling could flourish in contrast to the East. Manfred explains this contrast as having something to do with the difference between the writers Henry James and Mark Twain. In an extemporaneous speech given November 12, 1966, at Pullman, Washington, "On Being a Western American Writer," Manfred speaks of the "Siouxland language" that he learned on the farm and in small towns while growing up. He told his audience it was as worthy of preservation as the vernacular around Hannibal, Missouri, that Mark Twain used in his novels.[33] Manfred recalled that at Calvin College in Grand Rapids, Michigan, where he attended, two of his teachers tried to make him write like Henry James:

> But in truth I was a Mark Twain man. It took some while for me to understand that my natural tongue, the language I talked back home in Siouxland, was not English but something else. It was English-American. A different language.
>
> This understanding has become very important to this someone who lives west of the Mississippi and who writes about the Midlands and the Far West. It is my conviction that a new language is being created out here west of the Mississippi.[34]

Manfred went on to suggest that language had to change violently but naturally as settlers moved into the interior of North America, encountering weather and landforms they needed to talk about in new ways. "The swamps and the mountains, the heat and the cold, the rainstorms and the snowstorms (or as we Western Americans say now, 'the cloudbursts and the blizzards'), the grasslands and the deserts, all these new things, were something the users of the English language had to somehow describe and, if possible, accept. And this is what the Western American writer is doing more than any other American writer."

Surely there is some validity to what Manfred is saying. Walter Prescott Webb's classic study, *The Great Plains*, gives an etymology for blizzard (possibly derived from *blitzartig*, lighning-like) and seems to concur with Manfred in locating the weather phenomenon's true home not far from Siouxland: "Blizzards occur rarely in the East, and their real home is on the northern Plains."[35] Similarly, there are other instances in which the interior of America dictated new terms. Patrick Gass, a member of the Lewis and Clark Expedition, later published his own journal of that expedition, in which he finds it necessary early on to footnote the word "prairie" for his readers ("Prairies are natural meadows, or pastures without trees and covered with grass.").[36]

Manfred argues that new phenomena such as tornadoes in the interior of North America demanded new words. "It's as though a place finds its voice through whatever creatures happen to live in that place, rooted or footed, trees or people moving about; as though a place shapes a people and then shapes the language they use.…We all can't help but be shaped by the place in which we live. That is something that the Eastern critic and the Eastern scholar and the Eastern reviewer and the Eastern editor can't get through his head. He keeps thinking we should talk and write like he does."[37]

One could argue that Frederick Manfred's homegrown term for the Big Sioux River valley and its larger cultural region is itself an example of what he is talking about. "Siouxland" is a new word that a writer from a western watershed has added to the English language to describe a region with a distinct history and way of life. Manfred might even have argued that the river valley itself has conjured up the term, for in speaking of western writers, Manfred went so far as to suggest there is "a primordial voice that is still alive in the American land and that speaks through us."[38]

In the end, what may have been most important about Siouxland to the writer Frederick Manfred is what it *wasn't*—it wasn't the East; it couldn't be described in terms an Eastern writer such as Henry James might use. Here is where Sioux City Public Library Director George H. Scheetz's 1991 discussion of Siouxland as a "vernacular region" is singularly apt, for the term sums up the shared history, interests and identity of people with a strong, mutual sense of place.[39] The Siouxland of Frederick Manfred is emphatically such a region, named by a writer who is proudly regional and provincial. His work is rooted in the western soil and fertile language and stories told by those people who dwell in a river valley where Iowa and Minnesota brush shoulders with South Dakota and Nebraska.

Notes

[1] Wallace Stegner, Foreword, in *Conversations with Frederick Manfred*, moderated by John R. Milton (Salt Lake City: The University of Utah Press, 1974), xiv.

[2] Edward S. Curtis, *The North American Indian: The Complete Portfolios* (Cologne: Taschen Bibliotheca Universalis, 2018), 143.

[3] Frederick Manfred, interview by author, June 18, 1993 (original typescript in archives of the Center for Western Studies, Augustana University), 10.

[4] Frederick Feikema Manfred, "The Making of Lord Grizzly," *South Dakota History* 15:3: 214-15.

[5] John R. Milton, Foreword, *Lord Grizzly*, Bison Book edition (Lincoln: University of Nebraska Press, 1983), xii.

[6] Frederick Manfred (Feike Feikema), map of Siouxland, *This is the Year* (Garden City: Doubleday & Co. Inc., 1947), inside front and back covers. The map is also available in Harry F. Thompson, "Preface—West from Here," in *The Interior Borderlands: Regional Identity in the Midwest and Great Plains*, ed. Jon K. Lauck (Sioux Falls: Center for Western Studies, 2019, xviii.

[7] Frederick Manfred, map of Pier's Farm and neighborhood, *This is the Year*, inside back cover.

[8] John Calvin Rezmerski, introduction to *The Frederick Manfred Reader*, ed. John Calvin Rezmerski (Duluth: Holy Cow! Press, 1996), xv. For examples of the critical reception to Manfred's novels, see Nancy Owen Nelson, ed., *The Lizard Speaks: Essays on the Writings of Frederick Manfred* (Sioux Falls: Center for Western Studies, 1998).

[9] Ibid., xvii.

[10] Frederick Manfred, *The Wind Blows Free* (Sioux Falls: Center for Western Studies, 1979), 13.

[11] Frederick Manfred, *Milk of Wolves* (Boston: Avenue Victor Hugo, 1976), 248-50.

[12] Manfred, interview by author, 7.

[13] Manfred, *Milk of Wolves*, 248.

[14] Ibid., 250.

[15] Frederick Manfred, *The Selected Letters of Frederick Manfred, 1932-1954*, ed. Arthur R. Huseboe and Nancy Owen Nelson (Lincoln: University of Nebraska Press, 1988), 273.

[16] Frederick Manfred, *Conversations with Frederick Manfred*, moderated by John R. Milton (Salt Lake City: The University of Utah Press, 1974), 73.

[17] Frederick Manfred, interview by author, 9-10. See also Manfred's definition of a resident of Siouxland in his essay "The Siouxlander," in Frederick Manfred, *Duke's Mixture* (Sioux Falls: Center for Western Studies, 1994), 221-27.

[18] Manfred, *This is the Year*, xii.

[19] George H. Scheetz, "Whence Siouxland?" *Book Remarks* (Sioux City Public Library), May 1991, 2.

[20] A. B. Guthrie, Jr., *The Blue Hen's Chick: An Autobiography* (Lincoln: University of Nebraska Press, 1993), 172.

[21] Manfred, *The Selected Letters of Frederick Manfred*, 401.

[22] Manfred, interview by author, 10.

[23] Wikipedia, "Siouxland," accessed January 17, 2021, https://en.wikipedia.org/wiki/Siouxland.

[24] Frederick Manfred, *This is the Year*, map of Siouxland.

[25] Wikipedia, "Siouxland," accessed Dec. 31, 2020, https://en.wikipedia.org/wiki/Siouxland.

[26] Joseph M. Flora, "Frederick Manfred," Western Writers Series, No. 13 (Boise: Boise State University, 1974), 8-9.

[27] Stegner, Foreword, in *Conversations with Frederick Manfred*, xiv.

[28] Manfred, *Conversations with Frederick Manfred*, 155.

[29] Manfred, interview by author, 9.

[30] Ibid.

[31] "Marilynne Robinson, "When I was a Child," in *When I Was a Child I Read Books* (New York: Farrar, Straus and Giroux, 2012), 85-86.

[32] Ibid, 87.

[33] Frederick Manfred, "On Being a Western Writer," in *Prime Fathers* (Salt Lake City: Howe Brothers, 1988), 128.

[34] Ibid.

[35] Walter Prescott Webb, *The Great Plains* (New York: Grosset & Dunlap, 1931), 25.

[36] Patrick Gass, *A Journal of the Voyages and Travels or a Corps of Discovery Under the Command of Capt. Lewis and Capt. Clarke of the Army of the United States, from the Mouth of the River Missouri through the Interior Parts of North America to the Pacific Ocean, During the Years 1804, 1805 and 1806.* (Minneapolis: Ross & Haines, 1958), 17.

[37] Manfred, "On Being a Western Writer," 133.

[38] Ibid.

[39] Scheetz, 1.

Chapter 11

Lorena King Fairbank and John King Fairbank: South Dakotan Cosmopolitans

Gregory Rohlf
University of the Pacific

In 1982 John King Fairbank was asked to reminisce about his child-hood years in South Dakota for the *Sioux Falls Argus Leader*.[1] Fair-bank was born in 1907 in Huron and spent his childhood in Sioux Falls. He went on to a fifty-year career as professor of modern Chinese history at Harvard University and became one of the most influential shapers of U.S. public opinion toward China in the twentieth century. His publications reached a wide audience, but his influence was felt more broadly through his training of scores of graduate students who filled faculty ranks across North America; and through his public advo-cacy for China studies as an interdisciplinary and social science-driven enterprise that was vital to U.S. interests.[2] In part because of his long career at Harvard—he was an undergraduate student there, too—he appeared to some to be a quintessentially blue-blooded New England gentleman-scholar. After leaving South Dakota, he was educated and polished up at elite Anglo-American institutions: Phillips Exeter Acad-emy, Harvard College, and at Balliol and Oxford in England. But Fair-bank was purposefully a man of the world, a cosmopolitan, rather than a stuffy provincial. Some found him to be a personification of China, an inscrutable "mandarin," a Confucian-style gentleman who gladly shared his home with his students and visiting scholars. Fairbank and his wife and fellow China scholar, Wilma, hosted countless graduate students for afternoon teas at their home near the Harvard campus and at their New Hampshire mountain cottage for weekend retreats. He was revered by his students as an intimidating but kind teacher with an impish wit. Yet in 1982, just after his retirement from Harvard, when Fairbank recalled his childhood, he suggested that South Dakota had always been with him. He recalled for readers of the *Argus Leader* that the two-week trip to the Badlands and Black Hills of western South Dakota in 1914 "beat anything I ever experienced later in the U.S.A., Europe, Japan or China."[3]

In this chapter we examine John King Fairbank as a cosmopolitan South Dakotan at home in the world but always attached to his place of birth. We will see that this quality was no accident and was not generated solely by his personality, birthplace, schooling, or travels. In his memoir, Fairbank credited his mother, Lorena, with being the greatest influence on him, in particular his aspiration to a worldly education and globe-trotting habits that led him far from home.[4] In fact, Lorena King Fairbank was a formidable and accomplished woman in her own right. Although son John achieved fame as a nationally- and internationally-renowned China scholar, his mother had a more profound and enduring influence on South Dakota through her pioneering work in the American Association of University Women. Here we examine the lives of John King Fairbank (1907-1991) and his mother Lorena King Fairbank (1874-1979) to better understand the role of place in historical processes and identity formation. We will consider the mother and son together as a lineage of South Dakotans shaped by a particularly important phase in the history of the state and the Big Sioux River valley. Although the arcs of their lives were different, and ranged far and permanently distant from their heartland places of birth, South Dakota stayed with them in observable ways.

Lorena King Fairbank, Educator, Dramatist, and Social Reformer

Lorena's life story shows the imprint of the unquenchable impulse to build a public life of consequence through liberal personal and social striving powered by higher learning. She was one of four daughters— Gwyneth, twins Lorena and Leona, and Grace—born to John H. and

Permelia King. The drive that animated Lorena's life certainly drew in part from her father's adventurous and high-achieving example. John H. King (1845-1906) was a mover and shaker in the settlement and opening of Dakota Territory. He was born on an Iowa farm, studied law, was admitted to the Iowa bar in 1870, and was elected to two terms in the Iowa statehouse, starting in 1877. Though seemingly poised for a distinguished career as a lawyer and legislator in his state of birth, he resigned his seat in the middle of his second term and departed for Dakota Territory in 1880 with Permelia, his daughters and a group of settlers to found the town of Chamberlain.[5] But John King was no humble homesteader. He rubbed shoulders with senators and federal officials in the land politics leading up to statehood for North Dakota and South Dakota as well as the politicking between cattlemen, settlers, and Indians.[6] The family moved between Chamberlain, Rapid City, and Huron over two decades, with trips to the nation's capital mixed in. King took his daughters, Lorena and Gwyneth, to two presidential inaugural balls, Gwyneth to Republican William McKinley's and Lorena to Democrat Grover Cleveland's second term.[7] A newspaperman called King the "biggest toad in the puddle" in 1888 for his work lobbying Congress to gain speedy access to Sioux lands that were being held back from settlement.[8] At his death in 1906 in Huron, "Colonel" John H. King was remembered as one of the most important and well-known citizens in the state.[9]

The King girls moved to Dakota Territory in the 1880s when the lines between the Anglo world and the Indian world were not yet as defined and hardened as they would soon become. Gwyneth's reminiscences about a trip down the Missouri River in 1881 as a teenager offers a window into the world Lorena grew up in.[10] On that riverboat trip, a party of four teenaged girls and their chaperones traveled from Chamberlain to Fort Randall, where Chief Sitting Bull was being held after returning to the U.S. from Canada. Gwyneth recalled that on more than one occasion during the multi-day trip, Sioux men asked of the girls' chaperones if they could buy one of the girls with a number of ponies. That the offer was even made and freely declined with amusement rather than indignation, horror, or disgust, suggests the way in which inter-ethnic relations were "in play" at this historical moment.[11] Gwyneth recalled a sense of unsettledness about white-Indian relations, remarking that the "[purchase] offer was unusual because they [the Indian men] could scarcely have been unaware that in this section white women did not marry Indians."[12] At Fort Randall she interacted with Sitting Bill, his mother, and other Indian women through an interpreter and in their encampments. In her reminiscence 60 years later, she recalled the exchanges with respect and admiration for Sitting Bull and the Sioux:

> He looked the commander, the leader. But he appeared in no sense pompous. It seemed a benevolent face. Yet here was the victor of what was recorded as the worst massacre in our history. When General Custer led an attack on Sitting Bull's tribe in 1876, not one white man of that battalion was left alive. Although there was now a touch of pathos and humor about this figure in the shabby, unpressed army suit, no army officer could have worn it with greater dignity.[13]

Gwyneth's memory may have been burnished by the subsequent destruction of Indian dominance in these lands and the conversion of the territory into a U.S. state in 1889. This process contributed to a view of the Indian past that was tinged with melancholy and romance, even as families like the Kings celebrated and profited from the march of liberal progress that accelerated the merciless destruction of the Indian world. Lorena was just five or six years old when the family moved to Dakota Territory and was not part of the adventure that led to Gwyneth's one-on-one conversation with Chief Sitting Bull. But she was sixteen at the time of the massacre at Wounded Knee in late 1890; we can easily imagine how U.S. victories over the Sioux informed Lorena's sense of historical change and the passing of an era.[14]

Perhaps in response to the rushed state-building that she witnessed—the building of new towns and institutions from the ground up—and as a public school student in Rapid City, Lorena began a lifelong effort to bring the high culture of literature, drama, and elocution to the "crudity" of the newly settled white communities.[15] By the age of fifteen, she had begun doing recitations for public events, such as at the Grand Army of the Republic campfire in Rapid City in February 1889.[16] Her performance—one of many over several decades—at this patriotic event honoring Union veterans also presaged her lifelong sense of duty toward a public life. By the fall of 1892, at about the age of 18, Lorena completed a training course for teachers in Chamberlain. [17] She subsequently took a teaching position at a middle school in Hope, North Dakota, where she also served as the secretary for the Women's Christian Temperance Union and attended the statewide WCTU meeting with three other women.[18] Hers was a purposefully public life lived in full awareness that women who stepped into public roles were held up to scrutiny and ridicule at least as often as they were admired. The *Hope (*North Dakota) *Pioneer* reported on the women's trip to the WCTU meeting in 1899 in a way that both captured Lorena's intrepid spirit of adventure while also poking fun:

> [The four women chartered a carriage and booked train tickets but] asked no questions of the men folks, but just quietly skipped out, and returned when they got ready—sorter independent women like—which leads us to think they believed in women's rights.[19]

Women's suffrage in South Dakota became an issue of national interest during the run-up to South Dakota statehood. Well-known women's suffrage figures crisscrossed the state building support for women's enfranchisement, which was to be put to a vote in 1890. The *Argus Leader* reported in 1974 that Dr. Anna Howard Shaw and Carrie Chapman Catt had been guests in John and Permelia's home during this period, no doubt making a deep impression on Lorena.[20] The outcome of the voting on the referenda—enfranchising Native American men but *not* white women—brought into sharp focus the limits of progressive politics at the time. Most white women suffragists looked down on people of color, so the enfranchisement of Indian males was a humiliating, racially-tinged slap in the face for white women who hoped to participate in democratic politics through voting.[21]

In 1901 Lorena completed her teacher's college degree at the North Dakota State Normal School and was offered a job in Fargo public schools.[22] But Lorena sought more than technical or professional training. She enrolled in 1899 as a 25-year-old at University of Chicago, where she studied literature and speaking performance, a liberal arts degree that made her part of the larger world of ideas and scholarly inquiry.[23] At Chicago she made a splash on stage, playing the role of Portia in the *Merchant of Venice*, for example, and Celia in *As You Like*

It.[24] Of her work on stage, the text accompanying a standing photographic portrait of Lorena in costume noted that Lorena "ha[d] been a leader in university dramatics for two years," the duration of her time at the university.[25] Altogether, her performances as a widely known elocutionist in South Dakota, her professional development and service as a teacher, her habit as a joiner of groups and associations, her work on stage in Chicago, and her University of Chicago B.A. led naturally to her joining the Association of Collegiate Alumnae in 1904, which later became the premier mission-driven American organization serving educated women, the American Association of University Women (AAUW).[26]

On April 4, 1906, Lorena's father John King died in Huron, somewhat suddenly. Twelve days later, at age 32, she married Arthur Boyce Fairbank, a well-to-do lawyer about her age.[27] In a year's time they would be parents; their only son John King Fairbank was born on May 24, 1907. The Indiana-born Arthur (1873-1936) had completed his law degree at Washington University in St. Louis in 1901 and moved to Huron to practice law. He quickly made his mark as an attorney, and like Lorena's father, became a prominent member of the South Dakota establishment. He became a partner in his cousin Jesse Boyce's Sioux Falls law firm in 1912, and moved Lorena and John there from Huron.[28] He was elected president of the South Dakota Bar Association in 1926 and was the commencement speaker at State College graduation in 1930.[29] Boyce, Warren and Fairbank became one of Sioux Falls most prominent legal firms. The Boyce-Greeley building that the firm built remains a treasured historical property in the city; the firm itself lives on as the Boyce Law firm.[30]

The marriage seems to have been one of like-minded equals. Arthur was also a joiner of civic clubs who supported Lorena's public life, including her suffragism.[31] But their life together was more than a shared commitment to political participation; this was a power couple that liked to have fun and entertain. An account of his 34th birthday party was preserved on the society pages of the *Dakota Huronite* and suggests the home life of cultured performative entertainment for which the family became known. Arthur was born on Halloween, and in the second year of their marriage, they hosted a spooky-themed birthday party complete with Macbeth's witches—no doubt including Lorena at her finest dramatic eloquence—and a cauldron that brewed a "charmed potion" that was passed around to the jack-o-lantern-lighted room.[32]

Overall, what can be observed in Arthur B. Fairbank is a model of prosperous establishment equipoise in service of Lorena's cultured spirit of action and reform.[33] In his memoir, John Fairbank recalled his father as both a founder of the Minnehaha Country Club and as an outdoorsy type. He liked gardening and carpentry, for example, and was an avid Minnesota fisherman and hunter of duck and pheasant, qualities that presumably influenced John's affection for the country life at their New Hampshire cottage.[34] He also credited his father with imparting a secular mindset to him. What seems most important, however, was that he provided a genteel lifestyle for mother and son. He purchased a home on a large wooded lot in Sioux Falls, a home that became known for its cultured gatherings, with scenes from Shakespeare performed on the expansive wooded grounds in the evenings.[35] A family friend recalled in 1949 that "The family home fairly breathed culture and learning, yet there was a warm, informal, and hospitable air about it. Close in our memory are the many delightful and enriching hours spent there."[36] The pace and nature of Lorena's leadership as a society woman accelerated with motherhood, with John as her most important project. And, as Fairbank recalled, it was mainly Lorena's guidance that launched him on a career path that made him the single most influential U.S. scholar on China by the 1960s.

Lorena King and John King Fairbank at Home in the World and in Sioux Falls

The gentility of the Fairbank home was captured in its bucolic name, "The Cedars." The home had been built on land that had been a tree nursery, a telling measure of Sioux Falls' suburban expansion.[37] To this day, the large meandering lot has a wooded, idyllic feel; some of the namesake cedars still stand. Moreover, that the Fairbanks named their home certainly evokes an Old World, even aristocratic sensibility, more English country estate than Sioux Falls suburbs. Viewed in the context of her own childhood experiences, The Cedars was a manifestation of Lorena and Arthur's vision of how quickly and vigorously civilization can and *ought* to flourish with care and the right sort of education. It showed how the rudiments of civilized society—platted towns, tidy farmsteads, courthouses, newspapers, schools, churches, clubs—were brought to full flower through higher learning in the liberal arts. Moreover, for Lorena, educated people had a duty to participate in the process of liberal reform that began with personal improvement. In her own life—in the multiple public readings and performances of Shakespeare, for example—she insisted on the primacy of mastering Anglo-American high culture at its most refined levels. Thus, the world the future Professor Fairbank grew up in was more scholarly, Midwestern high society than it was frontier or rural. His upbringing in Sioux Falls was both an historical epoch and physical distance from the world that his mother had experienced in the 1880s and 1890s. Sioux Falls was no Rapid City in vistas or sensibilities.

Although young John lived in a world of important house guests, bridge games, frequent appearances on the society pages and afternoon teas, it nevertheless was outward- and political action-oriented. In 1908, before the move to Sioux Falls and when John was just a toddler, Lorena and her mother were the lead signatories or "patronesses" of a public appeal extended by the women of Huron to build a hospital there. The appeal called out a laundry list of Huron society groups to contribute funds for the project—"religious, medical, benevolent, social, railroad and business organizations"—to be sure these groups were aware of the responsibilities they would be held to by the patronesses.[38] In 1909 Lorena was elected treasurer of the South Dakota Equal Suffrage Association. She served in various statewide leadership roles in the suffrage movement over a decade and in the Minnehaha County League of Women Voters after the 19th Amendment was passed.[39] Then, as if her work and engagements were not enough to keep her busy, in 1911 Lorena took four-year-old John to Paris with law partner Jesse Boyce's wife, Etta, where they spent the winter in the heart of Paris.[40] The two women shared a passion for oral performance, and at the time the Boyces and Fairbanks shared a home as well. John recalled that Etta was a New England Conservatory graduate and promoter of classical concerts that brought touring musicians to their dinner table.[41] The historical record thus suggests that young John had spent a winter in France with his mother on a Grand Tour before he ever made his way west to the sites of the high plains, Indian reservations, or the Black

Hills, the 1914 trip he had reminisced about in 1982 that began this chapter.

In his memoir, Professor Fairbank recalled an awareness of his unusually high-minded and privileged home life. When he entered public school after his trip to Europe, he recalled that school bullies considered young John a delicate city boy in "knee socks." But Fairbank rejected the label and embraced a vigorous life of physical exertion, recalling with pride that he went out for the football team, much to the horror of his mother.[42] As a student at Harvard, he took a summer job on the Canadian railways in search of "red-blooded, muscular work," which the job indeed supplied.[43] In these qualities, we are reminded that personal and regional identities are claimed as much as they are inherited or shaped by geographical circumstances. Still Fairbank's Midwestern childhood placed him in the company of others of his generation from the region who rose to national prominence from small-town origins.[44] Fairbank's biographer, Paul Evans, reported that much later Fairbank had considered himself driven by an "expansionist-frontiersman spirit," a man of action who could make a new world with little regard to what had come before.[45] As the only child of high-powered parents, and a beneficiary of the prestige and connections bequeathed to him by well-traveled and accomplished grandparents and relatives, we can understand how Fairbank came to have a "brash" sense of pioneering great purpose and his own uniqueness.[46] So it is no surprise that he appears in the Sioux Falls newspaper society column as a young gentleman celebrating his eighth birthday in 1915:

> Master John King Fairbank was host to several of his little friends last Monday afternoon, entertaining them at the home of his parents...in celebration of the eighth anniversary of his birthday. The little folks spent a merry afternoon with games and visiting and at six o'clock, dinner was served.[47]

Fairbank remained a favorite son of Sioux Falls society even after he moved away permanently as a sixteen-year-old in 1923.[48] The *Argus Leader* kept readers up-to-date on his achievements, travails, and return trips to Sioux Falls to visit friends and relatives, in part because Lorena continued in her prominent leadership roles in the AAUW in South Dakota.

In fact 1923 turned out to have been a key turning point in the story of mother and son cosmopolitans. It was in that year that Lorena founded the Sioux Falls chapter of the AAUW at a gathering of 11 women at The Cedars.[49] Her leadership connected her with other prominent women nationally and locally. In 1927 she spent a month in New York and attended the national conferences of the AAUW in Washington. D.C., for example, representing South Dakota as state chapter president.[50] Over two decades, she hosted many meetings of the Sioux Falls chapter at her gracious home.[51] In 1938 an *Argus Leader* news story included a photograph of Mrs. A. B. Fairbank (Lorena) performing a program of Shakespearean conversation on the lawn at The Cedars before an audience of about 100 AAUW guests.[52] In 1974, on Lorena's 100th birthday, the South Dakota AAUW endowed a fellowship in her name for her pioneering work with the organization.[53] The Minnehaha County Historical Society commemorated the founding of the chapter and Lorena's role as first president by installing a historical marker on the campus of the University of Sioux Falls in 2006. Both milestones showed the enduring influence Lorena was to have on the Big Sioux valley, well past the 64 years that she lived there. In 1944, as a 70-year-old, she moved to Washington, D.C. to be near John, who was working for the U.S. government at the time.

The year 1923 was also a pivotal year in John's life. John left Sioux Falls to begin a global education that took him to four different institutions by 1930. He attended Exeter to finish high school, graduating as valedictorian; as a debater and Big Man on Campus at the University of Wisconsin; and then on to Harvard College for a more scholarly undergraduate education; and then to England as a Rhodes Scholar. By 1931 he landed in Beijing with his future wife and fellow scholar, Wilma Cannon, to begin his dissertation research.[54] In his striving for distant horizons, we certainly can observe the influence of his mother. The decision to head east to an elite private boarding school was made by John and his mother in a matter-of-fact way. Fairbank reported no dissatisfaction with Sioux Falls teachers, schools, or peers in his memoir. He was not fleeing from provincial attitudes or habits.[55] He and his mother simply felt that the public schools could not fulfill John's desire to learn.[56] John and Lorena looked at a few catalogs, consulted some New Englander friends in Sioux Falls, and selected Exeter. But there were other manifestations of Lorena's shaping of young John's intellect. Her prominence as an elocutionist and dramatic performer surely influenced his participation in debate in high school, at Exeter, Wisconsin, and Harvard as a self-described "disciple" of William Trufant Foster's debating style.[57]

Lorena looked up to John, just as he admired her. Mother and son, elegantly attired at their family home (The Cedars) in Sioux Falls, 1925. Courtesy of Holly Fairbank.

Although Lorena did shepherd John toward a scholarly life, neither her nor Arthur's influence played much of a role in Fairbank's decision to embark on a career studying China. Why indeed did he choose to write his dissertation about China when he knew not a word of the language in 1931 when he arrived in Beijing? It is a riddle that requires some examination because Fairbank was an outlier for scholars of his generation. He had no personal or family connection with East Asia prior to choosing China as the topic of his dissertation. Although the earliest U.S. connections with China, Japan, and Korea were formed by the trading firms of New England, and then later through trade and migration through the ports of San Francisco and Seattle, by the late nineteenth century, deep Midwestern connections with Asia were in fact flourishing.[58] Midwesterners were over-represented in the flocks of missionary couples and singles who built mission careers in China, for example, whose experiences were conveyed to small-town congregations in home fund-raising visits, published in memoirs, and shared at mission conferences and in local newspapers. Like Fairbank's public advocacy work later, these accounts shaped Americans' perceptions of China in a fundamental way and over several generations. Many of the "China hands" of the twentieth century were raised in China by missionary parents with Midwestern family ties. Other national figures, too—ambassadors, trade representatives, and journalists—have hailed from the heartland and shaped the national conversation and policies on East Asia right up to the present.[59] In his memoir, Fairbank described the preachers and missionaries in the Fairbank part of his family heritage but found no global soul-saving in his own motives. When he recalled the talks he gave on the Rotary Club circuit as a young scholar, however, starting with Sioux Falls in 1936, Fairbank saw an affinity with the work of his preacher grandfather, guessing that he had "addressed as many audiences as his grandfather had...I felt I was in his footsteps, though my line—America's salvation through China studies—had become a bit more narrow and specialized...."[60]

Fairbank's presentations to Midwestern Rotary Clubs and other general audiences to "save" Americans by making them more cosmopolitan in outlook, including understanding China as vital to U.S. national interests, is a defining element in his own internationalist and liberal reformist sensibilities.[61] In this he was part of broader efforts by Midwestern philanthropists and city leaders who wished to build citizens and a regional culture that transcended local biases and orientations, including through connections to Asia. Christa Adams explains the founding of cultural institutions such as Cleveland Museum of Art during this period as part of the "civilizing mission" of high culture in a way that was similar to Lorena's understanding of the role Shakespearean performance in social "uplift."[62] Just as in Lorena's performances, art museums served a dual role: they uplifted citizens into the somewhat borderless world of high culture while also bringing prestige to the city that built and supported it. In another example of this kind of collective striving for diverse local cultural landscape, the city of Sioux

Falls began building a Japanese garden in the 1920s on land that it had purchased to develop as a park. Significantly, the city built the Terrace Park Japanese Garden before it started work on a Mediterranean-style open-air theater in the same park in 1932, an indication perhaps of the priority the Japanese Garden had in planning and design for city leaders.[63]

By 1936, when John made his first presentation to a Rotary Club as a China specialist, his role as South Dakota cosmopolitan was cast: a South Dakotan by birth, member of Anglo-American elite by academic training and polishing, and expert on a foreign culture and government. John and Wilma had returned to Sioux Falls after four years in China and a U.K. doctorate in hand. Sadly, at the time, John's father Arthur was already ill with cancer. They made a "happy family outing across the South Dakota dust bowl to the Black Hills" in July, a poignant evocation of the journey John had made as a youngster with his father in his Cadillac in 1914.[64] In September of that year Arthur passed away at the age of 62.

So why did Fairbank choose China as the subject of his dissertation research and life's work? In his memoir, Fairbank suggested that the sense of wide open possibilities that he saw in the horizon-reaching vistas of the South Dakota plains had influenced him in some way to the field of China studies.[65] Biographer Paul Evans found that it was mainly the influence of his advisor at Harvard, Charles Webster, a British diplomatic historian who recommended a careful empirical study of documents on China's diplomatic history.[66] Fairbank's motives in studying China were "exclusively secular, professional and academic," qualities that were to outline the intellectual profile of Fairbank over his career.[67] During World War II, he served in various government positions in China and in Washington, D.C. as a "China Hand," including as director of the U.S. Information Service in China, a position that later made him a target for Congressional anti-Communists looking for scapegoats for the Communist victory.[68] As a scholar, he was focused on empirical study and the application of knowledge to problem-solving rather than the development or application of theories per se; his foray into government service was a manifestation of his interest in scholarship that served national interests. He departed from the tradition of philology that drove European Sinology and instead advocated for an area studies approach that integrated the social sciences.[69] He was center-right in his politics, and acknowledged the role of politics in the production of knowledge, but was wary of ideological lenses that could lead scholars astray from the empirically-generated documentary record. The intellectual profile that emerges in Paul Evans' superb biography paints him as a consummate professional, an educational entrepreneur for the field of China Studies. He was a tireless grant writer, appeared on television shows, and supported scores of graduate students. He was a compulsively diligent man who enjoyed being at his desk at work at 7:00 a.m. and yet found time to write a "letter to his mother every day."[70] There was no interpretive thread, no grand theory, that connected his writings other than his view that research should generate knowledge that was useful, solved problems, and contributed to the national interest of a well-informed citizenry.[71]

Fairbank returned to Sioux Falls as a favorite local boy at least six more times before his death in 1991, occasions that were covered in the *Argus Leader*. He proudly claimed his South Dakota roots, even as he centered his life with Wilma, daughters Holly and Laura in Cambridge, Massachusetts, and at their cottage in New Hampshire. It was a pattern that stretched back to his days as a Rhodes Scholar in England, for example, when he delighted in introducing himself as a South Dakotan, which typically was met with a blank stare and silence. Fairbank confessed enjoyment at seeing the confusion on the faces of the Englishmen and women he met, in effect, thumbing his nose at those ignorant of his state of birth. He relieved their "consternation" by disclosing his Harvard degree, and got the requisite affirmation of the hallowed Boston institution.[72] His colleagues and graduate students also observed in his habits and statements public affirmations of his Midwestern roots. Theodore "Teddy" White, a journalist who achieved fame as the China correspondent for *Time* magazine in the 1940s had been Fairbank's student just after he had taken up his faculty post at Harvard. White described him as "tall, burly, sandy-haired, a prairie boy from South Dakota."[73] Harvard librarian Yen-Tsai Feng remarked in a *Festschrift* that Fairbank was quick to bring up his South Dakota roots and "bragged about his pioneer ancestry. He was so fond and proud of the 'roughing it' state of their...cottage which until the later years was without running water and no heat."[74] In the same volume, historian Yen-p'ing Hao recalled waiting for Professor Fairbank at a train station as a graduate student en route to the cottage, but not recognizing him because he was dressed like a "rustic farmer," an outfit former student and colleague Paul Cohen described Fairbank consistently wearing to the office in his retirement.[75] The irony, of course, is that as we have seen, John's childhood was far from rustic, rural or "western," reminding us that a regional sense of identity is often a matter of choice, affinities, and perception more than it is a mechanical or natural process generated by physical landscapes or regional cultures.

Like a proud parent, Fairbank's successes and travails were shared by his state of birth. When Fairbank was accused of being a Communist sympathizer in 1951, the editorial writers of the *Argus Leader* launched a vigorous defense, ascribing to him the South Dakota virtues of forthrightness and lack of pretense that Fairbank himself also claimed:

> In every sense, [Fairbank] is a good American—a citizen with high purpose...an intellectual, a student and a scholar...[He is] now vacationing in Sioux Falls— his old hometown and in the state of his birth—... and he has been talking to friends—old friends— not so much as a professor of history at Harvard University but as a South Dakotan with the fresh and broad viewpoint of the prairies as a background. To say that Fairbank is a liberal is correct. To say that he is an advocate of Stalinism is asinine. The methods of Stalin are as repugnant to him as they are to most South Dakotans...Let us listen to men of Fairbank's understanding.[76]

John's affection for his home state was freely stated, too, although no doubt, as a favorite son, he knew that his sentiments would be well received by readers. A few days before the editorial defending him was published, Fairbank had been interviewed about the charges that he was a Communist sympathizer. To close the article, journalist David Smith reported Fairbank saying, "I still feel myself a member of this community. I have the impression that most of the best people in the east come from the middle west."[77]

The Big Sioux River Valley and the Fairbanks

Both Lorena and John came of age during a time when the Midwest was nationally prominent relative to other parts of the nation. It was a "Midwestern moment" in U.S. culture before shallow bicoastal truisms would insist that the Midwest is defined mostly by what it lacks.[78] Lorena and John's lives show evidence of many of the qualities associated with this moment in the nation's history especially high rates of civic participation, a commitment to public culture, educational and cultural uplift as well as emotional reserve and uprightness.[79] Moreover, as Jon Lauck described, Midwesterners identified more with the national culture, almost as an "anti-region," again relative to other parts of the country, some of which asserted proud regional peculiarities driven more by the ethnic and cultural histories as Yankees or Southerners, for example.[80] Certainly, we can discern identification as "nationals" as part of the Fairbanks' cosmopolitan rejection of what they viewed as biases or parochialisms—such as irrational religious piety in John's view—in favor of a more nationally inflected universal and secular culture of liberal learning and uplift.

Although Lorena "retired" from public life in Sioux Falls at the age of 70, she lived another 35 years in Washington, D.C. The *Argus Leader* continued reporting on her life and its significance to South Dakotans as it did for her more nationally famous son. In 1971, for example, the newspaper reported a news story that had been sent in by a reader. Mary Ann Lenker reported that her "distant relative," 97-year-old Lorena, had attended an AAUW reception in Washington, D.C., "'elegantly clad in an ivory chiffon and beaded lace gown…that she had worn to the 1929 A.A.U.W. convention in New Orleans.'"[81] Three years later, Mrs. Fairbank was visited by a *Washington Post* reporter on the occasion of her 100th birthday. The birthday interview with the grande dame of the Washington, D.C., chapter was also reported in the *Argus Leader*. Lorena's life and personality zing across the decades, all the way back to the late nineteenth century. Hers was an Anglo-American cosmopolitanism oriented to the great centers of culture at places like New York and London. She treated the journalist to an afternoon glass of sherry, for example, a detail included by the journalist to emphasize her "Old World," almost aristocratic personal style. Lorena explained that she was more interested in contemporary issues than in rehashing the past, an affirmation of her currency as a liberal social reformer oriented to the future. In the same phrase, however, she displayed her displeasure at the decay in social norms that she observed in the youth culture of the 1970s. Lenker quoted Lorena's "charming and typical" remark that she could not bear the "costumes, the customs, the lack of courtesy in the world," an affront to the sense of uprightness and the importance of following social norms that had defined her own life. The stolid and unsmiling portrait that accompanied the text showed her to be a curmudgeonly grande dame, proudly insisting on timeless and higher cultural standards in all things; as well as her conviction that she still had a role to play in the purpose and process of reform.[82]

In reviewing their lives, we can see that South Dakota shaped Lorena and John in different ways. Lorena spent her formative years building civic culture in territorial western South Dakota from the ground up in public performances, membership groups, political participation, and her dogged pursuit of higher learning for herself and suffrage for women. John's life was cast in Lorena and Arthur's fully formed and prosperous world of Anglo-American high culture at The Cedars, her insistence on social striving and political participation, and the liberal duty of personal improvement and uprightness. John spent just the first sixteen years of his life in South Dakota, and then enrolled at two of the finest, private, elite, East Coast, Anglo-American institutions of learning, surely the antithesis of the way many Midwesterners perceive educational opportunities. But he was a proud son of the plains who knew the virtues and educational value of pioneering. It seems, too, that joining the elite Anglo-American world only enhanced his sense of belonging to both South Dakota and the wider world. Building something anew with one's own hands and the social leveling generated by swinging an axe oneself, rather than paying someone else to do it, had become part of him and the way he lived at the cottage in New Hampshire.[83] John's cosmopolitanism became more global than Lorena's by virtue of his subject of study. He promoted China studies as vital to U.S. interests at all levels; it was his life's work, more so even than his scholarship. Like Lorena, he was driven to lead a public life of consequence driven by education and the spirit of improvement that transcended borders. In a letter to his parents in 1932 Fairbank wrote that his home life had given him a mix of good health, ambition, and "few encumbering or warping prejudices."[84] It was this aspiration to liberal universalisms and freedom from provincial and local biases that ultimately marked mother and son as cosmopolitans, at home in South Dakota, Washington, D.C., Massachusetts, China, and the world.

Gender roles, too, were fundamental to how their life stories played out in South Dakota and in the world. His mother's life and work showed an insistence to improve and uplift South Dakota, to *change* it, to make it more like other places in the Anglo-American world in line with the homogenizing spirit of progressive reform. These were activities and habits of mind she shared with other Progressive society women of her time. For John it is clear that South Dakota as place played a different role in his sense of self. It needed no ornamentation or improvement. Instead he sought to *preserve* his South Dakota origins intact as a set of virtues and habits through which he channeled his prodigious energies. He likely would have agreed with Lloyd Wendt, another South Dakota native profiled in the 1982 *Argus Leader* news story that featured Fairbank, who asserted that the state had endowed him with "hard work, frugality, self-reliance and trust of my fellow citizens."[85] In asserting a uniquely Midwestern identity, Fairbank bore the imprint of the Midwestern Moment, as did others of his generation. Through their aspirations and travels, Lorena and John became citizens of the world but always maintained their connections with the lands of the Big Sioux River. At her death in 1979, Lorena was buried next to her husband, Arthur, in Minnehaha County, South Dakota, and finally came to rest.

Notes

[1] *I would like to thank Holly Fairbank for her generosity in sharing photos and reminiscences of her father and grandmother. Paul Evans provided thoughtful direction to this project in conversation and encouragement. My University of the Pacific colleague and U.S. Women's historian Jennifer Helgren also shaped my analysis through her careful reading of a draft of this project. All errors are mine, of course.*
He was one of six men profiled from different professional fields, including two military men, a journalist, and a vintner. Like Fairbank, they built careers outside the state. Anson Yeager, "Prominent S.D. natives take nostalgic glimpses at the past," *Argus Leader* (Sioux Falls, SD), May 2, 1982, 27.

[2] One of his most highly regarded books, *The United States and China,* was first published in 1948 and has been in print ever since: John King Fairbank, *The*

United States and China, 4th ed. (Cambridge, MA: Harvard University Press, 1983). The significance of his life and work were the subject of Paul Evans' excellent biography. Evans reports that Fairbank's Ph.D. students went on to positions at more than 100 universities in the U.S. and around the world. Paul Evans, *John Fairbank and the American Understanding of Modern China* (New York: Basil Blackwell, 1988), 2.

[3] Yeager, "Prominent S.D. natives take nostalgic glimpses at the past," 27.

[4] John King Fairbank, *Chinabound: A Fifty-Year Memoir* (New York: Harper & Row, 1982), 6. Paul Evans documented multiple points at which Fairbank himself credited his mother with endowing him with self-confidence and steering him toward ceaseless striving, such as his decision to leave the University of Wisconsin and its campus life oriented toward socializing for the rigors of Harvard scholasticism. Evans, 13-14.

[5] "Representative John Hereford King" from 33 GA (1909) House Journal Memorial Resolution, *The Iowa Legislature*, accessed April 28, 2021, https://www.legis.iowa.gov.

[6] A full examination of the career of John H. King would provide more context for the King and Fairbank families in South Dakota politics, particularly around the statehood drive, Anglo-Indian relations, the suffrage movement, and the Republican Party. "Colonel John H. King dies at his home," *The Mitchell Capital* (Mitchell, SD), April 13, 1906, 1.

[7] "Dakota Pioneer Marks 100th Birthday," *Argus Leader* (Sioux Falls, South Dakota) March 29, 1968, 3. J.Y. Smith, "Lorena King Fairbank, 105, Marched for Women's Vote," *The Washington Post*, October 17, 1979, accessed April 28, 2021, https://www.washingtonpost.com.

[8] The phrase "toad in a puddle" seems to have been used favorably by the author, referring to King's efforts to open Indian lands "without their consent." "What John Believes," *The Black Hills Daily Times* (Deadwood, SD), Jan. 14, 1888, 3.

[9] The military title appears to have been honorary; King was not a veteran. "Colonel John H. King dies at his home" *The Mitchell Capital* (Mitchell, SD), April 13, 1906, 1.

[10] This reminiscence, first published in two installments in 1947, and then later drawn upon for a commemoration of her one hundredth birthday in 1968, was likely drawn from an unpublished autobiography that Gwyneth had begun writing in the 1930s. The account is evocative of the time rather than a reliable primary source. Warren Morrell, "Thru the Hills," *Rapid City Journal* (Rapid City, SD), December 12, 1947, 9. "Dakota Pioneer Marks 100th Birthday," *Argus Leader* (Sioux Falls, SD), March 29, 1968, 3.

[11] As noted above, it is not possible to determine the veracity of Lorena's account of the request or the way in which it was received. Warren Morrell, "Thru the Hills," *Rapid City Journal* (Rapid City, SD), December 12, 1947, 9.

[12] Morrell, 9.

[13] Morrell, 9.

[14] One wonders, for example, what Lorena would have thought of the Americanization of young Indians through federally-run boarding schools launched after this time. Holly Fairbank, John's daughter, reported that Lorena

had seen the mistreatment of Indians when she was a girl and that these impressions had influenced her father's views of the U.S. and human rights. Holly Fairbank, personal email to the author, April 11, 2021. The politics around male Indian suffrage was complex as well. The *Argus Leader* reported, for example, that "Lorena shared her father's indignation when Dakota Territory became two states with a constitution that gave Indians the vote but denied it to women," presumably based on Lorena's own reflections on her life at age 100. "AAUW to Honor Lorena Fairbank on 100th Birthday," *Argus Leader* (Sioux Falls, SD), June 30, 1974, 32.

[15] The conceptualization of territorial and early statehood South Dakota as marked by "crudity" comes from John Fairbank's memoir, to explain Lorena's enrollment at the University of Chicago as a 25-year-old undergraduate. Fairbank, *Chinabound,* 7. Lorena was a high achieving student in the Rapid City Public schools. "Honor Roll," *Rapid City Journal* (Rapid City, SD) December 23, 1888, 1.

[16] "The Journal," *Black Hills Weekly Journal,* (Rapid City, SD), February 15, 1889, 4. Her recitation at the Grand Army of the Republic campfire was "Spinning Wheel," perhaps the Irish ballad poem. It was one of three recitations and four songs. In 1917, at the State Federation of Women's Club meeting, she recited "The Melting Pot," presumably the play by Israel Zangwill about Jewish immigrants in the U.S. "Club Women of State Will Meet at Huron," *Argus Leader* (Sioux Falls, SD), September 21, 1917, 16. Oral performance and debate were interests that her son, John, would later take up.

[17] "Teacher's Institute" *The Kimball Graphic* (Kimball, SD), July 2, 1892, cited in the superb biographical profile by Liz Almlie, "Lorena King Fairbank," *History in South Dakota*, accessed April 28, 2021, https://historysouthdakota. wordpress.com.

[18] "Women's Christian Temperance Union," *The Hope Pioneer* (Hope, ND), November 25, 1892, 4.

[19] "Pick-ups [social column], *The Hope Pioneer,* (Hope, ND), September 28, 1899, 2.

[20] "AAUW to Honor Lorena Fairbank on 100th Birthday," *Argus Leader* (Sioux Falls, SD), June 30, 1974, 32.

[21] For more on the politics of woman suffrage and Indian male suffrage, see Getrude Simmons Bonnin, "Woman versus the Indian" in *Recasting the Vote: How Women of Color Transformed the Suffrage Movement*, Cathleen Cahill, ed., (Chapel Hill: University of North Carolina Press, 2020), 11-24.

[22] "Local News Notes," *The Hope Pioneer* (Hope, ND), January 3, 1901, 4.

[23] Fairbank, *Chinabound*, 7.

[24] "Co-eds will present plays at the university," *The Inter-Ocean* (Chicago, IL), May 17, 1903, 7.

[25] "Girls to Take Part in University Play," *Chicago Tribune* (Chicago, IL), June 7, 1903, 3.

[26] She attended the Association of Collegiate Alumnae national meeting in St. Louis in 1904 with organization founder Marion Talbot. Suzanne Gould, "Jail, Picketing, and Resolutions: AAUW and Suffrage, *AAUW Community*," accessed

February 28, 2013, ww3.aauw.org. On her participation as an "elocutionist" at the State Federation of Women's Clubs, see "Convention at Huron," *The Lead* (Lead, SD), June 7, 1905, 1. See also Liz Almlie, "Lorena King Fairbank."

[27] The wedding had been a small one, with just a few immediate relatives as guests, so it is possible that the decision to marry was made suddenly, prompted at least partially by her father's death. "Fairbank-King: Prominent Huron Young People United in Marriage," *Argus Leader* (Sioux Falls, SD), April 17, 1906, 2.

[28] "J. W. Boyce Dies At Home in This City," *Argus Leader* (Sioux Falls, South Dakota), September 13, 1915, 3.

[29] "Sioux Falls Attorneys Honored by Bar Association," *Argus Leader* (Sioux Falls, SD), August 12, 1926, 16. "22 Receive Diplomas at State University," *Argus Leader* (Sioux Falls, SD), July 19, 1930, 5.

[30] Jodi Schwan, "Boyce Law Firm marks 140 years with focus on future workforce," *SiouxFalls.Business*, accessed April 28, 2021, https://www.siouxfalls.business.

[31] He served as the president of the newly founded Sioux Falls Rotary in 1918, for example, and was an active member of the Masons, Shriners, and the Elks lodge. "Sioux Falls Attorneys Honored by Bar Association," *Argus Leader* (Sioux Falls, SD), August 12, 1926, 16.

[32] "Hallowe'en Frolic: A Happy Hallowe'en Gathering at the Fairbank Home," *Dakota Huronite* (Huron, SD), November 14, 1907, 7.

[33] He was a Republican, as had been his father-in-law, John H. King. Lorena's oldest sister, Gwyneth, had married Gilbert Roe in 1899, the law partner of the progressive Republican senator from Wisconsin Robert LaFollette, which also linked the Fairbanks with the progressive Republican figures and politics of the day.

[34] The description of Arthur Fairbank comes from Fairbank, *Chinabound*, 5-6, and from Evans, 9-11.

[35] The recollection is by family friend Joanna Downs Lee, who referred to Lorena as "Aunt Looey." Ms. Lee went on to a career as a dancer and dance instructor and was part of the arts community that Lorena participated in and shaped. Paul Cohen and Merle Goldman, compilers, *Fairbank Remembered* (Cambridge, MA: Harvard University Press, 1992,) 3.

[36] "Authority on China," *Sioux City Journal* (Sioux City, IA), January 16, 1949, 6.

[37] "Souvenir Program, Dedication of the 'AAUW Sioux Falls Branch,'" The Cleveland Center, University of Sioux Falls, Sioux Falls, South Dakota, September 6, 2006, Minnehaha County Historical Society. The records of the Sioux Falls Chapter of the AAUW are located at the Center for Western Studies, Augustana University.

[38] "For County Hospital," *The Dakota Huronite* (Huron, SD), September 10, 1908, 8.

[39] Liz Almlie, "Lorena King Fairbank." See also Suzanne Gould, "Jail, Picketing, and Resolutions: AAUW and Suffrage."

[40] John was in the charge of an "old family nurse" hired from Sweden. Fairbank, *Chinabound*, 7-8. John and Lorena would sail for Europe again in 1925 as a recent high school graduate. "Mrs. Fairbank to Spend Summer Abroad," *Argus Leader* (Sioux Falls, SD), June 6, 1925, 7.

41 Etta and Jesse Boyce were also giants of Sioux Falls society. Their early deaths—Jesse at age 55 in 1915 and Etta five years later at age 57—were terrible losses for Lorena and Arthur and for Sioux Falls. "Mrs. Etta Boyce Dies Suddenly," *Argus Leader* (Sioux Falls, SD), April 2, 1920, 15.

42 Fairbank, *Chinabound*, 8. Teddy Roosevelt's embrace of Dakota Territory as testing ground for vigor in the ranching he did there comes to mind as an expression of the progressive spirit of the times, with the Dakotas as a place of opportunity for the enterprising.

43 Fairbank, *Chinabound*, 8. Paul Evans reported that Fairbank suffered from exhaustion-related illnesses from relentless study. His work on the railways was intended to be an antidote to all the time sitting at a desk. Evans, 22-23.

44 In the introduction to *Small-Town Dreams,* historian John E. Miller suggests different ways of understanding how Midwestern origins shaped people of Fairbank's generation, including the relative prominence of the region in the generation of "leadership, energy and creativity" on the national level. Henry Ford, George Washington Carver, and the historian Frederick Jackson Turner were some of the men Miller profiled in his book that he argues were generated by a particular Midwestern social milieu. John E. Miller, *Small-Town Dreams: Stories of Midwestern Boys Who Shaped America* (Lawrence: University of Kansas Press, 2014), 9. For his own musings on the physical environment of his childhood, see chapter 1, "How I became Oriented" in Fairbank, *Chinabound,* 3.

45 Evans, 22, 40.

46 Gwyneth King Roe is another example of a high achieving person in Lorena's and John's world. In 1888, 20-year-old Gwyneth was a teacher in the Rapid City high school where Lorena was a ninth-grade honor student. "The Honor Roll," (Rapid City, SD), March 30, 1888, 4. By 1899, 31-year-old Gwyneth crisscrossed the U.S. teaching the Delsarte system of bodily movement or interpretive dance. In that year, she married Gilbert Roe. The marriage enhanced family connections with Progressive politics through Roe's law partner Robert La Follette, who became Wisconsin governor and U.S. Senator. Lorena and Gwyneth both lived to be more than 100 years old, outliving their husbands by fifty years. "Local News Matters," *Mitchell Capital* (Mitchell, SD), September 22, 1899, 5. Paul Evans uses the phrase "brash optimism" to describe Fairbank's sense of self, 22.

47 "Week in Society," *Argus Leader* (Sioux Falls, SD), May 29, 1915, 5.

48 A summer 1924 visit from Exeter was covered on the society pages and again displayed the prominence of the Fairbanks in Sioux Falls. The *Argus Leader* reported that Fairbank spent that summer "motor[ing] through [Sioux Falls] in an Italian motorcar with his cousin from New York, Jack Roe." Jack Roe was Aunt Gwyneth's and Uncle Gilbert's son. Fairbank later attended the University of Wisconsin where Jack was also a student. "Society," *Argus Leader* (Sioux Falls, SD), July 22, 1924, 7. On Jack Roe and John Fairbank at Wisconsin, see Evans, 13.

[49] Souvenir Program, Dedication of the 'AAUW Sioux Falls Branch,'" The Cleveland Center, University of Sioux Falls, Sioux Falls, SD, September 6, 2006, Minnehaha County Historical Society.

[50] Lorena surely met Iowa-born Lou Henry Hoover, the wife of President Herbert Hoover, on this trip. Mrs. Hoover hosted a tea at her home in Washington as part of the AAUW meeting. Lorena joined the Washington D.C. chapter of AAUW when she moved there in 1944, the year of Lou Henry's death at age 69. Both Lorena and Lou Henry had been born in 1874. "Mrs. Arthur Fairbank Home From Conference," *Argus Leader* (Sioux Falls, SD), April 9, 1927, 17.

[51] "A.A.U.W. to Entertain National Secretary," *Argus Leader* (Sioux Falls, SD), October 18, 1924, 7. "Prominent Women Taking Part in A.A.U.W. Convention, *Argus Leader* (Sioux Falls, SD), April 27, 1929, 17.

[52] "One Hundred Guests Attend AAUW Fall Meeting Held at 'The Cedars' Saturday," *Argus Leader* (Sioux Falls, SD), September 18, 1938, 4.

[53] "AAUW to Honor Lorena Fairbank on 100th Birthday," *Argus Leader* (Sioux Falls, SD), June 30, 1974, 32.

[54] John and Wilma married in 1932 in Beijing. Wilma's sister Marion would later marry Arthur Schlesinger, Jr., also a prominent historian at Harvard, who spent part of his childhood in Iowa City, graduated from Harvard, and was a veteran of U.S. government service in Washington during World War II. "Sioux Falls Youth Planning Study at Chinese University," *Argus Leader* (Sioux Falls, SD), July 22, 1931, 2. On John and Wilma's life in Beijing as newlyweds and scholars, see Evans, 25-34.

[55] Paul Evans, interview by author, November 27, 2019.

[56] Fairbank, *Chinabound*, 9.

[57] At Harvard, he encountered British-style parliamentary debating which he distinguished from Foster's debating style that he and other Midwestern disciples practiced. Fairbank, *Chinabound*, 15.

[58] For a superb elaboration of this theme, see Jeffrey Wasserstrom, "Of Exports, Envoys, Boxers, and Books — Midwestern Links to the Middle Kingdom," accessed April 21, 2021, Los Angeles Review of Books blog (BLARB) blog. lareviewofbooks.org, February 15, 2017.

[59] Former Iowa governor Terry Branstad, who served as ambassador to China from 2017-2020, was one of many envoys from the Midwestern states to serve in that role. Wasserstrom, "Of Exports, Envoys, Boxers, and Books — Midwestern Links to the Middle Kingdom."

[60] Fairbank, *Chinabound*, 4-5.

[61] He cited talks in places like Peoria, Minneapolis, Brookings, Northfield, Grinnell, and Wichita that evoked for him the work of his traveling preacher grandfather, a comparison that suggests own sense of mission. Americans risked disasters if they did not understand China; this was his main rationale for his talks and his cosmopolitanism. Fairbank, *Chinabound*, 4-5.

[62] The Cleveland Museum of Art was founded in 1913 and came to have a strong collection of Asian art. Christa Adams, "Creating a Site of Midwestern Cosmopolitanism: Heterotopia, East Asian Art and the Cleveland Museum Of

Art," in *The Making of the Midwest,* Jon Lauck, ed., (Hastings, NE: Hastings College Press, 2020), 249-63.

63 "Terrace Park and Japanese Gardens," [National Register of Historic Places Registration Form], United States Department of the Interior, National Park Service, accessed June 14, 2021, www.nps.gov/nr/feature/places/pdfs/15000566.pdf.

64 On the trip west, see Fairbank, *Chinabound,* 141-42. "Fairbank, Prominent S.D. Attorney Dies," *Argus Leader* (Sioux Falls, SD), September 14, 1936, 3.

65 Fairbank, *Chinabound,* 3.

66 Evans, *John Fairbank,* 16-17. Fairbank's memoir confirms the role of his advisor. Fairbank, *Chinabound,* 17-18.

67 This section draws heavily from Evans, *John Fairbank,* 16, 37-50.

68 "'They can't pin red label on me,' Avers John King Fairbanks [sic]." *Argus Leader* (Sioux Falls, SD), July 27, 1951, 3.

69 A sample of titles in his oeuvre demonstrate his interests in diplomacy, politics, and broad synthesis rather than theoretical analysis. The textbook *East Asia: Tradition and Transformation* first published in 1960 with Edwin Reischauer and Albert Craig was the standard work for many years and also appeared in revised editions. John King Fairbank, Edwin Reischauer, and Albert Craig, *East Asia: Tradition and Transformation,* (Boston: Houghton-Mifflin, 1973). John King Fairbank, *China: A New History* (Cambridge, MA: The Belknap, 1992) was his final work. He passed away just after completing the manuscript. It is also still in print in a second enlarged edition.

70 William Youngman, who knew Fairbank in the 1930s and 1940s, reported on the frequent letter writing, in Cohen and Goldman, 7.

71 Evans, *John Fairbank,* 44-46.

72 Fairbank, *Chinabound,* 29.

73 "Harvard's China Scholar: A man who helped the twain meet," *Boston Globe* (Boston, MA), September 22, 1991, 131.

74 Her comments were published in Cohen and Goldman, 29.

75 Also see Cohen and Goldman, 115. Paul A. Cohen, "John King Fairbank" *Proceedings of the American Philosophical Society* 137:2 (June 1993): 280.

76 "Dr. Fairbank Speaks With Understanding," *Argus Leader* (Sioux Falls, SD), August 1, 1951, 4.

77 "'They can't pin red label on me,' Avers John King Fairbanks [sic]." *Argus Leader* (Sioux Falls, SD), July 27, 1951, 3.

78 The phrase "Midwestern moment" comes from Jon K. Lauck, ed., *The Midwestern Moment: The Forgotten World of Early Twentieth-Century Midwestern Regionalism, 1880-1940,* (Hastings, NE: Hastings College Press, 2017), ix-xv.

79 See the sections on nineteenth-century political and cultural evolution; and on enduring sensibilities in Jon K. Lauck, "Soft, Democratic and Universalist: In Search of the Main Currents of Traditional Midwestern Identity and a Grand Historiographic Synthesis," *Middle West Review* 6:1-2 (Fall-Spring 2019): 69-72, 76-79.

80 Lauck, "Soft, Democratic and Universalist," 70-71.

[81] Mary Ann Lenker, "Town Talk" *Argus Leader* (Sioux Falls, SD), April 18, 1971, 12.

[82] Lenker, "Town Talk" *Argus Leader* (Sioux Falls, SD), July 14, 1974, 29.

[83] The very first sentence of his memoir is a whimsical reference to the trees that he felled at their New Hampshire cottage to clear trails. Fairbank, *Chinabound,* 3.

[84] Evans, 11.

[85] Yeager, "Prominent S.D. natives take nostalgic glimpses at the past," 27.

Chapter 12

James Seaton of Sioux City: A Biography of a Midwestern Intellectual

Jeremy Seaton

Dr. James Everett Seaton, an English professor of 46 years at Michigan State University who challenged many of academia's prevailing orthodoxies, passed away in March of 2017 at age 72. Though many—including his colleagues—have cast him as a defender of the so-called "Canon" of established literary classics and a critic of postmodernism, he is better characterized as a champion of what he termed the "Humanistic Tradition" of literary criticism. This approach prioritized literature before theory and cautioned against the tendency to engage in what Seaton viewed as Romantic excess in the defense of great literature as well as the temptation to render literature subservient to one's political or cultural goals. Literature, according to the Humanistic Tradition, was important because it could teach us about human beings as well as possibly entertain us in the process. He was also a father, a husband, a native Iowan, and a lifelong Midwesterner.

During a talk at Michigan State University, Seaton explored the relationship between the Midwest and the thought of another MSU professor, Russell Kirk. What, he wondered, did Kirk, the scholar, have to do with Kirk, the Midwesterner? He ultimately concluded that, while Kirk's most famous work, *The Conservative Mind*, had little apparent connection to the Midwest, "in *The Roots of American Order*, his true magnum opus, Russell Kirk returned to his Midwestern roots."[1] And so, one might fairly ask, what of James Seaton? Did his life as a Midwesterner, or for that matter, as an Iowan, have much, if anything, to do with his work as a writer?

On the face of it, given that Seaton published virtually nothing of an autobiographical nature, the most obvious answer might be that his writing had nothing to do with Iowa or the Midwest at all. Indeed, much of what he wrote was on the subject of literary criticism, or, as some have put it, "criticism of literary criticism," subject matter seemingly twice removed from the common human experience and entrenched firmly in the deepest recesses of academia, accessible and meaningful only to a select few. Is there any room in such a body of work, for the influence of either Iowa or the Midwest or one's home river valley? Though his personal history was largely absent from his published works, presentations, and talks, Seaton did write about his upbringing in personal letters. From these, one can gain an insight into his earlier life and, through it, an insight into what role that upbringing came to play in his career as a writer and academic.

Born in Cedar Rapids, Seaton's family moved to Sioux City shortly after his father, John Everett Seaton, returned from World War II following a stint in Patton's Third Army. John Everett grew up in Spencer, Iowa, where his family ran the Seaton Hotel, which also served as their living quarters. It was often a tight fit between guests and family; the children would either sleep in spare rooms or on cots in the hotel lobby if the rooms happened to be full. Though Seaton never knew his grandfather, he did have a few photos of him, one of which displayed a stern-faced man with a square jaw and focused, serious eyes. It was a deceptive picture, as by his father's account, he was a very kind-hearted and gentle man. Taking care of the hotel was not easy work; Seaton's father had a number of stories regarding rats that would invade the Seaton Hotel, only to be repeatedly fended off by the family's collective efforts. Strongly built, John Everett played as a lineman in high school football, where his teammates referred to him as "Horse." Following high school, he entered the University of Iowa, working as a milkman and doing chores for Grant Wood to pay his way through. It was there that he met Frances Kopecky, a Home Economics major. Graduating with a law degree in 1941, he wed Frances a year later. Not long after, he left to join the war effort.

John Everett Seaton returned from Europe with a number of decorations, which he explained as being for brushing his teeth, making his bed, and other such tasks. He claimed to have been rejected by the Marines for his inability to march in step, though he'd passed their exams. Later in life, his son James recalled his youthful surprise at the revelation, thinking that his father would have failed the exams. His mother took the opportunity to explain that, though his father was humble and self-effacing, he was actually far smarter than he let on.

After the war, John Everett would work for the Hartford Insurance Company until his retirement. Writing of his experience with the company, he would remark that, although he knew people "who felt that their lives were darkened by drudgery at their job" and that "his own children have often wondered how I could be so happy about going to work," he "loved the Hartford Insurance Company."[2] He noted that it was "particularly important to me that I have been given the opportunity to be forthright and honest in all of my business endeavors."[3] He felt that, "as a Claims Man, you are engaged in many adversary proceedings so, therefore, you must feel that you are armed with the ability to do the right thing or you find yourself discouraged."[4] With Hartford, he had "never found myself in this position."[5] Yet as much praise as he had for Hartford Insurance, he also insisted that he had the "duty to constructively criticize the corporation for whom I work."[6]

The Seaton house at 1101 W. 5th Street in Sioux City had a white picket fence, where "in the back yard there was rhubarb from which Mom would make rhubarb pie." Growing up without a television in the house, James Seaton found himself going next door for *Howdy Doody* and *I Love Lucy*, but noted that

> The best entertainment was the war stories Dad would tell at bedtime, always involving him and his buddy O'Gara. As I recall, they never involved anything violent but were always funny, usually Dad in some way making fun of himself. He also would tell stories about Charlie Chaplin and Jackie Coogan that were pretty similar in most ways to the war stories.[7]

Carrying on in the tradition of the Seaton Hotel, John Everett took in roomers at their Sioux City home, including one Seaton recalled as a "fast talker" who often joined in family Monopoly games. It later turned out the man was a bank robber. Not all the regular guests were boarders, however. Occasionally, Seaton remembered, a man named Arthur would visit with his family: "They were a Jewish family that Dad had helped get to the USA."[8]

The family attended Whitfield Church, where his parents "belonged to the 60-60 club for married couples at Whitfield. The idea," he recalled, "was that each partner in the marriage should go more than halfway in accommodating the other."[9] Seaton would meet the Reverend Whitfield's daughter Jeanie on his way to school when he passed their house and accompany her the rest of the way. His walks back home, however, could be much more precarious. "What really haunted me for years," he recalled, "were the packs of dogs that would swoop down on me, as it seemed, when I was walking back in the afternoon. I was scared of dogs for years afterwards, and those memories are one reason why I've never owned a dog. I never got bitten, but there was a lot of barking, and they seemed awfully big to me." [10]

At a young age, Seaton became a voracious reader. He "loved going to the library in Sioux City," where he "read all the Thornton Burgess animal stories in the library" before he "graduated to the even better *Freddy the Pig* books by Walker R. Brooks," of which, the English professor attested, decades later, "I still love." It was also at the Sioux City library that he "became a fan of the New York Yankees." This was not so much because of their success, but because he read "*A History of the Yankees* by Frank Graham where I learned about Lou Gehrig." His youthful admiration of Gehrig remained unshaken in his adult years, remarking that "his farewell speech stands up today as one of the most moving speeches on record."[11]

Beyond the library, he was also a devoted follower of illustrator and author Carl Barks' *Donald Duck* and *Uncle Scrooge* comic-books. Back in those days, subscriptions were offered for the *Donald Duck* comics but not *Uncle Scrooge*. Not wanting to risk missing an issue, Seaton wrote a letter to the publisher, asking if they could subscribe to both magazines. It was apparently persuasive, as from then on they received the adventures of both ducks in the mail.

Participating in the local Cub Scouts chapter, he enjoyed mixed results in his pursuit of merit badges; "the year Mom was the den mother …I got a lot of merit badges. The next year…when the neighbor lady was the den mother, not so many." He also practiced the piano under the tutelage of the "long-suffering Mrs. Cruikshank," recalling that he "couldn't carry a tune, my fingers were clumsy and I didn't like to practice." Nonetheless, he concluded that he "must have gotten something out of those lessons."[12]

The Seatons frequented Sioux City's drive-in movie theater. On one occasion, Seaton's "fourth-grade teacher, Miss Bartels, had recommended *Shane*, so we went to see it as a family." However, the recommendation turned out to be a controversial one. "Looking back," Seaton remembered, "I have to say Miss Bartels had good taste, but I remember Mom and Dad commenting that this was perhaps not the kind of movie that a fourth-grade teacher should recommend to her students. For me the most memorable part was the fight scene in the general store, which spills over into the tavern. It seemed so much more realistic than the fights I had seen in television shows or other movies." *Shane* would remain his favorite movie into adulthood, where family viewings of the film became something of a tradition.[13]

Seaton's mother had grown up in Shueyville, Iowa's Czech immigrant community, the daughter of Adolph and Mary Kopecky. Like John Everett, she had worked her way through school, teaching fifth-grade math following her graduation, a position she held most of her career. Though she had never played herself, she coached women's basketball, leading her team to a state championship. Her parents "did not own a farm but a few acres with a large vegetable garden, a small orchard, pigs, chicken and a couple of milk cows." Seaton had fond recollections of his visits to his maternal grandparents' homestead, recalling that "it seemed a wide open, strange and wonderful place." Seaton felt "very lucky to have been able to visit our grandparents in Shueyville and be part of a way of life so different from the way we lived in Sioux City or later in Glen Ellyn."

> [He was]…used to houses with small lots in a city, but they had lots of room for all sorts of things. It was, unfortunately, a long trip to the outhouse. It was

also a long trip to the pump, which was surrounded
by flowers. The path to the pump was in the summer
surrounded on both sides by crops that were taller than
we were. There was a long porch in front, and in the big
front yard there was a tree that was great for climbing.
I remember spending a lot of time on my back in the
front yard looking at the clouds and trying to see what
shapes they were taking.

His memories of his maternal grandfather were scant, but he recalled
that on occasion he fell into violent arguments with his Uncle Bill, who
was given to alcoholism. In these moments, he yearned for Sioux City
and his parents, who "didn't curse or swear or get in violent arguments
with each other."[14]

From Sioux City, the family moved to Glen Ellyn, Illinois, when
Seaton was in the fourth grade. Upon entering high school, sparked
by Will Durant's *The Story of Philosophy*, Seaton became interested in
philosophy, even humorously advertising himself as a "Consulting Philosopher," replete with a business card that promised "Enlightenment
possible—for a price!" Perhaps his local church took the offer seriously,
as on one occasion he was asked by the minister to explain existential-
ism to the congregation. By high school in the year of 1961 his reading
list had developed. By now it included (among more than fifty other
authors) the Beats, Allen Drury, Susanne Langer, Shakespeare, and Lao
Tzu. Of all these authors, it was the famed Ionian poet, Homer, author
of the *Iliad* and *Odyssey*, who would make the greatest impression upon
him.

Seaton also took up the sport of wrestling, receiving the distinction
of "Most Fundamentally Sound Wrestler" his sophomore year. As a
senior, he would horrify his mother by jumping from 165 pounds to
180 at his coach's direction. The gamble paid off. Though significantly
undersized for the division, Seaton nonetheless took home a district
championship at the weight. That tenacity was not limited to the mat.
His high school report cards told the tale of a determined student. He
sometimes began his classes with mediocre marks but studied hard and
seemed to pick up steam throughout the semester. Very often, classes
in which he started off with C's ended with A's. He also tested well and

would receive mention in the local paper for his high scoring in the National Merit competition.

Although he received an academic scholarship to Columbia (Lou Gehrig's alma mater), the school's tuition was still too costly for his parents. Instead, Seaton remained closer to home, attending the University of Illinois, where he joined the wrestling team and majored in English. It was in one of those English classes that he met Sandra Browne, a fellow English major. Though his wrestling career would end after his sophomore year, his interest in literature and Sandra Browne would sustain for the remainder of his life.

Following his graduation, he wed Browne and returned to Iowa to pursue his Ph.D. under the tutelage of Roger Hornsby. His Uncle Bill, now sober, was a frequent visitor to the couple. In place of alcohol, his car trunk was always filled with Shasta cola, which he shared generously. Seaton and his wife, who was black, "both appreciated his kindness and good wishes at a time when a lot of people were not ready to accept a couple like us."[15] During these years, Seaton laid pipe alongside itinerant construction workers to support his budding family, which by now consisted of a young daughter, Ann. Perhaps fittingly for a life at that point largely dominated by academic and physical labor, Seaton's graduate thesis was on Vergil's *Georgics*, a series of poems by ancient Rome's most celebrated poet, the topic of which was, in essence, labor.

He would critique the *Georgics* through the lens of Herbert Marcuse's critical approach, which presumed that the purpose of art was "to articulate the difference between the kind of world in which human beings actually live and the kind of world which would truly satisfy their needs."[16] Although the *Georgics* is often seen as a work that "celebrates a life of labor" and Marcuse contended that "in historical societies labor has been inherently unrewarding" and further, that "a glorification of ordinary labor is inherently 'ideological' and false,'" Marcuse's critical approach seemed the best choice, Seaton believed, because it addressed the tensions present in Vergil's work.[17] At times, Vergil seemed to be exalting rustic labor whereas at other times, he seemingly draws attention to the turmoil and suffering of the laborer, the warlike nature of the work he engages in and the ways in which even the most devoted labor could, by the whims of fate, be robbed of its fruits. This seeming inconsistency need not be seen as a weakness, but rather as a tension.

According to Seaton, "following Marcuse's theory, the poem may be seen as a dialectical unity arising out of the presentation of opposing values which are not reconciled at all."[18]

If Marcuse's theories were applied to more than just Vergil, it would seem to indicate a vast gulf between the critic and those lucky enough to be enlightened by his thought on the one hand and the mass of ordinary people who unwittingly subscribed to the value of work, unaware of their own best interests. It was a view that was very flattering for the intellectual, but not so much for everyone else. This implication was, perhaps, like the tensions present in the *Georgics*, unresolved.

Amid work and study, Seaton's marriage endured an early scare. At some point, his wife became aware that there was a certain box in their apartment that the erstwhile doctoral student had been keeping hidden. By the size of the box, she deemed that it was holding magazines. Somewhat aghast that her husband was secretly stowing away what she felt certain were adult magazines under her nose, she snuck out the box to see for herself when he was out, ready to confront him with its lurid contents on his return. The box contained, it turned out, a collection of classic *Uncle Scrooge* and *Donald Duck* comics. Embarrassed about his continued love for Carl Barks' duck books, or at least embarrassed about his wife finding out about it, he'd opted to keep his hobby a secret to her.

Upon completion of his studies at Iowa, he would move with his family to East Lansing, Michigan, to teach English at Michigan State University. In 1977 he published the article "A Rationale for Teaching General Humanities," in which he argued that it was not for a teacher of the humanities to "convert students," even to a posture of "impartiality," but rather to "nurture in students the ability to make moral and aesthetic judgments, whatever the ideological context of those judgments."[19] The purpose of humanities instruction and the nature of a humanities instructor's duties was a topic he would explore and return to many times over the course of his career.

Over time he began to distance himself from the thought of Marcuse. Instead, he found sympathy with the intellectual journey of Christopher Lasch, who, like Marcuse (and Seaton himself), had at one time been under the influence of Freud and Marx, but who came to believe that "it was not socialist revolution but the traditional family that seemed to provide the best hope."[20] Seaton would come to see in Lasch an example of "the moral and spiritual depth that becomes possible when an intellectual disdains the consolations offered by the intellectuals' view of themselves as morally and mentally superior to the rest of humanity."[21]

He would go on to publish four books, as well as numerous articles in *First Things*, *The Weekly Standard*, *Humanitas*, *The University Bookman*, and *The Wall Street Journal* among other outlets. His last book, published in 2014, is titled *Literary Criticism from Plato to Postmodernism: The Humanistic Alternative*. The book contends that the history of literary criticism can be broadly conceived as a conversation between three different, though sometimes overlapping, trends: the Platonic, which presumes that literature itself has nothing unique to teach readers but instead is only good or bad to the extent that it promotes the right ideologies; the Neoplatonic, which elevates great poets and writers above ordinary people and views their work as a means of accessing transcendent spiritual truths; and finally, the Aristotelian or, as Seaton referred to it after the tradition of Matthew Arnold and Irving Babbitt, the Humanistic Alternative.

The first tradition makes references to Plato's expulsion of the poets, including even Homer, from his ideal Republic, whereas the Neoplatonic tradition, somewhat ironically, is named for the thinkers that followed Plato, who, perhaps taking their lead from Plato's speculation in the *Ion* that poets may be divinely inspired, saw poetry and art as a means of accessing ultimate truths. On the other hand, Aristotle claimed for poetry—by which he in essence meant literature—the ability of telling us about the sorts of things that certain people might do, in contrast to history, which merely tells us what has happened. Crucially, for Seaton, Aristotle's approach did not entail Plato's presumption that literature had nothing special or unique to teach him or other similarly enlightened readers. Whereas Plato, at least in *The Republic*, approached literature from the position of someone who already knew the important answers to life's questions and was able to therefore simply work out whether or not the poets were conveying the right messages or the wrong ones. Aristotle acknowledged that literature, at least good literature, could indeed deepen our insights into human nature. Though Seaton believed that Aristotle's claims for poetry may have been too narrow, the basic notion that literature wasn't either a mere vehicle for ideological instruction or a gateway to special metaphysical insight, but rather more modestly, an unscientific, yet meaningful way of learning something of human tendencies and situations, rang true to him and became foundational to his own approach.

Finding sympathy with George Santayana's skepticism of man's capacity for moral or intellectual certitude, Seaton therefore thought it prudent to seek out guidance not only from traditional cultural and social institutions, but also from "the experience embodied in the *Iliad*."[22] That is, one can find a "critical filter" for the "dominant social and cultural nostrums of one's one day" in great literature as well as through consultation with the virtues and practices that have abided through previous generations and which are our inheritance.[23]

A chastened reader may be humbled by the discovery that vileness possessed by a character in one area of life may live side by side with great virtue in another, that nobility of spirit does not guarantee success or even competence, that life confounds all, and that while the true, the good, and the beautiful may be one in Plato's heaven they are mismatched often on Earth. These paradoxical realities, inconvenient to the propagation of any political program or philosophical system but often conveyed by the great authors, remind readers that life is not so easily sorted out and that humanity extends even to people you dislike. Not only does good and great literature offer the possibility of a guide, but a guide chosen not on the basis of the tastes and prejudices of the chooser, but on the basis of decades and even, in certain cases, several centuries worth of recommendations from critics and readers. It is an imperfect guide, to be sure, but the complexities of life coupled with man's moral and intellectual limitations make it all the more valuable.

And so we return to the question of the presence and influence of the Midwest and specifically, Iowa, in James Seaton's work. Perhaps most obviously in the fact that so many of the thinkers and writers Seaton wrote on, such as Irving Babbit, Christopher Lasch, Russell Kirk, Alan Bloom, and of course, Abraham Lincoln, were themselves Midwesterners. But it is also present in his very thought and analysis itself, and indeed a strong presence in his arguments for the continued importance of Humanistic literary criticism.

In order to see the influence of the Midwest in James Seaton's approach to literary criticism, first one must take note of how he himself viewed the region. On the one hand, he was certainly not a "Northern Agrarian" or someone who romanticized the region. And yet his affection for the region does come through in his writing. For example, according to Seaton, "not even the most enthusiastic defenders of the cultures of New England or the south or the coast argue that their region is a true heartland rather than the Midwest."[24] A number of times, he quoted approvingly perhaps the most famous Midwesterner of them all, Abraham Lincoln, in his characterization of the Midwest and its occupants as "the order-loving citizens of the Land of Steady Habits."[25] Seaton identified these "Steady Habits," at least in part, with "middle-class values" such as "family, work and love"; unromantic virtues whose commission may not lead to esteem or attention but fidelity to which nonetheless has shown to yield a durable civil order.[26] Seaton observed that, even as the "middle-class values" prevalent in the Midwest seem dull and prosaic at a first glance, on the other hand, "the promise of exemption from the common human lot is immensely seductive," leading many to "reject the claims of family and everyday obligations in the name of some 'authentic' moral gesture."[27] However, he cautioned "most human beings, those who are not saints descend below when they seek to rise above" such obligations.[28]

As noted earlier, those familiar with Seaton's public writings will find very little of a personal or autobiographical nature. And yet there is at least one exception: a paper Seaton gave, in 1998, which, though it did not involve him as the subject, was indeed of a deeply and explicitly personal nature. Its topic was not literature or the criticism of it, but rather the life and character of a recently deceased native Iowan: his father, John Everett Seaton. When Seaton delivered his father's eulogy, he refrained from waxing philosophical. He did not call upon his vast knowledge of literature and poetry to make allusions to classic works. He made the point, simply and clearly, that his father had been a good man. And it was clear that for James Seaton, to be a good man, a man who was honest in his dealings, dutiful, and loving to his family and kind to others, was something of immense importance. John Everett Seaton was, he suggested in so many words, a man of "Steady Habits."

A year prior, on quite a different stage, before a crowd of professors and writers and the cameras of C-SPAN, James Seaton presented another paper, regarding the life of another Midwesterner, Indianan Alan Bloom, and the legacy of his most famous work, *The Closing of the American Mind*. Responding to the sentiments expressed in Bloom's contention both that "life lived without the illumination of a philosophical conversion is a second rate affair at best" and that "men may live more fully in reading Plato and Shakespeare than any other time because then they are participating in essential being and forgetting their accidental lives," Seaton remarked that one may "appreciate his passion for the great authors and still feel that the dismissal of family, work and love as accidental is a romantic error."[29] Yet he credited Bloom with seeing beyond this error when he paid "tribute to a very different version of morality" in his observation that "There is a perennial and unobtrusive view that morality consists in such things as telling the truth, paying one's debts, respecting one's parents and doing no voluntary harm to anyone. Those are all things that are easy to say and hard to do; they do not attract much attention and win little honor in the world."[30] This seemed to elicit from Seaton some of his strongest praise for Bloom, as he found it to his "credit that he articulated this prosaic morality so sympathetically."[31]

Of all the authors who gave talks that evening at the University of Chicago conference on *The Closing of The American Mind*, Seaton was the only one who seemed compelled to dwell on the subject of traditional morality or what some might call "family values."

Particularly, he addressed the seductive "promise of exemption from the frustrations and difficulties of the common human lot" offered by the Romantic view of literature.[32] As much as he truly loved literature, he could not embrace a view of literature that belittled the aforementioned "prosaic morality" or prided itself on offering an escape from its perceived banalities.[33] Here, perhaps, we can detect a sense of the gratitude he'd later state in a more explicit manner, for his own father's commitment to the difficult, unglamorous duties of providing a decent and loving home for their children and instilling values necessary for a moral life.

This ability to appreciate and understand the value and meaningfulness of principles, customs, and experiences of everyday life against the temptations of various manifestations of the romantic impulse can be, according to Seaton, aided by the Humanistic approach to literary study and criticism. On the one hand, Dr. Seaton observed that the literary critic is not a "noticeably better person" than the average one, observing that in his experience "members of departments of English …don't seem particularly superior in wisdom or goodness to people who have not been privileged to spend much of their lives reading good books."[34] On the other hand, he believed that literature could be turned to "as a source of insight about human life" and that "one is less likely to believe that a currently fashionable philosophy is the summation of human wisdom if one is able to measure the current fashion not only by one's own experience but by the experience embodied in *The Iliad, The Divine Comedy* and *Pride and Prejudice.*"[35] And if great literature provides some window into the complexities and difficulties that abound in the human experience, then seemingly banal things like the basic order of everyday life might be seen to be more precious, more fragile, and harder to replace than one might apprehend upon first reckoning.

The long shadow cast by literary classics and social conventions can certainly seem at times an oppressive one. For many, reading the works of Homer is a long and arduous task, the completion of which is often followed by an even greater challenge: making sense of it. The act of conforming one's behavior to traditional morality and custom can also be difficult and seemingly unrewarding in a myriad of ways. Advocacy for classic literature can leave one appearing every bit the snob and elitist, just as advocacy for traditional morality may render one backward-looking, uncritical, or even prejudiced. Yet to "deprive" one's self of "such guidance" as offered by either is potentially disastrous, presuming as it does, that the individual is resourceful enough to come up with something superior to what he is rebelling against.[36]

Just as the Humanistic Tradition of literary criticism was best characterized, in Seaton's mind, as a continuing conversation between sometimes opposing voices rather than as a doctrine, the humility to consult custom and tradition rather than presume superiority to it does not preclude one from questioning it. In fact, one of the values Seaton saw in the Humanistic Tradition was that it could potentially "refine" and "clarify" traditional sensibilities and customs in addition to offering readers a means of tempering the romantic inclinations that so often lead to their disdain and dismissal.[37] In considering the recommendations left behind by past generations in our inherited traditions, one might also consider themselves not as a blind subject but, again, as a participant in a conversation with past and present generations.

Though skeptical of literature's ability to elevate one above the concerns that dominate everyday life, Seaton still viewed it as something of great importance; he believed that works of literature that succeed in capturing something of the human experience have the potential to not simply entertain us, but to provide us with a certain sort of instruction as well. Good literature, he asserted, can provide a "critical filter" for the popular nostrums of a given age and time, so that we might not give in too easily to the temptation to discard as anachronistic those principles and customs which might not fit entirely with the thought and fashion of the day.[38] It might, upon reflection, lead some to honor those very principles, even the sorts of principles that one might be reared on in a place like Sioux City, Iowa, by a man like John Everett Seaton.

Notes

[1] James Seaton, "Russell Kirk as a Midwestern Author" (paper delivered as part of a panel at the Society for the Study of Midwestern Literature, Michigan State University, June 2, 2015). Other panelists included Gleaves Whitney, James E. Person Jr., and Jon Lauck, 1:47:34, https://kirkcenter.org/audio-and-video/russell-kirk-as-a-midwestern-writer/.

[2] John Everett Seaton, "A Claims Man Views the Hartford Insurance Co.," (n.p., 1976), 1.

[3] Ibid., 2.

[4] Ibid., 2.

[5] Ibid., 2.

[6] Ibid., 3.

[7] James Seaton, personal email to author, January 29, 2011.

[8] Ibid.

[9] Ibid.

[10] James Seaton, personal email to author, June 11, 2012.

[11] Ibid.

[12] Ibid.

[13] Ibid.

[14] James Seaton, personal email to author, November 17, 2013.

[15] Ibid.

[16] James Seaton, *A Reading of Vergil's Georgics* (Amsterdam: Adolf M. Hakkert, 1983), 11.

[17] Ibid., 11

[18] Ibid., 15.

[19] James Seaton, "A Rationale for Teaching General Humanities," *Journal of General Education* 29:3 (1997): 218.

[20] James Seaton, "The Gift of Christopher Lasch," *First Things*, August 1994, http://www.firstthings.com/article/1994/08/the-gift-of-christopher-lasch.

[21] Ibid.

[22] James Seaton, "Teaching Literature," Joyce Carol Oates, A. B. Yoshua, Frank Kermode, Werner Dannhauser. C-Span, May 17, 1997, video of lecture, 2:00:30, https://www.c-span.org/video/?81303-1/teaching-literature#.

[23] Ibid.

[24] Ibid.

[25] Ibid.

[26] Seaton, "Teaching Literature."

[27] Ibid.

[28] Ibid.

[29] Ibid.

[30] Ibid.

[31] Ibid.

[32] Ibid.

[33] Ibid.

[34] James Seaton, "Literary Criticism and the Cultural Politics of Value" (paper, Critical Institutions, Michigan State University, March 2006).

[35] Seaton, "Teaching Literature."

[36] Ibid.

[37] Ibid.

[38] Ibid.

Chapter 13

"Harvey Dunn Colors":
The Art of the Big Sioux River Valley

Christopher Vondracek
Forum News Service

M y old musician friend, Jim, and his wife, Jill, live out near an exhaustedly-leaning barn, stripped of most of its redness, east of Rowena, South Dakota, and a softball's toss east of the Big Sioux River. It's a river he knows well, this curly-Q, irascible, sod-smeared river that curiously flushes northward over purple cliffs down in Sioux Falls only to slosh hard against steep, sodden walls beneath the watchful gaze of a pig slaughterhouse and then pass under charcoal-steel railroad bridge after railroad bridge buffered with a football field's length of untrammeled woodland and cow-tromping fields on its way down toward the Missouri in Sioux City, Iowa.

Jim has the eye of an artist, running a framing business in Aberdeen in the 1980s, so he gave me pause, when, some summers ago after a musical gig of ours in Canton, South Dakota, another Big Sioux port, with the sun still clenching to life in the orange sky, Jim told me he was taking the "scenic route" back up to their home east of Rowena.

"The *scenic* route?" I asked, incredulously.

"It goes right along the Big Sioux," Jim explained, holding his guitar with one hand and rubbing the other wide hand over his balding head. "Prettiest little river road no one knows about."

᪥

Those of us who live in those lands between the Mississippi and Missouri rivers haven't been allowed to claim any largesse of natural beauty. The land in the dead middle of this—an area Frederick Manfred called "Siouxland"[1]—is a glacial-scarred, tilled, farm country brown with dirt in the spring before planting, topped with a litany of green row crops in the summer into the brown fall, and buried beneath suffocating white snow in the winter. It is a plane upon which we build lives, with few topographical aesthetics or roving oil painters. Sure, there are hiatuses of geological prominence that might've spurred the great American watercolorist and essayist Thomas Cole to pen a paragraph in his traveler's notebook. There's the Coteau des Prairies up near Sisseton, South Dakota, where the hills rise like the backs of slumbering giants up from the north-flowing Red River Valley's auspicious beginnings. Or there's Blue Mound State Park in southwestern Minnesota, where Manfred lived in a pink quartzite ranch home near an improbable plateau topped with bluestem.

But, curiously, it's this *absence* of majestic wildness, of dark forests, of inchoate spills of running water, that seems to dissipate the farther inward you travel in this tract. Life may still hold some electric, spirited photographable potential along the banks of the Des Moines River, which plunges through a prairie valley around Jackson, Minnesota, or farther west in the Jim River, that non-navigable waterway bifurcating East River South Dakota and bursting its banks as often as cowboys thrown from the bareback of wild broncos out of the chute to the tune of some Aaron Copland suite. But, *aesthetically* speaking, which is a language perhaps appreciated only by *plein air*[2] painters and long-haul truckers, once you reach the South Dakota border, once you hit that unspectacular crest of interstate preceding Sioux Falls, dotted with billboards for petting zoos and feed companies, where a minor glacial end moraine passes for a ski slope, you've perhaps hit the dullest stretch in all of America.

That's why Jim's words felt like the delusions uttered about a high school girlfriend who got away decades earlier. I wanted to say, *this is what happens to us when we're stuck. We start hallucinating.*

But then I drove that road. A month later, coming north out of Sioux City, with Jim's jest still in mind, I stayed off the interstate back to Sioux Falls and drove a side road hugging the eastern banks of the

Big Sioux River, cutting through woods and hills, noting distant farms, and by the time I reached Westfield, Iowa, amidst a cottonwood savannah, I felt like the narrator in *Big Fish*,[3] who discovers at his father's funeral that the obvious lies his father had been telling his whole life about befriending a beautiful circus witch and a top-hat-wearing giant was absolutely, no-stitch-of-fraud true.

This little road, this little river country *was* breath-taking. I'd just missed it the whole time. No one had ever told me about tangled wilds of the Big Sioux. But, then again, I hadn't been hanging out with painters.

My dad complained just the other day, as we rolled back home from Blue Earth to Wells, Minnesota. "It's one big garden," he said.

He said it like it was a *bad* thing. But, of course, Harvey Dunn's *The Prairie Is My Garden*,[4] the painting of a woman holding a bouquet of prairie flowers and a shears, protecting her daughter from a coyote or approaching traveler with two farmhouses in the background and a slice of blue creek winding through the pasture, is about the closest thing to a postage stamp this region possesses.

Born amidst the Dakota Boom in the mid-1880s in Manchester, South Dakota, in Kingsbury County, Dunn encountered a portentous art instructor at South Dakota Agricultural College in Brookings and took flight to Delaware to study painting.[5] While he lived in New Jersey along the Hudson, Dunn painted of places he'd seen, the European Front during World War I, but also the Dakota prairie, such as in *Dakota Woman*, with a woman sitting astride a parasol out on the prairie, blocking the sun over an infant's head, with a J-shaped farmhouse in the background.

His school was American Naturalism, and while Dunn *physically* lived out east, teaching classes atop Grand Central Station, his creative output mediated the prairie's imagination for persons who never lived there: wide-open, desolate, but hauntingly beautiful fields, where (often) women and children eked out civilized existences, strewn from the east coast's fineries, to dig, cook, care for, build up, and withstand natural and unnatural impulses found for the generation after pioneer life.

When I interned at *South Dakota Magazine* in the summer of 2007, fresh after college graduation, it didn't take long for me to encounter and learn the depths of Dunn's impact upon the local imagination as so many readers wrote in about him, our articles obliquely referenced him, and his splashes of robust, unrestrained country living worked through the publication's veins.

And that Americana hypnosis has retained its hold.

In early August of 2020 a group of amateur painting enthusiasts under the guise of the Harvey Dunn Society gathered for a virtual "plein art" festival across eastern South Dakota.[6] On a hot day, with his water-bottle at the ready to spritz down his drying canvas, Sioux Falls artist Steve Randall recorded the festival's top-viewed video on a homestead near De Smet, South Dakota, roughly 40 miles west of the Big Sioux, painting what appeared to be, by any other angle, a simple road passing behind some cottonwoods.

"I'm going to focus in on that space between the two big cottonwoods" said Randall, using the clinically formal description of his "center of interest." "We'll do that with some green and sienna and ochre. That's a good Harvey Dunn color, isn't it?"

A Dunn painting does not speak imaginatively to a person who is yet to understand or think critically about the eccentricities that belong to the Dakota prairie or the color brown. His colors *aren't* terribly pleasing, after all. They look like what I found out my bus window on the way to school: a third of blue sky, a third of brown/green ground, and in the middle, something ordinary that people are up to. They are, in other words, *plain* images. But the older I've gotten the more I realize this plain sense of home is itself the mystery. *We are the place without mountains, the place without metropolises.* We are Tom Brokaw's accent-less voice. And Dunn gave us that, lustily and sentimentally, in a square.

The Harvey Dunn Society understands this. As Randall scraped acrylics onto his Gessobord, the painter opened up the raw materials that anyone must work with in this region: sky, country roads, and most frustratingly, cottonwoods.

"The tree mass on this side gets pretty wild," remarked Randall, adding like an inside joke, "It's a cottonwood."

By day's end, so many of the day's participating painters had cottonwoods, baroque and gangly. But each also had something spiritu-

ally of southeastern South Dakota. There were plenty of Van Gogh-y
wetlands, with thick, brush-stroked grasses lining lily-popping ponds.
There were green-and-tan hillsides, green-and-tan treescapes, brown
roads cutting up green fields under wide, blue skies, and even an occasional railroad bridge, like those crossing the Big Sioux.

But there was a curious element at play, too. While Dunn had lived
and worked in the New York City region, painting persuasively of the
Dakota topography and social relations, in painter after painter participating in the Harvey Dunn Society event, that is, painters who lived
and worked *in* South Dakota, somehow couldn't muster a faithfully
accurate painting *of* the Dakotas, I thought. The images they produced
of the Big Sioux valley, rather, were nostalgic, romanticized, and for
someone who lives in this region, a little too much like aspirational
postcards.

It's not surprising that America's most famous painting school sprung
from the eponymous river, that rises in the Adirondacks and flows
down into New York Harbor. From the get-go, American artists secured an Emersonian relationship with the nation's rivers that, while
not unique in world history, probably felt the most pragmatic. Rivers
provided access points west, north, south, and *away* from the city, to
the pretty stuff…and then back again to sell paintings of what they'd
seen. It's no coincidence that New York City (and its art market) sits at
the base of the Hudson. Yet when you visit the Hudson River for the
first time you can see why painters took up brushes. The bulkhead of
bluffs—mountains really—loom over the blue river that widens and
weaves its way down to the Atlantic. On a summer's day, even now,
you can stand in Haverstraw, New York, look out at the white triangles
of sailboats dotting the river at its widest and feel compelled to grab a
paintbrush and report what you see.

Other regions felt this way, too, about their rivers. Thomas Jefferson called the wide Ohio the "most beautiful river on Earth."[7] That
liquid backbone of America, the Mississippi River, drew nineteenth-
century oil painters, such as Ferdinand Richardt,[8] who typified the upper stretches of the river along St. Paul as some Edenic paradise. There
was John Steuart Curry,[9] one of the triumvirates of American regionalists along with Grant Wood and Thomas Hart Benton, who in *The*

Mississippi idealized a Black sharecropper family stranded and praying on a rooftop amidst a swollen Mississippi River. And there are more splendid, artistically-realized rivers, too. One practitioner of the Hudson River School, Thomas Moran,[10] went west to paint romantically of the Colorado River, jostling through pink-and-purple canyons, which he painted in watercolor numerous times, toiling below jagged, solemn cliffs rich with alpenglow.

But more than affection for *rivers*, what the Hudson School gave American visual artists (and, by extension, the public) was a humorless, often overly optimistic view of our own backyard. And like a river, those of us temporally downstream feel what happened above us.

A quick survey of other painters working commercially in the Big Sioux River valley suggests the painters' inclination in that Saturday festival are not unique to the amateurs. They, too, give us a Hudson River valley patina of our backyard that we'd like to hang on the walls of the Westward Ho Country Club.

Mary Groth is perhaps one of the more commercially successful painters in the Big Sioux River region. Groth's paintings[11] *do* engage with the region's humor. I've spotted her personable paintings at Bracco Restaurant, in the Sioux Falls Regional Airport, and in an old downtown Sioux Falls grocery store. But her paintings are also stories. A young woman in a puffy blue sweater on a beach holding a Labrador. Another is of a young couple circa *Mad Men* in front of an American flag at a country wedding, maybe meeting for the first time and ready to mingle.

Another contemporary painter who works ostensibly more with water, with the Big Sioux, is Madison-based oil painter John Green,[12] who talked to me about painting downtown Sioux Falls images—like the purple, granite-exposed falls along the Big Sioux or the merchant-friendly Phillips Avenue that he remembered from his youth.

"People like to hang pictures that they can relate to, you know," said Green, toward the end of our conversation.

Green's latest paintings are of faces of the dead superimposed over a Dairy Queen in Madison. It's a peculiar image, a charity's raffle as much as a painting. But he has an entrepreneurialism in his subject-matter, using Mount Rushmore or snowmobiles in what looks like the Tetons, or a misty Jesus Christ rising above the harvest.

And then, of course, there is Terry Redlin.

Godfather of the Midwestern hunting-lands-at-sunset-set, Redlin grew up[13] (and returned to live) in Watertown, South Dakota, a regional hub of the glacial lakes region in the rectangular state's upper-right corner, located on an adolescent stretch of the Big Sioux. Perhaps incuriously, Redlin barely acknowledges the river in his paintings.

The only Terry Redlin painting that prominently, explicitly features the river that partly supports his hometown's namesake comes in 1994, when Redlin reminisces upon some Rockwellian boyhood memory of fishing along the Kemp Bridge spanning 10th Street over a smaller, narrower Big Sioux River in Watertown. In classic Redlin patina, an almost pixelated, snow-globe realism with cherubic kids and adolescent nostalgia, *Spring Fishing*[14] is lovely as a Seurat stand-in, with boys standing astutely with long poles awaiting a bounty of carp or shiners or disagreeable bullheads, the gurgle of waterfalls under the bridge, and with his caption writer—who I've been told was Redlin himself—embellishing the scene's lackadaisical potential by writing, "And, of course, there's plenty of pop and snacks waiting on the picnic table."

But even this painting, again, seems to hold a deceptive quality: it is not exactly what that place *looks like*, after all. Suspecting this, one spring Saturday, I asked my sister-in-law, Amy, while a resident physician's assistant in Watertown, to hunt down the exact location of some of Redlin's paintings. What she found was a host of local Redlin inspirations—a house near a tree swing, a grain elevator sans the pheasants Redlin planted in the foreground. And there, at the end, was the one of the river. While Redlin places a farmhouse with a stout, stone chimney with a tree-topped knoll around the river, Amy's photo shows a less grand rise of a grassy shoreline, mixed with muck. There are Canada geese in both the painting and photograph, but rather than an old hunting lodge glimmering in the distance, Amy caught what appears to be a Ford Taurus skipping over the bridge, and one of those movement-sensing lights over a dull, sided garage. Only the bridge itself, a squat, Hellenistic viaduct, appears to bear any resemblance to the image Redlin got.

⟨≈⟩

If you stand looking north out of Sioux Falls, at that little pedestrian bridge over the Big Sioux between 6ᵗʰ and 8ᵗʰ streets, you can see green hills in the distance. According to Google Maps, what you're looking at when you stand upon that bridge is actually a smattering of the South Dakota State Penitentiary or—perhaps—Smithfield Foods meat-processing center, one of the nation's largest pork slaughterhouses. You also see Raven Industries, maker of weather balloons and high-tech farm system technologies, and across the river from Raven, you can see Cherapa Place, a tower where locals started *605 Magazine,* and at the bottom of which sits a restaurant with some optimal views of the river, so long as you're not catching smells of the aforementioned slaughterhouse.

About the most popular artistic representation of the Big Sioux, both the region and the river, is the namesake of Sioux Falls. And it's captured more often in photographs than in paintings. Photographers use slow shutter speeds to suggest running water, though there's often a Coca-Cola-colored hue to the falls, and they'll often capture the river at night, under eerie lights, with black-and-white representations to obscure the water's visual contaminants. These are the paintings you can buy at mall kiosks and on dentist office walls. Understandably, photographers (and buyers) fixate on the hiatus of prairie with Lourdes-like splashing water, delighting in the spontaneity of these granite brooks as the earliest inhabitants must've bathed or swam or lived near them. But the challenge for the Big Sioux painter is to turn *inward, to see the city.*

⟨≈⟩

There are museums in the city, of course, doing this work. Ipso Gallery, run by Groth's daughter and painter, Liz Heeren, sits in an advertising agency downtown in the historic Gourley Building. Artist Jennifer White runs Post Pilgrim in a record store off East 10ᵗʰ Street. At Rehfeld's Art & Framing, one night I ran into the Black Hills water colorist John Crane. These painters all, one way or another, speak to neighbors about this region.

But on that Saturday for the paint-off in 2020, after all the other painters presented their images of pastoral South Dakota, eventually came another artist, Miguel Hugo Jimenez, who set his easel up along Phillips Avenue in crowded downtown Sioux Falls and painted a scene

I'd yet to see: a street intersection, with unceremoniously parked cars, and even with one of the city's ridiculous sculptures, a gigantic, rising guitar, in the foreground.[15] In Jimenez's video about his painting, cars honk horns and speed up at the light. Pedestrians stroll past. But Jimenez is *part* of the scene he paints. In his video, he describes his painting by saying, "It is what I got from right here. I'm on Phillips and 11th Street."

In *Beauty in the City,* historian Robert Slayton[16] takes on the Ashcan School at the turn-of-the-century in New York City, largely suggesting that what prompted the development of a grittier subject-matter for painting was reaction to the Impressionist movement's arrival in America. He says artists such as Edgar Degas fell in love with the beauty of the Parisian upper class and of the bourgeois. He quotes historian David Shi saying that Degas and Monet "populated their canvases with fashionable people in shops, cafes, theaters, ballet and opera houses, at city parks and gardens."

In *Place de la Concorde,*[17] two wealthy little sisters in fancy horse-riding caps and their greyhound take a stroll along the dank streets. In Monet's *Argenteuil, la berge en fleurs,* for example, a smattering of white lilies rest in the foreground while a hellish, yellow urban-scape resides in the background. "Industry can be recognized, but not labor," wrote British art historian T. J. Clark, of the central tenet of Impressionist painting of the cities.

And I think something similar is at play in the Big Sioux. For two decades, the Sioux Falls Area Community Foundation has placed paintings[18] of the Big Sioux on the cover of its annual reports. There are turquoise river scenes and photographic cottonwood orchards. The classic painting, though, is one like Jim Sturdevant's *View from Good Earth State Park*, a green-and-blue landscape, hyper-realistic, shot from seemingly an outcrop from the park looking south down the ox-bowing blue river as it roams green fields. Politically, I understand the roots of this faith in a bonhomie version of the river. The foundation, a philanthropist group, wants to raise money to save the river, to improve water quality, to build recreational opportunities upon the river. They, then, operate by the same faith as the storm runoff muralist who painted cartoonish fish and turtles along sewer grates in downtown

Sioux Falls to make people more aware of water quality and what they dump down the drains. *If we show them we have a beautiful river,* seems to be the thought, *then maybe they'll care about saving it.*

But I wonder if the opposite is true.

We often think that the problem of our pollution is in money, but what if we blame our understanding of the river itself? The river, as you've likely read elsewhere in this collection, literally makes a national list as one of the most polluted rivers in America. In 2012 the river hit #13 on advocacy group Environment America's[19] list of dirtiest rivers in the country. The high levels of *E. coli* and other contaminants give folks reason to pause before recreating or fishing or really doing much of anything on the river. And while a riparian dead-zone, replete with sunken cottonwood, bags of trash, and a float of fish might not be the image you want to reach for on the cover of the foundation's annual, this painting would, like J. M. W. Turner's *The Slave Ship*,[20] show us a world that we should stop trying to ignore.

In 2020 during the South Dakota legislative session,[21] during debate about whether to pass a bill that would state-wide prohibit municipalities from passing straw legislation (i.e. requiring reusable straws), a Republican legislator from Pierre, Sen. Jeff Monroe, stood to say, "It doesn't bother me....It's habitat for bait fish. It's habitat for crayfish. I really don't have a problem with that."

The pregnant antecedent to which the "it" was referring was a plastic coffee tub "getting tossed into the river."

Four years earlier, in 2016, legislators tried to clean up the river by passing a set-back law—called riparian buffer strips—in the state, forgiving certain taxes for landowners, such as those who might own cattle, to push back operations 50 feet away from the river and instead grow four inches of perennial grasses in that patch to help water quality. It was similar to a law passed in neighboring Minnesota. But Gov. Dennis Daugaard vetoed the bill, suggesting it unfair to taxpayers. Two years later, they passed the measure, barring county approval, but few have taken part in the voluntary program. In fact, in the 2021 legislative session, while the state merged agencies overseeing agriculture and the environment, the departmental secretary, Hunter Roberts, noted the merger will give "a lot more validity" to the fledgling buffer strip program.

In short, it turns out, few are doing the program.

"It's a profitability issue," Jim Ristau, sustainability director for South Dakota's Corn Growers association told *The Otter* in the summer of 2020,[22] a newsletter published by Friends of the Big Sioux River. "The areas where buffers can be grown can be productive land, and although offering a tax incentive is an effort in the right direction, one serious issue facing landowners is trying to equate growing and maintaining a buffer versus growing and producing a cash crop."

This is the central problem, the unshakeable reality that land is money. And when land is money, when it is reduced solely to one of its applicable uses, rather than a panoply of possibilities, it's tougher to collect memories from its belly.

It is certainly not impossible for an artist to paint their own backyard, their own garden faithfully. But I wonder if it's easier to see South Dakota from New Jersey, as Dunn did. Or to faithfully remember through staggered engagements with a place that mostly lives in your imagination. In short, the reimagining of the Big Sioux will require an entire region, not just the painters, to reorient itself toward the river.

Both my grandparents were born in Union County, South Dakota, whose eastern edge borders Iowa and the Big Sioux River. They married on a Monday morning at an old church just a couple miles west of the Big Sioux, and from them I inherited a palimpsest of objects, dance halls, churches, and personalities that were never mine. On an emotional map, I can point to a homestead I'd never actually visited or the old St. Mary's Church with the cemetery (that I *had* visited, though never stepped inside), and I knew these old tales about how the Norwegian Lutherans approached my great-great-grandfather Thomas Fitzgerald to buy a few acres of his rolling farmland to build a Lutheran church with a steeple you might see all the way to Iowa, and my ancestor—a Catholic—refused them.

"I won't sell you that land," he said, according to family legend. "But I will give it to you."

In all these years, over 30, coming to Beresford, I'd heard these stories, like images from a movie playing in my head, but we never heard about the river growing up. When I asked my mother, she came to me with geography. "Well, because, remember, Mom grew up in Gerryowen. That was still about five, ten miles away from the river. The closer you got to the river, I think, those were Norwegians. Mom's family, of course, was all Irish."

Then Mom slipped into some memory that her great-aunt, Tillie, had told her.

"Those Norwegian kids used to swear at the O'Connors in Norwegian," Mom said. "And since they didn't know any swear words in any other language, the O'Connors just yelled back at them in Latin."

My uncle, Tommy McGill, though, said he remembered his own mother, my grandmother, talking about the Missouri flooding "below the bluffs" in Vermillion, sending the whole town packing for the hillside.

"I don't know why we never heard about the river," said my uncle. "Probably because we were told to 'stay away from the frickin water!'"

As the population centers of the Big Sioux grow, the region will necessarily begin attracting voices and visual artists who do not enlist in the region's varied campaigns, nor to the ancient screeds to flee the water, to stop it up, or dredge it, or merely dump into it. Then, the paintings of the Big Sioux will become paintings *not* of the Big Sioux as it's remembered, but as it has become, or as it's always been. Although, this will require engaging with the river directly. As such, there will always be a place for those living along the river, who've stayed faithful to this place, as the riparian buffers winnow and wax.

I texted Jim when I started working on this assignment and asked him for the prettiest view on the river. "Try Klondike Bridge," he texted back.

Having moved back to South Dakota, I drove down and found a scene, just above the rock rapids of the East Klondike bridge, northeast of Canton and northwest of Inwood, Iowa, and I went upstream for about a half hour. Every time I dipped my oar in, the yellow flipper disappeared beneath the mud, and when I returned to where I started, other than a few trumpeting Canada geese and some bored Sunday afternoon fishermen, the most drama-filled encounter was the chicken hawk who sat bowing a tree branch high above with its side eye watching me as I dashed my paddle into the brown river. I watched him as I moved downstream, treading carefully, watching the hawk watch me, wondering what image played off its iris, and whether it saw anything other than food, than function, or whether it, too, saw something it liked in the scene of it all, in this kayaker in a green life-jacket and a yellow paddle moving slowly up the brown river, through the Harvey Dunn colors.

Notes

1   Frederick Manfred, *This is the Year* (New York: Doubleday, 1947), introductory map.

2   "En Plein Air," Wikipedia, Wikimedia Foundation, August 19, 2021, https://en.wikipedia.org/wiki/En_plein_air.

3   *Big Fish*, dir. Tim Burton (2003; Culver City, CA; Columbia Pictures, 2003), film.

4   Harvey Dunn, *The Prairie Is My Garden,* 1950, oil on canvas, 9 x 12.25 x 0.25 inches, Brookings, SD.

5   "Harvey Dunn's Biography," South Dakota State University, accessed September 2, 2021, https://www.sdstate.edu/south-dakota-art-museum/harvey-dunns-biography.

6   Steve Randall, "Today's Second Demonstration Was from Artist Steve Randall," Harvey Dunn Society (Facebook, August 7, 2020), https://www.facebook.com/harveydunnsociety/videos/726364204589614.

7   Thomas Jefferson, *Notes on the State of Virginia* (Paris: Abbe Morellet, 1786), 8.

8   "(Joachim) Ferdinand Richardt." The Society of California Pioneers, accessed September 2, 2021, https://www.californiapioneers.org/collections/art/artists/joachim-ferdinand-richardt/.

9   John Steuart Curry, *The Mississippi,*1935, tempera on canvas, 36 x 48 inches, St. Louis.

10 "Thomas Moran," Smithsonian American Art Museum, accessed September 2, 2021, https://Americanart.si.edu/artist/Thomas-moran-3406.

11 Lance Nixon, "Dakota Life: Picturing a storied land, the art of Mary Groth," *Capital Journal,* published Feb. 19, 2015 (updated Sept. 24, 2019), accessed on September 2, 2021, https://capjournal.com/news/dakota-life-picturing-a-storied-land-the-art-of-mary-groth/.

12 John Green, interview by author, June 2020.

13 Keith G. Olson, *The Art of Terry Redlin: Master of Memories* (Italy: Hadley House, 1997), 12.

14 Terry Redlin, *Spring Fishing,*1996, oil on canvas, 41 x 26.5 inches, Watertown, SD.

15 "Miguel Jimenez was live" (Facebook, August 7, 2020), https://www.facebook.com/migue.jimenez.39/videos/3116690538457554,

16 Robert Slayton, *Beauty in the City: The Ashcan School* (New York: Excelsior Editions, 2017).

17 Edgar Degas, *Place de la Concorde*, 1879, oil on canvas, 46.3 x 30.9 inches, St. Petersburg, Russia.

18 "Supporting Local Art," Sioux Falls Area Community Foundation, accessed September 2, 2021, https://www.sfacf.org/about-us/supporting-local-art.(b) "Supporting Local Art," Sioux Falls Area Community Foundation, accessed September 2, 2021, https://www.sfacf.org/about-us/supporting-local-art.

19 The Associated Press, "South Dakota's Big Sioux among dirtiest rivers in nation," *Rapid City Journal*, May 7, 2012, accessed September 2, 2021, https://rapidcityjournal.com/news/soust-dakotas-big-sioux-among-dirtiest-rivers-in-nation/article.

20 J. M. W. Turner, *The Slave Ship*, 1840, oil on canvas, 48 x 36 inches, Boston.

21 Christopher Vondracek. "South Dakota weighs outlaw of bans on plastic bags, straws," *The Washington Times*, January 28, 2020, accessed September 2, 2021, https:/www.washingtontimes.com/news/2020/jan/28/south-dakota-weighs-outlaw-of-bans-on-plastic-bags/.

22 "Boosting Buffers," *The Otter* (Summer 2020), accessed September 2, 2021, https://friendsofthebigsiouxriver.org/newsletters.

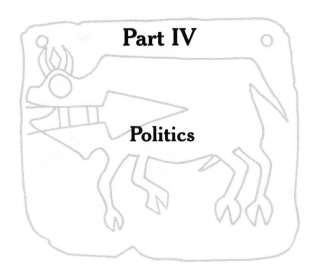

Part IV

Politics

Chapter 14

The Politics of the Valley

Matthew Housiaux
Kiplinger

It is hard to overstate the Big Sioux River's importance to South Dakota. Today, the nine counties through which the river flows (Brookings, Codington, Grant, Hamlin, Lincoln, Minnehaha, Moody, Union) account for over 40% of the state's population and nearly half of its GDP, shares that have only grown in recent decades.[1] Sioux Falls—South Dakota's biggest city, named for the iconic rapids of the river that flows through it—alone accounts for over 20% of the state's population.[2] The region is also home, by birth or migration, to some of South Dakota's most important political figures, from the state's first governor, Arthur C. Mellette (Codington County) to its current one, Kristi Noem (Hamlin County).[3] Because of the region's dominant position in the state, its political culture has, in some ways, come to define the political culture of South Dakota as a whole—one of small-r civic republicanism built upon an economic foundation of family farming.[4] At the same time, these factors also distinguish the Big Sioux valley from other parts of South Dakota, in particular the mining-and-ranching-dominated western half of the state.[5] Moreover, the region itself has evolved over the years—thanks to the growth of Sioux Falls and the emergence of new industries, such as finance and health care—in ways that have also changed its politics.[6]

Along with small-r republicanism, so too the Republican Party has long held sway in state politics and along the Big Sioux River. Indeed, the foundations for Republican rule were laid well prior to statehood. As historian John Miller has noted, "The types of people who flocked into southern Dakota after the [Civil War] leaned heavily toward the party of Lincoln," including New England Yankees, Midwestern transplants, German and Scandinavian immigrants and Union Army veterans, many of whom ultimately settled in the Big Sioux valley.[7] At the time of the 1890 census, the first taken after South Dakota achieved statehood, the nine Big Sioux River counties accounted for nearly a quarter of South Dakota's population.[8] They also strongly backed the GOP during the state's first major elections in 1889. Among the Republican victors was Arthur C. Mellette, a Midwestern transplant (originally from Indiana) who first came to Dakota Territory in 1879 after receiving a job in the Office of Public lands in Springfield. The office and his job soon moved to Watertown, where Mellette built both a mansion on the bluffs above the Big Sioux River and a successful career in territorial politics.[9] In 1889 he became both the last governor of Dakota Territory and the first governor of the state of South Dakota, winning election to the latter post with over 69% of the statewide vote and 74% of the Big Sioux River county vote.[10]

Despite the state's predilection for Republicans, South Dakota also boasts a tradition of agrarian radicalism that has allowed for periods of sustained two-party competition, as well as the occasional independent or third-party reform movement. This tendency emerged early in the state's history with the rise of Populism, which coincided with a downturn in the agricultural economy. In 1890 farmer anger stemming from high debt, low commodity prices, and drought conditions inspired the formation of an agriculture-focused Independent Party. Henry Loucks, a farmer from Deuel County, became the party's candidate for governor and received 32% of the vote in that fall's election—good enough for second place against the incumbent Mellette, who saw his share of the statewide vote fall to 44%.[11] Along the Big Sioux River, Loucks made significant inroads with the region's sizable population of Norwegian farmers, who traditionally favored Republicans but backed many of the candidate's proposed reforms, including government ownership of railroads and the free and unlimited coinage of silver. This strong showing put both Loucks and the Big Sioux valley at the forefront of a growing movement that would soon coalesce into the national Populist Party. Loucks would even preside over the party's first national convention in Omaha in 1892.[12]

Despite some electoral success, South Dakota Populists didn't have a real breakthrough until 1896, when they joined with the Democrats to form the state's first viable opposition party. Populist candidate Andrew Lee won the governorship, carrying four of nine Big Sioux River counties: Brookings, Minnehaha, Moody, and Union. In the presidential race, Democrat William Jennings Bryan, the Populist standard bearer, also won the state, carrying the same four Big Sioux River counties as Lee.[13] Crucial to their victories were German and Norwegian farmers, who voted disproportionately for Populist candidates. Such voters were not hard to find along the Big Sioux River, particularly Norwegians, who had settled in the area in large numbers during the Great Dakota Boom of 1878-1887. By 1900 the state's heaviest concentration of Norwegians was in the Big Sioux valley, with particularly large numbers in Minnehaha County and other parts of southeastern South Dakota.[14]

The Populist era proved to be rather short lived. Lee would narrowly win reelection two years later, improving on his electoral performance along the Big Sioux River; he flipped Lincoln County and won by even bigger margins in Brookings, Minnehaha, Moody, and Union. But Republicans took back control of the state legislature and in 1900, the governorship too. The gradual recovery of the farm economy also undermined support for William Jennings Bryan, who lost decisively in his 1900 rematch with Republican William McKinley. In South Dakota, a state Bryan narrowly won in 1896, the Democratic nominee garnered only 41.1% of the vote and failed to win a single Big Sioux River county.[15] Nevertheless, Populism did have a lasting impact on state and regional politics in two ways: (1) through policy achievements, such as the creation of the initiative and referendum process, which allowed the voters themselves to propose and vote on new laws; and (2) by establishing a pattern of political reform and retrenchment that would play out many times throughout South Dakota's history.[16]

While Populism gradually withered away, the reform spirit endured in South Dakota with the emergence of the Progressive Movement. Progressivism originated in the 1890s as a municipal reform movement, focused on rooting out corruption and addressing social and economic problems stemming from America's rapid urbanization and industrialization in the late nineteenth century: Industrial monopoly, labor conditions, machine politics, consumer protection, etc. In South Dakota, the movement was more agrarian in both style and substance, but nevertheless appealed to a diverse coalition of farmers, laborers, small businessmen, clergy, educators, women, and others. The diversity of this coalition was reflected in Progressives' legislative accomplishments, which ranged from establishing a pure food and drug commission to providing farmers with low-interest loans and hail insurance.[17]

At the ballot box, Progressivism was even more successful than Populism along the Big Sioux River. In part, this was because Progressives in South Dakota existed primarily as a faction within the dominant Republican Party, rather than as an opposing party. The region's high concentration of Norwegian voters, among the strongest backers of Progressive Republicans during this period, may also have given such candidates an added boost.[18] Indeed, Progressive candidates frequently did better along the Big Sioux River than they did in the state overall. In 1906 Republican Coe I. Crawford, South Dakota's first Progressive governor, received nearly 70% of the vote in Big Sioux River counties, versus 65% statewide.[19] The region also strongly backed President Theodore Roosevelt during both his 1904 reelection campaign and his 1912 comeback bid on the Progressive, or Bull Moose, Party ticket.[20] Even as the movement's strength started to wane in the 1920s, the Progressive label could still be an asset. During the 1924 presidential election, renowned Progressive Senator Robert "Fighting Bob" LaFollette (R-WI) won five Big Sioux River counties (Codington, Grant, Lincoln, Moody, and Roberts) running as an independent against Republican Calvin Coolidge and Democrat John W. Davis.[21]

LaFollette's second-place finish in South Dakota during the 1924 presidential election was yet another testament to the fact that, in the early years of state politics, most meaningful competition occurred within the GOP. Democratic candidates, with a few notable exceptions, generally struggled to break through.[22] The agrarian revolt of Populism in the 1890s represented the first major break with that trend. The second, also led by farmers, was the New Deal, which opened another temporary window of two-party competition. The roots of this political shift in the 1930s lay in the depressed farm economy of the 1920s. While much of America prospered during the "Roaring Twenties," farmers in South Dakota and elsewhere were plagued by falling commodity prices, bank failures and, eventually, drought—a situation made worse by the collapse of the stock market in 1929 and the resulting Great Depression.[23]

As would prove true many times over the next few decades, bad news for farmers translated into good news for Democrats at the ballot box, starting with William J. Bulow (Union County). A Beresford-based lawyer and politician, Bulow in 1926 became the first Democrat elected governor in South Dakota, despite capturing only 47% of the statewide vote. He fared much better in the Big Sioux valley, his home region, winning 52% of the vote and carrying seven of nine counties.[24] Bulow was hardly a transformative politician. By most accounts, he got along well with the GOP-controlled state legislature and avoided partisan politics.[25] But that was enough to help him win a second term as governor in 1928 and a Senate seat in 1930.[26] More importantly, Bulow's success set the stage for additional Democratic victories over the next decade. In 1932 Franklin Roosevelt became only the second Democrat to win South Dakota in a presidential election, carrying all nine Big Sioux River counties in the process. That same year, Tom Berry became South Dakota's second Democratic governor, though the West River politician fared much worse than Roosevelt along the Big Sioux River, carrying only five of nine counties.[27] Notably, Berry's Republican opponent, Warren Green, hailed from Hamlin County, and thus may have had something of a home-region advantage in the contest. Green had the misfortune of taking office at the height of the Depression, and his refusal to provide direct aid to struggling farmers played a major role in his ultimate defeat.[28]

This initial period of Democratic dominance did not last long. By 1938 the GOP was back in control of the governor's mansion, the state legislature, both House seats and one of the state's two Senate seats (they would reclaim the other one in 1942).[29] The Big Sioux valley presaged this trend. While Roosevelt and Bulow won reelection in 1936, both did worse along the Big Sioux than they did in the state overall.[30] One leader of the GOP resurgence was Karl Mundt (Minnehaha County), a Humboldt native who captured South Dakota's East River congressional seat in 1938. Mundt would go on to serve five terms in the House before being elected to the Senate in 1948. A debilitating stroke forced him out of office in 1973 after 24 years in the chamber, making him both the state's longest-serving member of Congress and one of the Big Sioux valley's greatest political success stories.[31]

Republicans once again dominated South Dakota politics during the 1940s and much of the 1950s, a reflection of both the GOP's underlying strength in the state and America's gradual shift from New Deal liberalism to Cold War conservatism. Several Big Sioux valley politicians were key players during this period. In Washington, D.C., Karl Mundt played a crucial role in fellow Senator Joseph McCarthy's (R-WI) controversial campaign to suss out Communists in the U.S. government. Mundt was also instrumental in the creation of Interstate 29, which runs through all nine Big Sioux River counties and has since played a crucial role in the region's population growth and economic development.[32] In Pierre, Sigurd Anderson—a native of Norway whose family later settled in Lincoln County—became one of the most successful governors in state history, at least from an electoral perspective. In 1952 Anderson secured 70.2% of the vote in his gubernatorial reelection campaign, a record that would later be broken by Bill Janklow in 1982.[33] The GOP landslide of 1952 marked the peak of the party's success during the postwar era, both statewide and in the Big Sioux valley. In the presidential election, Republican Dwight Eisenhower cruised to victory, carrying all nine Big Sioux River counties, five of them (Brookings, Hamlin, Lincoln, Minnehaha, Moody) with over 70% of the vote. Sigurd Anderson, meanwhile, won 71.5% of the Big Sioux River vote, slightly better than the 70.2% he got statewide.[34] Republicans also claimed all but two seats in the state legislature.[35]

Two things helped revive Democratic fortunes in South Dakota. One was Eisenhower Agriculture Secretary Ezra Taft Benson, whose effort to roll back farm price supports earned him the title of "worst Secretary of Agriculture in history" among many in South Dakota.[36] The other was George McGovern, a war hero and college professor who helped rebuild the state Democratic Party, in part through diligent organizing, and in part by capitalizing on Benson's enormous unpopularity. In his effort to revive the state Democratic Party, McGovern notably touted the achievements of the New Deal, from farm price supports to rural electrification, and their current benefits to farmers. This strategy finally bore fruit during the 1956 elections.[37] While Eisenhower easily carried South Dakota on his way to a landslide reelection, his share of the vote fell both statewide and in every single Big Sioux River county. McGovern, meanwhile, managed to get himself elected in South Dakota's East River congressional district, carrying six of nine Big Sioux River counties. One of them was Codington County, home to McGovern's Republican opponent Harold Lovre.[38] Lovre's loss on his home turf was perhaps the strongest sign that Republicans had, at least temporarily, lost credibility on agricultural issues, opening the door for McGovern and a resurgent Democratic Party.

McGovern's political ascendancy, which culminated with him winning the Democratic nomination for president in 1972, also coincided with the growing importance of the Big Sioux valley to winning elections in the state, especially for Democrats. For one thing, the region possessed a growing share of the state's people, and thus votes. By 1960 Big Sioux River counties accounted for 28% of South Dakota's population, up from 23% in 1930. That number would only continue to grow in the years to come, thanks largely to the growth of Sioux Falls (Minnehaha County), the state's largest city, which by itself accounted for nearly 10% of the state's population in 1960.[39] Perhaps more importantly, the region also contained over 22% of the state's farms, up from 18% in 1930. This elevated the region's political importance at a time when the farm vote was increasingly up for grabs, even though the overall number of farms in the state and the Big Sioux valley was declining, after peaking in 1930.[40]

McGovern learned the hard way the importance of the Big Sioux valley during his first run for Senate in 1960. His GOP opponent, Karl Mundt, carried five of nine Big Sioux River counties, while winning the election by nearly five points.[41] McGovern would prevail in his second attempt two years later, going on to win reelection twice (1968, 1974) before his 1980 defeat at the hands of Republican Jim Abdnor. In each of McGovern's Senate victories, he won a majority of Big Sioux River counties. In each of his defeats, he did not. This rule also applied during McGovern's ill-fated 1972 presidential run, in which he lost his home state—and six of nine Big Sioux River counties—to Republican Richard Nixon.[42] As arguably the most successful Democratic politician in South Dakota history, McGovern's experience is strongly indicative of what other Democrats needed to win in the state in the postwar era—namely, a strong personal brand, credibility on rural issues, and some crossover support from Republicans.[43] Add to that list a strong showing along the Big Sioux River.

Other Democrats would follow in McGovern's footsteps, but not for some time. Except Democrat Ralph Herseth's single term as governor (1959-1961), Republicans continued to dominate state politics in the years following McGovern's first election to the House in 1956. In 1960, the same year McGovern lost his first Senate bid, Republican Archie Gubbrud narrowly defeated Herseth in the governor's race, winning 50.7% of the statewide vote (52.3% along the Big Sioux River). He would handily win reelection in a rematch against Herseth two years later.[44] A successful farmer from Alcester (Union County), Gubbrud was one of two Big Sioux valley politicians to serve as governor in the 1960s. The other was Nils Boe, a Sioux Falls attorney (born in Baltic, Minnehaha County). Both men were Republicans of Norwegian descent who embraced modernization as governor, particularly in the form of support for education.[45]

Boe's first election to the governorship in 1964 coincided with a rare event in South Dakota: A Democratic presidential victory. Lyndon Johnson became the third and, to date, the last Democrat to carry the state in a presidential election, winning 55.6% of the vote statewide and 56.7% in the Big Sioux valley.[46] A major factor working in Johnson's favor: His controversial Republican opponent, Barry Goldwater. While Goldwater drew criticism for his views on several issues, from Civil Rights to Vietnam to Social Security, what really cost him in South Dakota was his initial call for the "prompt and final termination" of farm subsidies and general neglect of agricultural issues during the campaign. Goldwater would later change course, at the advice of farm-state politicians, including Karl Mundt. But it was too late to win over many skeptical farmers.[47] GOP weakness at the top of the ticket may have played a factor in Boe's relatively close, three-point victory over Democrat John Lindley in the governor's race. Like Lyndon Johnson, Boe also did slightly better along the Big Sioux River than he did statewide, winning 53.5% of the vote in those nine counties, versus 51.7% overall.[48] Such ticket-splitting indicates the strength of voters' attachment to the GOP, despite their willingness to reject Republicans who failed to meet certain criteria, especially on agricultural issues.

South Dakota's attachment to the GOP reached perhaps its weakest point in the early 1970s, when Democrats benefited from a string of stellar candidates as well as (yet again) antipathy towards a Republican White House's farm policies. Oddly enough, the true apex of Democratic success came in 1972, the same year Richard Nixon clobbered George McGovern in the presidential election. While McGovern went down to defeat, Democrat Richard Kneip was easily reelected as governor. Democrat Frank Denholm (who spent most of his life in Brookings County) was reelected to a second term representing South Dakota's East River congressional district. And Democrat Jim Abourezk won the state's open Senate seat, following the retirement of Republican Karl Mundt. All three men won every single Big Sioux River county. Kneip and Abourezk both did better in the Big Sioux valley than they did in the state overall.[49] Democrats also gained seats in the state legislature, good enough for a majority in the Senate and a 35-35 tie with Republicans in the House. But once again, the party's time in power was short-lived. In 1974 Kneip would win reelection to a third term as governor, once again carrying all nine Big Sioux River counties, but at considerably reduced margins than two years prior; Kneip remains the last Democrat to win a gubernatorial election in South Dakota. Denholm by contrast would lose his congressional seat to Republican Larry Pressler, despite an otherwise banner year for congressional Democrats in the aftermath of the Watergate scandal.[50]

A native of Humboldt, like Karl Mundt, and a political moderate, Pressler would go on to win Mundt's old Senate seat in 1978, after Jim Abourezk declined to seek reelection. He was one of two "maverick Republicans," in the words of John Miller, who would help reestablish GOP dominance in South Dakota following Democrats' unprecedented success in the early 1970s. The other was Bill Janklow of Flandreau (Moody County). Janklow's rise was fueled, in part, by many South Dakotans' desire for "law and order" amid the turbulence of the late 1960s and early 1970s. Appointed by Attorney General Kermit Sande to oversee cases involving the American Indian Movement, Janklow would soon take his boss's job, besting Sande in the 1974 attorney general race.[51] Janklow would win not just every Big Sioux River county (most notably

Minnehaha County, where he garnered nearly 68% of the vote), but every county in the state.[52] Four years later, he would be elected for the first time as governor, ushering in the so-called Age of Janklow.[53]

If any South Dakota politician deserves an entire era to himself, it's Janklow. In two decades, he was elected governor four times (1978, 1982, 1994, 1998). His two eight-year stints in Pierre (1979-1987, 1995-2003) were interrupted only by term limits and the election of George Mickelson, another important Big Sioux valley politician (Brookings County), to the governorship in 1986. Few politicians did more to shape the state and the Big Sioux valley as they are today. Perhaps Janklow's greatest contribution in this regard was luring the credit card industry to Sioux Falls by signing legislation that eliminated the state's cap on interest rates, which helped transform the city into a major financial hub.[54] Janklow was also, in many respects, a trend-setter. His first gubernatorial victory in 1978 came two years ahead of the 1980 "Reagan Revolution," which cemented conservatism as the driving force in U.S. politics.[55] Like Janklow, Ronald Reagan was also quite successful in the Big Sioux valley. The Republican was one of only three U.S. presidential candidates to twice win all nine Big Sioux River counties during his 1980 and 1984 presidential campaigns.[56]

While Janklow was a Republican—and generally a staunch social and fiscal conservative—the Age of Janklow was not a uniformly Republican era. For one thing, Janklow had an iconoclastic streak and was at times willing to break with party orthodoxy to score political points or do what he felt was best for the state, depending on one's point of view. See, for example, the government's takeover of hundreds of miles of track from struggling railroads during his first term in office.[57] For another, South Dakotans routinely sent Democrats to Washington during the Age of Janklow, including Tom Daschle and Tim Johnson, who succeeded in part by following the old McGovern playbook of appealing to farmer/rural interests, while downplaying controversial social issues, such as abortion. Case in point, Daschle's first election to the Senate (he had previously served four terms in the House) and Johnson's first election to the House in 1986 came in the middle of that decade's farm crisis, which hammered rural South Dakota.[58] Both men cleaned up along the Big Sioux River, winning eight and nine counties, respectively.[59] Johnson would join Daschle in the Senate in 1996, the same year his opponent, Republican Larry Pressler, voted in favor of the controversial Federal Agriculture Improvement and Reform (or Freedom to Farm) Act, which dismantled many of the last vestiges of the New-Deal-era federal farm safety net.[60]

The conventional wisdom at the time was that South Dakota sent Democrats to Washington to bring money back to the state, while electing Republicans back home to keep taxes low.[61] The 1998 midterm elections offer some evidence for this thesis. Voters overwhelmingly reelected both Republican Janklow as governor and Democrat Daschle as senator. Interestingly, both men did better along the Big Sioux River than they did statewide, a testament to their powerful personal brands and considerable appeal in the region.[62] Notably, the success of Daschle and Johnson did not extend to other Democrats at the national level. Democrat Bill Clinton came close, but never won South Dakota during his 1992 and 1996 presidential campaigns, despite some success along the Big Sioux River.[63] And in addition to being shut out of the governorship and most other statewide offices during the Age of Janklow, Democrats also never controlled the state legislature, minus a brief stint in charge of the state Senate (1993-94), in which four of the party's 20 seats came from Minnehaha County alone.[64]

Since the beginning of the New Millennium, South Dakota and the Big Sioux valley have largely returned to the Republican fold, as polarization between America's two main political parties has increased and ticket-splitting by voters has declined.[65] President George W. Bush easily won the state in 2000 and 2004, carrying first nine, then eight Big Sioux River counties.[66] Bush's strong showing in 2004 contributed to Daschle losing his Senate seat to Republican John Thune, who accused his Democratic opponent of being out of step with the state's conservative electorate and an obstructer of the Bush agenda.[67] While Daschle still carried five of nine Big Sioux River counties, his margin of victory in vote-rich Minnehaha County fell considerably from his previous election in 1998, which in turn helped cost him the state.[68] Meanwhile, Republicans maintained their lock on the governor's mansion with Mike Rounds, a state senator who was elected in 2002 to succeed Bill Janklow (and would be easily reelected four years later). Janklow, in turn, went after South Dakota's at-large congressional seat, scoring a decisive seven-point win over Democrat Stephanie Herseth.[69]

But months after taking office, he was involved in a fatal traffic accident that resulted in a conviction and jail time for vehicular manslaughter, forcing him to resign from his post in January 2004. Herseth would narrowly win the special election to fill Janklow's seat, notably improving on her earlier performance along the Big Sioux River, where she won seven of nine counties.[70]

The 2008 elections would be Democrats' last big hurrah in South Dakota. Both Johnson and Herseth would easily win reelection, carrying all nine Big Sioux River counties in the process. In the presidential election, Democrat Barack Obama lost the state but won four Big Sioux River counties, all of which in some way spoke to the national Democratic party's growing reliance on young, urban and non-white voters: Brookings County, home to South Dakota State; Minnehaha County, home to the state's largest city, Sioux Falls; and Moody and Roberts counties, both home to substantial Native American populations.[71] As some observers have noted, Obama's 2008 presidential victory in some ways fulfilled the promise of George McGovern's 1972 presidential campaign of uniting "the minorities, youth vote and highly educated liberals" into a winning political coalition.[72] Nevertheless, it is still not a winning political coalition in South Dakota, as evidenced by subsequent election results. Herseth would soon be wiped out in the Republican midterm wave of 2010, despite winning five of nine Big Sioux River counties. Her replacement: Republican Kristi Noem.[73] Obama would lose the state again in 2012, only winning one Big Sioux River county (Roberts).[74] Johnson, meanwhile, opted not to run for reelection in 2014 and was succeeded by Republican Mike Rounds, the former governor.[75]

While Republicans returning to dominance in South Dakota may seem like history repeating itself, the party has, in fact, continued to evolve. Perhaps the best illustration of that fact is the political careers of the state's two most recent governors, Dennis Daugaard (2011-2019) and Kristi Noem (2019-present). Both are Republicans hailing from the Big Sioux valley, in Daugaard's case Minnehaha County, in Noem's case Hamlin County. But while Daugaard quietly rose through the ranks of state government to reach the governor's mansion, Noem followed a more haphazard path, jumping from a seat in the South Dakota House to one in the U.S. House in 2010, then returning to the state to run for governor in 2018. Unlike Daugaard, who easily won two terms as governor in two Republican-friendly years (2010, 2014), Noem has faced a genuinely competitive statewide race; her roughly three-point victory over Democrat Billie Sutton in 2018 was the closest South Dakota gubernatorial election in over 30 years.[76] Also unlike Daugaard, she has become a national political figure, thanks to her close ties with Donald Trump, the populist businessman turned Republican president (2017-2021) who has, fairly or not, drawn comparisons to Bill Janklow.[77]

What does the recently concluded Trump presidency say about the future of politics and two-party competition in South Dakota, in general, and the Big Sioux valley, in particular? Trump himself proved to be a potent political force in the region, winning all nine Big Sioux River counties in both his winning 2016 and losing 2020 presidential campaigns.[78] Republicans, meanwhile, continue to dominate at virtually all levels of state government, no surprise given the party's overwhelming advantage among rural voters, who make up a much larger portion of the electorate in South Dakota than in other states.[79] And yet the Trump era also offered a glimmer of hope to South Dakota Democrats in the form of Billie Sutton, whose strong showing in the 2018 gubernatorial race garnered national attention.[80] A pro-life ex-rodeo star who frequently sported a cowboy hat on the campaign trail, Sutton was in many ways a throwback candidate, one whose rural bona fides likely gave him an edge over other Democrats and contributed to his strong showing both statewide and in the Big Sioux valley, where he bested Republican Kristi Noem by just over 1,000 votes.[81] Time will tell if Democrats can build on Sutton's success, holding their own with rural voters while benefiting from the continued growth of the Sioux Falls metropolitan area, where growing numbers of young urban professionals in such industries as education, finance, and health care could work in the party's favor.[82] In the meantime, Republican dominance of South Dakota and the Big Sioux valley looks set to persist for years to come.

Notes

[1] U.S. Bureau of Economic Analysis, "Gross Domestic Product By County, 2019," news release (December 9, 2020), https://www.bea.gov/sites/default/files/2020-12/lagdp1220_2.pdf; US Census Bureau, "2020 Population and Housing State Data," The United States Census Bureau, August 26, 2021,

https://www.census.gov/library/visualizations/interactive/2020-population-and-housing-state-data.html.

2 U.S. Census Bureau, "Population Estimates, July 1, 2019 (V2019)—Sioux Falls city, SD," *Quick Facts*, accessed May 1, 2021, https://www.census.gov/quickfacts/siouxfallscitysouthdakota.

3 Tony Venhuizen, "Governor Arthur Calvin Mellette," Trail of Governors Foundation, July 22, 2020, https://www.trailofgovernors.com/governor-arthur-calvin-mellette/; Office of the House Historian, Kristi Noem, Biographical Directory of the United States Congress, accessed May 6, 2021, https://bioguideretro.congress.gov/Home/MemberDetails?memIndex=N000184.

4 Jon K. Lauck, "The Foundations of Political Culture in East River South Dakota," in *The Plains Political Tradition: Essays on South Dakota Political Culture*, ed. Jon K. Lauck, John E. Miller, Donald C. Simmons, Jr. (Pierre, SD: South Dakota State Historical Society Press, 2011), 29.

5 Discussion of the Big Sioux valley in this chapter is limited to the nine counties through which the river flows, as mentioned in the introductory paragraph. Furthermore, this chapter explores how political trends in the Big Sioux valley compare with those of South Dakota as a whole since statehood; it does not provide a comprehensive overview of major Big Sioux valley politicians, meaning some important figures, such as South Dakota's first U.S. Senator, Richard Pettigrew (Minnehaha County), who did not make the cut.

6 U.S. Bureau of Labor Statistics, "South Dakota Economy at a Glance," (U.S. Bureau of Labor Statistics), accessed May 9, 2021, https://www.bls.gov/eag/eag.sd.htm.; U.S. Bureau of Labor Statistics, "Sioux Falls, SD Economy at a Glance" (U.S. Bureau of Labor Statistics), accessed May 9, 2021, https://www.bls.gov/eag/eag.sd_siouxfalls_msa.htm.

7 Indeed, devotion to the Union cause is evident in the names of several Big Sioux River counties: Grant, Hamlin (named for Abraham Lincoln's Vice President Hannibal Hamlin), Lincoln, Moody (named for Civil War veteran and later South Dakota Senator Gideon C. Moody), Union. John Miller, "Setting the Agenda: Political Parties and Historical Change," in *The Plains Political Tradition* (see note 4), 78-79; John Miller, "Politics Since Statehood," in *A New South Dakota History*, 2nd ed., ed. Harry F. Thompson (Sioux Falls, SD: The Center for Western Studies, 2009), 194.

8 William C. Hunt, *Population of South Dakota by Counties and Minor Civil Divisions* (Washington, D.C.: Census Office, 1901), 2.

9 Herbert T. Hoover, "Territorial Politics and Politicians," in *A New South Dakota History*, 115.

10 J. E. Hipple, *South Dakota Legislative Manual, 1903* (Pierre, SD: State Publishing Company, 1903), 175.

11 Hipple, *South Dakota Legislative Manual*, 177.

12 Terrence J. Lindell, "South Dakota Populism" (1982), Open-Access* Master's Theses from the University of Nebraska-Lincoln. 32, http://digitalcommons.unl.edu/opentheses/32; Miller, "Politics Since Statehood," 196.

13 Hipple, 184 and 186.

14 Miller, "Politics Since Statehood," 198; Gary Olson, "Yankee and European Settlement," in *A New South Dakota History*, 125-27.

[15] Hipple, 189 and 191.

[16] Miller, "Politics Since Statehood," 198.

[17] Miller, "Politics Since Statehood," 201-03.

[18] U.S. Bureau of the Census, Thirteenth Census, Volume 3, Population: Reports by States Nebraska-Wyoming, South Dakota (Washington, D.C.: U.S. Government Printing Office, 1913); Dorothy Burton Skardal, *The Divided Heart: Scandinavian Immigrant Experience through Literary Sources* (Lincoln: University of Nebraska Press, 1974), 162-63.

[19] L. M. Simons and James W. Cone, *South Dakota Legislative Manual, 1907* (Pierre, SD: State Publishing Company, 1907), 338.

[20] Simons and Cone, 329-32; Frank M. Byrne and W.D. Johnston, *South Dakota Legislative Manual, 1915* (Pierre, SD: State Publishing Company, 1915), 357-60. Roosevelt's impressive 1912 showing in South Dakota and the Big Sioux valley is somewhat colored by the fact that then-Senator Coe I. Crawford launched a successful effort to exclude Republican nominee William H. Taft, whom he regarded as insufficiently progressive, from state ballots. See, for example, Leonard Schulp, "Coe I. Crawford and the Progressive Campaign of 1912," in *South Dakota History* 9:2 (1979): 116-30.

[21] "Official Election Returns for South Dakota: General Election, November 4, 1924," https://sdsos.gov/elections-voting/election-resources/election-history/official-election-returns.aspx. Unless otherwise noted, all electoral statistics are accessed from this website.

[22] One of those exceptions: Democrat Edwin S. Johnson, who became South Dakota's first popularly elected senator in 1914, winning five of nine Big Sioux River counties in the process. Frank M. Byrne and W. D. Johnston, *South Dakota Legislative Manual, 1915* (Pierre, SD: State Publishing Company, 1915), 432.

[23] Lynwood Oyos, "Farming Dependency and Depopulation," in *A New South Dakota History*, 230-32.

[24] Official Election Returns for South Dakota: General Election, November 2, 1926."

[25] Miller, "Politics Since Statehood," 205.

[26] "Official Election Returns for South Dakota: General Election, November 6, 1928"; B.W. Baer and D.W. Forbes, *South Dakota Legislative Manual, 1931*(Pierre, SD: State Publishing Company, 1931), 251.

[27] "Official Election Returns for South Dakota: General Election: November 8, 1932."

[28] Tony Venhuizen, "Governor Warren Everett Green," Trail of Governors Foundation, July 14, 2017, https://www.trailofgovernors.com/governor-warren-everett-green/.

[29] "Official Election Returns for South Dakota: General Election, November 8, 1938"; "Official Election Returns for South Dakota: General Election, November 3, 1942."

[30] "Official Election Returns for South Dakota: General Election, November 3, 1936."

[31] Miller, "Politics Since Statehood," 210, 218.

32 Rex Myers, "Transportation and Tourism," in *A New South Dakota History*, 194; Brad Tennant, "Bringing Interstate 29 to South Dakota," in *Papers of the Fiftieth Dakota Conference*, comp. Kari Mahowald (Sioux Falls, SD: Center for Western Studies, 2018): 298-307.

33 Miller, "Politics Since Statehood," 213.

34 Don W. Beaty and Catherine Pulles, *South Dakota Legislative Manual, 1953* (Pierre, SD: State Publishing Company, 1953), 150-51.

35 Miller, "Politics Since Statehood," 213.

36 Miller, "Politics Since Statehood," 215.

37 Jon K. Lauck, "George S. McGovern and the Farmer: South Dakota Politics, 1953-1962," *South Dakota History* 32: 4 (2002): 331-33.

38 "Official Election Returns for South Dakota: General Election, November 6, 1956"; Office of the House Historian, Harold Lovre, Biographical Directory of the United States Congress, accessed August 28, 2021.

39 U.S. Bureau of the Census, U.S. Census of Population: 1960. Volume 1, Characteristics of the Population, Part 43, South Dakota (Washington, D.C.: U.S. Government Printing Office, 1963).

40 U.S. Bureau of the Census, U.S. Census of Agriculture: 1959. Volume 1, Geographic Area Series, Part 19, South Dakota, State and County Data (Washington, D.C.: Government Printing Office, 1962).

41 "Official Election Returns by Counties for the State of South Dakota: General Election, November 8, 1960."

42 "Official Election Returns by Counties for the State of South Dakota: General Election, November 6, 1962"; "Official Election Returns by Counties for the State of South Dakota: General Election, November 5, 1968"; "Official Election Returns by Counties for the State of South Dakota: General Election, November 7, 1972"; Official Election Returns by Counties for the State of South Dakota: General Election, November 5, 1974"; Official Election Returns by Counties for the State of South Dakota: General Election, November 7, 1980."

43 Matthew Housiaux, "The Two George McGoverns: The Rise and Fall of a Prairie Populist, 1956-1980," in *Papers of the Forty-Seventh Annual Dakota Conference*, comp. Erin Castle and Nicole Schimelpfenig (Sioux Falls, SD: Center for Western Studies, 2015): 122-48.

44 "Official Election Returns by Counties for The State of South Dakota: General Election, November 8, 1960"; "Official Election Returns by Counties for The State of South Dakota: General Election, November 6, 1962."

45 Miller, "Politics Since Statehood," 216-17.

46 "Official Election Returns by Counties for The State of South Dakota: General Election, November 3, 1964."

47 Bruce Laurie and Ronald Story, *The Rise of Conservatism in America, 1945-2000: A Brief History With Documents* (Boston, MA: Bedford-St. Martins, 2008), 59-61; William H. Chafe, *The Unfinished Journey: America since World War II* (New York, NY: Oxford University Press, 2011), 224-25; "Issues: Backdown on the Farm," *Time*, October 30, 1964), http://content.time.com/time/subscriber/article/0,33009,876302,00.html.

48 "Official Election Returns by Counties for the State of South Dakota: General Election, November 3, 1964."

49 "Official Election Returns by Counties for the State of South Dakota: General Election, November 7, 1972."

50 "Official Election Returns by Counties for the State of South Dakota: General Election, November 5, 1974."

51 Jason A. Hepler, "The American Indian Movement and South Dakota Politics," in *The Plains Political Tradition* (see note 4), 276-79.

52 "Official Election Returns by Counties for the State of South Dakota: General Election, November 5, 1974."

53 Miller, "Politics Since Statehood," 221.

54 Miller, "Politics Since Statehood," 223.

55 Bruce Laurie Story, *The Rise of Conservatism in America*, 20-22.

56 "Official Election Returns and Registration Figures for South Dakota: General Election, November 4, 1980."

57 Miller, "Politics Since Statehood," 223.

58 Cory M. Haala, "Replanting the Grassroots: Remaking the South Dakota Democratic Party from McGovern to Daschle, 1980-1986," in *The Plains Political Tradition: Essays on South Dakota Political* Culture, vol. 3, ed. Jon K. Lauck, John E. Miller, and Paula E. Nelson (Pierre, SD: South Dakota State Historical Society Press, 2018), 189-90, 195-96.

59 "Official Election Returns and Registration Figures for South Dakota: General Election, November 4, 1986."

60 "South Dakota Official Election Returns and Registration Figures: General Election, November 5, 1996"; Oyos, "Farming Dependency and Depopulation," 251; "Federal Agriculture Improvement and Reform Act: Roll Vote No. 57."

61 Miller, "Politics Since Statehood," 222.

62 "South Dakota Official Election Returns and Registration Figures: General Election, November 5, 1998."

63 "Official Election Returns and Registration Figures for South Dakota: General Election, November 3, 1992"; "South Dakota Official Election Returns and Registration Figures: General Election, November 5, 1996."

64 "Official Election Returns and Registration Figures for South Dakota: General Election, November 3, 1992."

65 Gordon Heltzel and Kristin Laurin, "Polarization in America: Two Possible Futures," *Current Opinion in Behavioral Sciences*, August 2020, 179; "Large Shares of Voters Plan to Vote a Straight Party Ticket for President, Senate and House," Pew Research Center—U.S. Politics & Policy (Pew Research Center, May 25, 2021), https://www.pewresearch.org/politics/2020/10/21/large-shares-of-voters-plan-to-vote-a-straight-party-ticket-for-president-senate-and-house/.

66 "South Dakota Official Election Returns and Registration Figures: General Election, November 7, 2000"; "South Dakota Official Election Returns and Registration Figures: General Election, November 2, 2004."

67 Jon K. Lauck, *Daschle vs. Thune: Anatomy of a High-Plains Senate Race* (Norman: University of Oklahoma Press, 2016), 176, 195; "Leader Daschle Loses Senate

Seat," CBS News (CBS Interactive, November 3, 2004), https://www.cbsnews.com/news/leader-daschle-loses-senate-seat/.

[68] "South Dakota Official Election Returns and Registration Figures: General Election, November 2, 2004."

[69] "South Dakota Official Election Returns and Registration Figures; General Election, November 5, 2002."

[70] "South Dakota Official Election Returns and Registration Figures: Primary and Special Congressional Election, June 1, 2004."

[71] "South Dakota Official Election Results and Registration Figures: Primary Election and General Election, June 3 and November 4, 2008."

[72] Jeff Bloodworth, "Obama: Urban Liberalism's Ascent," *PS: Political Science & Politics* 50:1 (2017): 44, https://doi.org/10.1017/s1049096516002080.

[73] "South Dakota Official Election Returns and Registration Figures: Primary Election and General Election, June 8, 2010 and November 2, 2010."

[74] "South Dakota Official Election Returns and Registration Figures: Primary Election and General Election, June 5, 2012 and November 6, 2012."

[75] "South Dakota Official Election Returns and Registration Figures: Primary Election and General Election, June 3 and November 4, 2014."

[76] "Official Election Returns and Registration Figures for South Dakota: General Election, Nov. 4, 1986"; "South Dakota Official Election Returns and Registration Figures: Primary Election and General Election, June 5 and November 6, 2018."

[77] Kevin Woster, "Comparing Bill Janklow and Donald Trump? Well, You Might Actually Get an Apology from One of Them," SDPB, March 3, 2017, https://www.sdpb.org/blogs/kevinwoster/headline/.

[78] "South Dakota Official Election Returns and Registration Figures: Primary Election and General Election, June 7, 2016 and November 8, 2016"; "South Dakota Official Election Returns and Registration Figures: Primary Election and General Election, June 2, 2020 and Nov. 3, 2020."

[79] Nathaniel Rakich, "How Urban Or Rural Is Your State? And What Does That Mean For The 2020 Election?," FiveThirtyEight, April 14, 2020, https://fivethirtyeight.com/features/how-urban-or-rural-is-your-state-and-what-does-that-mean-for-the-2020-election/.

[80] "A Democrat with a Chance in South Dakota," *The Economist*, February 10, 2018), https://www.economist.com/united-states/2018/02/10/a-democrat-with-a-chance-in-south-dakota.

[81] "South Dakota Official Election Returns and Registration Figures: Primary Election and General Election, June 5 and November 6, 2018."

[82] "South Dakota Economy at a Glance," U.S. Bureau of Labor Statistics (U.S. Bureau of Labor Statistics), accessed May 9, 2021, https://www.bls.gov/eag/eag.sd.htm.; Richard Florida, "Why Is Your State Red or Blue? Look to the Dominant Occupational Class," City Lab, November 28, 2018.

Chapter 15

The Western Watershed:
Lake County and Its Water

Jon Hunter
Madison Daily Leader

M ost of the lakes, streams and creeks of Lake County are tributaries of the Big Sioux River, but they have a rich history
of their own. From dry lakes in the 1930s to flooding events
more than a half-century later, water flows and lake levels have been a
continual source of debate, politics, speculation and action, including
questionable environmental and surreptitious activity.

With the exception of a small part of Lake County which runs into
the Vermillion River valley, all of the surface water in the county is in
the watershed feeding lakes and streams that eventually drain into the
Big Sioux River. In general, the watershed begins in northwest Lake
County and moves southeast.

Small creeks and streams from agricultural areas in the northwest
part of the county feed into Lake Herman. Since the sod busting of
the late 1800s, the creeks also bring sediment into the lake, making it
shallower each year. A comprehensive study was published in 1969 by
Dr. Clyde Brashier of Dakota State University and T. W. Edminster of
the United States Department of Agriculture.[1] Funding came from the
U.S. Department of the Interior, presumably with the urging of U.S.
Sen. Karl E. Mundt, a long-established senator who was considered a
conservationist and had also taught at Dakota State University.

The paper, entitled "New Life for Prairie Lakes," was a moment of reckoning. The opening sentence of the paper stated "The inevitable end for prairie lakes is that of death." It concluded that the southeast end of Lake Herman would be filled in by silt in 15-20 years, and the entire lake could be consumed by silt in 25-30 years.

Brashier was not a native of South Dakota, but he embraced his adopted state. He received his bachelor of science at Louisiana Tech University, his masters and Ph.D. at the University of Nebraska, all in botany. He accepted a position at the University of Wisconsin-Superior, and at the age of 32 became the youngest tenured professor in the Wisconsin public higher education system. He came to Dakota State University in Madison in 1967 and immediately began studying water in the county. Brashier later became dean of instruction, and even ran for the U.S. Senate.[2]

Brashier and Edminster's paper was a call to action, and local, state, and national officials took note. Not long after, silt dams were constructed on a number of creeks to reduce the flow of silt into Lake Herman, and a six-year dredging project commenced to remove silt already in the lake. More than 2,000 acre-feet of silt was removed from the lake, or nearly 25 percent of the silt at the bottom of the lake, and placed on a field to the north of the lake. However, silt continued to flow into the lake during the dredging years, reducing the net effect of dredging. Eventually, funding ran out for dredging, but a substantial portion of the lake is deeper, and its long-term health appears more stable today.

Brashier, along with Constance Churchill and Dan Limmer, published another paper in 1975 entitled "Evaluation of a Recreational Lake Rehabilitation Project." Again, the study was comprehensive and made evaluations of the effects of dredging, both positive and negative, to all aspects of Lake Herman. Brashier pushed hard to boost efforts to stop silt from flowing into the lakes and to reduce shoreline erosion, stating that dredging is worthless unless the inflow is stopped. Some maintenance work has been conducted on the silt dams, but some observers believe much more is needed to maintain their effectiveness.[3] Brashier was inducted into the Dakota State University Academic Hall of Fame in 2019, partly due to these works and their impact on water in Lake County.[4]

Silver Creek leaves Lake Herman on its eastern edge and flows east through additional agricultural areas and through the City of Madison on its way to Lake Madison, the largest of all county lakes at about six miles long and one-half to one mile wide. Memorial Creek starts north of Madison, and flows through the city, joining with Silver Creek just before Lake Madison.

Water leaves Lake Madison at its eastern edge, and flows into Round Lake, which flows into Brant Lake, then into Skunk Creek, one of the largest tributaries of the Big Sioux River. Battle Creek drains the north-central section of the county, flowing east to the Big Sioux River out of Lake Badus.[5] Several other bodies of water and creeks in the county, including Buffalo Creek, North Buffalo Creek, Wolf Drain, Milwaukee Lake, Green Lake, Reynolds Slough and Buffalo Slough, drain east into the system as well.[6]

The earliest known history of lakes in the county states that Native Americans camped on the lake shores while traveling to and from the pipestone quarries in Minnesota. In 1870 William Lee, Herman Luce, and Joseph Mason left Sioux Falls looking for land to settle. They decided that Lee would settle on the first body of water they found, and Luce the second. They camped at what is now called Lake Madison, where Lee settled, then traveled west to what is now Lake Herman, where Luce assumed squatter's rights, built a cabin, and named the lake after himself. The cabin still stands today in Lake Herman State Park. Luce and his son plowed two or three acres, sowed rutabaga seed, and returned to Minnesota. Luce later became a local postmaster and land grant officer.[7]

The area was used for camp meetings, religious gatherings, and picnics. Suffragist Susan B. Anthony spoke on November 18, 1889 at a large farm picnic there.[8] A dance pavilion was built and orchestras, including the Lawrence Welk Orchestra, played there in the 1920s and 1930s. Lee built a store and planted the first wheat sown in the county in the spring of 1872, and his land was near where the Lake Madison Chautauqua would be located. He later became sheriff of Lake County.[9]

Small communities were settled on both Lake Madison and Lake Herman in the early 1870s. The towns, appropriately called Madison and Herman, merged and moved to a central site in 1881 where the

Chicago, Milwaukee, and St. Paul Railroad would place a depot. The merged town was first known as "new" Madison, then later Madison.

The new location would straddle both Memorial Creek and Silver Creek. About a mile of Memorial Creek in the center of Madison would later be lined with stone walls to convert a marshy area into a beautiful park. The walls would also help control erosion and prevent flooding in certain areas. They were built as a Works Projects Administration project under President Franklin Roosevelt's New Deal. Construction began in 1936 at the north end and worked its way south, using primarily granite and quartzite. The rock had been mined at Dell Rapids and used for a rail line across a dry portion of Brant Lake. When the rail line was abandoned, the rock became available for the Memorial Creek project. About 100 men were working on the project at any one time.[10] Maintaining the integrity and beauty of the stone walls on Memorial Creek would require constant funding and work over the coming decades.

While the original settlements on Lakes Herman and Madison are gone, there has been substantial construction of seasonal cabins and permanent residences on both lakes. In the earliest years, small wooden structures such as chicken coops were even brought to the lake and converted into a summer relaxation spot. In recent years, more substantial year-round homes have been constructed on the lakeshores, as well as in the area surrounding the lakes. Without swimming pools in the cities, nearly everyone in the county who learned to swim did so in local lakes. Presumably, among those was Madison native Eugene Vidal, who participated in the decathlon in the 1924 Olympics in Antwerp, Belgium.[11]

In addition to casual recreation, more permanent facilities and organizations were established. The Lake Madison Chautauqua ran on the northwest shore of that lake from 1890 to 1932, and provided boating, fishing, swimming, camping, music, education, cultural events, speakers, and other entertainment. Speakers over its history included Booker T. Washington, William Jennings Bryan, and ex-President William Howard Taft.[12]

A tragedy was associated with the Chautauqua on July 4, 1919, when the pleasure boat *The Reliance* sank and nine people drowned. The launch had been giving pleasure trips on Lake Madison all day.

That evening, the boat was traveling southeast across the lake and hit a sunken tree about 80 to 100 feet from the shore, causing a panic among passengers. As they scrambled to one side of the boat, the imbalance caused the boat to roll twice. One passenger swam to shore and phoned the Chautauqua hotel. Small boats were sent out and saved 23 people. It was later determined that if the passengers had not panicked, they could have gotten out on the shore side of the boat and waded to safety. But in the darkness, all they could see were the lights of the Chautauqua far away.[13] The Chautauqua movement started fading in the 1920s, with radio providing more entertainment and automobiles providing easier transportation to other cities.[14]

Years later, another structure was built at the same site, called at different times The Grandview or The Resort, with a dance hall upstairs above a restaurant (perhaps most notable was Jack's Surf & Sirloin Supper Club), bar, and bait shop. Regional bands such as Myron Lee and the Caddies and the Outer Limits would help pack the dance hall, while occasionally national performers such as Jerry Lee Lewis would perform. The Ink Spots, a pioneering black vocal group who appeared on The Ed Sullivan Show three times, even performed at Lake Madison.[15] Additional restaurants such as Smith's Park Resort, Wentworth Park Resort, the Hillside, The Broadwater and The Shipwreck (at Brant Lake) all offered dining, musical entertainment, and in some cases, lodging.

At Lake Herman, the Madison Chapter No. 16 of the Izaak Walton League of America was founded in March 1925. Members moved a double garage near the shore to hold meetings. Six months later, two hoboes built a fire too close to the structure and it burned down. The fire spurred fundraising and construction of a new fieldstone building in 1934.[16] It continues to provide gun-safety courses for youth and recreational shooting.

In 1941 the city of Madison purchased 298 acres adjacent to Lake Herman from the Limmer estate with the idea of building an airport and park there. When the government decreed that the land was unsuitable for an airport, most of the land was sold. In 1946 118 acres were donated to the South Dakota Department of Game, Fish & Parks. The GF&P purchased two more tracts of land nearby to complete the current size of Lake Herman State Park at 227 acres.[17]

Today, the park is one of the best and most-visited state parks in South Dakota. An extension of Lake Herman State Park is state-owned Walker's Point Recreation Area on the south shore of Lake Madison. Both locations offer camping, fishing (all-year round), boating, and other recreation.

Also in 1941 the Lake County 4-H clubs dedicated a State 4-H Youth Camp to be known as Camp Lakodia. The land was again donated by the City of Madison, and construction of 15 buildings was performed by the Works Projects Administration. Sears, Roebuck and Company furnished appliances, Sioux Valley Empire Electric built 6½ miles of line to provide power, and the state Game, Fish & Parks provided landscaping.[18] Many years later, the camp was completely renovated and used as a summer camp for deaf children.

In 1946 the Lake Herman Recreation Association was formed with the intent to build a golf course. The association bought a private golf course from an individual in St. Cloud, Minnesota, and moved all the golf facilities to Lake Herman, including the greens, tee boxes, water pumps, mowers, sprinklers, and pipes. A fieldstone clubhouse (using the same architectural style as the nearby Izaak Walton League building) was completed in 1949.[19] The original nine-hole course was expanded to 18 holes in 1989.

In the 1990s a former cattle feedlot between the east end of Lake Madison and the west side of Round Lake was developed into a substantial enterprise called The Lakes Community, which includes a golf course, housing development, marina, motel, campground, and restaurant.

Lake County owns land on the southwest shore of Lake Madison that was used for many years as a gravel mine. In 2017 a portion of it was developed to become Scott Pedersen Memorial Park, in memory of an admired former county commissioner.

Winter and frozen lakes don't prevent some people from enjoying the outdoors. Ice fishing is popular, and snowmobile races and ice sailing are occasionally seen.

Much of the development around the lakes depends on stable water levels, which aren't part of the climate of eastern South Dakota. Wide ranges of annual precipitation lead to varying depths of Lake County lakes, streams, and sloughs. Because the largest lakes have been developed with housing and recreation, both higher and lower levels cause consternation.

In 1893, and to a greater extent during the 1930s, the lakes became nearly dry, or at least became more like sloughs than lakes. Trees and other vegetation grew in the lake beds. During that time, some of the cabins were removed permanently from the former shorelines of the lakes. Each time, snowmelt and rains would bring the lakes back to more normal levels.

In the mid-1960s low lake levels caused a number of sandbars to become small islands at Lake Madison. In an effort to hold more water in Lake Madison, there were times when unauthorized persons surreptitiously approached the east spillway in the middle of the night and placed wooden planks across the span. Once discovered, the planks were removed, although they sometimes mysteriously reappeared. Heavy snows in the winter of 1968-69 refilled the lakes, and there have been very few dry years since.

Excessive water became a problem a number of times, most notably in 1993, when heavy rains in early July caused flooding throughout Lake County. Damage to shorelines was substantial, and a shore stabilization program (funded by the Federal Emergency Management Agency) followed soon after. Another flood occurred in September 2019, although much less damage took place.

Each of these events caused federal, state, and local officials to create flood mitigation projects, including buying out homes near creeks at risk of flooding, stabilizing shorelines with rock, and constructing new bridges and culverts to allow more water to pass. For the most part, flooding events have not permanently changed the course of any waterways in the Lake County watershed.

There has been some intentional change to the waterways, most famously the "ditching," or draining, of Milwaukee Slough in the late 1920s. A series of local landowners decided they could increase the size of their farms by draining swampy areas on their land in the northeast portion of Lake County. A straight ditch was created to draw water out of Milwaukee Slough and other low-lying areas and send it east to Bachelor Creek. Landowners placed drain pipes (also called drain tile) under their fields that fed into the ditch.

Beginning around 2000 additional drain tile was placed that drained water into the ditch. The combination of additional inflows plus silt buildup over many decades caused the ditch to flood over its banks onto adjacent landowners' property. There continues to be disputes about who should pay for maintenance of the ditch, and who should be able to drain into it.[20]

Substantial additional drain-tiling throughout Lake County since 2000 has also increased the speed of water from rain events reaching creeks and streams, sometimes causing them to exceed their banks. Fewer wetlands now act as detention ponds to handle large rain events or to prevent nutrients from flowing into streams and lakes.

Naturally-occurring phosphorus concentrations (and to a lesser extent, nitrates) in the soil have always made their way to Lake County creeks, streams and lakes, but additional quantities have been added through development of cities, residences, and farms. These elements have contributed to algae blooms in the lakes, and uncontrolled waterways have added silt.

Over recent years, lakes in the county regularly fail to meet South Dakota Department of Agriculture and Natural Resources water quality standards for permanent fish life propagation, swimming, livestock watering, and wildlife propagation. A study by a Dakota State University professor and students in the late 1990s and early 2000s concluded that the lakes would need a 50 percent reduction in phosphorus input to recategorize Lake Madison to the next level of improved clarity and water quality standards.[21]

In fact, local officials identified problems with water quality through most of the twentieth century. A study commissioned by the City of Madison in 1959 determined that an adequate quantity of water was available for municipal use, but that the quality was poor. The city was pumping water from seven shallow wells ranging from 24 to 50 feet deep. At that time, the City of Madison was dumping its sewage into a creek that flowed into Lake Madison.[22]

Shallow and deep wells continued to provide all the drinking water to the city into the twenty-first century, until a portion of its water supply began being supplied by the Big Sioux Community Water System in 2017. That water comes from the Big Sioux Aquifer near Egan, South Dakota. The city and its water users have made a substantial financial commitment to the Lewis & Clark Rural Water System to bring Missouri River water to Madison via pipeline by 2030.

Substantial efforts over many decades to improve water quality have been undertaken, although results have not been as hoped for. One such program, the Lake County Watershed Improvement Project, operated from 2000 to 2006 with a goal of decreasing the phosphorus load of Lake Herman/Lake Madison/Brant Lake by 50 percent each. Final calculations indicated a reduction of 6 percent, 4 percent, and 27 percent at those three lakes, respectively. The principal reason for not achieving the goals was the voluntary nature of landowner compliance.[23] A study was undertaken to dredge Bourne Slough to the northwest of Lake Madison, but was not executed.

Construction of a sanitary sewer system at Lake Madison was a success, while a similar system at Brant Lake resulted in lawsuits and a huge financial burden for homeowners. A system at Lake Herman has been debated but never constructed, so septic tanks are still used around the lake for waste disposal.

Many attempts to address the algae problem in Lake County lakes have been tried over the years, including the now-questionable applications of copper sulfate and alum. County government even funded a company that installed a large underwater "fan" to push the algae to the lake floor to create clear water at the surface. It was not successful.

A State of South Dakota program passed by the legislature to encourage the planting of grassy strips along waterways to reduce erosion and leaching of phosphorus and nitrates into the water has had very limited success. Shoreline along 11,000 miles of South Dakota streams and rivers and adjacent to 575 lakes is eligible for the program, but in the first year, only 31 landowners from across the state enrolled 318 acres into the program. The following year, 35 landowners received tax reductions on 426 acres, and a good share of the second-year participants had also enrolled the first year.[24] The South Dakota legislature passed improvements to the program in 2021 to encourage more acres to be planted.[25]

Surface water has long defined Lake County and will continue to do so. Decisions made each year about use and treatment of water assets will determine the future of this portion of the Big Sioux River watershed.

Notes

1 Clyde Brashier and T. W. Edminster, "New Life for Prairie Lakes" (1969), conference proceedings.

2 "Dr. Clyde Brashier—Academic Hall of Fame Induction Ceremony 2019" (2019), PowerPoint, 11.

3 Clyde Brashier, "Evaluation of a Recreational Lake Rehabilitation Project" (1975).

4 "Dr. Clyde Brashier—Academic Hall of Fame Induction Ceremony 2019" (2019).

5 Jay Gilbertson, Manager/Treasurer of East Dakota Water Development District, telephone interview by author, July 28, 2021.

6 *History of Lake County* (Lake County Historical Society, 1995), 18-20.

7 *History of Lake County*, 43-44.

8 *History of Lake County*, 455, 891.

9 *History of Lake County*, 42-46.

10 *History of Lake County*.

11 *Wikipedia*, s.v. "Eugene Luther Vidal," accessed July 24, 2021.

12 *History of Lake County*, 443-52.

13 *History of Lake County*, 954-55.

14 W. Cory Christenson, *The Early History of the Lake Madison Chautauqua* (M.A. thesis, University of South Dakota, 1956); *History of Lake County*, 444-46.

15 Mary Gales Askren, "Lake Madison Ballroom: Gone but not forgotten," *Madison Daily Leader*, March 1, 2018, 1.

16 *History of Lake County*, 123-24.

17 *History of Lake County*, 455-56.

18 *History of Lake County*, 127.

19 *History of Lake County*, 457-58.

20 Jay Gilbertson, telephone interview by author, August 13, 2021.

21 D. L. Droge and C. H. Hamblin, "Phosphorus Concentrations in Tributaries and Lakes of the Lake Herman and Lake Madison Watershed," Proceedings of the South Dakota Academy of Sciences 94 (2015): 372.

22 Donald S. Hanson, "Water resources of Lake and Moody Counties, South Dakota," U.S. Geological Survey Report 84-4209, www.pubs.usgs.gov, accessed July 25, 2021.

23 Lake County Watershed Project, accessed August 1, 2021, https://denr.sd.gov/dfta/wp/documents/madisonscrapbook.pdf.

24 "Improving South Dakota's Riparian Buffer Program," *The Otter* (Summer 2020).

25 Robert Hunter, Secretary of the South Dakota Department of Agriculture and Natural Resources, *The Lake News*, 2nd ed., (2021), 20-21.

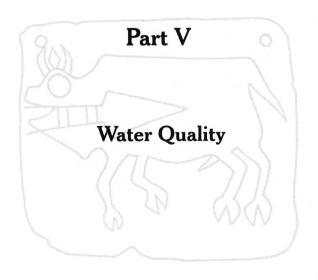

Part V

Water Quality

Chapter 16

The Big Sioux River Watershed: Changing Perceptions of River Health and the Role of State Soil and Water Conservation Districts in Twentieth Century South Dakota

Dale Potts
South Dakota State University

The study of the Big Sioux River watershed and the topic of pollution requires an understanding of local, state, and federal history while acknowledging environmental impacts from industrial, municipal, and agricultural sources. As an interstate watershed, the river constitutes a critical feature of eastern South Dakota and surrounding states. Actions to positively affect the health of this watershed in South Dakota, as in the case of many states, initially developed in the twentieth century reflecting a utilitarian usage of water sources commensurate with Progressive Era wise-use policies. Efforts to mitigate pollution, whether during the Progressive Era, the Dust Bowl 1930s, or the era of the modern environmental movement of the 1960s, reflected economic, political, and cultural ideas about the uses of water at local, state, and national levels. What began as a focus on topsoil loss and river siltation, later emphasized the need to address pollution from industry and municipalities, connected pollution to infrastructure changes including flood control, all the while wrestling with more complex discussions of pollution from agriculture and livestock production.

State conservation districts, and affiliated agencies, played a significant role in assessing pollution sources and levels by the 1940s. However, it is important to trace the development of conservation districts, understanding antecedents that emerged during the Great Depression, as well as state and federal agencies that emerged by the 1960s and 1970s. To understand long-term changes to the river's health, it is necessary to ascertain the complex interrelationships between industrial and municipal growth, as well as agricultural and livestock practices. Within this framework, the creation of twentieth century conservation districts at the state level indicated a shift brought about by necessity in how South Dakotans perceived agriculture's effects on the river and, in a related context, how urban centers similarly possessed the ability to impact river communities far beyond a city's borders.

The first major identifiable pollution source related to the Big Sioux River involved topsoil runoff. Large-scale runoff became prevalent as agricultural production increased in the latter half of the nineteenth century. Once called "'the Silvery Sioux,' because of its clarity," the Big Sioux River possessed different characteristics before the advent of large-scale agriculture. The river once possessed gravelly and sandy bottoms as well as different aquatic life, but an initial reduction in habitat diversity occurred due to silt "covering gravel substrates and filling in deep holes."[1]

Topsoil loss occurring in the nineteenth century, increased rapidly by the early decades of the twentieth. As an example of "nonpoint pollution," meaning its origin was diffused and its sources could not be directly pinpointed, topsoil clogged rivers along with fertilizer runoff from fields.[2] In the case of lost topsoil, knowledge of good practices took time to develop. In the nineteenth century, soil science was a field restricted to university professors whose knowledge of positive practices, such as the "growth of sufficient cover," remained underutilized on "the more sandy textured soils" found in eastern South Dakota.[3] To prevent feedlot runoff, in addition, it was problematic to keep livestock back from a river's edge when rivers provided a ready source of water that the animals required.

Although attention to river pollution sources from industry and municipalities was at the forefront of river cleanup campaigns in the nation during the Progressive Era, albeit with limited overall results, such pollution sources as topsoil runoff remained largely unnoticed by a disinterested public.[4] Instead, at the national level, early-twentieth-century river pollution discussions focused debates on the impacts of industrial and municipal waste, by and large, east of the Mississippi River. In New England's major river systems, as John T. Cumbler writes, state boards of health contended with corporations that "resisted pressure to stop dumping wastes into local streams and smoke and noxious fumes into the air, and towns resisted pressure to stop dumping their wastes into the nearest running water."[5]

Government agencies acknowledged both point and nonpoint sources of pollution as problematic in the early-to-mid-twentieth century, but while point pollution sources might be more readily identified, nonpoint sources, including those from agriculture, could not be as readily determined. This time frame coincided with national farm legislation including the Smith-Lever Act of 1914, which established the Cooperative Extension Service, in part, to increase knowledge of soils. In 1919 the South Dakota Legislature "appropriated $10,000 for soil survey work," which led to cooperative soil surveys for Beadle and McCook counties by the following year.[6] It would take time for states like South Dakota to establish such services as extension work across the state for rural communities, but by the 1930s the role of the State Cooperative Extension Office in addressing Dust Bowl conditions became critical.

Large-scale efforts to avoid topsoil loss likewise began in the 1930s with federal governmental agencies like the Soil Erosion Service (later the Soil Conservation Service), the Civilian Conservation Corps, and the United States Army, with all three organizations often working in tandem.[7] The United States Department of Agriculture's State Soil Conservation Districts, as part of the Soil Conservation Service, spearheaded efforts to preserve soil health, the very foundation of the region's agricultural economy, while the Civilian Conservation Corps, already providing labor in places such as national parks and forests, demonstrated techniques to prevent erosion alongside the SCS, thus also actively working to conserve soils in the state.

Soil health became a national issue with federal legislation helping to define the role of individual states in assessing problems and developing solutions. As the State Soil Conservation Districts Law of 1936 found, "improper land-use practices" caused "progressively more serious erosion of the farm and grazing lands" and that it was necessary that "appropriate soil-conserving land-use practices be adopted and carried out."[8] As Donald Worster writes, leadership of the Soil Conservation Service in Washington believed "that new farming methods would be more acceptable if they came not from federal experts, but from community groups run by those affected," a belief that allowed "local people to set up, through petition and referendum, their own district."[9] It would take several years before some counties in South Dakota organized their conservation districts, but the ideas behind the district concept were already at work through different agencies in the mid-1930s. By 1936, in the Big Sioux River watershed, CCC Camp SCS-3 (DPE-211) at Alcester, south of Sioux Falls, appeared as a drought-relief camp where "soil erosion projects" on private land consisted of "terracing and dam building" under the direction of the newly-renamed Soil Conservation Service.[10]

The camp's "main project consisted of the application of conservation practices on the farmlands in Union, Lincoln, and Clay counties" while, in general, "enrollees [of the CCC camps] constructed dams, sod waterways, grade stabilization structures, and terraces," while also renovating "the old woodland areas" that included a nursery in Vermillion.[11] Building on the County Extension Service, demonstration farms, and the work of the Civilian Conservation Corps, state scientific experts in the 1930s promoted agricultural practices such as contour farming, riverbank revegetation, reforestation, as well as terracing and overall water conservation.[12]

Through the work of the Soil Conservation Service, with logistical direction from the U.S. Army, many farmers observed firsthand how conservation practices could mitigate erosion through field windbreaks, contour furrows, contour strip-cropping, and terracing, as demonstrated at camps at Alcester, Huron, Chamberlain, and Sturgis.[13] The camps worked to rehabilitate the landscape while demonstration farms exhibited best practices for soil health, and in each case scientific expertise remained instrumental in educating the farm population. Dr. J. G. Hutton, Head of the Soils Department at South Dakota State College, working with the Soil Erosion Service, was credited with influencing general public acceptance of implementation of Soil Conservation Districts in the state.[14]

Judging from the example of Minnehaha County, a 1941 referendum and subsequent votes in 1944 added the entirety of the county to the Minnehaha Soil Conservation District.[15] In another case, Brookings County identified corrective measures to address soil erosion by demonstrating restorative practices involving gully control, contour farming and terracing, the establishment of grassed waterways, a cropping system to maintain cover, and the encouragement of "subsurface tillage on sandy soil."[16] Throughout this time, the overall emphasis remained on retaining topsoil in the fields rather than attempting to rehabilitate the ecosystems of the river.

By World War II, the federal government phased out the CCC, although the Soil Conservation Service continued to work with conservation districts. The South Dakota Association of Conservation Districts was established as a formal organization by 1942.[17] During World War II, the State Soil Conservation Committee, headed by directors of state agencies such as the Extension Service, the State Agricultural Experiment Stations, and others, increasingly attended to issues related to flood control; and by 1961, after the *South Dakota Watershed Act of 1957* authorized the creation of water conservation districts, the committee formally became the Soil and Water Conservation Committee responsible for the continued goal of promoting watershed projects.[18]

Over the same time frame, when it came to urban industrial and municipal waste, however, eastern South Dakota faced similar challenges when it came to discussion of these sources of pollution. As Samuel P. Hays writes, these efforts originated with federal resource policy that responded to environmental degradation, economic downturns, and evolving scientific expertise during the Progressive Era in order "to promote efficient development and use of all natural resources."[19] Despite an ideology that originated in the early decades of the twentieth century, however, this federal policy continued to influence perceptions of water use long after World War II's conclusion. With an emphasis on efficiency, civil engineering and scientific knowledge of water quality in the post-war years led to the start of improved water treatment facilities in urban centers.

Along the Big Sioux River, near Sioux Falls, populations were keenly aware of the levels of pollution as early as the 1920s. The *Report of the Sioux River Sanitary Survey of 1923*, by the Division of Sanitary Engineering of the South Dakota State Board of Health, related "numerous complaints" to the State's Attorney's and County Commissioners' Offices in Minnehaha County, namely "that the river is badly polluted below Sioux Falls by the wastes from a packing house, city sewage and other industrial wastes" with evidence provided by farmers living miles below the city who had to close their windows on summer evenings due to the smell of hydrogen sulfide.[20] It would take until after World War II to see actions related to urban point pollution and that would occur most often when the issue was bundled with that of flood control.

The work of the conservation districts, then, would correlate with state and federal agencies to create plans and reports that assessed and attempted to limit pollution levels in the Big Sioux River watershed, but also to foster watershed projects. Congress passed the *Watershed Protection and Flood Prevention Act of 1954* "authorizing the Department of Agriculture to assist local sponsoring organizations to develop watershed management projects for the nation's tributary basins," an action that benefited the City of Sioux Falls.[21] An extensive flood control project begun by the Army Corps of Engineers two years later in and around the city was completed in 1965 with "10.8 miles of channel improvement through the city, 2.7 miles of new diversion channel, and 27.1 miles of levees."[22]

An indication of the continued importance of flood control at the state and national level, South Dakota Senator Karl Mundt, as a member of the Senate Appropriations Committee, secured funds for dam and reservoir projects on the Missouri River through the Civil Functions of the Department of the Army, in Public Law 163–July 15, 1955, while earmarking funds for "flood control, and rescue work, repair, restoration or maintenance of flood control projects threatened or destroyed by flood" for the Mississippi River and its tributaries.[23] Election campaign materials from the late 1950s point out Senator Mundt's record, indicating his attention to "River Progress in South Dakota," including Missouri River development and flood control around Sioux Falls.[24]

Instilling a public need for soil rehabilitation required an increase in general knowledge of soil conservation practices. Conservation districts alongside other agencies, such as the Extension Service, promoted information to the public on agricultural practices to keep soils out of the river systems. In the 1950s a regional program known as the Great Plains Conservation Program came about through an Act of Congress and, connected with the Soil Conservation Service, by the late 1950s promoted similar attention to soil rehabilitation and "acreage diverted to grass" on a larger scale.[25] By the 1960s, with Soil Conservation Districts, Extension Service agents, demonstration farms, and other federal and state agencies in place providing information and guidance, a gradual, if uneven, transition occurred that promoted conservation practices in agriculture. Nonpoint pollution sources, such as topsoil loss to the river as well as fertilizer and feedlot runoff, existed as challenges for conservation agencies. For instance, the South Dakota State Association of Soil and Water Conservation District Supervisors published the *South Dakota Soil and Water Conservation Needs Inventory* in 1962, which found that of the 299 watersheds studied in the state, 98 indicated a need for action.[26] And although there had been restorative practices engaged in since the 1930s, the need for new and continued actions remained significant.

The *Needs Inventory* identified the scale and significant cost necessary to address these issues. Knowing that federal aid was crucial to assist both rural and urban communities for various developments, the report reiterated the long-established goals "of flood prevention, agricultural water management," as well as "nonagricultural water management.[27] As federal directives continued through the *Water Quality Act of 1965*, the government required by 1967 that states like South Dakota mandate "water quality standards for the interstate surface waters within their boundaries" and "to formulate a plan to implement and enforce these standards."[28] While investigations into the status of the Big Sioux River watershed typified an evolving concept of river health, overall the goal of both federal and state enforcement efforts still emphasized a multiple use ideology, with some limited attention to ecosystem rehabilitation. With many constituent interests, the limits of legislating the environment became evident, as enforcement, in the form of direct regulation, contained a "principal method" whereby the government did not necessarily work to eliminate pollution sources but "to prohibit emissions beyond prescribed limits."[29]

With the passage of the *National Environmental Policy Act of 1970*, state departments of Environmental Protection assumed a larger role in directing conservation efforts. The South Dakota Department of Environmental Protection, in 1976, after testing water conditions along the river, found considerable variance in water quality by locale. Near its headwaters, the river at "low flow" displayed "pooled water, organic and nitrate pollutants from agricultural fertilizers and livestock feedlots that have spring runoff," while at the Sioux Falls monitoring station below the city, the report stated that the "discharge greatly degrades water quality."[30]

In 1971, one year prior to the *Clean Water Act*, South Dakota's Committee on Water Pollution, working from federal guidelines, sponsored the creation of the *Interim Basin Plan of 1971* for the Big Sioux River which reported that "the waste treatment problems of numerous small cities in the Big Sioux River Basin" would lead to expected grant applications "for construction of waste treatment facilities in the near future" (or improvement of existing facilities).[31] Federal legislation in 1972, in the form of the *Clean Water Act*, codified many requirements regarding water quality and necessitated that states meet federal standards "to restore and maintain the chemical, physical, and biological integrity of the Nation's waters."[32] To achieve these ends, federal funds would assist municipalities with addressing waste water treatment issues.

In 1973 the Environmental Protection Agency, through its National Field Investigation Center, Denver, Colorado, investigated the health of the Big Sioux River and reported on conditions created by urban centers like Sioux Falls. At the time, Sioux Falls water treatment was not unlike other such treatment facilities across the nation. It consisted of "a two-stage, trickling filter system for industrial-waste pretreatment, followed by a complete-mixed activated sludge system that treats both the pretreated industrial wastes and domestic wastes"; however, the actual physical plant at that time did consist "of a potpourri of units, vintage 1920-1960s."[33]

By contrast, small communities in the last few decades have used simpler systems, treating sewage in lagoons and allowing aerobic bacteria to break down organic matter where sewage water would be pumped into a different lagoon to purify over time.[34] The field investigation report determined that in periods of low-flow conditions around Sioux Falls, the river was subject to "severe depletion of oxygen resources and by excessive ammonia concentrations downstream," resulting from municipal water treatment facilities that treated the city's domestic waste as well as that of two meat-packing plants, John Morrell and Company and Meilman Food Industries.[35] The 1973 EPA report on water quality recommended that a waste permit issued to Sioux Falls include "specific effluent limitations," "continuous disinfection" of "fecal-coliform bacterial density," and furthermore, that Sioux Falls "establish enforceable pretreatment standards for those pollutants that are not susceptible to treatment by the municipal system."[36]

In the 1970s plans to address pollution in river systems evolved through investigation of conditions and reportage to the Environmental Protection Agency as well as by state efforts, the latter as evidenced by the *Interim Basin Plan of 1971*. Seven years later, the South Dakota statewide *208 Water Quality Management Plan*, created by the South Dakota Department of Environmental Protection, proposed actions to address point and nonpoint pollution in the state. For point pollution sources, namely industrial and municipal sewage treatment, this plan provided municipalities with federal funds through the Construction Grants Program and provided 75 to 85 percent "of the cost of planning, designing, and constructing a wastewater treatment plant."[37] To monitor the effectiveness of the treatment plants and to gauge the need for future upgrade efforts, the National Pollutant Discharge Elimination System (NPDES) issued permits to facilities and established a self-monitoring program.[38]

The *Interim Basin Plan of 1971*, and subsequent reportage on nonpoint sources of pollution from agriculture and feedlot runoff, by contrast, illustrated that "agricultural runoff and wastes from cattle feeding operations were significant pollution sources in the basin," while the impact they had on the environment "could only be estimated" at that time.[39] In the context of the *Clean Water Act*, the focus of investigations into pollution sources initially pinpointed, and sought to limit, the amount of pollution entering river systems from factories and municipal water treatment plants, and while their efforts in these instances had some successes, they were less effective in "limiting 'nonpoint' pollution from farms, feedlots, timber clear-cuts, mines," and other sources.[40]

The relationship between the agricultural sector, state agencies, and federal agencies included programs that directly or indirectly addressed the river's watershed by the late 1970s. The Agricultural Stabilization and Conservation Service, at that time under the Department of Agriculture, provided funds to foster best management practices, while other programs mitigated soil erosion and provided funds for feedlot operators "in the reduction of pollution to waterbodies from feedlot operations."[41] An amendment to the *Clean Water Act* in 1977 expanded regulation and proved "fairly effective at limiting 'point sources,'" while the 1987 amendments "established incentives for polluters to reduce their nonpoint releases."[42]

Addressing nonpoint pollution sources resulting from agriculture and livestock was a complex proposition in 1978 as expressed in South Dakota's *Statewide 208 Water Quality Management Plan*. As the plan reported, the "effects of nonpoint source (NPS) pollution in South Dakota are varied and extensive" and that "the major effects of nonpoint source pollution are caused by solid materials or sediment carried by the water, and by the input of nutrients such as nitrogen and phosphorus that are associated with nonpoint runoff."[43]

The connection between topsoil loss and chemicals finding their way into river systems, as examples of nonpoint pollution, have historically been difficult to determine when compared to point pollution. In various reports of this era, such nonpoint pollution sources were acknowledged, but not addressed as directly as point pollution sources. By the mid-1980s, the nation's Environmental Protection Agency noted in a study of pesticides in South Dakota's ground water that "agricultural activities have been reported as a source of contamination, but not ranked for seriousness."[44]

If federal and state reports on pollution abatement did not actively address ecosystems within the rivers as part of their overall approach, they did reflect the effects of pollution more generally. Instilling the need for improved water quality continued to be directed through agencies such as the Extension Service, as well as other government outlets and publications. In 1969 the Wildlife Management Institute, Washington, D.C., advised farmers to allow marshes, streams, and

ponds to remain as integral parts of their farms, "holding surface water on the land" and allowing some to "trickle down through soil and
rock to replenish the 'ground water.'"[45] And echoing the work of CCC
camps in the 1930s in places such as Alcester, the guidebook advised
farm operators that "the banks of streams under nearly all conditions
should be protected with vegetation," and furthermore, "maintain
them in a wooded condition."[46]

Efforts to slow point pollution sources in the twentieth century
met with a measure of success spurred on by federal and state legislation, governmental agencies, and by conservation districts and the
personnel who helmed them through the decades. Today, conservation
districts continue the work they began in the 1940s, "implementing
conservation practices that maintain the health of our air, land, water,
plants and animals," while also "teaching the value of natural resources
and encouraging conservation efforts," including the prevention of soil
erosion.[47]

In the twenty-first century, the Big Sioux River watershed continues to exhibit a focus on multiple use, retaining its importance for a
variety of constituents throughout the state. There are indications that
perspectives on river health have changed in the last forty years. Idling
of agricultural land to reduce crop surpluses and provide acreage seed-
ed to grasses has had a significant role to play in the river's health.[48] In
addition, the South Dakota Conservation Reserve Enhancement Program (CREP) "provides for the establishment of buffers, grass plantings, forbs [flowering plants] and shrubs to improve and enhance water
quality" in watersheds across the state.[49]

By the mid-1990s the South Dakota Department of Environmental and Natural Resources reported that "today, about 40% of the river
meets water quality requirements for contact recreation."[50] Changes
enacted over the decades with regard to the river's health reflected the
historical contexts of those times. If, as in 1968, the winter "outflow
from the Sioux Falls sewage treatment plant was greater than the flow
of the river," with low dissolved oxygen levels, by the 1990s the situation had somewhat improved.[51]

The Big Sioux River today continues to be heavily utilized and, as
such, is still impacted by topsoil loss, industrial and municipal pollutants, as well as agricultural runoff. In the late 2010s, the river was still

classified as an "'impaired water body' for the purposes of swimming and even 'limited-contact' recreation such as kayaking and canoeing."[52] The Sierra Club notes that the primary pollutants in the Big Sioux River continue to include *E. coli*, sediment, nitrates, chemicals, and trash.[53] Organizations like Sierra Club as well as Friends of the Big Sioux River offer the public opportunities for annual cleanup efforts and outline best practices related to topsoil loss, livestock runoff, and "chemical conservation" to keep substances out of the river.[54]

While urban point pollution sources are perhaps better understood than nonpoint pollution sources, both remain issues for state and federal conservation agencies, including those responding to increased desires for public recreation. Public interest in recreational fishing is evident by surveys conducted by the South Dakota Game, Fish and Parks Department, and in 2010 these surveys yielded in-state comments that identified agricultural "runoff" as a practice believed to be a cause for dwindling fish populations.[55] Relatedly, some respondents hoped for better ways to control invasive carp populations.[56] Invasive species such as Asian carp, introduced into the American South in the 1960s "to eat aquatic weeds and clean aquaculture ponds," have thrived in such low-oxygen environments found in many stretches of the Big Sioux River watershed.[57]

From the nineteenth to the twenty-first centuries, different constituencies have utilized the Big Sioux River watershed, while more recently, public debates have increased on the subject of river health. In the 1960s, ecologist and wildlife specialist Paul L. Errington wrote, "in attempting to safeguard what naturalness we can, we may of course find here and there—sometimes even in metropolitan areas—minor tracts very well worth preserving, along with the plant and animal life properly associated with them."[58] For over a century, public perceptions of the role of river systems in the economy as well as the social fabric of South Dakota society influenced, and were influenced by, legislation and the actions of governmental agencies. Present early on, the conservation districts played a significant role in maintaining a focus on the Big Sioux River watershed and its importance to different constituencies. With growing public interest in river ecosystem health, the debates over river conditions will likely continue.

Notes

1. Douglas J. Dieterman, "The Influence of the Clean Water Act and Tributaries on the Fish Community of the Big Sioux River, South Dakota" (M.A thesis, Wildlife & Fisheries Science, South Dakota State University, 1995), 1, 8.

2. John T. Cumbler, *Reasonable Use: The People, the Environment, and the State, New England 1790-1930* (New York: Oxford University Press, 2001), 163.

3. Harry H. Martens et al., *History of South Dakota's Conservation Districts* (Pierre, SD: Association of Soil and Water Conservation Districts History Committee, 1969), 3.

4. Thomas L. Thelen, "Water Quality Management Study for the Big Sioux River Basin" (M.A thesis, Civil Engineering, South Dakota State University, 1976), 1.

5. Cumbler, 132.

6. "South Dakota Conservation History Timeline–Developed April 2010," South Dakota Department of Agriculture, accessed February 8, 2021, https://sdda. sd.gov/conservation-forestry/conservation/history-sd-conservation-district/ PDF/103%20SDConservationHistoryTimelineApril2010.pdf.

7. Martens, 4-5.

8. *A Standard State Soil Conservation Districts Law, Prepared at the Suggestion of Representatives of a Number of States*, PDF Download (Washington, D.C.: U.S. Department of Agriculture, Soil Conservation Service, 1936), 2-3, accessed April 10, 2021, https://www.nrcs.usda.gov/Internet/FSE_DOCUMENTS/ nrcs143_021255.pdf. The law itself would be enacted by Congress in 1937 and sent to state governors as a guide for preparing state soil conservation legislation, Martens, 7.

9. Donald Worster, *Dust Bowl: The Southern Plains in the 1930s* (New York: Oxford University Press, 1979), 219.

10. Lyle A. Derscheid, *The Civilian Conservation Corps in South Dakota (1933-1942): A Historical Report Sponsored by Chapter 61 of NACCCA* (Brookings, SD: South Dakota State University Foundation Press, 1991), 271-72.

11. Martens, 6.

12. *A Standard State Soil Conservation Districts Law*, 19.

13. Martens, 4-5.

14. Ibid., 7.

15. Ibid., 90.

16. Ibid., 135.

17. "South Dakota Conservation History Timeline."

18. Martens, 7, 10-11.

19. Samuel P. Hays, *Conservation and the Gospel of Efficiency: The Progressive Conservation Movement, 1890-1920* (Pittsburgh: Pittsburgh University Press, 1999), 2.

20. *Comprehensive Water Quality Management for the State of South Dakota–303 (e) Basin Report for the Big Sioux River Basin* (Pierre: South Dakota Department of Environmental Protection, 1976), 34-35.

21. Thelen, 42-43.

22 "Missouri River Division–Water Resources Development, South Dakota," PDF Download (Omaha: Department of the Army, Missouri Division Corps of Engineers, 1979), 16, accessed June 26, 2021, https://usace.contentdm.oclc.org/digital/collection/p16021coll7/id/6606/.

23 *Public Works Appropriation Act*, 84th Cong., 1st sess., July 15, 1955, H.R. 6766, 363, accessed April 3, 2021, www.govtrack.us/congress/bills/84/hr6766.

24 "Your Senator, Karl Mundt," Karl E. Mundt Collection, Digital Library of South Dakota, accessed May 1, 2021, https://explore.digitalsd.org/digital/collection/mundt/id/652/rec/9.

25 Douglas Helms, "The Great Plains Conservation Program, 1956-1981: A Short Administrative and Legislative History," PDF Download, in *Readings in the History of the Soil Conservation Service* (Washington, D.C.: U.S. Department of Agriculture, Soil Conservation Service, 1992), 145, accessed August 21, 2021, https://www.nrcs.usda.gov/Internet/FSE_DOCUMENTS/stelprdb1043484.pdf.

26 State Soil and Water Conservation Needs Committee, *South Dakota Soil and Water Conservation Needs Inventory* (Huron, SD: South Dakota State Association of Soil and Water Conservation District Supervisors, 1962), 4.

27 Ibid., 81.

28 Thelen, 1-2.

29 Roger W. Findley and Daniel A. Farber, *Environmental Law in a Nutshell* (St. Paul: West Publishing Company, 1988), 59.

30 *Comprehensive Water Quality Management for the State of South Dakota*, 85, 90.

31 Thelen, 17.

32 "U.S. Code and the Clean Water Act of 1972," Legal Information Institute, Cornell University Law School, accessed July 18, 2021, https://www.law.cornell.edu/uscode/text/33/1251.

33 "Report on Water Quality and Waste Source Investigations, Big Sioux River & Selected Tributaries," PDF Download (Denver, CO: Environmental Protection Agency–Office of Enforcement, 1973), 62, accessed April 9, 2021, https://nepis.epa.gov.

34 Randy Hascall, "Strict Rules Govern Wastewater Dumping," *Argus Leader*, July 18, 1999, A5.

35 "Report on Water Quality and Waste Source Investigations,"1.

36 Ibid., 13.

37 *South Dakota 208 Water Quality Management Plan* (Pierre: South Dakota Department of Environmental Protection–Office of Water Quality, 1978), 20.

38 Ibid., 20-21.

39 Thelen, "Water Quality Management," 17.

40 Daniel McCool, *River Republic: The Fall and Rise of America's Rivers* (New York: Columbia University Press, 2012), 191.

41 *The South Dakota 208 Water Quality Management Plan*, 16.

42 McCool, 190-91.

43 *The South Dakota Statewide 208 Water Quality Management Plan*, 24-25.

44 "State Program Briefs Pesticides in Ground Water," PDF Download, Environmental Protection Agency–Office of Groundwater Protection

(Washington, D.C.: U.S. Environmental Protection Agency, 1986), 74, accessed June 28, 2021, https://nepis.epa.gov.

[45] Durward L. Allen, *The Farmer and Wildlife* (Washington, D.C.: Wildlife Management Institute, 1969), 38.

[46] Ibid., 41.

[47] "South Dakota's Conservation Districts," The Association of Conservation Districts, accessed June 10, 2021, www.sdconservation.org/sdcd.

[48] Harry F. Thompson, ed., *A New South Dakota History*, 2nd ed. (Sioux Falls: The Center for Western Studies, 2009), 250.

[49] "South Dakota CREP (Conservation Reserve Enhancement Program–James River Watershed," Farm Service Agency, accessed March 1, 2021, https://gfp.sd.gov/userdocs/docs/crepfacts-2021.pdf.

[50] Dieterman, "The Influence of the Clean Water Act," 1.

[51] Ibid., 7-8.

[52] John Hult, "Will it ever be safe to swim the Big Sioux?: The river is still a mess, with complex challenges, but there have been recent successes," *Argus Leader*, April 29, 2017, A3.

[53] "Big Sioux River Watershed," Sierra Club, accessed June 1, 2021, www.sierraclub.org/south-dakota/big-sioux-river-watershed.

[54] "Friends of the Big Sioux River Rural Position Statements," Friends of the Big Sioux River, accessed May 30, 2021, www.friendsofthebigsiouxriver.org/rural.

[55] Larry M. Gigliotti, *Fishing in South Dakota–2010: Fishing Activity, Harvest and Angler Opinion Survey* (Pierre: Game, Fish and Parks, 2010), 98.

[56] Ibid., 56-57.

[57] Andrew Reeves, *Overrun: Dispatches from the Asian Carp Crisis* (Toronto: ECW Press, 2019), 1.

[58] Paul L. Errington, *Of Predation and Life* (Ames: Iowa State University, 1969), 262.

Chapter 17

Don't Drink the Water: Bacterial Contamination of the Big Sioux River

Kelsey Murray
Western Dakota Tech

Linda DeVeaux
New Mexico Tech

Introduction

The Big Sioux River, as it runs through eastern South Dakota, represents a vanishing rural landscape in the United States. It is emblematic of "rural flight," the movement of people from agrestic to urban areas, a phenomenon rooted in the industrialization of agriculture. In its relatively short length (~420 miles), the Big Sioux weaves among three of the five largest cities in the state (Watertown, Brookings, and Sioux Falls) while also moving through some of the most sparsely populated regions in the country.

In the span of just two centuries, the Big Sioux has transformed from a crystal-clear river abundant with fish and wildlife to one of the most highly polluted bodies of water in the United States. Water resources across the globe are profoundly impacted by humans in both their quantity and quality, and the Big Sioux River is no exception. The river has a history of hydrologic instability, as evidenced by frequent and often severe flooding. The diminished water quality results from a combination of factors: periodic flooding, as well as urban, industrial, and agricultural sources of pollution.

In rural western states like South Dakota, there are significant problems with human and animal waste contaminating surface waters in both populated and uninhabited areas. Of the 9,726 miles of perennial rivers and streams in South Dakota, about 4,000 miles are affected by unacceptably high levels of excrement. The Big Sioux River and many of its tributaries are moderately to highly polluted with such waste. High levels of waste, either human or animal, in a body of water increases the likelihood of spreading of infectious diseases and provides an environment for emerging diseases to breed.[1]

Across the globe, infectious diseases are emerging at an unprecedented rate. Water serves as an interface between the environment and human health. Water-related infectious diseases are already a major cause of illnesses worldwide, and the problem is only expected to grow. Classic water-related pathogens (bacteria, virus, or other microbes that cause disease), including those responsible for causing typhoid and cholera, account for much of the disease burden, especially in developing countries. However, polluted streams and rivers, especially those found in the United States and Europe, are a source of new types of infectious disease and re-emergence of established pathogens. Contamination of streams and rivers, such as the Big Sioux, with waste, especially when coupled with changing climate, will inevitably lead to new types of diseases, outbreaks, and deaths. It is important to gauge the risks of such contamination as the consequences will be a mounting challenge to both the water and public health sectors.[2]

A Short Microbiology Lesson

In the late 1800s, the German pediatrician Theodor Escherich published a landmark study in the field of microbiology. He isolated gut bacteria from infants, including the now famous *E. coli*, and described their role in digestion and disease. In the time since its discovery, *E. coli* has been widely used in the laboratory to help scientists understand a variety of biological processes, where it has played a role in major scientific advances in the fields of molecular biology, genetics, medicine, and biotechnology.[3] We now know that such *E. coli* (as well as other closely related microbes, termed "coliform bacteria") are a normal part of the guts in mammals. In fact, most *E. coli* is good for us; they help us digest food and make vitamin K for our bodies to use. Because it is a normal inhabitant of our body, particularly our gut, when *E. coli* is present outside of the body in the environment, perhaps in places such as the Big Sioux River, it serves as an indicator that there is waste from humans, cattle, or other mammals present. Water testing routinely checks for levels of *E. coli* to ensure that our drinking water supply is safe from human waste contamination.[4]

From a microbiologist's standpoint, *E. coli* is an interesting species. These bacteria have a great range of diversity in their hereditary material, DNA. If you compare the DNA of any two humans, they differ by only 0.1%, meaning we are all 99.9% genetically identical to one another. In *E. coli*, however, two individuals may only share about 20% of their DNA. So up to 80% of the genetic makeup of *E. coli* is variable.[5] Perhaps even more interestingly, *E. coli*, like most bacteria but unlike humans, can change their DNA over their lifetime. As humans, we are "stuck with" the DNA we are born with, but bacteria have the ability to copy-and-paste DNA from other microbes into themselves. So, as bacteria age, they gain DNA. The extent at which this exchange happens can be prolific. Some *E. coli* have gained up to 18,000 genes from other organisms. (For reference, humans have approximately 30,000 genes in total.[6])

But why do bacteria need to seek out more genetic information? The genetic adaptability of bacteria is important for their very survival; it is the literal definition of survival of the fittest. Each segment of DNA that is added to the repertoire can make *E. coli* more resilient to stress and extreme changes in their environment. For instance, the trip from the cozy safety and comfort of a cow gut (microbes like it there) to the extremes of the South Dakota landscape can be a rough one. The bacteria don't know their ultimate destination; they are just along for the ride. They might land in the Big Sioux River on a hot, humid day or a pasture during a frigid winter snowstorm. So by collecting an arsenal of genetic tools, bacteria can be prepared for any scenario.

While the ability to swap genes gives bacteria a leg up, it also inadvertently leads to problems for humans. Often the same segments of DNA that keep *E. coli* alive are those that change them from helpful gut bacteria into human pathogens. The more of these "bad" genes a single bacterium can pick up, the higher the danger to human health. Infection with an *E. coli* with one or two "bad" genes may lead to mild or moderate diarrhea. *E. coli* that have gained several more genes can cause worse disease, including hemorrhagic colitis (bloody diarrhea) and hemolytic uremic syndrome (kidney failure), an often lethal condition in children and the elderly, and even death. These more-dangerous *E. coli* are close relatives of other human pathogens, including *Salmonella*, *Klebsiella*, and *Yersinia*, the germ responsible for Bubonic Plague. To complicate matters, bacteria can also pick up genes that make them resistant to medical treatment with antibiotics.[7] So, if you get sick, the treatment options are limited.

In the United States, infections by pathogenic variants of *E. coli* account for more than reported 265,000 illnesses and billions of dollars in medical costs.[8] The actual number is probably significantly higher as many people won't seek medical care for mild to moderate diarrhea.

Another Microbiology Lesson: Shiga-Toxigenic *E. coli* (STEC)

Shiga-toxigenic *E. coli* (STEC) is one example of "good" bacteria that have gone "bad" through acquisition of genes from their neighboring microbes. The hallmark of STEC is the ability to make toxic chemicals called Shiga toxins. These toxins, just like they sound, are poisons that contribute to the severity of infection. Since the emergence of STEC in 1982, followed by a major outbreak associated with contaminated hamburgers sold at Jack-in-the-Box in 1993, it has become the most widely recognized type of *E. coli* in the United States and other developed nations.[9] When you hear about *E. coli* contamination of lettuce or meat from the news, it is more than likely that STEC is the culprit. While many types of *E. coli* lead to disease in developing countries, STEC has a higher prevalence in developed countries such as the United States and European countries. Interestingly, the vast majority of recent STEC outbreaks in the United States were linked to water sources (either directly or indirectly) impacted by human and animal waste.[10]

A prominent STEC outbreak occurred in 2001 in Germany, where consumption of contaminated sprouts (irrigated with waste-contaminated water) led to over 4000 illnesses. Eight-hundred people developed severe kidney failure. Fifty-three people died. When the responsible *E. coli* was analyzed by scientists, it was found that this particular strain had picked up a new combination of genes, including those for Shiga toxins, that resulted in a never-before-seen pathogen.[11]

You might be wondering what Shiga toxigenic *E. coli* and outbreaks in Germany have to do with South Dakota and the Big Sioux River. As of the 2012 National Enteric Disease Surveillance STEC Report, the state of South Dakota ranked third in the nation for the number of STEC infections per total population, and first for rate of one particular STEC strain (O157:H7).[12] In 2019 South Dakota had a record 128 reported cases of STEC. Rates of STEC infection have been steadily rising since 2013, and in 2019, the incidence was 14.5 (meaning there are 14.5 infections for every 100,000 people in the state). This is the highest rate in the United States; the average national rate for STEC infection is 1.39.[13]

The Big Sioux River as a Bacterial Mixing Pot

E. coli need a large catalog of genes to ensure their survival. But where do they find the genes? Mostly, they obtain DNA from their nearest neighbors, usually (but not necessarily) from other bacteria. Since *E. coli* is originally a type of gut microbe, it receives much of its genetic information from other gut microbes. This means that where you find high levels of fecal bacteria (bacteria that are found in human or animal waste) you also find high levels of DNA transferring. Places such as the Big Sioux River, where fecal contamination is high, are hotspots for this exchange.

So how much fecal bacteria (waste) is in the Big Sioux River and its tributaries? The short answer: lots. The Environmental Protection Agency (EPA) is the authority for setting water quality standards. Allowable bacteria levels are based on how we use the water. Segments of the river are designated as domestic water supply, fish and wildlife habitat, recreational-use water (both immersion and limited-contact recreation), and as a source of irrigation water. Depending on its designated use, the acceptable level of bacteria is between 126-630 colony forming units (CFUs) per 100 milliliters of water. So, if we scoop water from the Big Sioux into a shot glass, we should find, at most, an average of 630 bacteria.[14] If we want to go swimming, we hope to find far less. (Think about how much water you accidentally swallowed the last time you went swimming; now imagine swallowing fecally contaminated water). The Big Sioux River, especially in the summer, has high average levels: 1500 or more bacteria in the shot glass. Skunk Creek, a tributary of the Big Sioux, has exceeded 24,000 bacteria in a single sample. That's a lot of *E. coli.* (Especially if you accidentally take it in a gulp.[15])

You might be thinking, poop (or more scientifically, feces) in the water is not new. For as long as there have been animals, including humans, there has been fecal contamination of water. This is true. Why then should we care about the high levels of fecal contamination in the Big Sioux River and other rivers in midwestern states?

Historically, gut bacteria from two different species only had the opportunity to intermittently meet and swap DNA. For instance, fecal bacteria from a cow rarely encountered fecal bacteria from a human. The waste from cows and humans was naturally physically separated in different environmental compartments after excretion. Therefore, their genetic information remained largely unavailable for sharing.

Humans, however, are affecting the environment dramatically. Changing land-use practices (particularly those associated with industrialized agriculture), urbanization and development, and local population growth are expected to have a profound effect on water quality and quantity.[16] Now, fecal contamination of watersheds, such as the Big Sioux River drainage basin, is a consequence of continuous inputs from multiple sources, both rural and urban in origin. Urbanization and industry can lead to major changes in freshwater environments through contamination with various chemicals and microbes.

There is large-scale deposition of feces from humans and our wastewater into the environment. Approximately 240,000 people live in the area of the Big Sioux River watershed. There is also large-scale deposition of feces directly from agricultural animals. In South Dakota, as of the 2020 census, cows outnumber people 7 to1 (for a total of about 6.4 million cattle). In regions adjacent to the Big Sioux River, this ratio can be as high as 12:1. There are more than 2 million hogs and more than 4.5 million turkeys. It is estimated that the total fecal input from all of these sources in the region is equivalent to that of 168 million people.[17]

Local land use practices and subsequent stormwater runoff also contribute additional fecal bacteria to the Big Sioux River. In South Dakota about 89% of the total land (by area) is used as farmland.[18] Applying manure-based fertilizer leads to more bacteria entering surface water through runoff. Fecal material from wild animals, such as deer or birds, and domesticated animals, such as dogs, also inevitably ends up in the water, again mostly through stormwater runoff.

We, through anthropogenic pressures, are creating diverse wildlife-livestock-human interfaces that did not exist in the past. Thus, the Big Sioux River acts as a mixing pot for fecal bacteria that would have never intermingled without such human intervention. These newly acquainted bacteria are now able to copy and give their neighbors their previously isolated genetic material. The consequences of this include increasing the total possible combinations of genes. This means more potential for disease. Given the high concentrations of E. coli in the Big Sioux, this mixing is happening frequently.[19]

Once fecal bacteria enter the environment, they have to find their niche. While some bacteria are found in the water, some sink to the bottom and find a home in streambed sediments. It is here that they find food and shelter. Sediments are prime real estate for bacteria to multiply. As a result, sediments can often harbor 100 to 1,000 times more fecal bacteria than the overlying water.[20] When the sediments get stirred up, they can add to the measured total daily loads of bacteria in the water. So it is not always new input of bacteria we are measuring. Changes in streamflow, wave height, wind speed, human recreation, natural turbulence, among many other variables can resuspend bacteria into the moving water. This may lead to transportation of potentially dangerous bacteria downstream.

The Big Sioux River and its sediments, thus, likely serve as a large, central reservoir for agents of infectious disease, including STEC. Storm events, particularly those that result in large scale flooding, are the big spoon that helps stir the pot.

Adopting Best Management Practices along the Big Sioux River

It has been known for over a decade that fecal bacterial levels in the Big Sioux are not within safe limits, as set by the EPA.[21] In order to address the excessively high levels, the Natural Resources Conservation Service (NRCS), the South Dakota Department of Environment and Natural Resources (DENR), and the City of Sioux Falls funded a water quality improvement project along Skunk Creek. Skunk Creek contributes significant flow to the Big Sioux River (sometimes it is responsible for 100% of downstream stream volume, as much of the Big Sioux is diverted around the Skunk Creek Confluence through a diversion canal), so it is anticipated that this project will have positive long-term impacts downstream. This Seasonal Riparian Area Management (SRAM) plan works to implement conservation practices in such a way as to lessen or eliminate agricultural impairment of waterbodies within a given watershed.[22] For Skunk Creek, this plan means suspending cattle grazing on a stretch of land near the creek during the official recreation season, which runs from May through September. (Remember that direct deposit of fecal bacteria by agricultural animals as well as local land use practices are a major contributor of *E. coli* to the Big Sioux River. Also remember that summer months are when *E. coli* levels and disease incidence peak.) Baseline levels of *E. coli* in the water are established upstream of the SRAM, and downstream sites are routinely monitored for changes in *E. coli* levels (in addition to other parameters related to overall stream health). Preliminary data from this SRAM show that this Riparian Management plan has been successful at lowering the total bacterial loads in the stream, which means less *E. coli*.[23]

The Big Sioux River as a Driver for Emerging Infectious Disease

From the "mini-microbiology" lessons presented above, we know that a very real concern is not necessarily that there is fecal contamination of the river, but more the quality of that fecal contamination. The current screening for fecal contamination of streams and rivers involves collecting water and counting *E. coli*. However, this type of test is unable to tell the difference between harmless *E. coli* and those that cause disease. This is potentially an important distinction. If all of the bacteria are "good," does it matter if you accidentally swallow it while kayaking or fishing? (It might be distasteful, but at least you won't get sick or die.) If the bacteria are "bad," that's another story. Of the worst kinds of *E. coli*, it takes ingesting only 10 cells to get sick, but a single drop of water can contain up to a million total bacteria.[24]

In order to explore the disease-causing potential of bacteria (and their ability to be treated with available antibiotics in a clinical setting) in the water, we developed a molecular tool called Path-STREAM (Pathogenicity Profiling: Shiga Toxins and Related E. coli Attributes Identification Method). Path-STREAM uses techniques from microbiology and molecular biology to analyze a surface water sample on a genetic level. Path-STREAM identifies those genes that contribute to changing E. coli from good to bad. It also looks at whether antibiotic resistance is prevalent in the bacterial community, which is clinically important information. If we get sick from a bacterial infection, we hope there are effective antibiotic treatments available. Path-STREAM is a method that allows us to see what genes are in the "mixing pot."[25]

Through our work, we have shown that the Big Sioux River harbors a large number of genes associated with "bad" E. coli. We found the ingredients for pathogens such as STEC (which might explain our relatively high number of cases in South Dakota). We also found combinations of genes that may be remixed to form a new pathogen. It is therefore postulated that surface water with abundant fecal bacteria, such as the Big Sioux River, is driving emergence of new disease. We, through continued work, may be able to show that clinically important bacteria are persisting in the environment and that such strains may be linked in space and time to outbreaks. Further supporting this hypothesis is that E. coli levels in aquatic environments vary seasonally. Higher levels of bacteria are found in the Big Sioux in the summer. Over 40% of all waterborne outbreaks occur during the month of June, and about half of all outbreaks occur between July and September. This holds true for STEC cases in South Dakota, where the majority are reported in the months of June, July, and August.[26]

The Changing Climate and Emergence of New Pathogens

Globally, climate is shifting. Extreme weather events, such as prolonged droughts and heavy rain events, have increased in intensity and frequency.[27] In South Dakota, the effects of climate change will differ depending on geographic location. In western South Dakota, drought will become more common. In eastern South Dakota, flooding is more likely. Summers are becoming increasingly hot and winters shorter in duration but with increasingly intense snowstorms. The whole state has recently seen an increase of 1-2°F in average annual temperatures.

These changing climate conditions have already had a profound effect on the Big Sioux River valley.

In 2019 the United States experienced the wettest year on record. During this "Great Flood of 2019," 14 million citizens were affected, 1 million acres of U.S. farmland was underwater, and new records were set for river levels in 42 different locations. In South Dakota, records were set for inches of rainfall in one day. More records were set for number of inches of rain in a single hour.[28]

Microbes have elaborate mechanisms for adapting to changes in their environmental conditions. Major storm events are part of the natural cycle of renewal and evolution of waterborne bacteria populations. As the frequency and severity of these events increase with a changing climate, bacteria will need to become more savvy in order to survive.

Climate extremes make bacteria stronger. Drought conditions require bacteria to collect genes that make them strong enough to survive. Subsequent storm events allow breeding of pathogens. Floods then disseminate these super-bacteria. It has been well documented in the scientific literature that extreme flooding, such as the 2019 event, is a major risk factor for spread of water-borne disease.[29] Bacterial profiles of flooded sites around the world show an abundance of pathogenic and drug-resistant bacteria.

The Future of the Big Sioux River

Where there are feces, there is potential for disease. The Big Sioux River may be unique in its sources of bacterial contamination, ranging from agricultural, domestic, and wild animals to storm water runoff, septic tank leakage, and wastewater and municipal discharge. This combination gives the Big Sioux an unacceptably, and potentially dangerously, high level of fecal bacteria, including *E. coli*. Clearly, the presence of *E. coli* in high numbers in the Big Sioux River presents a threat. However, while standard water quality testing allows us to routinely measure the quantity of bacteria, it gives us no information related to the potential danger of the water. Path-STREAM was created to give a more in-depth analysis of the good versus the bad bacteria in surface waters. It was designed to assess the potential for transforming normal *E. coli* into those that can make us sick. Ultimately, connecting the presence of emerging pathogens in surface water with clinical outcomes will help us understand the role of the environment in relation to human health.

Notes

[1] S.D. Department of Environment and Natural Resources, *The 2020 South Dakota Integrated Report for Surface Water Quality Assessment*, by S.D. Department of Environment and Natural Resources (South Dakota: Department of Environment and Natural Resources, 2020).

[2] K. E. Jones et al., "Global Trends in Emerging Infectious Diseases," *Nature* 451:7181 (February 21, 2008), https://dx.doi.org/10.1038/nature06536.

[3] S. T. Shulman, H. C. Friedmann, and R. H. Sims, "Theodor Escherich: The First Pediatric Infectious Diseases Physician?," *Clin Infect Dis* 45:8 (October 15, 2007), https://dx.doi.org/10.1086/521946.

[4] U.S. Environmental Protection Agency, "Water Quality Standards: Regulations and Resources," United States Environmental Protection Agency, https://www.epa.gov/wqs-tech.

[5] A. Leimbach, J. Hacker, and U. Dobrindt, "*E. Coli* as an All-Rounder: The Thin Line between Commensalism and Pathogenicity," *Curr Top Microbiol Immunol* 358 (2013), https://dx.doi.org/10.1007/82_2012_303.

[6] J. C. Venter et al., "The Sequence of the Human Genome," *Science* 291:5507 (February 16, 2001), https://dx.doi.org/10.1126/science.1058040.

[7] Soumya Jaya Divakaran et al., "Insights into the Bacterial Profiles and Resistome Structures Following the Severe 2018 Flood in Kerala, South India," 7:10 (2019), https://www.mdpi.com/2076-2607/7/10/474.

[8] P. D. Frenzen et al., "Economic Cost of Illness Due to Escherichia Coli O157 Infections in the United States," *J Food Prot* 68:12 (December 2005), https://dx.doi.org/10.4315/0362-028x-68.12.2623; Health and Human Services, *National Shiga Toxin-Producing Escherichia Coli (Stec) Surveillance Overview*, by U.S. Centers for Disease Control (2012).

[9] National Center for Emerging and Zoonotic Infectious Diseases, *National Enteric Disease Surveillance: Shiga Toxin-Producing Escherichia Coli (Stec) Annual Report*, by U.S. Centers for Disease Control (2012).

[10] J. M. Rangel et al., "Epidemiology of Escherichia Coli O157:H7 Outbreaks, United States, 1982-2002," *Emerg Infect Dis* 11:4 (Apr 2005), https://dx.doi.org/10.3201/eid1104.040739.

[11] Elzbieta Brzuszkiewicz et al., "Genome Sequence Analyses of Two Isolates from the Recent Escherichia Coli Outbreak in Germany Reveal the Emergence of a New Pathotype: Entero-Aggregative-Haemorrhagic Escherichia Coli (Eahec)," *Archives of Microbiology* 193:12 (2011/12/01 2011), https://dx.doi.org/10.1007/s00203-011-0725-6.

[12] *National Shiga Toxin-Producing Escherichia Coli (Stec) Surveillance Overview.*

[13] S.D. Department of Health, "Infectious Disease Surveillance," South Dakota Department of Health, https://doh.sd.gov/statistics/surveillance/; *National*

Shiga Toxin-Producing Escherichia Coli (Stec) Surveillance, by U.S. Centers for Disease Control (2016).

14 S.D. Department of Environment and Natural Resources, *The 2020 South Dakota Integrated Report for Surface Water Quality Assessment.*

15 K. E. Murray, "Path-Stream: Development and Implementation of a Novel Method for Determining Potential Risk from Pathogenic Bacteria in Surface Water Environments" (South Dakota School of Mining and Technology, 2017).

16 S. Marcheggiani et al., "Detection of Emerging and Re-Emerging Pathogens in Surface Waters Close to an Urban Area," *Int J Environ Res Public Health* 12:5 (May 22, 2015), https://dx.doi.org/10.3390/ijerph120505505.

17 "The Big Sioux: A Brief Environmental History," *eco In The Know*, 2020, http://ecointheknow.com/uncategorized/the-big-sioux-a-brief-environmental-history/.

18 Acretrader, "South Dakota Agriculture Overview," 2020, accessed 5/2/2021, https://www.acretrader.com/resources/south-dakota-farmland-prices.

19 Murray.

20 C. M. Davies et al., "Survival of Fecal Microorganisms in Marine and Freshwater Sediments," *Appl Environ Microbiol* 61:5 (May 1995), https://dx.doi.org/10.1128/AEM.61.5.1888-1896.1995.

21 Environmental Protection Agency, U.S. "Water Quality Standards: Regulations and Resources." United States Environmental Protection Agency. https://www.epa.gov/wqs-tech

22 S.D. Department of Agriculture & Natural Resources, "Skunk Creek Nwqi Project," DENR South Dakota, https://denr.sd.gov/dfta/wp/NWQIskunkcreek.aspx; U.S. Environmental Protection Agency, "Seasonal Riparian Area Management Improves Water Quality in Skunk Creek," U.S. Enviornmental Protection Agency, 2019, https://www.epa.gov/sites/production/files/2019-07/documents/sd_skunkcreek_1771_508.pdf.

23 U.S. Department of Agriculture and National Agricultural Statistics Service, "USDA's National Agricultural Statistics Service South Dakota Field Office," United States Department of Agriculture, https://www.nass.usda.gov/Statistics_by_State/South_Dakota/index.php.

24 P. Schmid-Hempel and S. A. Frank, "Pathogenesis, Virulence, and Infective Dose," *PLoS Pathog* 3:10 (October 26, 2007), https://dx.doi.org/10.1371/journal.ppat.0030147.

25 Murray.

26 S.D. Department of Health.

27 P. R. Epstein, "Climate Change and Emerging Infectious Diseases," *Microbes Infect* 3:9 (July 2001), https://dx.doi.org/10.1016/s1286-4579(01)01429-0.

28 R. Bagwell and B. Peters, *Analysis of the 2019 Midwest Us Flooding Using Nasa Data, American Geological Union Fall Meeting* (San Francisco, CA: 2019).

29 Jones et al.

Part VI

Personal Reflections

Chapter 18

Life, Loss, and the Literature of Loess

Ryan Allen

For the self I would know is ever a self that is lost [...]
For I am this great river, ever emptying myself
Of myself, that I may take in more and ever more

—Clif Mason (from "Big Muddy")

I know what it means to be lost. To lose connections. To forget where I come from. I've lived in many places in most regions across America in my life: Kentucky, New Hampshire, South Dakota, Idaho, Oregon, and Alaska were a few. Now, so many years and miles later, it's Iowa, it's Sioux City, where South Dakota, Nebraska, and Iowa meet at the Missouri River. But in getting here, and now after over a decade of *being here*, I've come to find myself still wandering, still a transplant wondering where I am, who I am, and how did I get here? And where is *here*, after all? I can almost hear David Byrne and the Talking Heads in the background singing, "and the days go by" and "same as it ever was."

Maybe here is *Siouxland*, what has been called a "'vernacular region', a distinctive area where the inhabitants consider themselves interconnected by a shared history, mutual interests, and a common identity."[1] Maybe here is the *Loess Hills*, the 200-foot bluffs in places above the flat plain for a 200-mile band alongside the Missouri River, formed over the last 160,000 years or so from wind-borne silt and glacial flour remnants from the last Ice Age.

But maybe *here* is less tangible, more elusive, like an idea that lives and dies on that wind, here one moment somewhere else the next. I'm

361

a spectator to a game I don't understand. I want to sometimes say I see and feel something I don't. I want it to be easy even though I know it is hard. I want to just *feel the wind* and to press my feet into the earth and for it to all make sense, to matter. I want to feel like I belong. But when I spy through my camera eyes, I'm witness to a picture of a world gone mad. I try but can't find any sense. I turn the lens inward, and I get even more confused. Where am I supposed to go? How am I supposed to be? I can't seem to find my place. I'm in-between worlds of clarity and madness, between being a father and being a son, and between a prairie of wild grass and a forest of planted trees.

And I'm not sure why. From one angle, it all looks like the crisis of loss. From another vantage point, a promise of opportunity, of renewal. I teeter on an edge, stuck at this threshold, unable to cross. I'm a fringe species, it seems, forever roaming across uneven terrains of place, space, consciousness, and imagination.

I'm not the only one.

In search of signs, I look to the past to guide me, to the book of life that is our collective, shared memory, written in the history of this land, its people and culture; and I look to the mythology of my own creation, to my family to light the way. And in those brief moments of stillness when I can sharpen the lens of time, and I see it all so clearly—the connections, the hopes, the forgiveness, the healing. It's all so brief, though. There are so many forces still standing in our way.

They look like us.

The search begins again.

The name *Siouxland* originates from author Frederick Manfred (*Lord Grizzly*), who coined the term in 1946 when he used it in the prologue to his third novel, *This is the Year*, which included his own drawn map of Siouxland for its cover, and encompassed the entire Big Sioux River drainage basin, including areas of Minnesota, Iowa, Nebraska, and South Dakota. In the Sioux City Public Library's May 1991 *Book Remarks*, Manfred is quoted as saying, "I wanted to find one name that meant this area where state lines have not been important."[2] So since its inception, "Siouxland" has always been a created place, one imagined or conjured from the mind of the artist, shaped by its inhabitants, by ones capable of seeing space where pre-determined political or topographical lines aren't mapped.

This type of vision and understanding is important for the Loess Hills of northwestern Iowa because of the threats it faces from external forces and its own internal instability and fragility. Loess (pronounced "luss") is German for loose or crumbly. It's gritty, lightweight, and porous. According to the USGS, "Loess is the source of most of our Nation's rich agricultural soils"[3] and also at about 40 tons/acre/year, has some of the United States' highest erosion rates. So this place I'm grounded in, this land of loess, is a space of loss and renewal, of constant change. The wind-blown silt that's formed here is the remnants of a geographic and topographic trauma thousands of years in the making. And it's not just the land that I'm looking at. It's me too. What's outside is a manifestation of intentions we share inside.

We have no concept of what might be lost.

I feel I am a witness—watching, waiting, gazing at past and future through my present eyes. From my vantage point, I see what's happening in the Hills in my own family. I feel and see it in the life and death of my grandmother, her brothers and sisters, children of the Depression, war after war, love and loss. I see it in the cancer inside my dad, the childhood trauma in my mom, the all-too-soon loss of friends, a global pandemic. Why does it all look and feel so much like an ending? Back home in Louisville, Kentucky, for a family funeral and walking Bardstown Road, remnants of Covid and reminders that *Black Lives Matter* and of George Floyd and Breonna Taylor are everywhere.

Whatever *it* is, it's not going to go on forever. One day we'll all be ghosts in a graveyard.

So, when standing at our family plot in St. Croix, Indiana, staring down at what's left of my grandmother, Elnora, her brothers Patrick, Edwin, Paul, Mark, and Ambrose, her sisters, Catherine, and now Lucille, their parents, John and Ida, and so many more, I find myself searching, seeking a sign, looking for dots to connect, a story to tell.

And that's why I think I'm struggling so much now—not because of the death of life, but because of the loss of words.

Where is the space for stories? I'm asking this a lot these days.

I'm not the only one.

᳇᳇

"Not too many folks are that interested in reading anymore,"[4] my friend and colleague and editor of *The Briar Cliff Review*, Tricia Currans-Sheehan, sadly said to me in a recent conversation. She talked about how it feels like we've lost our ability to enjoy being lost, to losing ourselves in a good book, in a compelling story.

We're all feeling this loss. I feel it personally as I lose family and friends. I feel it professionally in the cutting of the English major at my university, Briar Cliff, in the loss of my department, and in the loss of my job. I see and feel it all slipping away. Those who came before, my connection to them. My profession. My discipline. My hopes for the humanities and the liberal arts.

The crystal ball looks more like a hazy IPA.

A health crisis. A climate crisis. A crisis of conscience.

How will we ever find our way back home? Is it even possible at this point?

I gaze out beyond my view and I see a country that's now crossed over 780,000 lives lost from Covid-19, with new variants on the loose, a politics of mutually assured destruction, and a climate showing us we're on the brink of collapse. In "Unnatural Writing" (1995), Gary Snyder says, "Nature's writing has the potential to becoming the most vital, radical, fluid, transgressive, pansexual, subductive and morally challenging kind of writing on the scene. In becoming so, it may serve to help halt one of the most terrible things of our time—the destruction of species and their habitats, the elimination of some beings forever."[5] We could of course use a good dose of this vitality, but this is a big responsibility for artists—to carry this torch *of* and *for* civilization. But this is our job nonetheless—to bear witness to this ecological and cultural genocide.

And yet, it can all be too much to grasp, and certainly too elusive to hold onto.

I asked Tricia what it will mean when *The Briar Cliff Review* is gone. *What will be left*, I wondered out loud to her. "A big hole," she replied, emphasizing the sentiments of the *CLMP* (Community of Literary Magazines and Presses). "We promote literature for the small market. The backstage work of American literature is done in small presses," she expresses, "and we're losing something. We're watching it be lost and we don't really know how to get it back."[6]

In the Spring 1991 issue of *The Briar Cliff Review*, longtime Briar Cliff University English and writing faculty and poet Phil Hey observes in his essay, "The Relevance of a Liberal Arts Education from the Perspective of my Discipline, Writing," how so many students act only as if "they were preparing to execute someone else's instructions" and, quoting Richard Sloma from *No-Nonsense Management*, that "[y]ou have to have something to say."[7] Look around. Nobody's talking anymore. We're shouting past one another on Twitter and cable news, or simply tuning out completely. So maybe it's just that we've lost our capacity to listen, to sit with information that challenges our worldview, to walk a mile in another's shoes, to be able to feel something for someone who is hurting even if we don't know how to understand the pain. It's about equity way more than equality. "When two elephants fight it's the earth that suffers" is the old wisdom I learned from my environmental education days at Nature's Classroom in New England. It's the civilians, the innocent bystanders caught in the crosshairs, who pay the heaviest price, who feel the weightiest burden. That's me: trying to hold my grandmother's hand through a grave from eight hundred miles away.

We know what we've left behind and that once it's gone it never comes back the same again. And yet, although I may live in Sioux City, Iowa, that place where my grandmother is will always be my home. We return to where we came from. I know what it is to be rooted in a place even as the rest of the world above the ground spins. I'm still lost, but now it's different. Now a father myself, I feel a few things as true.

Like how no matter how many years I live in Iowa, I'm still *from* Kentucky. It never leaves you, even when you leave. And I've taken this part of me everywhere I've gone. Taken the bluegrass and the limestone and the bourbon, taken the Ohio River Valley, the hills and bluffs of Otter Creek. To my own children, this Kentucky will only be the place where their dad is from, where they visit on vacation. They will, though, I hope, be able to drink their own land's elixir. They are from *here*, from these Loess Hills of northwestern Iowa. My Ohio River is their Missouri. My limestone, their silt-blown loess.

This gives me solace—as a father and as a writer. Geography can be destiny, as the poet Joseph Brodsky once suggested. I find hope that my destiny is tied to this place, that I am part of the "squatter regionalism"[8] that has defined the postwar Program era—that I am just one link in a very long chain of creative, artistic transplants spending a lifetime "consulting the genius of the place."[9] This is what I've learned in my years living in Sioux City, Iowa, in traveling and immersing myself in these Hills, in working at Briar Cliff University for ten years, and in being one of the nonfiction and Siouxland/Voices of the Great Plains editors for *The Briar Cliff Review*. I've learned that I'm not alone, that this place has value, and that its voice needs to be shared. That's why years ago a group of students and I set out to create *The Loess Hills Oral History Project*, whose mission was to give a voice to residents and others in the Loess Hills region in order to better understand the landscape and to preserve it. This yearning to understand has been happening at the Loess Hills Prairie Seminar in Onawa, Iowa, each summer since 1977. Conservationist and author Sylvan Runkel said of the Seminar: "Getting people–getting children–acquainted with what's out here will make people concerned about what is happening here. If we get acquainted with natural communities, we feel at home. Any place we feel at home, we feel like protecting."[10] And Seminar founder Carolyn Benne often espoused how when we get connected to the natural wonders in our backyard, we get connected to our values.

What Runkel and Benne described is exactly the work *The Briar Cliff Review* has engaged in its close to 35 years of publication, especially in its "Siouxland," now "Voices of the Great Plains," section that has forever preserved these Midwestern voices and engrained them in our collective cultural consciousness. Since its inception in 1989, *The Briar Cliff Review* has always had a section devoted to this region, to its people and way of life. This part of the magazine has magnified a history, culture, and art of the people of the Big Sioux River basin in South Dakota, Minnesota, Iowa, and Nebraska in the ways that Manfred envisioned, but that will only be measurable when it's gone, when we look into the space of what *was* to better understand what *is*.

The literature of loess has deep roots in this region and *The Briar Cliff Review*, as the voice of the region. The 2000 issue, for example, was rich with the themes and imagery of "Big Muddy," most notable in Robert Kelley Schneiders' "Majestic Waters: The Missouri Then and Now," in Jim Redmond's "Winter Camp Out in the Loess Hills," and in Clif Mason's poem, "Big Muddy." In her editor's note for that 2000 issue, Tricia Currans-Sheehan, referencing Mason's poem, writes, "We are seeing that the flow of creativity leaves behind permanent things— art."[11] This is what the wind carries, this is what's in the silt: there are minerals, sedimentary debris, and trauma, yes; but there're also stories and art and resilience too.

If not for magazines like *The Briar Cliff Review*, we could never know the stories of people like Doc Hagedorn, "the last medicine man of Sioux City."[12] We wouldn't know about Sioux City native Josephine Herbst, "the best writer Iowa has ever produced."[13] If not for *The Briar Cliff Review*, an event like the crash landing of the DC-10 United Flight 232 in Sioux City would only be a blurb on one night of weekly news broadcast. Because of *The Briar Cliff Review*, we have a record for posterity of the words of orthopedic surgeon David Paulsrud, who wrote in his essay, "Trauma," from the 2008 issue, "To my horror I saw a thick column of black smoke rising into the clear blue sky. I sorted casualties in the ER and then went into surgery [...]."[14] Or about the role Briar Cliff University played in housing and caring for survivors and families unless we have the record Marcia Poole created in her piece, "Close Enough to Feel," in the 1999 issue. We wouldn't know the history of Buffalo Bill and Sioux City unless we had the poems of Ann Struthers or the essays of Leslie Duling. As William Faulkner noted in his 1950 Nobel Prize speech, "The poet's voice need not merely be the record of man, it can be one of the props, the pillars to help him endure and prevail."[15] The artist isn't here to sit on the sidelines and take notes. Our work is in saving humanity from itself for itself and for the sake of all creation.

This is the value of a liberal arts education. As Phil Hey notes, it's exactly "what can give the professional's mind the beginning of a lifetime of worthwhile figures–words, images, algorithms, heuristics from which he or she can create."[16] As more and more colleges and universities cut humanities departments and small presses close their doors, we're not only removing our ability to document this living history, but also our capacity to save ourselves. Without the props, without the pillars, how can this house still stand? If all our graduates can do is complete checklists, how will our culture ever navigate this life to come?

Who will tell the stories when all the storytellers are gone?

In his poem "Pearly Everlasting," from the book *In the Blast Zone*, a collection chronicling a gathering of artists and scientists at Mount Saint Helens, Gary Snyder writes, "*If you ask for help it comes*. But not in any way you'd ever know."[17]

I find myself asking a lot these days. So I look to the Hills and wait for a sign.

In the Loess Hills of western Iowa, we exist in-between woodlands and prairie. A band of shrubs divide the landscape. Where there's more moisture there are trees. Where it's sun-drenched and drier there's the prairie. The southern Hills get more rain; the northerly, more wind and sun, especially on the upper slopes. But the line between grass and tree isn't always static. Things are always moving, you see. At the equator the Earth spins at over a thousand miles an hour but our feet stay planted. My mind races a million miles a second, it seems, but my brain still hasn't exploded. In the Loess Hills, distribution patterns have been dynamic since their dawn. A little tension, a little friction on the rope keeps things interesting. Crisis can be opportunity, right?

And yet I find myself asking, in a world of mountains, what feat are some hills? Who's to care for quartz and silt and exposed root systems? In 1910 Bohumil Shimek called the hills a "billowy expanse" and a "giant swell of a stormy sea [...] suddenly fixed."[18] With the long lens of time, I see an altogether different prairie. I see gullies and valley floors. I see dendritic drainage and catsteps and alluvial fans and terraces—I see these things, but I do not really know what I'm looking at.

So I look to history and I gaze out to a landscape of grass and sky.

Humans migrated eastward across Beringia in the late Pleistocene.

Today, the bridge to our shared past is submerged. Siberia and Alaska are disconnected even if Sarah Palin can see Russia from her house.

Twelve-thousand years ago people came to the Hills as major loess deposition tailed off.

Before the time of Christ, the Woodland Culture walked the Loess Hills. They developed pottery, created burial mounds, and innovated horticultural techniques. They ate deer and rabbits and squirrels and raccoons and badgers and birds and mussels. They gathered berries and nuts and seeds. They lived in-between worlds: on a prairie, but between the river and the woods, between the earth and heaven.

Sioux City is surveyed in 1854. Here, horse-drawn graders scrape seventy feet of loess from hilltops. By 1856 there were about 1,700 families in the six Loess Hills counties. That number was around 7,500 by the end of the Civil War. The transcontinental railroad is done by 1869.

I came to the Hills much more recently.

By the time of my arrival the megafauna are long gone. Not even a distant memory. Traveling from Sioux City to Omaha there are no mammoths or camels or bison. The only horses are not wild. The landscape's collective conscious, shaped by the Clovis spear and later Folsom points. And by our other innovations and explosions of technology and stupidity—like the wheel, the plow, the steam engine, and the bomb: all the things that transform our landscape. We play the God. We remake the world in our own image: we stretch our faces and contort our smiles as we kill our capacity to live. We subvert the skills we need to survive.

And by *we* I mean *me*.

The beat goes on and on and on: bigger, more, faster, more, faster, bigger, faster, more, more, more.

Progress. Destruction.

When will we stop mining loess to fill dirt? When will we stop plowing slopes for cropland? When will we stop degrading soil-holding prairies by grazing cattle? When will we stop baring soil? When will our need for the prairie outweigh our need for dirt bike and horse-back riding trails, our need for bluff-borne homes? We plant cottonwoods and soft maple and box elders and conifers, and we watch our prairie grasslands die. We watch our biodiversity slip away with it. When will we all learn to leave *well enough* alone?

We force the land to conform to us, to our expectations. Instead of molding our land use practices fitting the Hills topography, we simply slash and plow and graze ourselves into oblivion. And when we're done maybe only the pocket mouse, the box turtle, and cowboy's delight will remain. They've all survived fallouts before.

༄

Adjacent to the Hills, snow geese and ducks migrate along the Missouri River to escape pharaoh and winter. Bald eagles follow closely behind. At Squaw Creek, at the DeSoto refuge, the land shows it still knows how to care for itself.

It's not enough though. We have a part to play. Our fingers skim the same phlox and plantain as coyote and bobcat. Our feet walk the same path the prairie rattlesnake slithers. We're all in this together.

The Archaic atlatl, the ground stone axe, and the mano and metate, are relics hanging on a prairie museum wall. I will be there one day too, hanging in-between a hollow bird bone flute found in Cherokee, Iowa, and an ocher-covered skeleton wearing a shell bead necklace found at the Turin site in Monona County.

One day we will all be ghosts.

We forget the ancient maxim carved into mountaintops and plowed into corn crops: Just because you can do something doesn't mean you should.

We need to show some restraint. It's like we're coming to a precipice, and we can't slow our momentum enough to change our course. If we could, we'd remember to look to our shared past, our collective memories, to guide us. We'd remember our Gary Snyder and become the advocates and allies the Earth needs; and we'd recall our Wes Jackson who reminds us to hold "nature as measure."[19] In the introduction to Jackson's text, Wendell Berry writes, "For the remedies we must look to nature [...]. Since our health and wealth finally are indistinguishable from hers, we have no choice but to learn her ways, her limits, and her demands, and do our best to obey."[20]

So to see our way forward we have to look back. How else will we find our way through this *present*? *The Briar Cliff Review* has given us this lens to look for close to thirty-five years now, that glimpse into what Jon Lauck, in "Notes on Deep America" (2021), encourages us to listen for again. He argues for "a new sensibility—regionalist, civically-inclined, republican, decent, grounded in place and realism, moderate, non-radical [...]. [W]hat we have been doing has not been working—it leaves too many people out and our discourse impoverished."[21]

Snyder and Lauck are both right too. All things in moderation, even moderation. We need a new playbook.

It's time for a great renewal.
I look to the Hills.

We live in a world of extremes but we're running out of excuses. And time. We must find a little balance: a way for farmers to farm, a way for prairie and woodlands to play nice—a way to stop poisoning the well, a way to stop spoiling our supper, a way to leave *well enough* alone.

We need to take our medicine and follow the doctor's order: to minimize destruction, to maximize diversity, and to maintain integrity. I'm talking about the Hills. I'm talking about myself. We all need a little self-control. Because when we lose loess, we lose more. We lose ourselves. Richard Manning makes it clear: "Our culture's disrespect for its grasslands has produced an environmental catastrophe."[22]

Now is the time to stop *looking* and to start *living*.

For thousands upon thousands of years the prairie has been reborn time and time again. We have been too. Beginnings are ends. Ends are beginnings. We are born. We die. In between the fire burns and remakes us, the prairie, time after time, age after age.

It's happening right now. A fire burns on Five-Ridge Prairie. My grandmother gets closer to death as we await the birth of a child.

We breathe out. Breathe in.

For now, though, we wait: for babies to be born, for fires to subside, for wildflowers to rise from the ash.

We'll be ready this time we hope.

We know loess encourages long roots. The Yucca's forty-foot roots seek and find the deepest moisture.

We dig for the ghosts we need to believe in.

We adapt. We *give* to *get*. We have to change or we will die.

I look backward through time to my grandmother to find a way home.

I look to the loess, to the Hills, to the literature and love of place to guide me.

The plains spadefoot toad stays buried underground until early summer rains brings it to surface pools. The plains pocket mouse stores seeds in its fur-lined cheek pouches and doesn't need to drink water since it gets it from the food it ingests. A hairy covering on cowboy's delight and a waxy coating on great-flowered beardtongue prevent excessive evaporation. The silky aster has whitish hairs to reflect the sun's heat. Skeleton weed barely has any leaves to reduce moisture loss. Soil lichens are covered in gelatinous goo to withstand desiccation. Mosses help check erosion of fragile loess soils.

The prairie shows us how to burrow, how to look within ourselves to find the answers.

My grandmother knew adaptation too—a woman who survived the Great Depression and World War II. A woman who buried three siblings by the time she was twenty. A woman who made it through an abusive marriage, a divorce, and still raised two boys to become good men. A woman who knows how to get up each time she falls.

She survived trauma. But can we?

Can her grandson learn to live without her lighting his way?

Can we all adapt before we mutate into the people and things we no longer recognize? Into what we never wanted or intended to be? Before we destroy it all?

A community is the place where individuals interact. An ecosystem is the place where interdependent communities overlap. We don't have to go it alone. There's a star-seeded sky and a promise in grass to guide our way.

The moon still glows. The sun still shines.

Writers write. And if it's not *The Briar Cliff Review*, then some new delight will bloom from its ashes, some new voice will emerge.

Because it has to.

Sons and daughters morph to mothers and fathers, grandmas and grandpas. We become the ghosts we buried.

If my grandmother can learn to live without Louisville I can.

What we can't live or be without is each other.

Her survival is in our creations, in the art, in the loess, silt forever being blown into new formations.

I pray I'll learn this lesson before it's too late. So that I can still teach it. That we'll read the old stories. Together. And that we'll make some new ones together too. This is a hope worth waking for, a book worth reading.

For now, I pick up an old *Review* and run my fingers to a familiar site, a piece from a frequent contributor over the years, David Evans. In his 2016 piece, "Coming Home," he writes, "I left Sioux City over fifty years ago, but did I really leave?"[23] We are the places we rest our heads.

Outside, snow lines the branches of trees.

My eyes gaze and roll and wander to the Hills.

My breath, I see, circles to blue skies and to heaven.

Notes

[1] "Whence Siouxland," *Book Remarks* (Sioux City Public Library), May 1991.

[2] Frederick Manfred, quoted in "Whence Siouxland."

[3] United States Geological Survey, accessed May 20, 2021, https://pubs.usgs.gov/info/loess/.

[4] Tricia Currans-Sheehan, interview by author, June 9, 2021.

5 Gary Snyder, "Unnatural Writing," *A Place in Space: Ethics, Aesthetics, and Watersheds* (Counterpoint, 1995): 170-71.

[6] Currans-Sheehan, interview.

[7] Phil Hey, "The Relevance of a Liberal Arts Education from the Perspective of my Discipline, Writing," *The Briar Cliff Review* 3:1 (Spring 1991): 30.

[8] Nicholas M. Kelly, Nicole White, and Loren Glass, "Squatter Regionalism: Postwar Fiction, Geography, and the Program Era," *Journal of Cultural Analytics* 4 (2021): 75-109.

[9] Wes Jackson, *Consulting the Genius of the Place: An Ecological Perspective to a New Agriculture* (Counterpoint, 2004).

[10] Sylvan Runkel, *Loess Hills Prairie Seminar,* accessed August 23, 2021, http://iowaee.org.

[11] Tricia Currans-Shehan, "From the Editor," *The Briar Cliff Review* 12 (Spring 2000).

[12] Richard L. Poole, "Doc Hagedorn: The Last Medicine Man in Sioux City," *The Briar Cliff Review* 5 (Spring 1993), 28.

[13] Ona Lee Iverson, "Josephine Herbst: An Iowan" *The Briar Cliff Review* 8 (Spring 1996): 42.

[14] David Paulsrud, "Trauma," *The Briar Cliff Review* 20 (2008): 40-41.

[15] William Faulkner, *Nobel Prize Acceptance Speech,* accessed June 15, 2021, https://www.nobelprize.org/prizes/literature/1949/faulkner/speech/.

[16] Hey, 30.

[17] Gary Snyder, "Pearly Everlasting," *In the Blast Zone: Catastrophe and Renewal on Mount Saint Helens*, ed. Charles Goodrich, Kathleen Dean Moore, and Frederick J. Swanson (Oregon State University Press, 2008).

[18] Bohumil Shimek, quoted in Cornelia Mutel, *Fragile Giants: A Natural History of the Loess Hills* (Bur Oak Books, 1989), 88.

[19] Wes Jackson, *Nature as Measure: The Selected Essays of Wes Jackson* (Counterpoint, 2011).

[20] Wendell Berry, quoted in Jackson, *Nature as Measure.*

[21] Jon K. Lauck, "Notes on Deep America," *Local Culture: A Journal of the Front Porch Republic* 3:1 (Spring 2021).

[22] Richard Manning, *The Promise of Grass: The History, Biology, Politics, and Promise of the American Prairie* (Penguin Books, 1995).

[23] David Allan Evans, "Coming Home," *The Briar Cliff Review* 28 (2016): 40.

Chapter 19

"Follow Me," Said the River

David Allan Evans
South Dakota State University

Part 1: Sioux City: A Brief Memoir of Hills and Rivers

"Pigeons of My Youth"

They never give up,
those pigeons of my youth.
Look: under the bluff,
they nod, step quick,
picking up spilled corn
between the tracks.
When two box cars—
iron fists—
wham together
away they go

a fleet cloud rising
over the creosote steps,
over the hill street's
houses, up, up...
later, when the rusty
grains of noise
settle, look again: they're
picking up spilled corn
between the tracks.[1]

One of my favorite thinkers and writers is E. O. Wilson, the evolutionary biologist who has been called our modern Darwin and Thoreau combined. He has a chapter in his well-known book *Biophilia* called "The Right Place," in which he discusses the importance of habitat selection, which is of crucial importance for all animals. Considering the two-million-year history of humans, he says that we have a world-wide tendency to prefer a habitat with three main characteristics: first, "a savanna with an abundance of animal and plant food"; second, "some topographic relief" such as "cliffs, hillocks, and ridges," appropriate as "vantage points from which to make more distant surveillance" (I think of cheetahs in *Nature* programs standing on prominences, surveying for prey); and third, "lakes and rivers…with "fish, mollusks, and new kinds of edible plants." The water also creates "perimeters of defense." "Put these three elements together," Wilson writes: "…it seems that whenever people are given a free choice, they move to open tree-studded land on prominences overlooking water."[2]

Wilson goes on to say that when people visit other cities or countries they quite naturally notice and even move toward buildings on promontories—for instance, beautiful homes and other structures built to overlook water. My wife, Jan, and I have noticed in our travels that castles in the United Kingdom and temples in China were often built on high places—for instance, Edinburgh Castle in Scotland, and a Buddhist temple in western China built into a mountainside, overlooking a huge lake.

The three elements of what Wilson calls "the right place" are especially interesting to me, since they go a long way in delineating the landscape of my hometown, Sioux City, Iowa.

Rivers, for instance—"Only connect," wrote the British novelist E. M. Forster. According to an old origin story, War Eagle, a Yankton chief born in 1785 and well known as a peaceful man, befriended a French-Canadian fur trader named Theophile Bruguier, who one day told the chief that he had a dream about two rivers meeting at a point where a new settlement could begin. The rivers were the Missouri and the Big Sioux, and the place of the new settlement was close to what is now known as Riverside. Anyone driving today on Gordon Drive, which runs under and along the Loess Hills bluff into Sioux City, passes War Eagle's Monument, a sculpture of the image of the chief, holding up a peace pipe.

Up to the age of eight I lived in a house in the middle of a hill in what was called "The Valley." I remember watching horses pulling plows in the black soil below our house, with white gulls trailing in the air close behind. Above our house was a high hill, with horses and even a mule sometimes coming down and peering over our backyard fence. One day at the age of five I followed my older brother down the hill to watch the rushing water of a flashflood, and was swept off my feet and into a culvert and nearly drowned. Luckily, a neighbor man saw what was happening and was able to grab me when I came out the other end of the culvert.

When I was eight we moved into town and into a house across the street from the Railroad Bluff. I had a habit of standing on top of the bluff's creosote steps, and watching trains, especially passenger trains at night. I was fascinated by the profiled faces of passengers in the lighted windows, heading to Omaha and other places. I named my first book of poems *Train Windows*.

As a boy in my early teens I became obsessed with running and sports and, later, sprinting in track and on high school football fields. I still remember the feeling of exhilaration when running up nearby hill streets and even looking down at my knees and watching them pumping me upward, higher and higher.

At the age of 12, during the Great Flood in the spring of 1952 (after an extremely snowy winter), I stood with my father in a large crowd on a Loess bluff, looking down at the flood water. The Floyd and the Big Sioux rivers had crested and jumped their banks and flooded Springdale, Riverside, and parts of South Sioux City—but the water from the two smaller rivers and the Missouri combined was now swelling all over the lowland for mile after mile as far as we could see. Duck boats were moving about near the old Combination Bridge, whose closed-off deck by then was only a few feet free of water.

In the early fifties, across the tracks from our street (then called Wall Street but later re-named Floyd Boulevard, after Sergeant Floyd, the only member of the Lewis and Clark Expedition to die) was the baseball park of the Sioux City Soos, a class A farm club of the then New York Giants. I still have a strong memory of running alone in the headlights of cars in a long line after a game, especially up the steep 10th Street hill, and then up yet another hill to our house.

The steepest hill in the neighborhood was on Iowa Street, one block over from us. It was so steep that in winter we could ride our Flexible Flyers down it all the way to Strongin's grocery store, in the middle of the next level block.

Just after I turned 15, our family moved north across town to Leeds, where we lived at the bottom of another steep hill, on Fillmore Street. One block west of our street was the steepest hill in Leeds—almost straight up!—on Polk Street.

The Leeds swimming pool was at the bottom of what was known as Swimming Pool Hill. Standing on that hill in a certain spot, we boys in our middle teens could sometimes get a glimpse into the girls' dressing room (they were onto our act). My girlfriend and future wife, Jan, and I spent many nights walking around on that hill together. For us Leeds kids, there was always romance and magic in the phrase "swimming pool hill."

And then, too, there were those treacherous and aptly-named Roller Coaster Hills, a mile or so northeast of Leeds. In my sophomore year, the night before our Homecoming game, four of us boys were in a car coming down the last of the three hills so fast that our driver lost control and coming to a T in the road didn't make the turn, so we busted through a cattle fence and rolled over a couple of times, breaking the shoulder of my friend Gary and spraining a couple of my ribs, which kept me from suiting up for the Homecoming game. On those same perilous hills, one night after a rain my older half-sister, at 38, lost her life trying to push her and her husband's car out of the mud.

"You never know what is enough unless you know what is more than enough," wrote William Blake in the eighteenth century. Living in a place like Sioux City, Iowa, with its rich variety of topography, one becomes aware of another kind of contrast: "You never know what is low unless you know what is high, and vice versa."

Not only as a native Sioux Cityan but also as one interested in the biological and cultural elements that account for human nature, I'm always alert to how such a contrast is expressed in words. I've noticed, as the following examples show:

> we *look up to* those we respect; we like to think we always *seek the high ground*; we would certainly rather be *top dog* than, say, a *low-down cur* (the dog on the bottom); we like to think *we know up from down*; we remember Julie Andrews famously singing in the movie: *The hills are alive with the sound of music*; when Robert Frost says in a poem (referring to a divorced, discredited husband of a very strong woman), *You can come down from everything to nothing*, the emphasis is on the word *down*; we prefer to live in an *up and coming neighborhood*; we enjoy an *endorphin high* after a good

run or workout; religious or not, we appreciate the poetry in the words from the Bible: *I will lift up mine eyes unto the hills, from whence comes my strength;* we'd rather be *a high brow* than a *low brow*; we don't always like to do what *the higher ups* want us to do, but they're the ones who call the shots; we'd rather be feeling *up* than *down*, or *high* than *low*; taller people have *higher* salaries and get elected to office more often than shorter people; to have *status*, according to the dictionary, is to have *high standing*, and so on....

Over the nearly 60 years of my writing life I have re-visited Sioux City's hills and bluffs and rivers hundreds of times. It's as if E. O. Wilson's "the right place" became, early in my life, an inherent part of my mind and body. As I see it, a person can do a lot worse for a hometown.

Part II. Highlights from a Flat College Town

In 1968 I was teaching in my second year at Adams State College in Alamosa, Colorado, among mountains that I never quite felt comfortable being between and among, and Jan and I were missing our Midwestern life and landscapes. I called Jack Marken, head of the English Department at South Dakota State University (SDSU), and got a job on the phone! About all I knew about SDSU is that in my senior year in high school, the football coach, Ralph Ginn, and an assistant coach (years later I learned that it was Stan Marshall), came to our house in Sioux City and talked with my father and me about playing football at SDSU, and a possible scholarship. I recall my father suggesting that I have a T-shirt on so the coaches could see my "build."

Marken started me at an annual salary of $8,300. It didn't occur to me to ask for a bit more; at the time, I was too ecstatic to be told *no*. In the 1960s, jobs in English and other Humanities departments were fairly easy to get—it was a wide-open market. But in ten or so more years the market would drastically tighten. In my case, I had only a master's degree. Later on I would get my MFA at the University of Arkansas, a terminal degree that soon would become essentially the union card for teaching creative writing courses at the college level. I had so far published only a handful of poems, whereas these days, to get the same kind of job you need, in many cases, at least a published book showing on your resume.

Ah, to live among hills and then even mountains for so long, and then move to Brookings, South Dakota, a town flatter than a pancake at Perkins. There had to be other things than an interesting terrain that would keep me in Brookings. And as it turned out, overall, there were many.

Our first winter in Brookings, however, was one of the snowiest on record, with blizzards coming seemingly every weekend. I remember my cap flying off forever in a cold, fierce wind one morning when I was shoveling out our driveway. As the poet Carl Sandburg put it, "nothing like it ever was." At least for me and other Brookings residents, nothing like that winter of '68 ever was.

Over 39 years, as I said, there were plenty of highlights from the college town called Brookings. For instance, a living, albeit modest, for Jan and me, both of us being employed by the university. Excellent schools for our three kids. An administration that allowed me to travel in-state and regionally and even abroad to give readings and talks, and even do week-long Artist-in-Residence programs in K-12 schools for the South Dakota Arts Council. The competent, dedicated colleagues in my department and other departments on campus, some of whom became good friends. The track and exercise machines in the Stan Marshall complex.

And, especially, in the old Barn, the four racquetball courts. The game would become such an obsession for me that I once had to be pulled out of a court by our department secretary because I'd forgotten to show up for a final exam. And then, too, there were the Shotokan karate workouts in the Barn that were run by a nationally-known, multi-degree black-belt sensei named Dick Gould. Two years of karate opened up a whole new world for me: Eastern thinking, especially Buddhism and Daoism, which would intensify when I later was an exchange professor in western China and then a Fulbright Scholar, twice in eastern China, with the result of Jan and I spending a total of two years teaching and traveling in that incredible, ancient country.

The fishing, along with the beer and camaraderie, while I lived in Brookings were certainly other highlights. Oakwood Lakes, Lake Campbell, just ten miles south and near the Big Sioux—which I also fished in from the rickety bridge, without a lot of luck—and the much larger Lake Poinsett about 30 miles away.

During my tenure at SDSU I was able to help arrange readings and talks by well-known writers such as William Stafford, James Dickey, Charles Simic, Ted Kooser, Bill Kloefkorn, Dave Etter and Garrison Keillor.

When William Stafford visited, I had him over to my house for coffee one afternoon, and I mentioned that I was surprised that he hadn't written any fiction in his career, especially since some of his poems tended to contain characters. "I know exactly why I don't write fiction," he said, firmly. "I don't care enough about people." I assumed that by "people" he meant that fiction writing is all about characters in dramatic settings, which is true. But his response also seemed to suggest that "people" meant just that: people, even people he actually knew. Maybe (I was thinking at the time) he was in a bad mood? But he gave a good reading, though he was laid back compared to, say, James Dickey.

The visit by Dickey was by far the most memorable for me. There are poets, like Stafford, whose poems are meant mostly for the page. James Dickey was not only a poet of the page but also an outstanding presenter to audiences all over the country and beyond. The two of us knew each other from a writers' conference in Boulder, Colorado, when I was in my mid-twenties. I had been struggling with my writing after dropping out of the Iowa Writers' Workshop a few years earlier. (More on this subject later.) Not long after I left the workshop I happened to come across some of Dickey's poems one day in the Iowa University library and something clicked in my head: here was a poet I could truly identify with, especially since both of us had been athletes.

So I was excited to get the chance to attend the writers' conference in Boulder, where Dickey was the headliner. After just glancing at a few of my poems, Dickey—an outgoing, superbly articulate fellow well over six feet—turned to me and said in his Georgia drawl, "You're very good." Then in a private conference when I showed him my poem called "Pole Vaulter," he told me, "Shakespeare never did any pole vaulting." From that moment on, that statement would resonate in my development as a writer. It meant that as a poet I had my own things to say in my own way, which was altogether unique. Dickey would then recommend my work to Dabney Stuart, the editor of *Shenandoah*, a well-known literary magazine. Stuart would publish a number of my early poems.

One winter in the early seventies I invited Dickey to do a reading at SDSU. The night of the reading he was being driven down through a snow storm to Brookings by a friend from a gig at the University of North Dakota in Grand Forks.

The audience for the reading was already seated in the large ballroom of the Pugsley building. I was holding them there, and the time for the reading had already passed by a few minutes, so I had to announce (pretending not to be too agitated) that he would be there if they waited just a little longer—and that his friend had called me earlier and said they were driving through a snow storm and it would be slow going, but that they would be here in plenty of time. Finally, Dickey arrived, not only about 15 minutes late, but I knew he'd been drinking. The big guy, wearing a huge Russian snowcap and long winter coat, took his time shambling down the aisle to the stage. I smiled nervously, as if everything was fine, introduced him to the crowd, and Dickey gave his usual excellent reading.

He spent several days in Brookings, drinking a lot and eating out with some of us from the department. He was funny and as usual brilliant in his knowledge of poetry. He and I spent some time together. He spoke of the screenplay he had recently finished writing for the movie *Deliverance* (based on his best-selling book by the same name), a movie in which, near the end, he would play the role of sheriff. He spoke of the actual mountain men who had been hired as characters. Having lived not far from where the movie would be filmed in Georgia, he was able to speak in their dialect. We had other conversations too. At one point, speaking about dying, he said to me that he wanted to be "totally aware" of his dying in his final moments.

After his stay, I drove him to Sioux Falls to catch his plane. He had me pick up an eight-pack of beer, and on the way he downed every can, and finished off a bottle of Wild Turkey he had. I learned a whole lot about poetry in that 52-mile ride to the airport. Dickey's memory was truly impressive, as he quoted whole runs of lines from poems, one of them being "The Witch of Grafton," by Robert Frost. There was so much elation in the man, so much of the opposite of cynicism, a state of mind that he always disdained. And I knew it wasn't the result of his drinking; he wasn't any less animated when he talked to me sober. I've never known a person more informed and joyous about poetry than James Dickey. I will always say that he was the one who more or less launched my career as a poet.

I still have a vivid memory of a particular moment from my discouraging semester in the famous Iowa Writers' Workshop in the mid-sixties, a workshop with a number of young writers from eastern places including New York City, some of whom had already been published in well-known magazines. At a reading by Workshop poets in the Student Union, an articulate, confident-sounding student got up behind the podium, paused, and began by saying, very loud and very mockingly, the word "corn," drawing it out as "CORRRRRRRRRN!" There was plenty of laughter: most in the audience obviously enjoyed what they had just heard. But not me. What was I to think at that moment, as a young, unpublished novice from across the same state in Sioux City, listening to another young guy in a town in the same state, suddenly trashing poetry written about local, Midwestern things? Corn, or Iowa cornfields, for instance, which I had grown up among. And just as significant to me at the time was the fact that I had gotten substantial praise from my Creative Writing professor, Howard Levant (a poet himself), for my short stories and poems, in my senior year at Morningside College—an excellent four-year college in the region—and had even been the editor of the campus literary magazine.

At semester's end in Iowa City, with the feeling that what I was writing was simply not measuring up to the work I had seen on weekly "worksheets," I went to the office of the main instructor, Marvin Bell, and told him that I was dropping out of the Workshop. He said he was sorry I was leaving, and told me to "keep writing," which did seem like a final note of encouragement.

Between that moment in the Student Union in the sixties and 1975, when a student of mine named Doug Cockrell and I decided to start up a campus literary magazine, a lot had happened in Midwestern poetry toward dispelling the prejudice against regionalism, as well as a vigorous promotion of a New York-oriented poetry. It was as if the work of important American heartland poets such as Carl Sandburg, Edgar Lee Masters, and Vachel Lindsay in the early decades of the century, if not forgotten, had at least been looked past for a time. But now, in the 1970s, regionalism was emerging once again in poetry. In fact, the new awakening had led to what an edition of *Encyclopaedia Britannica*, published in the 1970s, called "a Midwest renaissance" in American poetry.

As a writer myself, in my twenties, I had had to begin to not only embrace but celebrate the value of the local, the near-at-hand. What else could I do, being from a small city in northwest Iowa, but write about things I had actually seen and done in that landscape?—pole vaulting in a neighborhood vacant lot, frogging in a farm pond, watching flocks of blackbirds opening and closing like Venetian blinds over cornfields, or working on the kill-floor at Armour's.

A major contribution to the new regionalism was the publication of Lucien Stryk's *Heartland: Poets of the Midwest*, two anthologies containing poems by such widely known poets as Robert Bly, Gwendolyn Brooks, Paul Engle, James Hearst, Thomas McGrath, and William Stafford. I was happy to have several poems included in *Heartland II* (published in 1975), along with poems by other Midwest poets, such as Philip Dacey, Judith Minty, Ted Kooser, Louis Jenkins, and Robert Dana.

My student Doug Cockrell and I decided that our new magazine, which we called *oakwood* (after the nearby Oakwood Lakes), should include not only work by SDSU students but also work by some regional writers. So with the help of several other students we published a magazine with a snazzy, realistic black-and-white picture (chosen by Cockrell) on the cover. We included work by writers such as my good friend Phil Hey in Sioux City, who was also in the Iowa Workshop in the mid-sixties (though we didn't know each other at the time), Ron Ikan, another Iowa poet, and Dave Etter, a well-known poet from Illinois.

I'm glad to say that *oakwood* is still going strong in the new century, produced by the English and Art departments.

A number of SDSU student writers I worked with went on to publish their poetry and even their own books. Not only Doug Cockrell from Redfield but Dennis Sampson from Pierre, who became an English professor with several books of poems published over his career. Another poet is Sheryl Nelms. After graduation she moved to Texas and became what was known as the most published woman poet in Texas, with hundreds of poems published in magazines and journals, and many of her own books.

Probably the most well-known poet in my tenure was a young man from Pierre, where his family owns a grocery store. His name is Chad Lee Robinson. Chad had done virtually no writing when he signed up for my Creative Writing class. He says that early on I wrote on the blackboard a poem by the great Japanese haiku poet Basho and that moment became an epiphanic moment in his life. He began to write haiku, and soon he would become well-known not only nationally but internationally.

In 2002 Governor Janklow appointed me as poet laureate of the state, a position I held for 12 years. My appointment was a new thing in South Dakota, since I was the first state laureate from academia. The most famous South Dakota laureate was Badger Clark (who liked to refer to himself as "poet lariat"), known for his popular, conventional verse, with its rime and meter. My poetry differs from the traditional poetry of laureates before me, since I write free verse (though I do employ rime now and then). As a result, my appointment was at first controversial. The South Dakota Poetry Society, which was one of the first state poetry societies in the country, is an exemplary organization, promoting and publishing poetry all over the state, and even a recent anthology—*South Dakota in Poems: An Anthology*—edited by the present poet laureate, Christine Stewart-Nuñez. The Society also established a chapbook series that publishes several individual poets in one volume. Another fine anthology of South Dakota poetry, *A Harvest of Words*, was recently edited by Patrick Hicks, Writer-in-Residence at Augustana University in Sioux Falls.

I always assumed that my job as poet laureate was to promote poetry in any way that I could, throughout the state and beyond. That meant doing workshops and talks, as well as writing blurbs and reviews. During my tenure I also attended a number of national gatherings of laureates from other states, meeting, for instance, in North Dakota, Indiana, and New Hampshire.

I would keep my job at SDSU for 39 years and then retire and move to Sioux Falls, where Jan and I had started out in South Dakota. I could not have chosen a better way to make a living. Being a poet and writer gave me a license to teach works of literature that I myself loved and was influenced by in so many good ways. I have often thought: what if I hadn't been able to get a football scholarship to college? (My parents couldn't have afforded to pay for a college education.) I might have ended up working at a Sioux City packinghouse. I never have been a very practical person. My talents and leanings, finally, have been in writing and teaching. How fortunate I have been to be able to make a living as a professor in a university, where writing was part of my job. The American poet Randall Jarrell once said that if he had a lot of money he would pay for the privilege of teaching. I would say the same thing about writing.

Part III: Of Time, the Two of Us, and the Big Sioux

The power of water is awesome. Poets, novelists, essayists, and scientists have always known this truth: "The peach blossom follows the moving water," wrote the Chinese Taoist poet, Li Bai, born in 701 A.D. "In its hurry to find the shining river, the mountain brook makes many mistakes," wrote an anonymous poet. "If your Niagara were a cataract of sand," wrote the nineteenth-century novelist Herman Melville in *Moby-Dick*, "would you travel your thousand miles to see it?"[3] The American novelist Thomas Wolfe entitled his novel *Of Time and the River*. And the recent evolutionary biologist Richard Dawkins entitled his book on human evolution, *River Out of Eden*. Yes, water—oceans, lakes, rivers, streams, and brooks—can quite naturally take on metaphorical and mythological relevance.

My wife, Jan, and I have been more or less following the Big Sioux River all of our lives. We were born and grew up in Sioux City, where the Big Sioux meets the Missouri; we moved north out of high school to Sioux Falls, where, like us, the Big Sioux at the Falls turns north for a time, just as we did later again, when (after a two-year interlude in Colorado) we moved to Brookings, which is not far from the Big Sioux; and then, after retiring from SDSU almost four decades later, we moved south again, just like the Big Sioux flowing in the same direction, back to Sioux Falls, where we live only a few blocks from the river, and have biked and walked on the trail along it on many mornings over many years.

In those first weeks back in Sioux Falls I quickly acquired the habit of getting up very early and driving down to Falls Park. I took notes and wrote about what I observed—for instance, in a poem I named "Sioux Falls": "...far off, a train whistle;/ some mallards and drakes gliding/on the calm, dark water,/ beneath the fixed, dependable crashing...." And I named my next book of poems, *This Water. These Rocks.*

The two of us, now in what is sometimes called our "advanced age," still enjoy spending time at the Falls, watching the water cascading and flowing on and on.

Notes

[1] David Allan Evans, *Hanging out with the Crows* (University of Missouri-Kansas City: BkMk Press, 1991), 10.

[2] Edward O. Wilson. *Biophilia* (Cambridge, MA, and London, UK: Harvard University Press, 1984), 110.

[3] Herman Melville. *Moby-Dick* (New York: Penguin Books, 1988), 5.

Author Biographies

Dr. Ryan Allen is an educator, consultant, artist, advocate, and coach. He is a nonfiction and "Voices of the Great Plains" editor for *The Briar Cliff Review* and the co-owner and chief executive of Lumin Therapy, LLC, an integrative healthcare and education provider devoted to helping individuals, families, teams, and organizations build resilience and accelerate transformation. Dr. Allen is also the board president for the non-profit organization FIRE Foundation of Northwest Iowa, whose mission is to provide children with disabilities the opportunity for an inclusive education in the Catholic schools they attend. He is the author of two books of poetry and his works have appeared in a variety of magazines, alt-weeklies, and academic journals. He lives in Sioux City, Iowa, with his wife and three kids.

John Bicknell was born, raised, and educated in Indiana. He was a journalist for more than thirty years, as a reporter, columnist, and editor in Florida and Washington, D.C. He is the author of two books on nineteenth-century U.S. political history: *America 1844: Religious Fervor, Westward Expansion and the Presidential Election That Transformed the Nation* and *Lincoln's Pathfinder: John C. Fremont and the Violent Election of 1856*; co-editor of the 2012 edition of *Politics in America*;

and senior editor of the 2016, 2018, 2020, and 2022 editions of *The Almanac of America Politics*. He lives in Haymarket, Virginia.

Renee Boen is the State Archaeologist and Director of the Archaeological Research Center in Rapid City, a program of the South Dakota State Historical Society. She received her undergraduate degree in anthropology at the University of South Dakota-Vermillion and her master's degree in anthropology/museum studies at the University of Nebraska-Lincoln. Her research interests include burial customs, tool stone identification, site management, and collections management and preservation.

Jeff Bremer is associate professor of history at Iowa State University. He is currently writing *A New History of Iowa, 1673-2020*. His first book, *A Store Almost in Sight: The Economic Transformation of Missouri from the Louisiana Purchase to the Civil War*, was published in 2014. He was a Fulbright Scholar in China and has published articles in *The Annals of Iowa*, *Kansas History*, and *Missouri Historical Review*.

Dr. Linda DeVeaux received her doctorate in Microbiology from the University of Virginia. Following two post-doctoral appointments, at the University of Illinois and the Fred Hutchinson Cancer Research Center, she became a faculty member in the Department of Biological Sciences at Idaho State University. At ISU, she established a radiation microbiology research group with the Idaho Accelerator Center. From 2012-2017, she was an Associate Professor at South Dakota School of Mines and Technology, and the associate director of the Biomedical Engineering graduate program. Dr. DeVeaux is currently Professor and Chair of the Biology Department at New Mexico Tech.

Dr. Mark Dixon has been a Professor of Biology at the University of South Dakota since 2006, where he teaches ecology, biostatistics, landscape ecology, and Introduction to River Studies. He received his B.S. in Animal Ecology from Iowa State University, his M.S. in Wildlife Biology at South Dakota State University, and a Ph.D. in Zoology at the University of Wisconsin-Madison. He was a postdoctoral research associate at Arizona State University prior to coming to USD. Dr. Dixon's main research focus has been on the drivers of vegetation and land cover change on riparian landscapes, and he or his students have conducted research along the Wisconsin, Snake (Idaho), Platte,

San Pedro (Arizona), Big Sioux, Niobrara, White (South Dakota), and (in particular) the Missouri rivers.

David Allan Evans grew up in Sioux City, Iowa. He began college— Augustana in Sioux Falls—on a football scholarship, majoring in English and minoring in Biology. His interest in literature and natural history began in his teens when his self-educated father recited Shakespeare and spoke often of Darwin's ideas. He was a professor of English and Writer-in-Residence at South Dakota State University for many years, as well as a Fulbright Scholar, twice in China, and poet laureate of South Dakota for 14 years. He has been awarded writing grants from the National Endowment for the Arts and the Bush Artist Foundation of Minnesota. In 2009 he received the Governor's Award for Creative Achievement in the Arts. The author of nine collections of poems, including *The Bull Rider's Advice* (2004) from the Center for Western Studies, as well as short stories and essays—some of the latter in the field of Literary Darwinism—his latest book is *The Maze*, a novella.

Sam Herley, Ph.D., has been the curator for the South Dakota Oral History Center at the University of South Dakota since 2015. He has served as an instructor at USD for the Department of History, Native American Studies Program, and Honors Program since 2011, and he also has taught for The Indian University of North America at Crazy Horse Memorial. He earned his doctorate in history of the American West from the University of Nebraska-Lincoln in 2010 and is a graduate of Gettysburg College. His areas of interest include the American Civil War, the post-Civil War West, the presidency of Harry Truman, and historical relationships between the United States and Native American tribal nations.

Matthew Housiaux was born in Brookings, South Dakota, and attended college at Augustana University in Sioux Falls. Since 2016 he has covered the White House and state and local government for *The Kiplinger Letter* in Washington, D.C.

Jon Hunter is Publisher Emeritus at the Madison (S.D.) *Daily Leader*, where he was publisher from 1990 to 2021. He is a native of Madison, with a Bachelor's degree from Arizona State University in 1981. He also worked in finance positions at The Clorox Company and Journey Investments in California before returning to Madison in 1990. He is past president of the South Dakota Newspaper Association, Karl E. Mundt Educational Foundation, Lake Area Improvement Corporation, past Chairman of the South Dakota Investment Council, and was a board member of the South Dakota Historical Society Foundation.

Dr. Joshua J. Jeffers received his Ph.D. in history from Purdue University in 2014, where he specialized in Native American history, environmental history, and U.S. settler colonialism. His current book project, *From Ohi'yo to Ohio: Conceptual Landscapes and the Transformation of Ohio Country, 1729-1847,* examines how beliefs about the Ohio landscape have shaped its history. He is currently an assistant professor of history at California State University-Dominguez Hills, where he teaches courses on Native American and early American history. He lives in La Mirada, California, with his wife and three children.

W. Carter Johnson's career spans 50 years educating scientists and students in five major areas: seed dispersal in fragmented forest landscapes; effects of dams on three major U.S. rivers (Missouri, Platte, Snake-Idaho); carbon budget of eastern U.S. forests; vulnerability of prairie wetlands and waterfowl to climate change; and economic and environmental benefits of restoring native grassland on Dakota farms. Dr. Johnson has held positions at Oak Ridge National Laboratory-Tennessee, Virginia Tech, and South Dakota State University (administration and faculty), and he is chairperson of EcoSun Prairie Farms, a South Dakota non-profit corporation. Dr. Johnson is now Distinguished Professor Emeritus at SDSU and recently completed a book with co-author Dr. Dennis Knight on the ecology of Dakota landscapes. Publication by Yale University Press is expected in late 2021.

Christopher Laingen is a Professor of Geography at Eastern Illinois University in Charleston, Illinois. He grew up on a family farm in southern Minnesota near the town of Odin, where much of his interest in the rural landscape and regional geography began. His research focuses on changes in farming and the landscapes of the rural Midwest and Great Plains, which has been published in *Great Plains Research, Focus on Geography, The Geographical Review,* and *The Professional Geographer.* He is also the co-author (with John C. Hudson) of the book *American Farms, American Food: A Geography of Agriculture and Food Production in the United States* (Lexington Books, 2016), and has contributed chapters for *The Interior Borderlands* (Center for Western Studies) and *Finding a New Midwestern History* (UNL Press).

Katherine Lamie is the Repository Manager at the South Dakota State Historical Society Archaeological Research Center in Rapid City. Originally from upstate New York and a graduate of the State University of New York (SUNY) at Geneseo, she started archaeological work in South Dakota after completing her master's degree at the University of Nebraska-Lincoln in 2008. Her research interests involve archaeological collection management, archival records, and various topics in historic archaeology.

Matthew J. Ley is vegetation ecologist and project manager at the Center for the Environmental Management of Military Lands at Colorado State University. He supports a variety of applied research projects for the Department of Defense at military installations and training lands around the world focusing primarily on habitat modeling and mapping as well as natural resource planning. He received his B.Sc. in Rangeland Ecology and Watershed Management from the University of Wyoming and his M.Sc. in Biology from the University of South Dakota.

Since 2018, **Dr. Kelsey Murray** has served as the Program Director of the Environmental Engineering, Controlled Environment Agriculture, and Pharmacy Technician Programs at Western Dakota Tech. She received her A.S. in Respiratory Care from Dakota State University, B.S. in Biochemistry from the University of Minnesota, and Ph.D. in Biomedical Engineering from South Dakota School of Mines and Technology (under Ph.D. advisor Linda DeVeaux). Dr. Murray's current research centers on establishing connections between the environment and human health, with emphasis on pathogenic and antibiotic resistance potential of microbes. Additionally, she is Principal Investigator on several award-winning sustainability projects, including those related to aquaponics and hydroponics, as well as operation of a deepwinter greenhouse. She also owns an apiary with over 20 beehives. Dr. Murray has been an invited lecturer at numerous conferences. She currently serves on the Live.Move.Be Farms (Co-Chair) and South Dakota Public Health Association (Vice President) boards of directors.

Lance Nixon is a freelance writer and part-time UPS driver near Pierre, South Dakota, where he previously edited the daily *Capital Journal* newspaper. He is also a past editor of *Montana Magazine*. He has a master's degree in English/creative writing from the University of North Dakota and a master's in journalism from South Dakota State University. His journalism about the Great Plains appears in national magazines such as *Cowboys & Indians* and *Wild West*, and in regional and industry magazines. His latest fiction about the plains appears in *Dappled Things* literary journal, where he is the winner of the 2021 J. F. Powers Prize in Short Fiction; and in the November 2019 and November 2020 issues of *Gray's Sporting Journal*, where another story is pending. He has twice been a semifinalist for the Iowa Short Fiction Award of the Iowa Writers' Workshop. He is married and has five children.

Dale Potts graduated with a doctoral degree in history from the University of Maine at Orono. He is an Associate Professor of History at South Dakota State University, where he teaches courses in U.S. and world history, environmental history, and U.S. cultural history. He currently researches popular nature writing in the twentieth century and how it relates to American conservation and environmentalism. He has published in journals such as *Interdisciplinary Studies in Literature and Environment* and *Studies in American Indian Literatures*. He contributed a chapter to the anthology *Rediscovering the Maine Woods: Thoreau's Legacy in an Unsettled Land* for the University of Massachusetts Press (2019). He is the recipient of the Kentucky Historical Society Scholarly Research Fellowship in 2016 and the James Phinney Baxter Award for best 2018 article in the journal *Maine History*.

Greg Rohlf is Professor of History at University of the Pacific in Stockton, California. He is author of *Building New China, Colonizing Kokonor* (Lexington Books, 2016), which examined Chinese state building in Tibetan regions of China, especially through agricultural resettlement. He is currently working on a project called "The World Builds a University: Tsinghua College and Transnationalism in Higher Education, 1890-1930."

James Calvin Schaap taught literature and writing at Dordt University, Sioux Center, Iowa, for 37 years before retiring. He has published many short stories and several novels, including *Romey's Place*, *The Secrets of Barneveld Calvary*, *Touches the Sky*, and *Looking for Dawn*. He is presently working with Marcella LeBeau, a 101-year-old Lakota elder, on her life story. His most recent publications include *Up the Hill: Folk Tales from the Grave* (stories) and *Reading Mother Teresa* (meditations). In addition, he's written non-fiction, including *Things We Couldn't Say*, the story of the Dutch Resistance fighter Berendina Eman. Since retirement, he's been running down stories drawn from regional histories, stories that make him giggle, or leave him in awe. Those "Small Wonder(s)" are broadcast on KWIT, 90.3, NPR, in Sioux City and available at the KWIT website or floydriverpress.com.

Jeremy Seaton is a freelance writer and editor from East Lansing, Michigan. He received his B.A. in Philosophy from Western Michigan University. After completing his B.A. at Western, Seaton received the university's Thurgood Marshall Fellowship for graduate study. His interests range from African American regional history, Christian apologetics and philosophy, conservative thought and Gothic literature to pulp fiction, penny dreadfuls and comic-books. Seaton has studied the history of combat sports and their portrayal in the media. He has written for *The University Bookman*, *Angels and Dragons*, *Scientific Wrestling*, and the *Lansing State Journal*.

Dr. David Swanson is a Professor of Biology and Director of the Missouri River Institute at the University of South Dakota, with research interests that include ecological physiology, the evolution of animal physiological diversity, and the use of natural and anthropogenic woodlands, wetlands, and grasslands by migrating and breeding birds in the northern Great Plains. He has published extensively on breeding and migratory bird use of riparian woodlands of the Big Sioux and Missouri rivers in comparison with human-planted farmstead woodlots. He is a co-author of the 3rd edition of *Birds of South Dakota* and author of *Birder's Guide to South Dakota*. Dr. Swanson is Secretary and Past President of the South Dakota Ornithologists' Union and an Elected Fellow of the American Ornithological Society.

Paul Theobald recently retired from a 42-year career as an educator, 35 of those years in higher education. He served as Dean of Wayne State College's School of Education from 1996 to 2004. He has published more than 50 journal articles and chapters, plus three books. Theobald has served as an expert witness in school consolidation cases and in cases dealing with the intentions of state constitution authors with respect to providing systems of free public education. In 2018 he ran unsuccessfully for Nebraska's Third District Congressional seat. He is currently President of District 7 of the Nebraska Farmers Union.

Christopher Vondracek is a journalist, piano-player, and poet living in South Dakota. His 2020 book, *Rattlesnake Summer* (Badger Clark Press), draws a poem for each of the state's 66 counties. He grew up in neighboring Minnesota. He covers the Dakotas for Forum News.

Index